PENGUIN PLAYS

JOKING APART AND OTHER PLAYS

Alan Ayckbourn was born in 1939 and educated at Haileybury. He has worked in the theatre since leaving school and has been a stage manager and actor at Edinburgh, Worthing, Leatherhead, Oxford, and with the late Stephen Joseph's Theatre-in-the-Round Company at Scarborough. He was a founder member of the Victoria Theatre, Stoke-on-Trent, and BBC Radio Drama Producer in Leeds from 1964 to 1970. He is now Director of Productions of the Stephen Joseph Theatre, Scarborough.

Since 1959 he has written numerous full-length plays, mainly for the Scarborough Theatre-in-the-Round. His London productions include *Relatively Speaking* (1967), of which there have also been fifty-one productions in Germany alone; *How the Other Half Loves* (1970), starring Robert Morley, which ran for over two years; *Time and Time Again* (1972); *Absurd Person Singular* (1973), which received the *Evening Standard* Best Comedy Award; *Absent Friends* (1975); *Jeeves*, a musical, written in collaboration with Andrew Lloyd Webber (1975); *Confusions* (1976); *Bedroom Farce* (National Theatre, 1977); *Just Between Ourselves* (1977), winner of the *Evening Standard* Best Play Award; *Ten Times Table* (1978); *Joking Apart* (1979), which received the *Plays and Players* Award; *Sisterly Feelings* (National Theatre, 1980); *Taking Steps* (1980); *Season's Greetings* (1982); *Way Upstream* (1982); and *Intimate Exchanges* (1984). *The Norman Conquests* (London, 1974), the comic trilogy, won the *Evening Standard* Drama Award for the Best Play of the Year, the *Plays and Players* Award, and the Variety Club of Great Britain voted him playwright of the year. Alan Ayckbourn's plays have been translated into twenty-four languages and performed all over the world.

Penguin also publish *Three Plays* (*Bedroom Farce*, *Absurd Person Singular* and *Absent Friends*) and *The Norman Conquests* (*Table Manners*, *Living Together* and *Round and Round the Garden*).

D1495106

ALAN AYCKBOURN

JOKING APART

AND OTHER PLAYS

PENGUIN BOOKS

PENGUIN BOOKS

Published by the Penguin Group
27 Wrights Lane, London w8 5TZ, England
Viking Penguin Inc., 40 West 23rd Street, New York, New York 10010, USA
Penguin Books Australia Ltd, Ringwood, Victoria, Australia
Penguin Books Canada Ltd, 2801 John Street, Markham, Ontario, Canada L3R 1B4
Penguin Books (NZ) Ltd, 182–190 Wairau Road, Auckland 10, New Zealand

Penguin Books Ltd, Registered Offices: Harmondsworth, Middlesex, England

Just Between Ourselves, Ten Times Table and *Joking Apart*
first published as *Joking Apart and Other Plays*
by Chatto & Windus 1979
Sisterly Feelings first published with *Taking Steps*
by Chatto & Windus 1981
Published in Penguin Books 1982
3 5 7 9 10 8 6 4

Just Between Ourselves, Ten Times Table and *Joking Apart*
copyright © Alan Ayckbourn, 1979
Sisterly Feelings copyright © Haydonning Ltd, 1981
All rights reserved

Made and printed in Great Britain by
Richard Clay Ltd, Bungay, Suffolk
Filmset in Monophoto Ehrhardt

CONTENTS

PREFACE

to *Just Between Ourselves, Ten Times Table*
and *Joking Apart*

Just Between Ourselves, Ten Times Table and *Joking Apart* could be described as the first of my 'winter' plays. Unlike their predecessors, which were all written in late spring for performance during the Scarborough summer season, these three were all composed in December for performance in January. I mention this not because I am a strong believer that the time of the year wields some astrological influence over what one writes (though I would never rule this out either). In a more practical way, though, this shift of my established writing pattern did, to some extent, alter my priorities. By the winter of 1975–6, the Scarborough Theatre-in-the-Round Company which I direct had made its first tentative steps towards a year-round playing pattern. This had long been an ambition of mine. After twenty years or so of being exclusively a summer rep. we were at last establishing some sort of deeper permanency within the town. To encourage and develop our much needed winter audience, I launched my latest play, *Just Between Ourselves*, at a time when it would, we hoped, do the most good for the box office. At the same time, the pressure that had always been on me to produce a play suited primarily to a holiday audience was no longer there.

As is customary, I wrote mainly at night – but this was my first experience of tackling a play whilst the North Sea storms hurtled round the house, slates cascaded from the roof and metal chimney cowlings were bounced off parked cars below my window, rebounding hither and thither like demented pinballs. Not surprisingly, the result was a rather sad (some say a rather savage) play with themes concerned with total lack of understanding, with growing old and with spiritual and mental collapse. Dennis, the husband, is no calculating villain. Nor is he, I contend, particularly unusual. Just a man pathologically incapable of understanding beyond a certain level. His wife's cries for help go unanswered not because he ignores them or fails to hear them but because he honestly hasn't the slightest idea what they're about. The wife, Vera, hampered by a lack of ability to express herself clearly or maybe too inhibited to do so, suffers from a conventional upbringing that has taught her that the odds on her being wrong and her husband being right are high. Slowly, the last vestiges of self-confidence are drained from her. Vera sits empty, huddled and withdrawn in the garden, unwilling to go back into a house that is no longer hers. Occasionally, and I'm glad to say it is only occasionally, it has been suggested that the whole piece might benefit from a more cheerful ending wherein Vera miraculously revives and all becomes right with the world. Perhaps a few years earlier, I might have paid such suggestions serious attention. In resisting them and allowing *Just Between Ourselves* to end as it does, I felt I took a large stride towards maturity as a playwright. It continued my small progress, first started in *Absent Friends*, towards my unattainable goal: to write a totally effortless, totally truthful, unforced comedy shaped like a flawless diamond in which one can see a million reflections, both one's own and other people's.

Ten Times Table, written exactly a year later, over Christmas which I missed completely that year, undoubtedly draws for its subject matter on experiences gained during 1976. We were due in October of that year to transfer from our present theatre home, the first floor of the Scarborough Public Library, to our new temporary housing, the far more commodious ground floor of the old Boys' Grammar School. For me, this entailed attending an interminable series of repetitive (and largely non-productive) committee meetings to finance and facilitate the move. Up till then, I had had little to do with committees. Little by little, their procedures and protocols began to intrigue me. And particularly the people involved and the way they used these procedures. Put a man behind the wheel of a car, they say, and his personality really starts to show itself. Similarly, a committee soon separates the goats. Apparent strong men weaken. Non-entities inherit the floor. Silent men gabble on inarticulately and to no point. Talkative men grow silent and merely emit low indecipherable moans of dissent and agreement. *Ten Times Table* is a study of the committee person. It breaks a pattern for me in that I leave my usual domestic setting for the more public surroundings of the ballroom of the quite awful Swan Hotel, where everyone at some time must have stayed, much against their better judgement. The play could be described, I suppose, as a predominantly sedentary farce with faintly allegorical overtones. In more innocent days, it would probably have been sub-titled a romp. Certainly, if in *Just Between Ourselves* I moved towards maturity, in *Ten Times Table* I reverted, happily, to my playwright's childhood.

Finally, *Joking Apart* which, at this time of writing, is my latest play and thus, naturally, my favourite of the three. I say naturally, since if it wasn't my favourite, I wouldn't have started it and certainly wouldn't have finished it. I have, at least, to convince myself I'm improving even if I fool no one else. Looking at the play as objectively as I can, I do feel that it does go some way towards combining the truth of *Just Between Ourselves* with some of the fun of *Ten Times Table*. Its most significant feature is the time span it covers – twelve years from start to finish. The characters all age from their late twenties to their early forties, save one who starts in her late twenties and retreats to eighteen. For it's important when reading *Joking Apart* to remember that Melody/Mandy/Mo/Debbie are intended to be played by the same actress.

The play was written when the 38-year-old author was confronted by his eighteen-year-old son, who was suddenly adult and growing more so each passing day. I think with *Joking Apart* I began to feel my age.

Alan Ayckbourn
Scarborough 1978

PREFACE to *Sisterly Feelings*

When *Sisterly Feelings* (1978) and *Taking Steps* (1979) were first produced in Scarborough, I called *Sisterly Feelings* a comedy and *Taking Steps* a farce.

The residents of Scarborough, it appeared, had no quarrel with these categories, though when the plays reached London in 1980 their descriptions provoked (as indeed I should have known they would) much lengthy and somewhat tedious discussion as to what precisely defined farce and where the boundaries should be drawn between that and comedy.

At the risk of adding another tube of lighter fuel to the bonfire, here are my own descriptions of what I consider to be the three main categories of play.

First, there is the drama or straight play which is usually rather short on humour but filled with Insights and other Serious Things and is thus, when successful, regarded as a Very Good Thing to See. Comedies, on the other hand, are straight plays with a sense of humour, often saying much the same thing only more enjoyably and therefore to a wider audience. A very few comedies can occasionally achieve the Very Good Thing category but generally only if (a) the director has removed all the humour from it by playing it with funereal solemnity or (b) the author is long dead, foreign, or preferably both. If the author is foreign, the chances are the translator will have killed off most of the humour anyway (cf. Molière, Goldoni). If very long dead, then most of the audience don't understand the jokes anyway (cf. Shakespeare).

Thirdly, there are farces which set out to be, and often are, funnier than comedies, though in order to achieve this, the author has necessarily had to jettison one or two things like deep character analysis or Serious Things.

Good farce explores the extreme reaches of the credible and the likely. It proceeds by its own immaculate internal logic and at best leaves its audience only at the end wondering how on earth they came to be where they are now. In other words, it takes the basic illusion of theatre whereby, as in all plays, the dramatist first creates a world and then convinces his audiences of its credibility – farce takes this illusion and stretches it to the limits and outside them.

For me, farce begins when I feel that I am now leading an audience into realms beyond the laws of human probability.

Thus, *Sisterly Feelings* contains nothing that *couldn't* happen. *Taking Steps*, frankly is, as a bare plot, unlikely and for its credibility it depends entirely upon its telling.

Sisterly Feelings is, or rather are, plays concerned with choice. Their distinctive feature is their variability whereby four combinations of alternative versions are possible depending first, on a toss of a coin at the end of the short prologue, then halfway through on a decision made by one or other of the sisters during the course of the action.

This device has the effect of stimulating actors, irritating stage managers and infuriating box office staff. By way of an apologia, I can only point out that the device is not employed merely out of cussedness. As I say, the plays are about choice. How much do we really control our lives and do we really make decisions or just think we do? In *Sisterly Feelings*, the last scene is always the same, though the emphasis in playing differs. Not that this is saying that I'm a believer in predestination and the inevitability of fate, but rather that I do believe that mostly we finish up with the friends and the partners in life that we deserve.

Of course, this variable device is an extremely theatrical one. It is not something that would work in any other medium. Which reflects my own total preoccupation with the liveness of stage writing. For the fact is that, of the other media, radio only attracts me slightly as a writer, films but mildly and television not at all.

At least with a stage play, with any luck, there will be a second and even third, fourth and fifth chance. There is always the slim possibility that, one night somewhere, the chemistry will be right. The right cast will meet the right audience in the right theatre and something rich and rewarding will be shared between them.

As a final footnote to this, I have resolved with any future plays I write to give them no description at all. Henceforth, they will all be plays. I will leave others to brand and pigeon-hole them if they want to. Ultimately, what matters is whether the play is good or not. Unfortunately, it's possible to gain only an inkling of a play's merit from reading it. The real test occurs on a stage or rather on several stages after many performances in different productions. Only then can a stage play's true quality begin to be assessed.

Alan Ayckbourn
Scarborough 1980

JUST BETWEEN OURSELVES

First produced at the Library Theatre, Scarborough, on 28 January 1976 and subsequently by Michael Codron at the Queen's Theatre, London, on 20 April 1977 with the following cast:

DENNIS	*Colin Blakely*
VERA	*Rosemary Leach*
NEIL	*Michael Gambon*
MARJORIE	*Constance Chapman*
PAM	*Stephanie Turner*

Directed by Alan Strachan
Designed by Patrick Robertson

ACT ONE
Scene One: February, Saturday morning
Scene Two: May, Saturday afternoon

ACT TWO
Scene One: October, Saturday evening
Scene Two: January, Saturday morning

ACT ONE
SCENE ONE

February. A garage attached to a medium-price executive house on a private estate belonging to DENNIS *and* VERA. *Our view is from the side of the house looking into the garage through its side wall. Its 'up and over door', furthest from us, remains closed throughout the action. Down one wall of the garage a workbench littered untidily with tools etc. In fact the whole place is filled with the usual garage junk, boxes, coils of rope, garden chairs etc. In the midst of this, sideways on, a small popular car, at least seven years old, stands neglected. Over the workbench a grimy window which looks out over a small paved or semi-paved 'sitting area'. On the other side wall a door, opening outwards, leading across a small dustbin yard to the backdoor of the house. There is also a paved walkway round the side of the garage, nearest us, leading to the 'sitting area'. A wrought iron or similar ornamental gate leads off the 'sitting area' and round to the front of the house and garage proper.*

DENNIS, *in his forties, is busy at his workbench. He is prodding at an electric kettle with a screwdriver muttering to himself. After a moment,* VERA, *his wife, a few years younger, emerges from the backdoor of the house. She is followed by* NEIL, *in his late thirties and smartly dressed in contrast to* DENNIS *who has on his weekend clothes.*

DENNIS [*frowning at the kettle*]: That goes in there ... and then that one goes ... through there to that one ... which should join up with the other one. In which case ...

VERA [*knocking gently on the garage door*]: Dennis ... Dennis.

DENNIS [*still absorbed*]: But in that case, that one ... should be joined to that one ... [*Calling*] Hallo ... [*Returning to the kettle*] ... unless that's the earth. In which case, it's that one.

VERA [*struggling with the door trying to open it*]: Dennis.

DENNIS: Come in. [*Back to the kettle*] On the other hand, if that's the earth, which one is the live one ...?

VERA: Dennis dear, can you open the door for me, please? It's stuck again.

DENNIS: Hang on, hang on, hang on. Live ... earth ... neutral.

VERA [*apologetically to* NEIL]: It's always sticking.

NEIL: Ah.

DENNIS: Earth, neutral, live.

VERA: My husband's going to fix it as soon as he has a moment but ... Dennis, dear.

DENNIS [*backing towards the door keeping his eyes fixed on the kettle*]: Right. In which case, if that's the earth it goes in there ... Hang on ... not in there ... right. Stand back.

VERA [*to* NEIL]: Stand back.

> [DENNIS *heaves against the door.*
> *It flies open.*]

DENNIS: I'll tell you one thing, the fellow who invented the electric kettle ... [*Seeing* NEIL] Ah. Afternoon.

NEIL: Good afternoon.

VERA: Dennis dear, this gentleman's come to look at the car.

DENNIS: At the car?

VERA: Mr ... sorry, I've forgotten your name.

NEIL: Mr Andrews.

DENNIS: Pleased to meet you, Mr Andrews, come in, come in.

NEIL: Thank you.

VERA: This is my husband, Mr Crowthorne.

DENNIS: Excuse the jumble. The place is due for a spring clean. Amazing what you collect.

NEIL: Yes, yes.

DENNIS: Amazing. I mean, where does it all come from? Just look at it. I mean, where does it all come from?

NEIL: Yes, yes. Accumulates.

DENNIS: Accumulates. That's the word, accumulates.

VERA: How's my kettle?

DENNIS: Coming along, coming along.

VERA: It just wasn't heating up at all. Your mother's making tea in a saucepan.

DENNIS: Well, I'll tell you, my love, I'll give you a little tip shall I? A little tip when you're next using an electric kettle. They work far better when you don't keep slinging them on the floor.

VERA: I couldn't help it. I just caught it with my elbow.

DENNIS [*to* NEIL, *laughing*]: Caught it with her elbow.

> [NEIL *smiles.*]

If I told you, Mr Andrews, the things my wife had caught with her elbow ...

VERA [*shy and embarrassed*]: All right.

DENNIS: You would not believe it, Mr Andrews, cups, saucers, dinner plates, radio sets ...

NEIL: Really.

DENNIS: Whole tray of glasses.

VERA: Dennis ...

DENNIS: And that's just for this month. You ever want a demolition job doing, Mr Andrews, she's your woman. [*He laughs.*]

  [NEIL *joins in halfheartedly.*
  VERA *less so still.*]

Elbows going away like pistons ...

NEIL: Well, I suppose we all tend to ... occasionally.

DENNIS: Yes, quite. [*Hugging* VERA] I was only joking, love, only joking. I'm always pulling her leg, aren't I, love? Eh? I'll have it fixed in a jiffy. I'll bring it in.

VERA: Right. I'll make you both some tea when the saucepan's boiled. Do you take sugar, Mr ...

NEIL: No, thank you. Unfortunately. I'm afraid I'm unable to take it.

VERA: Right then.

  [*As* VERA *turns to leave,* MARJORIE, *a woman in her sixties, comes out of the backdoor.*]

MARJORIE: Vera dear, there's a terrible smell of gas ...

VERA: All right, mother, I'm coming. Excuse me.

MARJORIE: I'm sure this stove still isn't right.

DENNIS: Check the pilot light, Vee. Check it hasn't blown out.

MARJORIE: It hasn't been right since I gave it that thorough clean.

VERA: All right, mother, all right.

DENNIS: Vee'll see to it, mother.

  [VERA *and* MARJORIE *go back into the house.*]

My mother, you met my mother?

NEIL: Yes, I met her on the way through to ...

DENNIS: Sixty-six.

NEIL: What?

DENNIS: Sixty-six years old.

NEIL: Really?

DENNIS: Not bad for sixty-six.

NEIL: No, no.

DENNIS: It's the pilot light, you see. It's in a cross draught. It's very badly sited that stove. They should never have put it there. I'm planning to move it. Right, now. You've come about the car, haven't you?

NEIL: That's right.

DENNIS: Well, there she is. Have a look for yourself. That's the one.

NEIL: Ah.

DENNIS: Now, I'll tell you a little bit about it, shall I? Bit of history. Number One, it's not my car. It's the wife's. However, now before you say – ah-ah, woman driver – she's been very careful with it. Never had a single accident in it, touch wood. Well I mean, look, you can see hardly a scratch on it. Considering the age. To be perfectly honest, just between ourselves, she's a better driver than me – when she puts her mind to it. I mean, look – considering it's, what now – seven – nearly eight years old. Just look for yourself at that bodywork.

NEIL: Yes, yes.

DENNIS: I bought it four years ago for her. It was then as good as new – virtually. Three years old and as good as new it was.

NEIL: It looks very good.

DENNIS: It is really, amazingly good.

NEIL: I suppose being under cover ...

DENNIS: Ah yes, well, quite. As I was just about to say, being under cover as it is.

NEIL: Important.

DENNIS: Vital. Vital to keep a car under cover. I mean, frankly that's why we want to get rid of it. I want to get my own car under cover. I don't know if you saw it when you were coming in, parked just out there, on the road there.

NEIL: Yes, I think I ...

DENNIS: It's doing it no good at all. It's an urgent priority to get that car under cover. You've got a garage, I take it?

NEIL: No.

DENNIS: Ah. Well, when I say that, with a car like this one, it's not as vital as with some cars. I mean, this one, [he slaps the bonnet] this is a very, very sturdy vehicle indeed. As a matter of fact, they're not even making them any more. Not this particular model. They took up too much raw material. They're not economic to make. There's a lot of raw material in this. Mind you, there's no problem with parts. They're still making the parts, they're just not making the cars. Not that you'll ever need a part. We've never needed a part not in four years. No, as a matter of fact, I'll let you into a little secret. This car has barely been out of this garage in six months.

NEIL: Really?

DENNIS: Barely been out. As a matter of fact, frankly, just between ourselves, the wife's had a few, what shall I say, health worries and she hasn't really been up to driving.

NEIL: Oh, I'm sorry to ...

DENNIS: Oh, she's better now. She's very much better now. But she's gone off driving altogether. You can see, look – look at that clock there – I'll be surprised if it's done fifty thousand. [Peering in] Here we are. Fifty-five thousand two hundred and fifty-two miles ... well, fifty-five, fifty thousand, round about that figure.

NEIL: Amazing.

DENNIS: Peanuts for a car like this. It's hardly run in.

NEIL: Right.

DENNIS: Have a look for yourself anyway. Feel free.

NEIL: Thanks.

[NEIL *wanders round the car aimlessly.*]

DENNIS: I'd let you have a test drive in it now but – actually it's a bit embarrassing – the up and over door there, you see it's gone and jammed itself somehow, can't get it open at all. Still, that's my next job.

NEIL: Oh. Well, it'll be important, won't it to ...

DENNIS: Oh, surely, surely. Wouldn't expect you to consider it without a run around. Still, you can have a preliminary look. See if it's the sort of thing you're looking for.

NEIL: Oh yes.

DENNIS: Here. We can have a butcher's at the business end. Just a tick. [*He releases the bonnet.*] There she is.

NEIL: Oh yes.

DENNIS: Not bad, eh?

NEIL: No.

DENNIS: Economic.

NEIL: Really.

DENNIS: Very smooth runner.

NEIL: Ah.

DENNIS: I'll tell you what I can do for you, I can turn it over for you. Then you can hear the sound.

NEIL: Oh well, that's ...

DENNIS: Keys are in it, I think ... yes, right. [*Sliding into the driver's seat*] I can't run it for too long, not in an enclosed space, you understand, but ... bit of choke ... right, stand by for blast off.

[*Engine turns over but fails to start.*]

She'll be a little bit cold.

[*Engine fails to start again.*]

Come along, my beauty. She's been standing, you see ...

[*He tries again. It fails to start.*]

Come on. Come on, you bastard.

[*Engine turns and starts to fire.*]

There we are. [*Climbing out of the car to join* NEIL *by the bonnet*] Listen to that. Purring like a kitten.

NEIL: Beg your pardon?

DENNIS [*yelling above the din*]: That's with the bonnet open, of course.

NEIL: Yes.

[*They stand and survey the turning engine. After a moment, it starts to misfire and peters out. Silence.*]

DENNIS: Battery'll be a little flat, I expect.

NEIL: Probably.

DENNIS: Once it's had a bit of a run round. Desperately needs a good run. Do you do a lot of driving?

NEIL: No. As a matter of fact, I don't drive at all.

DENNIS: Eh?

NEIL: No, I never got round to learning. My wife drives.

DENNIS: Oh, it's for your wife then, is it?

NEIL: That's right.

DENNIS: Oh I see, I see. Surprise, is it?

NEIL: That sort of thing, yes.

DENNIS: Surprise. That's nice. That's nice. Does she suspect? Does she know where you are today then?

NEIL: Yes.

DENNIS: Ah.

NEIL: She's here as well.

DENNIS: Here?

NEIL: I left her in your front room, talking to your mother.

DENNIS: Well, doesn't she want to come and have a look? Since she's here.

NEIL: No, I don't think so.

DENNIS: Well, of course it's an ideal woman's car. Not too big, you see. And it's got the radio. That comes with it, of course. It's a good radio. [DENNIS *turns it on. A buzzing noise. He turns it off swiftly.*] It won't work of course, not while it's in the garage. And then you've got your mirrors behind the sun visors here.

NEIL: Oh yes.

DENNIS: Little touches like that. Sort of thing a woman looks for.

NEIL: Handy.

DENNIS: Oh yes. Funny her coming all this way with you and then not wanting to see it herself.

NEIL: We hadn't far to come.

DENNIS: She prefers to leave it to the expert, does she?

NEIL: Oh, I'm not an expert. No, I was going to have this car delivered for her this morning from another man.

DENNIS: Ah.

NEIL: Only he let me down at the last minute.

DENNIS: It's undersealed, you see. Have a look underneath, see.

NEIL [*bending down to look*]: He sold this car of his to somebody else. Phoned me late last night. I didn't want to let her down. Oh yes, very nice.

DENNIS: Important to underseal.

NEIL: So I had to phone round in a hurry this morning. [*He suffers a mild spasm of indigestion.*] Excuse me.

DENNIS: You all right?

NEIL: Oh yes. Just a touch of indigestion.

DENNIS: Oh dear. Been living it up, have you?

NEIL: No, no. I only get it when I bend down. Nothing serious

DENNIS: That's odd. Sure it's indigestion?

NEIL: I think it is.

DENNIS: Could be something else.

NEIL: Could it?

DENNIS: Possibly. I'd get it looked at, if I were you.

NEIL: Think so?

DENNIS: No harm. I mean, nine times out of ten you're probably right it's indigestion, but the stomach's a peculiar thing.

NEIL: Is it?

DENNIS: Yes. I've had experience with stomachs.

NEIL: Have you?

DENNIS: Better safe than sorry.

NEIL: Anyway this chap let me down, you see, at the last minute. So I went through the small ads again this morning and, er, there was your advert. So I spoke to your wife.

DENNIS: I see, yes.

NEIL: I didn't want to disappoint her. Birthday, you see.

DENNIS: Birthday? It's your wife's birthday then?

NEIL: Yes.

DENNIS: Today?

NEIL: Yes.

DENNIS: Good heavens above. Pisces, eh?

NEIL: What?

DENNIS: Her star sign. Pisces.

NEIL: Oh yes.

DENNIS: You better keep an eye on her, mate.

NEIL: How do you mean?

DENNIS: They can get very moody, can Pisces. Very moody, brooding people. Unless you keep a very close watch on them. What sign are you, as a matter of interest?

NEIL: Er well, Scorpio I think.

DENNIS [*with a yell*]: Scorpio.

NEIL: Yes.

DENNIS: Living with a Pisces.

NEIL: Yes.

DENNIS: Good grief.

NEIL: Is that bad?

DENNIS: Perfect, perfect. Made for each other. Couldn't be better.

NEIL: Oh, good.

DENNIS: You don't look like a Scorpio. My mother's a Scorpio. She's a typical Scorpio. I mean, she's got the Scorpio bone structure. But you don't look a bit like a Scorpio. What date are you?

NEIL: 28th of October.

DENNIS [*with another wild yell*]: 28th of October! I don't believe it. I do not believe it.

NEIL: Eh?

DENNIS: You won't believe this. You will not believe this. You were born on exactly the same day as my mother.

NEIL: Oh.

DENNIS: Exactly the same day. Exactly the same day.

NEIL: Coincidence.

DENNIS: This was meant. I'm sure it was meant. It's extraordinary.

NEIL: Yes, yes it is.

DENNIS: Ah, well. Scorpio, eh? I'll have to keep an eye on you.

NEIL: Really?

DENNIS: Oh yes. Very deep waters, Scorpio. Very deep, secretive, scheming and occasionally, I regret to say, devious.

NEIL: Oh, well. I'll watch it then.

DENNIS: What a coincidence. Incredible. You don't have to worry about me though. I'm a Taurus.

NEIL: Oh good.

  [VERA *comes out from the kitchen with two cups of tea.*]

VERA: Dennis.

DENNIS: Ah ha. That sounds like Aquarius. The water bearer bringing the tea. [*He wrenches open the door.*]

VERA: Here's your tea.

DENNIS: Vee, now you won't believe this, Vee, we have just discovered that Mr Andrews here has exactly the same birth date as mother. Isn't that extraordinary?

VERA: Oh, coincidence.

DENNIS: To the day. Both Scorpios. Exactly the same date.

VERA: Not the same year though.

DENNIS: Same year? Oh yes, rather. Exactly the same year. Mr Andrews here will be sixty-seven next birthday, won't you, Mr Andrews?

VERA: No, I said not the same ...

DENNIS: Same year. Get on with you. Same year. [*He hugs her.*]

VERA: Careful. I'll drop them.

DENNIS: Well, it won't be the first time.

VERA: Dennis ...

DENNIS: Aquarius. You can tell, can't you? Typical bloody dopey Aquarius. Aren't you, my love?

VERA: Sugar's in it, Mr Andrews.

NEIL: Oh. Is it? Thank you.

DENNIS: You given Mrs Andrews some tea?

VERA: Yes, she's talking to mother.

DENNIS: Well, I don't know about talking to mother. I think she ought to be out here with me and Mr – look, can I call you by your Christian name, all this Mr this and Mr that.

NEIL: Neil.

DENNIS: Neil. Right, I'm Dennis. This is Vera. Vee she prefers.

NEIL: How do you do.

DENNIS: Well, don't you think we ought to ask, er – your wife ...

NEIL: Pam.

DENNIS: Pam – Brian's wife's called Pam, isn't she?

VERA: Yes.

DENNIS: Ask Pam out here. After all it's her present. I mean, assuming you're still interested.

NEIL: Yes. It's just that I don't think she's ...

VERA: Oh, is the car for your wife?

NEIL: Yes.

VERA: Oh I see. It's very good. It's a nice little car. I've had very little trouble with it.

DENNIS: Very little? Now be truthful, Vee, you've had no trouble. Be truthful.

VERA: It did break down that once on the ring road.

DENNIS: Petrol. That was petrol.

VERA: Oh yes.

DENNIS: It's not the car's fault if you don't put petrol in it, is it? Not the car's fault. Whose fault is it if there's no petrol in it?

VERA: Yes, all right.

DENNIS: Whose fault?

VERA: Yes all right, Dennis.

DENNIS: It's little Vee's fault. Vee's fault, that's whose it is. I tell you, Neil, I don't know if your wife's the same but if you do give her a car, watch her like a hawk. She'll never put petrol in it. She'll never put water in it. She'll never do the tyres and as for oil ... well, they've never heard of oil except on salads. Eh?

   [NEIL *laughs. A token laugh.*]

Except on salads, eh?

VERA: Shall I fetch Pam in here?

DENNIS: Yes, fetch her in, Vee, fetch her in. Let her have a look at it.

NEIL: I don't think she's that bothered actually.

DENNIS: Of course she's bothered. What is it, her first car is it?

NEIL: No, she had one a long time ago before we were married.

DENNIS: Well, nearly her first car. Her first car for some time. She'll want to see what she's getting. My God, if I was getting my first car, I'd be –

VERA: Yes all right, I'll fetch her. Drink your tea, Mr – Neil.

NEIL: Thank you.

VERA: Mother burnt herself on that saucepan, Dennis.

DENNIS: First Aid tin, top shelf over the boiler.

VERA: I know, I have already. She says it's the wrong stuff.

    [VERA *goes into the house.*]

DENNIS: Now, listen. We must do this thing properly. When Pam comes through the door everything must be right. She comes in the door, what does she see? She sees the car ... You all right?

NEIL: Yes, fine. I seem to have got the tea with the sugar in.

DENNIS: What? [*He takes a swig of his own.*] Here have this one. That's hardly got any sugar in at all.

    [*They exchange cups.* DENNIS *stands appraising the situation.* NEIL *takes a sip of* DENNIS'S *tea and reacts unfavourably. He puts the cup down.*]

She comes in, she sees the car and, how about if you were sitting behind the wheel, no, in the passenger seat, that's it, in the passenger seat and as soon as she sees you, you say to her – happy birthday, my darling Pam or whatever you usually call her, dearest, dear, how would you like this for your birthday?

NEIL: Well, I don't think she's the sort of person who goes for ...

DENNIS: Look, Neil, there is not a woman who has yet been born who does not respond to a romantic gesture. Come on, man, where's your romance?

NEIL: Do you mind if I leave this tea?

DENNIS: Is that too sweet as well?

NEIL: It's even sweeter.

DENNIS: It's all right, I'll drink them both. I'll drink them both.

    [VERA *comes out of the house with* PAM, *a woman in her mid to late thirties.*]

VERA: They're just out here.

DENNIS: Here they come. Here they come. Quick, get in the car, quick, quick, quick.

    [NEIL *does so without much enthusiasm.* DENNIS *leans against the garage door, till* NEIL *is in position.*]

VERA [*tugging at the door handle*]: Dennis. Dennis. Can you let us in?

DENNIS: Just a minute. Just a minute. [*Flinging open the door*]

VERA: Stand back.

    [*They stand back just in time.*]

DENNIS: Come in. Come in.

    [*He steps aside as* PAM *enters, followed by* VERA. PAM *sees* NEIL
    sitting in the car and stares at him.]

NEIL: Hallo.

PAM: Hallo.

DENNIS [*gesticulating wildly to* NEIL]: Go on.

PAM: What are you doing?

NEIL: Er – just looking at the car.

PAM: Oh.

NEIL [*getting out*]: What do you think?

PAM: I said, it's up to you.

NEIL: Yes, I know but – I mean you're going to be driving it.

PAM: As long as it goes.

VERA: Oh it goes. It did go anyway.

DENNIS: Still goes.

NEIL: What do you think?

PAM: Well.

NEIL: Yes?

DENNIS [*in another of his fierce undertones*]: Show her the radio. And the
   – [*he gesticulates*] the mirror.

    [PAM *opens and shuts a door listlessly.*]

NEIL [*in an undertone*]: What do you think?

PAM [*likewise*]: What's he asking?

NEIL: Four hundred.

DENNIS: Four hundred.

PAM [*moving further away from* DENNIS]: It's not worth four hundred.

NEIL: I don't know.

PAM: It's never worth four hundred. Offer him three fifty.

NEIL: Oh, you know I can't . . .

PAM: Three fifty. Settle for three seventy-five. He'd still be doing us.

NEIL: Oh, you know I can't do that sort of thing. You know I –

PAM: Yes, I know you. [*To* DENNIS] How long have you had it?

DENNIS: Three and a ha –

VERA: Four years.

DENNIS: Nearly four years.

VERA: Served me very well. Nice little car.

DENNIS [*bounding forward unable to restrain himself*]: Look, you see. It's
  got the mirror here.

PAM: Oh yes, so it has.
[NEIL *and* PAM *move away.*]
NEIL: Well, do you want it?
PAM: It's nothing to do with me, love, it's your money.
NEIL: No, it's our money.
PAM: Yours. You wanted to get a car. I didn't ask for one.
NEIL: But you did say you'd like one, didn't you? You said —
PAM: I said nothing of the sort.
NEIL: You said —
PAM: I have not said a single word on the subject. Not a word. It's entirely up to you.
NEIL: I just thought you'd ... that you could get out occasionally.
PAM: When am I going to get out occasionally?
NEIL: I just thought ...
PAM: Where the hell am I supposed to be going?
NEIL: I simply thought you'd ...
PAM: It's your money, love. If you want a car, you buy one.
DENNIS: Oh, by the way, just a point of interest. It is taxed for another three months. I forgot to mention that.
NEIL: Yes, well I ... I think we'll leave it for now if you don't mind.
DENNIS: Leave it?
NEIL: Just for the time being. It's a bit difficult deciding in a rush, you know. Till we've had a chance of a run out in it. You know.
DENNIS: Ah. Now, I'll have that garage door fixed in the next twenty-four hours.
VERA: Oh, do please. It's been like that for months.
NEIL: It's a bit difficult to decide just on the spur of the moment. It may be just a bit more than we were prepared to ...
DENNIS: Well, I said four hundred. Because that's the fair price, but I'll take a near offer. Three seventy-five?
NEIL: No, not just at the ...
DENNIS: Three sixty-five. There you are. Now I'm giving it away. Three sixty-five.
NEIL: No. Perhaps I could pop back sometime.
DENNIS: Yes, you're welcome to do that. But I must warn you I have one or two interested people.
PAM: Yes, I'm sure.
DENNIS: Yes. Well. Feel free to pop back.
NEIL: Thank you. [*He has another spasm of indigestion.*] Excuse me.
PAM: Don't do that.
NEIL: I can't help it.
PAM: Take one of your tablets.

NEIL: I left them at home.

PAM: Oh, God.

VERA: Anything the matter?

PAM: Heaven knows.

NEIL: No, no. Just a touch of indigestion I suffer occasionally.

VERA: Oh dear. Would you like some bicarb?

NEIL: No, no, that's . . .

VERA: No, we've got some milk of magnesia somewhere.

NEIL: No, no thank you. I have my own special tablets.

VERA: Oh I see.

DENNIS: I'd have a check up if I were you.

VERA: Can be nasty, indigestion.

DENNIS: Supposing it is indigestion.

VERA: Oh yes, supposing it is.

NEIL: Yes, well, thank you very much.

DENNIS: Not at all. We're always open.

NEIL: Leave you to get on with your kettle.

DENNIS: Yes, yes.

VERA: Have you far to go?

PAM: No, not far.

NEIL: Easterly Road.

VERA: Oh, Easterly Road. We used to live just off Easterly Road didn't we, Dennis?

DENNIS: That's right.

VERA: One of the new houses, is it?

PAM: No, the old ones.

NEIL: On the left just at the top.

VERA: Oh, I know them, yes. In that little block on its own. Didn't Mrs – er – whatever's her name – didn't she live up there, Dennis?

DENNIS: I didn't know they were still there, those places.

PAM: Just about.

VERA: What was her name, Dennis? She used to live there with her son who was a bit funny. You know, peculiar.

DENNIS: I thought those places were scheduled to come down.

NEIL: I hope not. We're still paying for ours.

DENNIS: I thought I read that somewhere.

VERA: Mrs – er . . .

DENNIS: For road widening.

NEIL: We've never heard anything about it, have we?

PAM: That's hardly surprising.

VERA: Mrs – um . . .

DENNIS: Yes, road widening. I'm sure it was that end of Easterly Road.

NEIL: Just be our luck, wouldn't it?

PAM: Well, we must get on.

VERA: Mrs Mandelsham. That was her name. Mrs Mandelsham.

NEIL: Mrs Mandelsham?

VERA: Do you know her?

PAM: She's my mother.

NEIL: Pam's mother. Living with us now.

VERA: Good gracious. Did you hear that, Dennis?

DENNIS: Yes, yes.

VERA: Then you must be Pamela Mandelsham.

PAM: I was.

VERA: Well. Isn't that extraordinary? We used to know Mrs Mandelsham ever so well. Do you remember, Dennis? The nice woman with the cakes.

DENNIS: With the cakes, that's right.

VERA: Of course, you weren't there when we were.

PAM: No, I was working away. I came back when I married Neil.

VERA: Of course we knew your brother. Graham, wasn't it?

PAM: Adam.

VERA: Adam. That's right. How is he?

PAM: Still a bit peculiar. He got married and moved to Liverpool. Haven't seen him for ages. Got masses of kids.

VERA: Oh well, fancy that. And your mother? How is she? Keeping well?

PAM: Fine.

NEIL: Yes.

PAM: She's babysitting for us.

NEIL: She's well. She's very well indeed.

VERA: Well, just fancy that. You must come round again. Bring your mother.

PAM: Yes. We must.

VERA: She made those wonderful cakes, didn't she, Dennis? She was always trying to teach me. I'd like to see her again.

PAM: Yes.

DENNIS: Yes.

NEIL: Yes.

     [*A pause.*]

PAM: Well. We better get on with it. Get Darren his tea.

VERA: Oh yes. Let me ... [*She leads the way out.*]

NEIL [*to* DENNIS]: Well, good-bye. Thanks very much again.

DENNIS: Not at all, Neil. As I say, look in any time. If you want a second look at this thing – just barge in. You're always welcome.

NEIL: Thanks.

DENNIS: Good-bye, Pam.

PAM: Bye.

DENNIS: Happy birthday.

VERA: Oh yes, happy birthday. Whose birthday is it?

DENNIS: Hers. Pam's. It's Pam's birthday.

VERA: Oh, happy birthday.

[MARJORIE *emerges from the house.*]

MARJORIE: I'm going to have to leave the potatoes to you, Vera.

VERA: Oh, mother. You shouldn't have started on that yet. It's far too early.

MARJORIE: I've been struggling with that little knife of yours.

VERA: We're not having dinner for hours.

DENNIS: Go on, mother, you clear off out of it. Let the Queen back in her kitchen.

MARJORIE: It's all very well. We've been having our meals later and later.

DENNIS: Bye.

NEIL: Bye.

[*They go into the house, leaving* DENNIS *alone in his garage.*]

DENNIS: Now then. Where were we? This little one comes up here and joins up with this one. Now which did we say was the earth?

[MARJORIE *comes from the house and into the garage.*]

MARJORIE: Come on then. Let's have your cups.

DENNIS: Help yourself.

MARJORIE: That's if I can carry them.

DENNIS: Your hands bad again?

MARJORIE: Not so good today.

DENNIS: Oh dear. Must be the weather.

MARJORIE: No, it's not the weather. I'm afraid it's age, Dennis. It's what happens when you get old, I'm afraid. Everything just stops working bit by bit. I'm afraid you'll soon find that out for yourself.

DENNIS [*unperturbed*]: Probably will, mother, yes.

MARJORIE: Someone hasn't drunk his tea.

DENNIS: He didn't take sugar.

MARJORIE: Oh. That was Vera. Did you sell the car?

DENNIS: No.

MARJORIE: No, I was talking to the woman. She didn't seem very keen. I don't think she wanted a car anyway. It was him. I told her. I said you don't want a car. They're more trouble than they're worth.

DENNIS: You told her that, did you?

MARJORIE: Well, I mean, look at Vera. She's had this car for years. She never drives it. I doubt if she's driven it once this year.

DENNIS: Ah well, in Vera's case ... you know.

MARJORIE: You want to keep more of an eye on her, Dennis.

DENNIS: How do you mean?

MARJORIE: She's a sick girl. She's not well, if you ask me.

DENNIS: No, she's better now, mother. She's much better.

MARJORIE: Now, don't let her fool you, Dennis. She's not a bit better. You don't get better. Not from that. When it's up here, in your head, it's there for good.

DENNIS: She seems all right to me.

MARJORIE: I've got a feeling she's got what our Joan had. God rest her soul.

DENNIS: Oh come on, mother, Auntie Joan went right round the bloody bend.

MARJORIE: Yes, I know. I nursed her. And she started just like Vera.

DENNIS: The doctor said she was better.

MARJORIE: Did he? Well.

DENNIS: Well, nearly better anyway. That was months ago.

MARJORIE: When she dropped that kettle, I was watching her closely. She just burst into tears, you know.

DENNIS: Not surprised. So did I. Nearly brand new this is. No, mother, if there's anything wrong with Vera it's because she's in a rut. She needs cheering up. Taking out of herself. She takes life too seriously. For that matter, both of you do.

MARJORIE: Well, Dennis, that might be your solution but I can tell you from my experience it is not the solution for Vera. Nor for me, I'm afraid. Nor was it for Auntie Joan, God rest her soul. I know they say laughter's a great tonic but there are some things it can't heal. You can't laugh everything off, Dennis.

DENNIS: I know that. I ...

MARJORIE: I've certainly never been able to. And nor was your father able to. I sometimes wish you took after your father, Dennis, I really do. Not in all ways but in some things. You could do well to follow him.

DENNIS: How do you mean?

MARJORIE: Well, for one thing he didn't try and laugh everything off. He had a deep and wonderful understanding of suffering. In fact, on occasions one could have said too much so. I think by the end, he had taken on everyone's suffering.

DENNIS: He was a miserable old sod when he died.

MARJORIE: And another thing your father always did. He always kept his garage tidy. He wouldn't have left it in this state. How do you ever find anything?

DENNIS: I can find things, mother, don't go on.

MARJORIE: Look at his tools, Dennis. Look at your father's tools. They're all over the place. It would have broken his heart to see them. Why don't you do what he did? Make yourself a proper rack for your tools screwed in the wall. He had little clips, you see. He had his chisels and his screwdrivers and all his hammers ...

DENNIS: I know. I know.

MARJORIE: And then on his bench itself, up one end he had all his little tins with his screws and nails and so forth. And he had them all labelled, you see. So whenever he wanted a little nail or a screw, he could just put his hand straight on it.

DENNIS: Yes, I know, mother, I was there.

MARJORIE: Now, I remember saving you some tins, Dennis. The ones I had my cough sweets in. What did you do with those?

DENNIS: I don't know. They're under that lot somewhere. I haven't got time, mother, to start putting things in tins. If I want a nail, there's a nail. I bang it in and that's that. If I can't find a nail, I use a screw. And if I can't find a screw, I don't bother.

MARJORIE: It'd break his heart in two to see it. Do you remember him working out there in his garage till all hours? Hammering away, making little things. Always beautifully finished. Do you remember his pipe rack?

DENNIS: Yes. Tremendous. It was a classic among pipe racks.

[*He applies himself with fresh fury to the kettle.*]

MARJORIE: He cut that with such care. Do you remember, Dennis? In fretwork, wasn't it? And he cut the letters out in fretwork as well. Pipes. P-I-P-E-S across the top.

DENNIS [*muttering*]: In case he forgot what it was for.

MARJORIE: That gave him more pleasure than anything. Till his eyesight went. Then he could hardly find his way to the garage at all, poor soul. Let alone his fretwork. Ah well, that's age, Dennis, that's age.

DENNIS: True. True. There's your kettle.

MARJORIE: It's not going to blow up, is it?

DENNIS: I've arranged it so it does.

MARJORIE: You're not very good at electrics. I'm still having trouble with that bedside light.

DENNIS: I've told you it's perfectly safe. The switch may be slightly faulty but it's perfectly safe.

MARJORIE: It's not the switch I'm worried about. The whole thing keeps falling out of its bottle. I had a lighted bulb in bed with me the other night.

DENNIS: I'll have another look at it.

MARJORIE: I daren't turn it on at all.

[VERA *comes out from the house.*]

VERA: Mother, you left the saucepan on with no water in it.

MARJORIE: No, that wasn't me, Vera. It wasn't me.

VERA: You made the tea. I haven't been near it.

MARJORIE: I may be getting old, Vera, but I wouldn't be stupid enough to put an empty saucepan back on a lighted gas. I'm not that old, Vera.

DENNIS: Now then, girls.

VERA: Well, it doesn't matter.

MARJORIE: I thank God that my mind is still perfectly clear.

VERA: What do you mean?

DENNIS: Yes, well as soon as it starts to go I'll send for the van, mother, don't worry.

MARJORIE: No, don't joke about it, Dennis, don't joke. It's only too true. Vera, could you carry these for me? I'm frightened I'll drop them. [*She gives* VERA *the kettle and both cups.*]

DENNIS: Well, don't give them to Vee.

MARJORIE: Can you manage?

VERA: Yes, I can manage.

DENNIS: I suppose I'll be mending that again in a minute.

VERA: Don't keep on, Dennis love.

DENNIS: Sorry. Sorry . . .

MARJORIE: Now don't tease her, Dennis. You're always teasing the girl. No wonder she's in a state.

VERA: I'm not in a state. I'm perfectly all right.

DENNIS: She's all right now, mother, don't keep on.

VERA: Will you be out here much longer, dear?

DENNIS: Why?

VERA: Oh, no reason. I've had the fire on in the front room. It's very cosy.

DENNIS: Lovely. Right.

VERA: Fancy that woman being Mrs Mandelsham's daughter.

MARJORIE: Was that Mrs Mandelsham's daughter?

VERA: Yes.

MARJORIE: Well, I never. Yes, she does. She looks like her.

VERA: Well, slightly.

MARJORIE: She will do when she's older.

VERA [*going to the door and pushing it open with her knee*]: Anyway apparently her brother, you know, the one we all thought was a bit peculiar, well – it's all right, mother, I can manage – well, he went to Liverpool and – [*A cup falls from its saucer. She attempts to catch it and succeeds in dropping everything.*] Oh God in heaven, this door.

DENNIS [*roaring with laughter*]: There she goes again. What did I tell you? [VERA *stands surveying the wreckage. On the brink of tears, unable to cope, she rushes into the house.*]

MARJORIE: There you are, Dennis, what did I say? What did I say?
DENNIS: She's all right, mother.
[MARJORIE *follows* VERA *into the house.*]
Oh, good grief ...
[*He starts whistling to himself cheerfully and tidying up his tool-bench.*]

ACT ONE
SCENE TWO

The same. It is now May and sunny. NEIL *is setting up a small garden table round the side of the garage in the 'sitting area'. After a moment,* PAM *enters from the house carrying a tray of teatime preliminaries.*

NEIL: Can you manage?

PAM: I can manage.

NEIL [*testing the table*]: I think this is secure.

PAM: Any chairs?

NEIL: I don't know. I couldn't find any.

PAM: Are we all supposed to stand?

NEIL: You can't find anything in that place. Oh God, are these cucumber?

PAM: You don't have to eat them.

NEIL: Why cucumber?

PAM: These are paste. Have the paste.

NEIL: We could have brought Darren, you know.

PAM: Oh no.

NEIL: He'd have been happy enough, playing out here. He couldn't have come to any harm.

PAM: I'd have been up and down all through tea. If there's something that child can get his hands on that he shouldn't do, he does.

NEIL: I don't know. He's –

PAM: You don't know. That's just the point. You're out all day, aren't you.

NEIL: No, what I'm saying –

PAM: I'm with him, remember. All day. Every day.

[NEIL *mooches about. After a moment*]

NEIL: If you'd let me buy you that car, you could've –

PAM: What was I supposed to do with it? Stick Darren in the boot and just drive off.

NEIL: No. Your mother would have looked after him. You could've gone off for the odd day.

PAM: He's getting too much for her now. I can't keep asking her. I trust him more than her.

NEIL: Well, in the evenings. You could've got to your night classes.

PAM: Night classes?

NEIL: Yes.

PAM: I think that was just a lovely dream, Neil. I'm getting too old for that.

NEIL: Too old? You're only ...

PAM: I know how old I am, thank you. I don't need reminding.

NEIL: I thought you said you wanted to go to night classes.

PAM: There's lots of things I want, Neil. But they're not to be, are they? If you follow me ...

NEIL: How do you mean?

PAM: You know.

NEIL: No, what?

PAM: You know perfectly well.

NEIL: What?

PAM: I'm not spelling it out, Neil.

NEIL: Oh.

PAM: Yes. That.

NEIL: Well.

PAM: That's what I'm talking about.

NEIL: Well I ... [*He picks up a sandwich, embarrassed, and chews it.*] It's not that I ... well ...

PAM: You're eating cucumber.

NEIL: Oh, God.

   [VERA *has come out of the house.*]

VERA: Thank you so much, Pam. If I'd carried it, I'd've probably ... oh, chairs. Have we got no chairs, Neil?

NEIL: I could only find this table.

VERA: Oh. Dennis put them away at the end of last year. First time we've brought them out this year. I hope we're doing the right thing today. Still, it's very mild.

PAM: It's lovely.

VERA: Considering it's May.

NEIL: Yes.

VERA: It shouldn't hurt mother's cold. She's over the worst. Neil, I wonder if you'd be very kind and ask Dennis if he would look out the chairs for us. They're probably tucked away at the back there somewhere. Only he's the only one who'll know where he put them.

NEIL: Right. [*A spasm of indigestion.*] Excuse me.

PAM: Neil.

NEIL: Sorry.

VERA: He was in the sitting room a moment ago watching the telly.

   [NEIL *goes in.*]

PAM: Your mother-in-law's better then?

VERA: Oh yes. Over the worst. It's something that's going round, I think. She got up at lunchtime. She wouldn't miss Dennis's birthday tea, that's for sure. She thinks the world of Dennis.

PAM: Yes, I gathered.

VERA: Won't hear a word against him.

PAM: I think Neil's of the same opinion.

VERA: Yes, you're right. They're very thick these days, aren't they?

PAM: Almost inseparable. Every other evening. I'm just going to have another look at that car, he says, and off he goes.

VERA: Well, he's no trouble. Hardly see them. Both shut away in that garage. He keeps Dennis out of mischief.

PAM: Yes. [*Pause*] I hope you don't mind me saying so, you don't look at all well.

VERA: Really? Oh ...

PAM: Sorry, I don't mean to ...

VERA: No, no. I've probably had a bit of a bug as well.

PAM: Oh.

   [*Pause.*]

VERA: Yes. It's a bit of a bug. Been going around.

   [*Pause.*]

PAM: Was it your idea to sell the car?

VERA: Er – yes. I think it was, yes. I mean, after all it's my car. Dennis bought it for me but it is mine.

PAM: Didn't you use it then?

VERA: No, not very much. I – well, if we're going anywhere I go with Dennis. So I go in his car.

PAM: But you go out on your own occasionally?

VERA: Not to speak of.

PAM: Still, I'd have thought it would have been very useful. Shopping, things like that.

VERA: Oh no. It's quicker to walk really. And then there's the parking and all that. It's very bad these days trying to park. Dreadful. [*Slight pause*] And then, well really I found I didn't really enjoy driving really. I used to get so tense, you know. All the other traffic and, er, I couldn't seem ... well, I'm not a very good driver. Dennis always said I couldn't concentrate. He used to hate driving with me. I mean, he didn't show it. He used to laugh about it but I knew he hated it really. And I just seemed to get worse and worse at it. So I gave up eventually. I think I'm a born pedestrian. That's what Dennis said. All thumbs, you know. [*Pause*] Would you like the car? I mean, supposing you wanted to buy it, would you like it?

PAM: Yes. Yes, I would.

VERA: Well, why don't you? I mean, if it's the price I'm sure I can get Dennis to ... I'm sure I could. It's better than having it stuck in the garage there.

PAM: I don't think I could even afford to pay for the petrol.

VERA: I expect Neil could though.

PAM: Oh yes, Neil could.

VERA: Well ...

PAM: But then if Neil bought it, it wouldn't be mine, would it? It would be Neil's.

VERA: Well, I suppose so. Technically.

PAM: Really it would. When I get a car, I'll buy it.

VERA: I can't say I can really see the difference. Still. Did you work before you were married?

PAM: Yes. I was a secretary. Then a supervisor.

VERA: Oh, really.

PAM: I was in charge of twenty-five girls at one time.

VERA: Twenty-five. Goodness.

PAM: I was the youngest supervisor they ever appointed. Then I was expecting Darren. I planned to go straight back to work as soon as I'd had him but it didn't work out like that.

VERA: No, well, your priorities change, don't they?

PAM: Yes.

VERA: You could probably go back now though, couldn't you? If only part time.

PAM: I'm not sure that going back to supervise a typing pool is really worth the effort. Even supposing they'd have me.

VERA: Well, no. I expect it's very hard work too, isn't it? And as you get older, you ...

PAM: Yes.

VERA: Not that you're old.

PAM: No.

VERA: Still.

PAM: What I'd really like to do is take a degree course.

VERA: A degree? You mean at a university?

PAM: And then teach perhaps. I'd like to teach.

VERA: Oh, that'd be nice. Teaching would be nice. Younger ones.

PAM: No. Older ones.

VERA: Oh. Well. I worked in Safeways. We had a really nice lot there. When I was there. Really nice. I don't see them much now. Most of them have got married.

PAM: You ought to get a job.

VERA: Me? Heavens above.

PAM: Do you good.

VERA: At my age? You must be joking. Anyway I'm far too busy for that. And I'm not qualified. You need qualifications these days. I mean, there was a time when I thought it would be nice to work with old folk, you know, but you need to have qualifications for that. To do it properly. Otherwise you can handle them wrong. I wouldn't want to handle them wrong.

PAM: There's nothing to stop you. If you really want to.

VERA: No, I suppose not. No more than you, really.

PAM: No.

    [DENNIS *comes from the house followed by* NEIL.]

DENNIS: Here I am then, here I am. Who wants me?

VERA: Oh, there you are.

DENNIS: Here I am. Here comes Taurus the Bull. [*To* PAM] Well?

PAM: Hallo.

DENNIS: No, not hallo. Happy birthday. Say happy birthday, Dennis.

PAM: Happy birthday, Dennis.

DENNIS: Thank you.

VERA: What about some chairs then, Mr Taurus? We're both standing around here like sore thumbs.

DENNIS: They're in the garage.

VERA: Well, can you get them please?

DENNIS: Oh dear me, they're not that heavy. [*To* NEIL] Dearie me.

VERA: Get on with you. I'm glad it's not your birthday every day.

DENNIS: Ah now, be careful what you say to me. We are two nil down at half time. You're looking at an anxious man.

VERA: Oh, sport, sport, sport.

DENNIS: Two nil down.

NEIL: Really.

VERA: Every Saturday afternoon, running, kicking, shooting, jumping. All afternoon.

DENNIS: You like the wrestling.

VERA: I don't like it at all. Great flabby things.

DENNIS [*bounding at her ape-like*]: Grrrrr.

VERA: Oh, get off, Dennis, get off.

    [DENNIS *laughing goes off round to the garage.*]

DENNIS: Can you give us a hand, Neil, there's a good lad?

NEIL: Right.

VERA: I'll just see how mother's managing, then I'll make the tea.

PAM: Can I help?

VERA: No, no. You stay out here. You might get a chair in a month if you're lucky.

DENNIS [*struggling vainly with the garage door*]: Oh, this damn door.

VERA [*passing them on her way to the kitchen*]: Why don't you fix it?

DENNIS: I'm going to when I've got a minute.

VERA: The up and under's still jammed as well. The electricity man got trapped in there the other day. He had to crawl through the window.

DENNIS: That'll teach him to read other people's meters. [*Successfully opening the door*] Ah, that's it.

[*The men go into the garage.* VERA *goes into the house.*
During the next, PAM *wanders out through the ornamental gate to the front of the house.*]

I'm really glad you came round today, Neil. I appreciate it very much.

NEIL: Oh, that's ...

DENNIS [*moving to the back of the garage and rummaging*]: Now where the hell did I put them last year? No, I really appreciate it. And Pam as well. I don't know what it is about birthdays. Some people, you know, they get to our age they start to forget about them but I've always – ever since I was a kid this is – I've always had this special thing about birthdays. [*Finding a chair*] Ah ha. Here's one – here, cop hold of that. I suppose one of the reasons is that I always had these marvellous birthdays when I was a kid. Marvellous. My Dad, you know. My father, he always made me something. Didn't just buy it. He made it. He'd go in the garage two or three days before my birthday – [*finding more chairs*] here's a few more – before my birthday and I wasn't allowed near. I used to hear him sawing away, hammering and that, every evening when he was home while I was lying in bed and I'd think – what's he making this year? What's he going to make for me this year? And then. On the morning he'd produce something I'd never dreamt of like a – well, one year it was a roundabout, you know. Little wooden horses going up and down. All painted. All wood. Beautiful work. Right, that's it. One, two, three, four, five. Five chairs, five of us. Oy, before you go. Don't forget to have another look at your car. Two hundred and fifty quid, it's yours.

NEIL: Well ...

DENNIS: Nobody else wants it. You won't get it any cheaper. In fact, if you leave it much longer, it'll become a vintage car and start going up again.

NEIL: Well, I'd buy it, yes. It's Pam, you see. I don't think she – well, she doesn't like the idea of me buying it for some reason.

DENNIS: Why not? You can afford it, can't you?

NEIL: Yes, I can afford it. She just doesn't want me to buy it. She wants to buy it.

DENNIS: Well then, give her the money as a present and let her buy it. What's the difference?

NEIL: No, it's not that. She's – odd like that. [*Suddenly wincing*] Ah ...

DENNIS: What's the matter?

NEIL: Nothing. Just this slight shoulder pain. I don't know what it is.

DENNIS: Oh.

NEIL: No, it's almost as if she resents accepting things from me. See what I mean?

DENNIS: Lucky fellow. Save yourself some money.

NEIL: It's as if she's trying to prove something. Only I don't know what it is. That she can do without me or something. But then again sometimes she's ... she's ...

DENNIS: What?

NEIL: Well, very amorous.

DENNIS: Really?

NEIL: At night time. I wake up and she's grabbing on to me. Digging in with her fingernails, you know ...

DENNIS: That's probably what's wrong with your shoulder.

NEIL: And scratching – I've got a terrible scratch mark.

DENNIS: Well, fancy that. She doesn't look the sort.

NEIL: No.

DENNIS: What do you do?

NEIL: Well, I say like – lay off, will you. I'm trying to get to sleep. I mean, it's about four in the morning she starts this.

DENNIS: You need your sleep.

NEIL: I do. I need eight hours. By the way I think the rumour you heard – about our house being scheduled for demolition – I think it was right. The bloke next door heard it too.

DENNIS: Oh. [*He ruminates for a second.*] Look, Neil, I've been meaning to ask you – if you're – if you were at some time considering buying this, it occurred to me you must have a bit of spare capital.

NEIL: Well, a bit, yes.

DENNIS: I was just curious. I hope you don't mind.

NEIL: No. It was a legacy. Got left it.

DENNIS: Oh, really. Somebody die then?

NEIL: Yes. My father.

DENNIS: Ah. What's it doing at the moment?

NEIL: Well, it's in the bank.

DENNIS: Ah. Well. Now. It's just that I heard something the other day.

Just between ourselves, there's this bloke who's working for this decorating firm and he's decided to set up on his own. And he's looking for capital. Just to get him started.

NEIL: Ah well ...

DENNIS: No, he's a good man. I've known him for years. And he's as sharp as they come. He's been slogging his guts out for this lot and finally decided he'd be better on his own. And you know the way these fellows work – I mean, if he leaves, you can bet your bottom dollar he'll take a lot of the best customers with him. But he needs premises, equipment, transport. It all costs money. Now you can say, it'll be a gamble, but to my way of thinking I wouldn't even call it that.

NEIL: Well, I don't know. I'm not much ...

DENNIS: No. Quite. What I'm saying is, if you've got, say, for the sake of argument, a thousand pounds to spare ...

NEIL: Oh, it's more than that.

DENNIS: More than that, fair enough. But for the sake of this discussion let's say a thousand pounds – now you can put that thousand pounds of yours in the bank and you can literally watch it depreciating even with the interest. By the time you're sixty-five or seventy, you've got the equivalent of thirty pence. Now this way, looking at it long term, he expands, you expand. His profit's your profit, see what I mean? When you come to sell out, you're laughing.

NEIL: Well, I suppose it's possible.

DENNIS: Look, I'm not trying to talk you into anything. Believe me. It's your money but – tell you what, I'll try and arrange for you to meet this fellow. Then you can make up your own mind about him. His name's George Spooner and, as I say, he's a good man. Just see what you think.

NEIL: O.K.

DENNIS: See what you think. He's a first-class workman. Wonderful. Did you happen to notice our lounge? That lounge in there?

NEIL: Oh yes, very nice.

DENNIS: Not the hall. That was somebody else. But he did the lounge. Beautiful work. You just have a look at the way that paper hangs when you next go in there.

NEIL: I will.

DENNIS: He's got terrific pride, that's what I like about him. Right, are you fit? You take those. I'll take these.

NEIL: Right.

[*They make their way round with the chairs. They meet* PAM *wandering back.*]

PAM: About time too.

DENNIS: Patience. Patience. Seldom found in woman. This looks good. Is mother coming down?

PAM: Vee went to fetch her.

DENNIS: I didn't think she'd miss out. [*Presenting* PAM *with a chair*] Madame.

PAM [*sitting*]: Thank you.

DENNIS: There you are, Cecil.

NEIL: Thanks.

DENNIS: Oh by the way, while we're alone, just a quick word ... Er – how shall I put it? Vee is a bit – well, I think looking after mother and me and all that – she's tended to get a bit – what shall I say? – tensed up. A bit tensed up. Nothing serious but if she – you know – drops anything or spills her tea or slips on her arse – anything like that – er – best to pretend not to notice. Don't laugh or anything.

PAM: Why should we laugh?

DENNIS: I don't know. I mean, if you felt like laughing.

PAM: I won't laugh. If somebody falls over, I don't laugh.

DENNIS: Well, that's fair enough. Fine. No problem. All I'm saying is if you did feel like laughing.

PAM: I won't.

DENNIS: Good. Then you're all right. Neil then?

NEIL: I wouldn't laugh.

DENNIS: Great. That just leaves me.

PAM: Just leaves you.

DENNIS: Good. Well. Fine.

[MARJORIE *comes out of the house in her coat. She carries a rug, a hot water bottle and her handbag.*]

MARJORIE: I don't know why we're eating out here, I'm sure. We'll all be in bed tomorrow.

[DENNIS *springs up and goes to her assistance, helping her to the table.* NEIL *rises and offers her his chair.*]

DENNIS: Here she is. Welcome back to the land of the living.

MARJORIE: We'll all be in bed with pneumonia tomorrow.

DENNIS: For tomorrow we die.

[DENNIS *passes* MARJORIE *to* NEIL *who supports her.* DENNIS *opens a chair.*]

MARJORIE: You'll be laughing at my funeral you will. I still haven't forgiven you for that kettle. Blowing up in my face.

[DENNIS *laughs.*]

DENNIS [*looking round*]: Which way's the wind ...

NEIL: From over there.

DENNIS: Right.

[DENNIS *takes* MARJORIE *from* NEIL *and moves her round the table.
He is about to help her into a chair. He hands* NEIL MARJORIE'S
handbag which is encumbering the operation.]

PAM: No, it's not. The wind's coming from here. From round here.

DENNIS: Right.

[*He moves* MARJORIE *again, forcing* PAM *to rise.* DENNIS *hands* PAM
MARJORIE'S *rug which is getting in the way. He is now hauling*
MARJORIE *round the table like a stuffed dummy.* VERA *comes out with
the teapot.*]

VERA: All right, everyone. Sit down now. [*Taking in the scene*] No, Dennis,
put her round there. She'll be out of the wind. She'll be out of the wind.

MARJORIE: I can't sit in the wind, I'm sorry.

VERA: You're not going to, mother. Dennis is putting you there. Put her
there, Dennis.

DENNIS: I am putting her there.

VERA: Yes, put her there ... All right then. Sit down, Neil. Help yourself.

NEIL: Right.

[DENNIS *has sat* MARJORIE *at some considerable distance from the
table, still in view of everyone but tucked round the corner.*]

VERA: We'll put the birthday boy here.

DENNIS: Fine.

VERA: Oh it's really nice, isn't it? I never thought we'd be able to.

NEIL [*who has been displaying signs of the cold*]: Very mild.

[MARJORIE *coughs.* VERA *reacts.*]

VERA: Could you pass me the cups, dear.

DENNIS: Coming up.

VERA [*starting to pour* PAM'S *tea*]: Just as it comes for you, Pam?

PAM: Please.

MARJORIE: I'll have to have mine weak.

VERA: Yes, you'll get it weak, mother. Just a minute.

DENNIS: Well, this is a nice spread. Very nice. This you, Vee, or mother?

VERA [*handing* PAM *her tea*]: I did this. [*Proffering plate of cucumber
sandwiches*] Have a sandwich, Neil.

NEIL: Er, yes. I'll stick to those if you don't mind.

[VERA *puts down the plate of cucumber, rather over-anxious.* NEIL, *with
a swift reflex gesture, prevents the plate sliding into his lap.* VERA *offers
the paste sandwiches.* NEIL *takes one. Meanwhile,* DENNIS *helps
himself to cucumber. Both men help themselves to side plates and napkins.*
VERA *offers a paste sandwich to* PAM. PAM *takes one.* VERA *puts down
the sandwiches and gives* PAM *a plate and napkin.* VERA *resumes
pouring tea, this time* NEIL'S *cup. As she starts this*]

MARJORIE [*suddenly*]: Where's his cake?

VERA: What?

MARJORIE: Where's Dennis's cake?

DENNIS: Ah – [*He rises expectantly.*]

[PAM *and* NEIL *also look more or less expectant.*]

VERA: We didn't make one this year, mother, did we?

MARJORIE: Dennis always has a cake.

VERA: Yes, but you've been ill, mother, remember.

MARJORIE: You could have made him a cake, Vera.

[VERA *gives* NEIL *his tea.*]

DENNIS [*mouthing, sotto, across to* MARJORIE]: It doesn't matter, mother.

MARJORIE [*mouthing likewise*]: She could have made you a cake.

[VERA *becomes aware of this silent conversation.* DENNIS *and* MARJORIE *continue mouthing and gesturing till* DENNIS *becomes aware of* VERA's *gaze.*]

VERA [*pouring* DENNIS's *tea*]: You know what I'm like with cakes. And I can't do all that icing like you do. I just get it all over everything. We should have asked Mrs Mandlesham ...

MARJORIE: You don't need to ask anyone how to ice a cake.

VERA: Well, I can't do it.

PAM: Nor can I.

DENNIS: It's all right, mother, it's all right.

[VERA *gives* DENNIS *his tea. She offers* DENNIS *a cucumber sandwich. He takes one. She offers* NEIL *who declines. She offers* PAM.]

PAM: What about your mother?

[*She takes the plate from* VERA *and offers the sandwiches to* MARJORIE. VERA *pours her own tea.*]

MARJORIE [*unaware of* PAM]: Ever since he was a little boy, he's always had his cake. Even when your father was dying, Dennis, I still made you your cake.

[PAM *gives up proffering the plate, waves it at* MARJORIE *somewhat 'V' signlike and replaces it on the table.*]

DENNIS: Yes, marvellous they were too, mother. Marvellous.

[*A long silence.* VERA *reaches for the hot water jug. She catches the sugar spoon with her wrist, sending sugar high in the air.* VERA *attempts to ignore this. The others concentrate their attention elsewhere. Shakily,* VERA *replenishes the teapot with hot water. The others find this, despite themselves, compulsory viewing. She returns hot water jug to the table, as it happens close to* NEIL's *place.* NEIL, *nervous, shifts his legs. Having safely negotiated this,* VERA *smiles round. Everyone looks away.* VERA *reaches for the remaining empty cup and saucer. She rattles it dangerously but places it in front of her. She puts milk in the cup. She starts pouring tea.* MARJORIE's *voice suddenly breaks the silence.*]

MARJORIE: Remember when you were in the army. [VERA's *tea-pouring experiences a hiccup.*] I parcelled them up and I sent them to you overseas.

VERA: Yes, well, I'm very sorry. [*She rises with the cup, preparing to take it across to* MARJORIE.]

MARJORIE: I think the least you could have done, Vera, is to make him a cake. It was really very thoughtless to forget ...

[*The teacup begins to vibrate uncontrollably in* VERA's *hand.*]

VERA [*through gritted teeth*]: Will someone take this cup, please? Will someone take this cup from me?

PAM [*taking the cup from her*]: Here. Here, all right.

[PAM *takes the cup to* MARJORIE. NEIL *rises, takes a couple of sandwiches, puts them on a sideplate and takes them over to* MARJORIE.]

NEIL: Would you like a sandwich, Mrs –

[PAM *returns and sits.*]

MARJORIE: Yes, I might as well have a sandwich.

[NEIL *returns and sits. Pause.*]

Seeing as she hasn't made a cake.

VERA [*spills a cup and saucer*]: Oh.

[*Tea pours all over the table, running down between the slats.* NEIL *and* PAM *rise hastily.* DENNIS, *still seated, suppresses his mirth.*]

DENNIS: Oh God.

PAM: It's all right. I'll do it. Don't you move, Vee, you'll have it all over everything.

VERA: I'm sorry, I –

PAM: No damage.

NEIL: Can I?

PAM: No, please don't.

NEIL: But if I held this, you could ...

PAM [*sharp*]: Please, Neil, leave it to me.

NEIL [*angrily*]: All right. All right. I was only trying to ... I'll keep my mouth shut in future. [*He takes a sandwich and jams it into his mouth.*] Oh.

DENNIS: Eh?

NEIL: Cucumber.

VERA [*in an undertone*]: If she says one more word about that bloody cake ...

PAM: There we are. All mopped up.

VERA: Thank you, Pam.

[*A silence.*

DENNIS *continues his struggle to contain his laughter.* NEIL *has an indigestion spasm.* PAM *glares at him.* DENNIS's *laughter erupts. He moves away from the table. At length recovers. Wipes his eyes. Stands surveying the miserable group, smiling.*]

DENNIS: Well.

[*Pause.*]

[*Softly*] Happy birthday to me.

Happy birthday to me.

Happy birthday, dear Dennis,

Happy birth –

[*He catches* NEIL's *eye.* NEIL *gently indicates* VERA. DENNIS *darts a look at* VERA. *He tails off into silence. They sit.*]

CURTAIN

ACT TWO
SCENE ONE

The same. October. The lights are on in the garage. Outside it is dark.
DENNIS has looped a string of coloured electric light bulbs high up
round the inside walls of the garage. Some of the bulbs are missing from the
sockets. He is at present working on his present for his mother. It is a
needlework box he has made. He is sanding it with an electric drill with sander
attachment. NEIL is perched on the bench, a glass of wine in his hand, the
bottle nearby. DENNIS's glass stands untouched. He is absorbed and hardly
listens to NEIL's conversation which, anyway, is intermittently drowned by
the sound of the drill.
    DENNIS *drills. He stops.*]

NEIL: . . . you see, my trouble – Pam's trouble is this. I think we –
    [DENNIS *starts drilling, the next is inaudible.*]
    – both expect things from each other. Things that the other one is not
    prepared to give –
    [DENNIS *stops drilling.*]
    – to the other one. Do you get me?
DENNIS: Uh–huh.
NEIL: I suppose it's nature really, isn't it?
DENNIS: Ah.
NEIL: You have your opposites – like this [*He holds up his hands to*
    demonstrate.]
    [DENNIS *starts drilling.*]
    This is me – that's her. And they attract –
    [DENNIS *stops drilling.*]
    – like a magnet.
    [DENNIS *starts again.*]
    Only with people as opposed to magnets, the trouble is with people –
    [DENNIS *stops drilling.*]
    they get – demagnetized after a bit. I honestly think Pam and me have
    reached the end of the road. [*He looks to* DENNIS *for a reaction to this.*]
    [DENNIS *drills.* NEIL *waits.* DENNIS *stops.*]
    I'm saying I think we've reached the end of the road. Pam and me.
DENNIS: Ah.

NEIL: It's a terrible thing to say. She's drinking as well, you know. I'm the cause of that.

DENNIS: Oh, I shouldn't think so. [*Holding up his work*] Does that look level to you?

NEIL: Looks it. I've reached a crossroads, you see, Dennis.

DENNIS: I've mislaid the spirit level.

NEIL: Suddenly I've got to decide. I've got to make decisions. That's not something that comes very easily to me. Frankly, I find it difficult to make decisions and that truly is what gets Pam. Decide, she says. You decide. She admires strength, Dennis. I think she admires you, actually.

DENNIS: Oh, does she? That's nice.

NEIL: Women need a rock, you see. A rock. Trouble is, I'm a bloody marshmallow.

[DENNIS *drills*, NEIL *drones on.*]

Weakness in a man. That's something a woman can never respect. Even today with all this equality, she still expects to find in a man someone she can rely on in a crisis. And if that man doesn't stand up to the test, God help him.

[DENNIS *stops drilling.*]

DENNIS: True. True.

NEIL: Well, you can't say I haven't tried. Anyway, she's given up clawing me to death in the night. [*Pause*] You can't say I haven't tried.

DENNIS: No.

NEIL: I mean, this business with George Spooner. That's a start isn't it? I decided that myself. I said, right, if Dennis says he's O.K., he's O.K.

DENNIS: He's O.K. is George Spooner.

NEIL: So I didn't even ask her. I just did it. I drew out the money, handed it to him and said there you are, George, there's three thousand, five hundred quid. Get on with it. Do your worst.

DENNIS: You won't be sorry.

NEIL: I know that. I know that. I liked him. I liked old George.

DENNIS: The only way you'll lose your money with him is, if he drops dead from overwork.

NEIL: That's what I told Pam.

DENNIS: What did she say?

NEIL: She said – she said I was an idiot. You idiot, she said.

DENNIS: We'll see, won't we?

NEIL: We will. We'll see about that. Did I tell you she's drinking? I can always tell when she's drinking. She gets very – abusive.

DENNIS: Ah well. Blows over.

NEIL: Vera's looking better.

DENNIS: Oh, she is. She's a lot better. She's getting better every day. Once she and mother can bury the hatchet, we'll be laughing.

NEIL: Are they still ...?

DENNIS: Not talking at all.

NEIL: Really.

DENNIS: Well actually, it's Vera who's not talking to mother. Mother comes in one door, Vera goes out the other. Ridiculous. Been going on for weeks. I said to them – look, girls, just sit down have a laugh about it. There's only one life, you know. That's all you've got. One life. Laugh and enjoy it while you can. We'll probably all be dead tomorrow so what's the difference? Do they listen to me? Do they hell. [*Admiring his handiwork*] That's not bad. Not bad at all.

NEIL: I took your advice by the way. Went to the doctor.

DENNIS: Oh yes?

NEIL: Yes.

DENNIS: And?

NEIL: He said there was nothing wrong with me.

DENNIS: Oh good. That must be a relief.

NEIL: The trouble is, can I believe him? Is he saying that genuinely or is he saying there is something wrong with me but it's so wrong that there's no point in telling me?

DENNIS: Oh, I don't think they do that sort of thing.

NEIL: They do. I have that on very good authority. They do just that.

DENNIS: Well, I'd look on the bright side.

NEIL: Yes, quite right. I had confirmation about our house this morning.

DENNIS: Oh really.

NEIL: It's definitely listed for demolition. They reckon in about a year.

DENNIS: Well, they'll rehouse you.

NEIL: Oh yes. We'll get rehoused. If we're still together.

DENNIS: Well, there you are then. Nice new house. Nothing wrong with that.

NEIL: No. No. True. [*Slight pause*] God, I sometimes feel like jumping off a bridge, Den.

DENNIS: Oh, come on. Cheer up. It's your birthday.

NEIL: If I wasn't able to come along and talk to you like this, I think –
      [DENNIS *picks up a hammer and bangs a loose joint into place.*]
   – I think I'd have gone and done away with myself –
      [DENNIS *stops hammering.*]
   – long before this.

DENNIS: There we are.

NEIL: Very good.

DENNIS: Now we'll see who's the joiner in this family. I'll show her.

NEIL: That your mother's birthday present, is it?

DENNIS: Yes. Needlework box.

NEIL: Thanks for the tie, by the way. Very nice.

DENNIS: Oh, glad you liked it. Mother chose it actually.

NEIL: Ah. Very nice. Good taste.

DENNIS: Yes, she has. Now then, what's next. Happy birthday, by the way.

NEIL: Oh, thank you.

DENNIS: No, you see, just between ourselves, I'm rigging up a little surprise for mother. Father always used to do that. He always had some little surprise for her on her birthday. I try to keep up the tradition.

NEIL: Is that what those are for?

DENNIS: The lights. Yes. Just a little touch. Had them left over from a barbecue. Look. [*He switches them on by the door. They fail to go on.*] Ah. Something wrong. I'll check those. Yes, look, some of the bulbs are missing. Steps? Stepladder . . .

NEIL: 'Course one of the problems is what to do with Darren.

DENNIS: When's that?

NEIL: When Pam and I separate.

DENNIS: Ah. What did she give you by the way?

NEIL: What?

DENNIS: For your birthday. What did Pam give you?

NEIL: Oh, I don't think she really had time. She's got her hands full with Darren at the moment.

DENNIS: There's a square box here somewhere with some coloured bulbs. Can you see if you can see them?

NEIL: – er . . . [*He starts to search.*]

   [PAM *comes out from the house. She rattles the doorknob of the garage.*]

PAM: Hey, you two. Open up.

DENNIS: Just a minute. Just a minute. [*To* NEIL] Quick, sling us that cloth.

NEIL: Eh?

DENNIS: To cover this up, quick.

PAM: Open up.

DENNIS: Right. Open up.

   [NEIL *struggles with the door.*]

Give it a shove. I must fix that. And the other one, come to that.

   [NEIL *manages to open the door.*]

PAM [*entering*]: What are you doing out here, for heaven's sake?

DENNIS: Hallo, hallo, here's trouble. Aha, a box of bulbs. These are they.

   [*He erects the stepladder, takes out a bulb and starts to climb.*]

PAM: Just what do you think you're doing?

NEIL: How do you mean?

PAM: We're all sat in there twiddling our thumbs waiting for you. What's going on?

DENNIS: Surprises, surprises.

NEIL: Just getting things ready, that's all.

PAM: And what are we supposed to do in the meanwhile? I mean, there's Vee and me in the kitchen, and Marjorie sitting on her own in the sitting room because Vee won't go in there if she's in there, and we're all having a marvellous time. I thought this was supposed to be a birthday party.

NEIL: Well, don't look at me.

PAM: I am looking at you. I want you to come in there and socialize.

NEIL: All right, all right.

DENNIS: Could you pass me one of those bulbs, please, from the box?

NEIL [*doing so*] : I'll be in in a minute.

PAM: No, Neil, I mean now. Right now.

DENNIS: Ta.

NEIL: Look, I can't at the moment, Pam. I'm –

PAM: I don't care what you're doing, I'm not sitting in there for another half hour.

NEIL: Look, don't keep on, Pam, for God's sake. Don't keep on. I've had it up to here.

DENNIS: And another one, please.

PAM: Oh, don't you start that one. You know what happens if you start that one.

NEIL: I know. I know.

DENNIS: Bulb, bulb, bulb.

PAM: Well, just you remember. You have absolutely no right to complain about anything ever. You've handed over total responsibility to me. You have forfeited any right to say anything ever again.

NEIL: What the hell are you going on about?

DENNIS: Another bulb, s'il vous plaît.

PAM: You have left me to deal with the running of the house entirely. You have left me to bring up your child and you have left me to nurse mother on my own.

NEIL: I don't know how you can say that.

PAM: Because it is true, my love. That is why I can say it.

NEIL: It isn't true.

DENNIS: Could somebody steady the steps, please.

NEIL [*placing a hand on the steps*]: It just isn't true at all.

PAM: Of course it's bloody true.

NEIL: Look, don't swear, Pam. Every time you get angry, you start swearing.

PAM: I'll do more than bloody swear in a minute if you don't come straight back in there with me this instant.

[*As she speaks, she grips the side of the steps in fury.*]

DENNIS: Look, steady, steady, I'll fall off in a minute.

NEIL: Look, don't do that with the steps, Pam, he'll fall off them.

PAM: Serve him right if he did. [*She shakes the steps.*]

DENNIS: Oy. Oy. Do you mind?

NEIL: Pam, he'll fall off them.

[VERA *comes in from the house.*]

VERA: Dennis. Dennis.

DENNIS: Hallo there.

VERA: Dennis, will you please come down at once. Come into the house, go into the sitting room and ask your mother, ever so nicely, if she would mind turning down the television.

DENNIS: Can't you ask her yourself, love, I'm a bit ...

VERA: I have asked her. Twice I have asked her. She has taken not a blind bit of notice. In fact, I think she's actually turned it up. Do I have to remind you there is a small baby next door?

DENNIS: Yes, all right. All right.

VERA: Who is very probably asleep.

DENNIS: Would somebody go and turn the television down, please?

PAM: I'll go.

VERA: No, I want Dennis to go. It's his mother. He can cope with her. I want him to see what she's like.

DENNIS: How can I go? I'm up a ladder.

PAM: It's all right, I'll go. [*She does so.*]

VERA [*calmer*]: What are you doing, Dennis? Will you please tell me what you're doing out here?

DENNIS: I'm just fixing up a little surprise, that's all. Like I always do.

VERA: Surprise?

DENNIS: For mother's birthday, love. It's her birthday.

VERA: Oh God, don't remind me. Sixty-seven today. I don't look sixty-seven do I, Dennis? Everyone was amazed when they heard I was sixty-seven.

DENNIS [*descending the ladder*]: Look, Vee, Vee, come on. Calm down, love, calm down.

VERA: And the butcher, he said – oh are you sixty-seven, Mrs Crowthorne. I'd never have guessed.

DENNIS: Vee, listen, it's her birthday. It's only once a year. Now go on.

Go in there and give her a smile. That's all she wants. Just a smile. Say – happy birthday, mother and give her a little drink.

VERA: She doesn't need a little drink. She's already downed half a bottle.

DENNIS: Vera. Now, Vera, for me. Come on, love, for me.

VERA: Oh God, Dennis, you just don't . . . you don't . . .

DENNIS: Now what is it? What don't I do?

VERA: You don't . . . look, would you mind very much, Neil?

NEIL: Eh?

VERA: Could you find somewhere else to go just for a minute?

NEIL: Oh, right.

DENNIS: He's all right. He's all right.

VERA: He's not all right.

NEIL: It's all right. I'm going.

DENNIS: Thanks, Neil. Thanks.

[NEIL *goes out of the door.*]

Now, Vee. What's the trouble?

VERA: It's just –

NEIL: I'll shut the door, shall I?

DENNIS: Thank you, Neil.

[NEIL *closes the door, contemplates whether or not to go into the house and finally opts to sit on a dustbin.*]

VERA: It's just – I think I need help, Dennis.

DENNIS: How do you mean, help?

VERA: From you. I don't think I can manage much longer unless I get your help.

DENNIS: Help. What way? With mother? Do you mean with mother?

VERA: Partly. No, not just her. You never seem to be here, Dennis.

DENNIS: What do you mean? I'm here. I'm home as much as most men. Probably more than most men.

VERA: Yes, but then you're out here, aren't you?

DENNIS: Not all the time.

VERA: Most of the time.

DENNIS: Well, I'm doing things. For the house. I mean, you're welcome to come out here too. There's nothing to stop you if you want to talk. Talk things over.

VERA: But we've got a home, Dennis. I spend all day trying to make it nice. I don't want to spend the evening sitting in a garage.

DENNIS: Oh, come on.

VERA: I mean, what's the point of my . . . doing everything? I mean, what's the point? I need help, Dennis.

DENNIS: Yes, but don't you see, you're not being clear, Vee. You say help but what sort of help do you mean?

VERA: Just help. From you.

DENNIS: Yes. Well, look, tell you what. When you've got a moment, why don't you sit down, get a bit of paper and just make a little list of all the things you'd like me to help you with. Things you'd like me to do, things that need mending or fixing and then we can talk about them and see what I can do to help. All right?

[VERA *does not reply*.]

How about that, Vee? All right? Does that suit you?

[VERA *moves to the door*.]

Vee?

[VERA *goes slowly out and into the house*.]

Vee. Vee.

[NEIL *sticks his head round the door*.]

NEIL: She's gone inside.

DENNIS: Oh well. All this house needs, Neil, is a little bit of understanding and a little bit more of people being able to laugh at themselves. [*He starts to ascend the steps*.] That's all it needs. Sounds simple enough, doesn't it? But when I think of the times I've said it and the times it's ... [*Suddenly, loudly*] Steady the ladder.

NEIL [*diving for the steps and steadying them*]: Sorry.

DENNIS: Blimey, I nearly went that time. One more bulb.

NEIL: One more bulb.

DENNIS: Now, I'm going to need you for the cake, Neil.

NEIL: Cake?

DENNIS: This is what happens. I want you, if you would, to wait in the kitchen. I've hidden mother's cake on the top of the shelf over the fridge. It's in a big maroon tin. Now. I'll call mother out here. As soon as she's through the kitchen, out with the cake and light the candles. She walks in here – [*Demonstrating*] you see, like this – I'll be hiding behind here, you see. Now as soon as she's through the door, I'll give you your signal. That'll be one long blast on the horn. O.K.? At the same moment, I jump up – happy birthday, mother – and uncover the present. Meanwhile, you have come in behind her with the cake – if you like, singing happy birthday, dear Marjorie or something – and if you can manage it, switching on these lights from here, you see? And at the same moment, Vee and Pam also come out of hiding. And you just watch mother's face. It'll be a picture. A real study.

NEIL: You're very fond of your mother, aren't you?

DENNIS: Yes, well, I suppose I am. I have to admit it. She's got her faults.

She's like Vee, you know. She gets a bee in her bonnet about things but you can soon joke her out of it. Easy as that.

[PAM *enters from the house with a broken glass in a dustpan.*]

PAM: Where do you keep your dustbins in this place?

DENNIS: Round the side there. Just behind you.

PAM: Oh yes. [*She lifts the lid and empties the dustpan.*]

DENNIS: Been a mishap?

PAM: Just a little one. Only one or two glasses. Nothing serious.

[*To* NEIL] Hallo, dearest.

NEIL: You all right?

PAM: Fine, dearest, fine.

NEIL: Right.

PAM: I'm getting very hungry. Is there any chance of eating soon?

DENNIS: Yes, we're nearly all set.

PAM: What have you been doing?

DENNIS: Never mind. You'll see. Eh, Neil?

PAM: As long as you haven't persuaded him to give away any more money.

NEIL: Look, it was my money.

PAM: Oh quite, quite.

DENNIS: Not unless he still wants to buy the car.

PAM: He can't afford it now anyway.

NEIL: Oh look, Pam, please.

PAM: Go to hell.

[NEIL *goes out into the house.*]

DENNIS [*at the back of the garage*]: Neil, would you mind ... oh, has he gone?

PAM: 'Fraid so.

DENNIS: Oh well, perhaps you wouldn't mind, Pam. I just want to clear a bit of space in here. Could you pass me that box?

PAM: This one?

DENNIS: Ta.

PAM [*handing him the box*]: You'll really have to do something about those two, you know.

DENNIS: Who do you mean?

PAM: Your wife and your mother.

DENNIS: Ah well. It's a traditional problem really, isn't it? Nothing much you can do. They rub along.

PAM: They do not rub along.

DENNIS: Oh well, not just at present. No. But these rows happen. You haven't seen us normally, Pam. I can tell you, there were times in the past when we three, we've sat round in there and we've laughed and pulled each other's legs about things. You'd be amazed.

PAM: I would. [*Indicating another box*] You want this one?

DENNIS: If you would, thank you.

[PAM *bends to pick up the box. She becomes giddy. She stands up and steadies herself.*]

You all right?

PAM: Wah. Yes, fine. You ever going to sell this thing?

DENNIS: Well, frankly, nobody seems really interested. And then I thought, well, it could be that in a few months Vee might get it into her head to want to start driving again. I mean, the way things are going she might. I mean, in general terms, she's getting better every day.

PAM: What exactly was wrong with her?

DENNIS: Oh well, she got these very gloomy depressions. You know. Nothing was right. She got very jittery so she went to see this doctor, psychiatrist, and he said primarily she was just to take it easier. She wasn't to rush at things. And she went on seeing him for a couple of months, and then she seemed to be feeling better and she just stopped going. I mean, I think we got the message. All Vee needs is a happy family atmosphere. To feel she has a home around her.

PAM: Could be. Good old Dennis.

DENNIS: Beg your pardon?

PAM [*holding up the bottle of wine*]: May I?

DENNIS: Help yourself. Help yourself.

PAM: I must say, you're very resilient. I think I'd have given up years ago.

DENNIS: Given up what?

PAM: Trying to spread jolly cheer.

DENNIS: Well. Smile costs nothing, does it?

PAM: True. True. Could you jolly me up, please, Dennis.

DENNIS: You? You're all right, aren't you?

PAM: Amazingly enough, no.

DENNIS: All right. You tell me your problem. I'll sort it out.

PAM: Well. Here am I, constantly being reminded by this avalanche of birthdays we all seem to be having, that I'm no longer as young as I'd like to be.

DENNIS: What does that mean, eh? For a start, what's that supposed to mean?

PAM: I feel old, Dennis – old, unfulfilled, frustrated, unattractive, dull, washed out, undesirable – you name it. And I've got absolutely nothing to look forward to. How about that to be getting on with?

DENNIS: Well, for a start you've got your kid. What about your little boy?

PAM: He'll soon go. As soon as he's strong enough to walk, he'll be gone.

DENNIS: Well, there's Neil.

PAM: Next.

DENNIS: Er – no wait. You can't just say that. What about Neil?

PAM: I don't really look forward to Neil as much as I used to, Dennis.

DENNIS: Really?

PAM: Really and truly.

DENNIS: Well then. I don't know.

PAM: Do you know what it's like, Dennis? To feel undesirable?

DENNIS: No. No. Can't say I do.

PAM: That's what he's done to me.

DENNIS: Sorry? Who's this? We're still talking about Neil, are we?

PAM: He's made me feel ashamed. Why should I be made to feel ashamed?

DENNIS: Depends what you've been up to, eh? [*He laughs.*]

PAM: He hasn't even paid me the compliment of going after another woman. I could accept that, just about. But to be frozen out, as if I was unnatural, some sort of freak. It isn't me, is it? It's him.

DENNIS: Neil?

PAM: There's something wrong with him.

DENNIS: Health worries, you mean.

PAM: That man is destroying me. He is systematically destroying me. I was the youngest supervisor they'd ever had. I had prospects. They told me. Prospects. They were grooming me for something bigger. That's what they told me when I left.

DENNIS: That a fact?

PAM: They had their eye on me. They said so.

DENNIS: Very good. You must have made an impression. Good.

PAM: You don't find me undesirable, Dennis, do you?

DENNIS: Ah well. Now remember, I'm a married man.

PAM: Presumably you've still got feelings.

DENNIS: Not if I can help them, I haven't. [*He laughs.*] No, you're very attractive. I mean, I'm perfectly sure, in another life, assuming such a thing existed, that you'd very probably attract me. I'd go so far as to say, I'd probably fancy you.

PAM: Then why the hell doesn't Neil?

DENNIS: What?

PAM: Fancy me, or whatever you call it.

DENNIS: Well, he possibly does. In fact, I'm sure he possibly does. But listen, Pam, when you get to our age, you have to slow down. We all do. I mean, I would do things ten years ago I can't do now. I used to be able to play forty-five minutes each way. Football. Down the road there. Couldn't do it now to save my life. Same with you, same with Neil. You need to adjust.

PAM: Is it age then? You think?

DENNIS: Probably nothing more than that. [*Pause*] That any help at all?

PAM: No, I'm sorry, Dennis, you're not doing a very good job . . . I'm still very depressed.

DENNIS: Well, I don't know. I mean, what do you want? Want me to do a funny dance for you or something?

PAM: Oh yes, please. Do a funny dance.

DENNIS: No, I mean seriously. Seriously I can't cheer you up unless you're serious about it.

PAM: Perhaps I should have said yes to the car.

DENNIS: Well, the offer's still open. Two hundred quid.

PAM: I can't afford two hundred pence, Dennis. I used to have some money. Quite a lot of money actually. That I'd saved. But now I'm a housewife so I'm not allowed to have any. And I spent all my money on curtains and pillow cases and lavatory brushes –
    [*She sits behind the wheel of the car.*] Brrm brrm.

DENNIS: Runs well.

PAM: Fasten your seat belts. Start her up, Dennis.

DENNIS: Haven't got the keys.

PAM: Start her up and let's slip away.

DENNIS: No, that door's still stuck, you see. I really must fix that.

PAM: Come on, Dennis, start her up.

DENNIS: You can't. Not in the garage. Not with the door shut.

PAM: Brrm brrm.

DENNIS: You all right?

PAM: Brrm.

DENNIS: Pam. Pam.

PAM [*loudly*]: BRRM.

DENNIS: Now come on, Pam. Pam.

PAM: Brrm – oh. Oh, Dennis.

DENNIS: What is it?

PAM: I think I'm going to be car sick.

DENNIS [*alarmed*]: Now hold on, hold on. Not on the upholstery. I'll help you out. Hang on.

PAM: Oh God.

DENNIS [*struggling with her*]: Come on, you're all right. Come on.
    [*He tries to tug her clear.*
    She appears to be tangled with everything, especially the seat belts and the steering wheel. DENNIS *tugs at her sweater sleeve. Her arm comes out of it.*]
    Oh, blimey o'reilly. Come on, Pam.
    [MARJORIE *comes out of the house in her party frock.*]

MARJORIE: Now, you can say what you like, Dennis, I am not sitting in there any longer. I want my surprise. Dennis? [*She enters the garage.*]

DENNIS: Oh mother, look, could you give me a hand?

MARJORIE: Oh, Dennis, you naughty boy.

DENNIS: Mother, please.

MARJORIE: It's all right, Dennis. It's all right. I've seen nothing. You needn't worry.

DENNIS: Mother. [*He continues to struggle.*]

   [MARJORIE *goes out and is closing the door when she is confronted by* VERA.]

MARJORIE: It's all right, Vera, there's no one in there.

VERA: What do you mean? Dennis is in there.

MARJORIE: No, Dennis is not in there, Vera. And I would prefer you didn't go in.

VERA: Oh, get out of the way. [*She pushes* MARJORIE *aside.*]

MARJORIE: I will not have my son being unjustly accused.

VERA: I said, get out of the way.

   [*She opens the door and goes in.*]

MARJORIE: All right. On your own head be it.

VERA: Dennis, I – [*Seeing them*] Oh, I'm sorry I ...

DENNIS: Vee, will you give me a hand?

MARJORIE: I told you not to come in. Serve you right. There are certain things it is best a wife doesn't know about.

VERA: You poisonous old woman. You're loving this, aren't you? It's what you've really wanted all along, wasn't it? For Dennis to go off with somebody. To break up my home.

MARJORIE: I don't know what you're talking about, Vera, you're being most offensive.

VERA: You nasty old toad. You've always hated me. You've always wanted my home.

DENNIS: Now, Vera.

MARJORIE: I don't know what's come over you.

VERA: Oh, I'd love to – I'd love to sandpaper your rotten face
   [*She picks up the electric drill.*]

MARJORIE [*screaming and running up to one corner of the garage*]: Vera. Vera.

DENNIS: Now, girls, steady. Girls.

VERA [*screaming above the drill whose cable is too short to allow her to reach* MARJORIE]: You sneaky, rotten, deceitful, sly, old toad.

MARJORIE: Now, you stop that. You stop that. Dennis, help me.

DENNIS [*releasing* PAM *and cautiously approaching* VERA *and the whirling drill*]: Now, Vee ...

[PAM, *released, slumps forward on to the steering wheel. The horn blasts loudly and continuously*.]

Now, Vee. I want you to stop that. I want you to put that down.

VERA: Bitch, bitch, bitch.

MARJORIE: Stop her, Dennis, stop her. Tell her to stop it.

[NEIL *enters from the kitchen bearing the illuminated cake. As he enters the garage, he switches on the lights, bathing the scene in a glorious technicolour*.]

NEIL: Happy birthday to you
Happy birthday to you
Happy birth –
[*He tails off*.]

ACT TWO
SCENE TWO

The same. January. A cold clear morning. VERA *sits in the garden in the 'sitting area'. She is enveloped in a large rug, with just her face showing. After a moment* DENNIS *comes in through the gate. He carries two large supermarket carrier bags. He has on his coat, scarf and gloves.*

DENNIS: There. That didn't take long, did it? I think I've got everything we need. Except the soup. I couldn't get your soup, Vee. Had to get another sort. But the man said it was just as good. Just as good. Now, are you sure you're warm enough out here?

VERA [*in a whisper*]: Yes.

DENNIS: Well, as long as you don't die of exposure on us. I'm not having that. See? I could get Mother to bring you out a hot water bottle. I mean, if you insist on sitting out here ... Very crowded in town today. Saturday morning, I suppose. Oh Vee, now this'll interest you. Listen to this. I heard something today. You remember old Spooner? George Spooner, you remember? The man who did our sitting room. Well, guess what happened? He's run off. With his secretary from his office. Drawn out all the money and done a bunk. Left his wife, his business, everything. What about that, eh? Would you credit it. Nobody knows where they've gone. All those poor people with half their wallpaper hanging off. Eh? Poor old Neil though. There goes his money. Well, we live and learn. Old George Spooner. I'd have laid my life on the line for George Spooner.

[MARJORIE *comes out of the house.*]

MARJORIE: Oh, Dennis, you're back. Did you get on all right?

DENNIS: I think so, mother. I can cope with a bit of shopping without falling down, you know.

MARJORIE: Well, knowing you. How is she?

DENNIS: She seems all right.

MARJORIE: As long as she's warm enough. If only she'd stay in the house, I'd feel happier. I could keep more of an eye on her. She won't have it. She doesn't like it. She gets so fidgety and restless.

DENNIS: Well, maybe the fresh air'll help her along.

MARJORIE: Did you get her soup?

DENNIS: Yes, we're well stocked up now.

MARJORIE: I'll try her with some at lunchtime. She had her rice krispies this morning so she's not doing so badly, are you, dear? Would you like to take those through to the kitchen, Dennis?

DENNIS: Will do. Will do.

MARJORIE: You must be nearly ready for your lunch.

DENNIS: I wouldn't say no to that, mother.

MARJORIE: I've got you a nice chop.

DENNIS: Lovely. Yum yum.

[*He goes into the house.*]

MARJORIE: Now, you're positive you're warm enough, Vera? [*Tucking her in more securely*] That's it. That's better. Now you just sit there quietly. You've no need to worry, do you hear? Dennis is being taken good care of. I'll see to him. You just look after yourself. We just want to see you get better. You know what Dennis has made for me? He's made me a little table. Little bedside table. You know, I've always needed one. And he mended my lamp. Wasn't that kind? Are you going to have a little soup for your lunch? Eh? Vera? A little soup? Would you like a little bowl of soup? Oh well, I expect you'll tell us if you want anything. I'll be back in a minute, dear. [*Calling*] Dennis dear, put the kettle on, will you?

DENNIS [*distant*]: Just a sec. Front door.

MARJORIE: Oh. Front door. Front door, Vera. I wonder who that can be?

[MARJORIE *heads towards the house.* DENNIS *emerges with* PAM *and* NEIL.]

DENNIS: Guess who? Guess who then?

MARJORIE: Well, fancy that. Hallo there.

NEIL: Hallo.

PAM: 'llo.

MARJORIE: We haven't seen you for ages, have we?

NEIL: No, no.

MARJORIE: Haven't been avoiding us, have you?

NEIL: No, no. Not really. We just – er ...

MARJORIE: How's your mother?

NEIL: Much the same.

MARJORIE: That's good. Have you come to see the patient?

PAM: If we could.

MARJORIE: She's just round there in the sun. I'll make us a cup of coffee, shall I, Dennis?

DENNIS: Lovely. Lovely, mother.

MARJORIE: Won't be a moment.

[MARJORIE *goes into the house.*]

DENNIS: Well, this is nice. Nice surprise.

NEIL: Well, we were ... we thought we'd —

PAM: How's Vee?

DENNIS: Well, in point of fact, she's a lot better. She's making giant strides. The doctor's delighted. He's over the moon about her. Here we are, Vee. Vee love, look who's come to see you. Pam and Neil, Vee. Come to see you.

PAM: Hallo, Vee.

NEIL: Hallo.

[VERA *looks at them blankly. They stand round her.*]

DENNIS: Say hallo, Vee. Say hallo. Hallo.

VERA [*faintly*]: 'llo.

DENNIS: There you are, you see. There you are.

NEIL: Well, that is progress.

DENNIS: Certainly is. I mean, last time you saw her, I don't honestly, to be absolutely frank, think she knew who you were. So you see, she's coming along.

NEIL: Oh yes.

DENNIS: I mean, yesterday was a breakthrough. An absolute breakthrough. She had, what — two good full bowls of soup. Now, that means her appetite is returning which is a very good sign. Two good bowls she had.

PAM: Is she all right out here? It's quite cold.

DENNIS: Ah well. Quite. But when she's in the house, she only frets.

NEIL: She what?

DENNIS: Frets. Starts fretting. She seems to be happier out here. I mean, we'd sooner she was in. Than sitting out here exposed to all the elements. I'd be happier. I think we'd all be happier if she was under cover.

NEIL: I'd have thought she ought to have been under cover.

DENNIS: Right.

PAM: What's the doctor say?

DENNIS: Well. Go along with her wishes. That's what it boiled down to. Good old rest, that's all she needs. I mean, we talked round the possibility of her, you know, going into a hospital but — er — on balance we decided that the home environment would probably do more for her in the long run. She always hated going away. Hated it. Never enjoyed hotels. That sort of thing. Always at her happiest at home. Home's where she belongs.

NEIL: Yes, I'd have thought so.

DENNIS: Of course, at the moment, she's still very much in herself.

NEIL: Yes, yes.

DENNIS: The doctor was explaining. A mental injury, which is what Vee's got, is not unlike in many ways a normal physical injury. Like, say, cutting your hand. It takes time to heal. Knit together again, you see. It's the same with her mind. That's what it's doing now. It's knitting together.

NEIL: Amazing.

DENNIS: Yes it is. It's amazing.

NEIL: It's a miracle of engineering, the mind.

DENNIS: True. True. Mind you, to her advantage she's always been a very fit woman. Physically very strong. She had a good home background, you see. Paid off.

NEIL: Ah.

DENNIS: Here, I'll let you into a secret, shall I? You know how old she is today? I know she wouldn't mind me telling you.

PAM: Oh, is it her birthday?

DENNIS: Yes, yes. But have a guess how old. You'll never guess. She's forty-two.

PAM: Really?

NEIL: Good gracious.

DENNIS: Now, you would have never guessed that, would you?

NEIL: No.

PAM: She's lucky. She's got a very good bone structure.

DENNIS: She was a lovely girl.

NEIL: Must have been.

PAM: Vera? Vee ... Vee ...

NEIL: Does she say much then?

DENNIS: Er, no, not really no. She says yes occasionally and no. That sort of thing. And you can get her to say hallo if you work at it. I mean, she can understand you. She'll understand what we're saying now.

PAM: Vee ...

DENNIS: I wouldn't bother, Pam. I really wouldn't.

[*Pause.*]

Neil. I've just heard about George Spooner.

NEIL: Oh yes.

DENNIS: Yes, I'm sorry.

NEIL: Yes.

DENNIS: I'm still absolutely amazed, I don't mind saying. I mean, he just didn't look the type, did he? Rushing off like that. With his secretary, was it?

NEIL: I understand so, yes.

DENNIS: Well. They're bound to catch up with him.

NEIL: Yes.

DENNIS: Bound to in the end. I suppose you'll have dropped a bit then?

NEIL: No. I dropped the lot actually.

DENNIS: Ah. Well, it seems like Pam was right for once. Eh, Pam?

PAM: Nothing to do with me.

DENNIS: No, you could really have knocked me down with a ... George Spooner. But you know the most unbelievable thing of all – what I really can't understand. He was a Capricorn.

NEIL: Ah.

DENNIS: Capricorns just don't do that sort of thing. It's not in their nature.

[*Pause.*]

[*Laughing*] As a matter of fact – er – talking of rumours, I'd heard that you'd both separated. Shows how much you can rely on rumours. Don't know where I heard that.

PAM: From your mother probably.

DENNIS: Oh?

PAM: Who got it from mine.

DENNIS: Ah.

PAM: We did separate for about a week.

DENNIS: Oh, I see.

PAM: Yes.

NEIL: But we're sort of together again now. Temporarily anyway. You see, we felt that Pam needed to get qualified. Before she could really start out on her own. What with Darren and that. So she'll probably be working on her qualifications for a bit.

DENNIS: You'll need qualifications.

NEIL: She will.

DENNIS: What are you planning to do, then?

PAM: Well, I was considering public relations.

DENNIS: Ah.

NEIL: I thought you said you were going into the prison service.

PAM: That was a joke.

NEIL: Oh.

[DENNIS *laughs. Pause.*]

DENNIS [*drawing them aside*]: Look – er – just between ourselves, I'm glad you came round actually. I was going to give you a ring. That car of Vee's. You know, the one you were interested in ...

NEIL: Oh yes?

DENNIS: Well, Vee obviously won't be up to driving it for quite some time – and, er, well, it's just lying there going to waste really. So I wondered if you'd care to have it. I know Vee would like you to have it.

NEIL [*exchanging a glance with* PAM]: Well ...

PAM: I don't think so, thank you.

DENNIS: I mean, as a gift, you know.

PAM: I don't think we'll be needing a car.

DENNIS: Oh.

NEIL: Thanks anyway.

DENNIS: Well, if you do change your minds ...

NEIL: Thanks.

[*Pause*]

DENNIS: Hey, guess what I did last Saturday?

NEIL: What?

DENNIS: I fixed those garage doors. What about that?

NEIL: I don't believe it.

DENNIS: I didn't have much choice. I had mother after me.

NEIL: Oh, I see.

MARJORIE [*distant*]: Woo-hoo.

DENNIS: Oh, there she goes. [*Calling*] All right, mother.

NEIL: She's looking well these days.

DENNIS: Oh, she's on top form at the moment. Wonderful. Sixty-seven, you know.

NEIL: Very good.

[MARJORIE *emerges from the house with a tray of coffee.*]

MARJORIE: Coffee up.

DENNIS [*hurrying to her*]: All right, mother, I'll take them. Are we going to have it out here then? It's a bit chilly.

MARJORIE: Well, yes it is. But what about the ...

DENNIS: Oh, my word yes. I nearly forgot. It's a good job you did come round today, you two. Bearing in mind who's twenty-one today, eh? Old Aquarius here. [*Drawing them aside*] Look, look, mother's made her a little cake, see? [*He displays a very small iced cake with a single candle on it.*]

NEIL: Ah.

MARJORIE: It's only a little one. Just a token.

DENNIS: No point in doing any more. She wouldn't really appreciate it. It's a good job you remembered, mother.

MARJORIE: Somebody's got to remember your wife's birthday.

DENNIS: Vee. Can you see? Mother's made you a little cake, see? Just to prove we haven't forgotten you.

[VERA *stares blankly.*]

I think she knows. I think she does.

MARJORIE: I don't know how she can sit out in this wind.

DENNIS: We can't keep her in the house, can we? Wouldn't you like to

come back in the warm, Vee? Be tucked up at home, eh? Wouldn't
that be nicer?

VERA [*after a pause, softly*]: No.

[DENNIS *looks at* MARJORIE.]

MARJORIE: No?

DENNIS: No. [*To the others*] She's still disorientated, you see.

MARJORIE [*handing out the coffee*]: Pam.

PAM: Thanks.

MARJORIE: Neil. That's yours. No sugar, is that right?

NEIL: Ah, thank you.

MARJORIE: And Dennis. That's sugared, Dennis.

DENNIS: Thank you, mum. Well, happy birthday to Vee, eh?

PAM: Vee.

MARJORIE:⎫
NEIL:　　⎬　Happy birthday, Vee.

[*Slight pause.*]

DENNIS [*singing softly*]: Happy birthday to you
　Happy birthday to you
　　[MARJORIE *joins in. She motions to* NEIL *and* PAM *who join in too.*
　　VERA's *lips move silently with them.*]
　Happy birthday, dear Vera
　Happy birthday to you.
　　[*The lights fade.*]

CURTAIN

TEN TIMES TABLE

First produced at the Stephen Joseph Theatre-in-the-Round, Scarborough, on 18 January 1977 and subsequently by Michael Codron at the Globe Theatre, London, on 5 April 1978, with the following cast:

RAY	*Paul Eddington*
DONALD	*Benjamin Whitrow*
HELEN	*Julia McKenzie*
SOPHIE	*Stephanie Fayerman*
ERIC	*John Salthouse*
AUDREY	*Matyelok Gibbs*
LAWRENCE	*Tenniel Evans*
TIM	*Christopher Godwin*
PHILIPPA	*Diane Bull*
MAX KIRKOV	*Rob Stuart*

Directed by Alan Ayckbourn
Designed by Patrick Robertson

ACT ONE

Scene One   At the meeting held on Wednesday 3 November

Scene Two. At the meeting held on Friday 17 December

Scene Three: At the meeting held on Thursday 19 May

ACT TWO

Scene One: At the emergency meeting held on Sunday 5 June

Scene Two: On Festival Day, Saturday 11 June

ACT ONE
SCENE ONE

*A committee room. In fact, the ballroom of the Swan Hotel. At one end a
stage where the band, when the room is in use, presumably play. One or two
'glitter' music stands. A mini – or possibly an upright piano. To one side, crash
doors to the street. To the other, the main entrance from the hotel. The room
is in bad repair. Dirty drapes. Dirty dim chandeliers. In the centre of the room,
isolated, the committee table with ten chairs round it (one at each end).
At the start, it is very gloomy indeed with only the emergency lights on.
In the semi-darkness, RAY, an enthusiastic man in his forties, enters. He
carries a briefcase and a half finished pint of beer.*

RAY [*to someone off behind him*]: Right, thank you. [*He turns.*] Hoy! Hoy
– I say. There's no light in here. Could we have some lights on in here,
please? Lights. Yes, lights ... [*Clicking of switches*] No ... No ...
No ...
   [*The lights go on.*]
That's it.
   [*The lights go off.*]
No. The last one you did. No. The one before that.
   [*The lights go on.*]
That's it. Thank you. Fine.
   [RAY *approaches the committee table, selects the end chair and stands
   emptying his briefcase. After a moment,* DONALD, *a grey man in his
   fifties, appears in the doorway.*]
DONALD: Ah. Good evening, Mr Dixon. Is this where we're met?
RAY: Yes. Yes. Come on, Councillor Evans, come in.
DONALD: Just one moment. I'll just fetch mother.
RAY: Right. Do you need any ...?
DONALD: No, no, no. I left her in the foyer while I found out where we
were. Save her a few steps. I thought we'd be in here. We usually are.
We meet in here with the Civic Society, you know.
RAY: Yes, well, it's a bit of a barn, I'm afraid. But it's cheap. They don't
have so many dances these days.
DONALD: No, that's true enough. Won't be a minute.
   [*As he turns to go, he passes* HELEN.]

Oh good evening, Mrs Dixon.

HELEN: Hallo there. Lovely to see you.

DONALD: I'm just fetching mother.

HELEN: Yes, I've been talking to her in the lobby. Doesn't she look fit?

DONALD: Yes, yes. Excuse me ...

[*He goes out.* HELEN *approaches the table.*]

HELEN: He's left that poor old lady sitting slap in front of the Gents. She keeps getting knocked sideways in the rush. Do you think she's going to be up to this?

RAY: How do you mean?

HELEN: Well, she looks a bit feeble. She didn't seem to understand a word I was saying.

RAY: Oh, it won't be very strenuous. Just a matter of taking a few Minutes. A little bit of typing now and again.

HELEN: She looks past it to me.

RAY: Well, with her being retired, I thought she might be glad of a few bob. I'll see her all right. She sounded very willing in her letter.

HELEN: God, it's freezing in here. I'm going to get my coat.

RAY: Mind you, she must be over eighty now, I suppose.

HELEN: Well, we'll have to speak very slowly for her, won't we?

[SOPHIE *enters. Early thirties. Still fresh-faced from much open air. She carries a large shopping bag. She is followed immediately by* ERIC, *bearded and suspicious.*]

Sophie, hallo.

SOPHIE: Hallo, Helen. Hallo, Ray.

RAY: Hallo, there.

SOPHIE [*indicating bag*]: Weekend shopping.

HELEN: I warn you, you're going to need a coat. It's freezing in here. Be warned ... [*Seeing* ERIC] Hallo. I don't think we've met, have we? Helen Dixon. How do you do.

ERIC: Hallo.

SOPHIE: Eric – Collins.

HELEN: Have you come along with Sophie?

SOPHIE: Oh no.

RAY: Hang on, hang on. Don't start that, my love, he's a married man. Haven't you met Eric, Helen? Eric, this is my wife Helen. Eric Collins who's teaching up at the school. The Catherine Stoker comprehensive.

HELEN: Really? The Catherine Stoker. How are you managing in that building?

ERIC: Well, it's ...

HELEN: Isn't it awful? Ghastly. Typical socialist monstrosity. Does your wife teach as well?

ERIC: Who? Oh yes ...

HELEN: Isn't that extraordinary? You know, they always come in pairs. Don't you find that? Teachers. Like Noah's Ark.

ERIC: She's not my wife.

HELEN: I beg your pardon?

ERIC: She's not my wife.

HELEN: Oh I'm sorry, I thought –

ERIC: We just live together.

HELEN: Ah well. That's convenient anyway. Excuse me, I must get my coat before I freeze.

SOPHIE: Yes, I think I will. It does seem rather –

HELEN: I said it was. Freezing. Absolutely freezing.

[HELEN *and* SOPHIE *go out*.]

RAY: Come and sit down, Eric. Very glad you could make it. You know, it just occurred to me we should have asked your – er – your Philippa to come on the committee as well. Then you could both ...

ERIC: No, she's – very busy.

RAY: Ah. Working?

ERIC: Babysitting. She loves babysitting. She's got a fixation about it.

RAY: Oh, I see. Now then, who have we got to come? You, myself, Mrs Evans, Councillor Evans, Helen, Sophie, Lawrence and Charlotte Adamson ... er – is that all? Yes.

[DONALD *brings in* AUDREY, *his mother. An old lady with an almost permanent smile*.]

DONALD: This way, mother.

RAY: Here we are. Can you manage?

AUDREY: Lot of steps. Awful lot of steps.

RAY: Yes, there are one or two.

AUDREY: I'm all right except for steps.

RAY: Would she like to sit here?

DONALD: No, I'll sit her up this end, Mr Dixon, I think. She's just a little bit hard of hearing and she'll be able to see most people from here. She's all right if she can see mouths.

RAY: Ah, I see.

DONALD [*sitting* AUDREY *down*]: There we are, mother.

AUDREY: Found I was sitting by the Gents.

RAY [*laughing*]: Oh dear, that won't do.

AUDREY [*to* ERIC]: By the Gents.

[ERIC *gives a wan smile*.]

RAY [*beckoning*]: – er – Councillor Evans – er – [*He is about to speak then turns away from* AUDREY.] – er – I'm just wondering whether you think your mother's going to be up to this?

DONALD [*also turned away*]: Well, if you recall, Mr Dixon, when you first approached me, I did I think warn you that – well, she's into her eighties, you know.

RAY: Yes, quite.

DONALD: I mean, she's still very active. She still gives the occasional piano lesson.

RAY: Does she really?

AUDREY [*ferreting in her bag under this. To* ERIC]: Getting out my pencil.

ERIC: Ah.

AUDREY: Ready for action.

DONALD: Well, you see her hands, although naturally they're not as supple as they were – they're still agile. I mean, she's given up the higher grades of course.

RAY: Well, we'll see how she gets on, shall we?

DONALD: Fair enough. Fair enough.

RAY: I can remember her doing the odd typing job for me very well indeed. But that was some time ago.

DONALD: Oh, that was some time ago. She's not worked for ten years.

RAY: As much as that?

AUDREY: Are we starting yet?

RAY: Er – [*looking towards the door*] – we're just hanging on for the others, Mrs Evans.

AUDREY: Are we ready to start?

RAY [*turning to her with emphasized mouth movements*]: No, we're just hanging on for the others.

AUDREY: We're hanging on for the others.

RAY: That's it.

AUDREY: Good, good. Perhaps they're in the Gents.

RAY [*laughing*]: Yes, that's right.

AUDREY: Everyone else seemed to be.

RAY [*laughing*]: Yes. Now, who are we missing? Has anyone seen Mr and Mrs Adamson?

DONALD: No, not this evening.

RAY: I hope they haven't forgotten. Haven't seen them for a few days. I meant to phone to remind them.

DONALD: I understood that Mr Lorne-Messiter would be attending this evening?

RAY: Yes. He was unfortunately unable to come at the last minute. I have apologies from him. I'll be reading it out.

ERIC: Is this Mr Bernard Lorne-Messiter?

DONALD: Yes, a very useful man to have on your side. Owns a lot of property round here.

ERIC [*grimly*]: Yes, I know he does.

[DONALD *slides along to* ERIC *and starts talking confidentially to him.*]

DONALD: You know, we hold all our Civic Society meetings in here.

ERIC: Oh yes.

[HELEN *and* SOPHIE *enter.*]

DONALD: We meet, I'd say on average, about a dozen times a year. We're mainly concerned with improving the life in the town – although we also keep a weather eye open for listed buildings and so on. And then once a year we generally have a function. That varies. We had a Whist Drive last year that was extremely successful. We raised over £80 for the old folk and this year, I understand, there is talk of a dance which we'll probably be holding here as well. I've been on the committee actually for twelve years.

ERIC: Ah-ha.

DONALD: So you can see there's quite a continuity there. My mother was actually Treasurer for over eighteen years until she unfortunately broke her hip and that I'm afraid forced her to give it up.

[*During the above, over* DONALD'S *monologue*]

HELEN [*as she enters*]: I love them. Where did you get them?

SOPHIE: Oh, they're very old.

HELEN: I love them. I want them. Where did you get them?

SOPHIE: Oh, I've forgotten now.

HELEN: Not round here, I can tell you that. How's Tim?

SOPHIE: Pretty well.

HELEN: Still breeding furiously, is he? [*To* ERIC, *across* DONALD'S *conversation*] Sophie and her brother breed lovely huge dogs – what are they? Old English, aren't they?

SOPHIE: That's right.

HELEN: Glorious. Ray won't let us have one.

RAY: What lies ... You said they come off on the carpet.

SOPHIE: They do a bit.

[DONALD *fades away through lack of an audience.*]

HELEN: Now where am I going to sit. I think I'll sit opposite Edward.

ERIC: Eric.

HELEN: Eric. Sorry. You look like an Edward. Well, are we off?

RAY: We're waiting for Lawrence and Charlotte.

HELEN: Well, where are they?

RAY: I don't know. They may have been delayed.

AUDREY: Could you ask them to speak down in this direction?

DONALD: We haven't started, mother.

HELEN: It's all right, my love, we haven't started.

AUDREY: You haven't started?

HELEN: No, we'll let you know when we start. We won't leave you out, don't worry. [*To the others*] Isn't she sweet?

RAY: We'll give them five minutes.

HELEN: It's very odd. Perhaps Lawrence has fallen over again.

RAY [*quietly*]: Helen ...

HELEN: Well, he could have done. He's continually falling over.

RAY: Yes all right, love.

HELEN: Well, he does hit the bottle. It's no secret.

RAY: No, well, that'll do ...

HELEN [*sotto*]: Like a fish ...

    [AUDREY *starts struggling*.]

DONALD: What is it, mother?

AUDREY: Very hot. It's getting very hot.

HELEN: Hot?

DONALD [*rising and helping her with her coat*]: Just a minute, mother, I'll ...

HELEN: My God, the woman's an Eskimo.

DONALD: Here we are.

AUDREY: Thank you. Can't bear being too hot.

HELEN: It's about minus ten in here.

SOPHIE: Will she be all right?

DONALD: Yes, mother has exceptionally good circulation. I'll just hang this up. Would you like me to telephone the Adamsons while I'm out, Mr Dixon?

RAY: Oh would you mind, Councillor, that's extremely kind ...

DONALD: Not at all. We don't want to be sitting around much longer, do we? Have we the number?

RAY: It'll be in the book, Councillor, under L. Adamson, 14 – is it? – Holly Drive.

SOPHIE: 14, I think ...

    [DONALD *goes out*.

    AUDREY *fumbles in her bag, brings out a bag of boiled sweets and eats one*.]

HELEN: Look, would someone mind telling me why – [*with a glance at* AUDREY] why we've – can she hear me?

RAY: Not if you keep your mouth this way.

HELEN [*turning off*]: Why we've got that awful little man in on this? He's most dreadfully boring.

RAY: Well, he happens ... [*He turns away*.] ... he happens to be on the Leisure and Amenities Committee and God knows what other committees and it's very possible he'll get us a grant.

HELEN: Well, as long as he's good for something.

AUDREY [*proffering the bag*]: Boiled sweet?

SOPHIE: No thank you.

AUDREY [*to* ERIC]: How about you?

ERIC: Oh, ta.

HELEN: Oh look, she's got her sweets. Isn't that charming? [*To* AUDREY, *loudly*] No, thank you. No, thank you. You keep them.

[RAY *waves declining the offer.*]

[*Aside*] She's not going to crunch all the way through the meeting, is she?

[*The lights go out.*]

SOPHIE: ⎫
HELEN: ⎬ Hey!

RAY: Oy – oy – oy. Lights! Lights, please.

[*The lights go on.*]

Thank you so much.

HELEN: What was that in aid of?

AUDREY: The lights went off.

HELEN: Yes, on again now.

RAY: It's that waiter, I think. Italian or something. He's got a thing about the lights. He keeps switching them all off.

SOPHIE: The Swan Hotel Economy Drive.

RAY: Something like that.

HELEN: They're certainly economizing on their dry cleaning. Have you seen their curtains out there? Filthy. And as for the heating. We'll all be frozen to death soon. Except for Eskimo Nell over there.

[DONALD *re-enters.*]

DONALD: Mr Adamson's here. He's arrived.

RAY: Oh good.

HELEN: Hooray.

[LAWRENCE, *in his forties, enters briskly. A big man. Florid. Tight-lipped. Tense. He carries a large whisky.*]

LAWRENCE: Sorry, everyone, sorry.

RAY: Come in, Lawrence.

LAWRENCE: Sorry.

RAY: Take a seat.

LAWRENCE: Sorry, Mr Chairman. Unfortunately I have to announce that my wife, Charlotte, won't be able to make the meeting this evening. She's regrettably – indisposed.

RAY: Oh, we're sorry to hear that, Mr Adamson. Nothing serious, I hope?

LAWRENCE: No, no, nothing. Well – nothing too serious anyway.

RAY: Right. Well. Good. All met. Well. Welcome everyone. Before we start, besides Mrs Adamson, I've had one apology for absence from Mr Lorne-Messiter who can't be with us. He has business in Sheffield.

HELEN: Shame.

RAY: I did however receive this telegram from him. I'll read it to you. 'Good luck to you and your endeavours. Look forward eagerly to your second meeting. Regards Bernard Lorne-Messiter.'

DONALD: Very nice.

LAWRENCE: Very nice indeed.

RAY: I know we'll look forward to welcoming him in due course. This is by way of an exploratory meeting. You'll all have had my circular, I hope, so you'll have a rough idea of what it's all about. There's some spare copies in the middle there if you wish to refresh your memories.

[*All except* LAWRENCE *and* ERIC *take a copy.* SOPHIE *offers one to* AUDREY *who accepts smiling.*]

DONALD [*confidentially to* RAY]: May I just – er –

RAY: Yes. Certainly, Councillor.

DONALD [*very quietly, to* RAY]: It's just, that – er – to be strictly in order before we start the meeting – we ought to elect a Chairman . . .

RAY: Ah. Yes, good point, Councillor. Councillor Evans has quite correctly just pointed out that before we start we ought – to be strictly in order – to appoint a Chairman.

LAWRENCE: Hear! Hear!

DONALD: To be strictly in order.

HELEN: I thought you were Chairman.

RAY: Ah, but I have to be elected.

HELEN: Well then, I elect you.

DONALD: He has to be proposed.

HELEN: Then I propose you.

DONALD: I will second that.

RAY: Right, well. Fine. If we're all agreed? All those in favour, then?

HELEN [*to* AUDREY]: We're electing him as Chairman, my love.

AUDREY: Oh yes, I second that.

RAY: All those in favour? Could we have a show of hands, please.

[*They are about to raise their hands when the lights go out. A chorus of protest.*]

HELEN: El illuminatos, s'il vous plaît.

[*The lights come on.*]

Merci. Gracias so much.

RAY [*crossing to the door and bellowing*]: Would you kindly leave those light switches alone, please. There is a meeting in progress. Thank you. [*Returning*] Right. Sorry about that. Did we get a vote?

HELEN: Yes, you're elected.

RAY: Fine. Well. To proceed then ...

DONALD [*very quietly, to* RAY]: Mr Chairman, I would just point out one minor discrepancy here. There is, in fact, a mis-spelling. [*Holding out roneod sheet*] There should be a second 'l', you see.

RAY: Ah yes. My secretary did do them in a bit of a hurry. Councillor Evans has pointed out an 'l' missing from the word 'dwelling' ... one, two, three, four, five, six lines down. If you feel like altering that.

HELEN: Good heavens, so there is. Well done.

DONALD [*very quietly, to* RAY]: And – er – I think this was meant to be a full stop, not a comma.

LAWRENCE: Oh my God ...

RAY: Yes. And there's a comma, one, two, three – several lines up from the bottom after the word 'it' which should be of course a full stop.

DONALD: Er –

RAY [*swiftly*]: So the next letter 'a', of course, will become a capital letter. Right now ...

HELEN: God, it's freezing in here. Absolutely freezing.

RAY: Now then. We're here to discuss the possibility of holding a First Pendon Folk Festival.

HELEN: I mean, it's an absolute disgrace. This is a three star hotel.

RAY: Helen, please. Would you mind? Thank you. Now, it seemed to me when I first had the idea ...

HELEN [*mouthing under her breath*]: Three star.

RAY: It seemed an exciting one to me in a number of ways.

DONALD: Mr Chairman, I wonder if you could direct your remarks a little bit more towards mother.

RAY: I'm sorry, yes.

DONALD: It was just I noticed she was having slight difficulty ...

RAY: Yes, sorry. In a number of ways. First, it is something new. Something I think that, if we handle right, could catch the imagination of everyone within the town. Second, [LAWRENCE *grunts in agreement.*] by making it a Folk Festival, that is to say by concentrating upon our own past with its crafts, its history, its bygone customs, we will in a real way be helping Pendon to regain its identity – an identity which I think and I'm sure you'll agree, under the pressure of modern life, is fast disappearing.

LAWRENCE: Hear! hear!

RAY: So the proposition is that we hold such a Festival next June. At that time of the year, obviously, we'd hope to attract a good number of visitors into the town for the occasion. Now, may I say immediately that since this is our first effort we shouldn't attempt to crawl before we can walk. Or rather vice versa. We start modestly. As indeed we shall probably have to, funds being limited. Although, may I add that we already have made application to the Council for a small grant to help us ...

DONALD: Mr Chairman, I do note that the application is on the agenda for the next meeting of the Leisure and Amenities Committee of which I am a member.

RAY: Grand. So, as I was saying, we start modestly. But the question is how? And with what sort of thing?

ERIC: Well, I suggest that we ...

RAY: Sorry, Eric. Would you mind? Sorry. Just let me finish. Well, we have in Pendon in fact the ideal starting point. [LAWRENCE *grunts in agreement*.] A piece of colourful history directly related to our own town that would indeed make an excellent basis for a modest pageant. I refer to an occurrence known by history apparently as the Massacre of the Pendon Twelve.

LAWRENCE: Of the what?

ERIC: Never heard of it.

DONALD: No, I can't say I have.

RAY: Well, it was a couple of hundred years ago. I came across it quite by accident myself.

DONALD: No, it's a new one on me. Mother might know.

HELEN: She was probably there.

DONALD: The Massacre of the Pendon Twelve, mother. Have you heard of it?

AUDREY: The Pendon Twelve? Was it recent?

DONALD: No, no. Some time ago.

AUDREY: No. Before my time.

RAY: No, anyway, I do happen to have located a brief description of these events which I came across in this book. I understand it's out of print now. It's called *Through Haunts Of Coot And Hern* by a bloke called E. Arnott Hutchings. I thought if I may, I'd read it to you. It's quite interesting. I've had a few copies made so you can take them away with you, if you like. Anyway, so – [*He opens the book*.]

HELEN: I think Mrs Evans ought to have a copy to read, darling. She'll never be able to follow this.

DONALD: Yes, I think it would be better.

[SOPHIE *passes a copy to* AUDREY.]

RAY: Right then. There's a copy, Mrs Evans. A copy of what I'm reading.

AUDREY: Thank you. [*She starts to read*.]

RAY: Here we go then. [*Reading*] The story of the Pendon Twelve is worth here, I feel, relating in some detail if the reader will forgive me. Following the increasing tide of discontent amongst agricultural folk brought about by these new taxation laws, two local men, Jonathan Cockle and William Brunt, began actively to ferment this feeling through a series of meetings when, according to one contemporary eyewitness, Cockle 'spoke with much fire and feeling' whilst Brunt 'would further inflame the crowd with his fierce appearance and wild gestures.' This pair, from all reports, through chance and circumstance brought together must have presented an incongruous couple. Cockle is described 'as a thin man with a choleric appearance ... an almost womanly complexion, resembling more a cleric or a scholar than one used to earn his living from the land.' Brunt, on the other hand, is said to have stood 'head above all others, a veritable giant with wild beard and besides much hair about his person as was visible to the eye ...' He (Brunt) 'would often for wagers toss his fellows high in the air to the amusement and recreation of all.'

HELEN: They sound the most unprepossessing people.

LAWRENCE: Hear! Hear!

RAY: Yes, Helen, let me ...

HELEN: Uggh! Horrid.

RAY [*continuing to read*]: The authorities ...

AUDREY [*finishing reading*]: What an interesting story. Is it true?

RAY: Yes, I haven't quite finished, Mrs Evans.

AUDREY: Haven't finished? Sorry.

HELEN: Does it go on much longer about these awful looking men?

ERIC: I shouldn't imagine they had a great deal of option as to how they looked.

HELEN: Oh, come now.

ERIC: These were men, may I remind you, who spent their working lives sweating their guts out for a living.

HELEN: My dear boy, there are people round this table who, as you charmingly put it, sweat their guts out for a living. I do for one but I don't go around covered in black hair throwing people in the air for fun.

ERIC: They were probably living at starvation level to start with.

HELEN: Oh, nonsense.

ERIC: What do you mean, nonsense?

HELEN: Oh, don't be so dim. You heard what he said. They were farmers. Perfectly capable of growing food if they wanted to.

RAY: Helen, would you mind?

HELEN: No, the trouble with them was they spent all their time making speeches. Getting drunk. Throwing people in the air. Serve them jolly well right.

LAWRENCE: Hear! Hear!

ERIC: How the hell you can sit there ...?

HELEN: They're all the same. Since time immemorial. Spend their lives belly-aching and complaining. It's the same these days with those whatever-they're-called, those Trotskys.

ERIC: What do you know, sitting there in your bloody fur coat, you stupid bourgeois bitch ...

RAY: Now, now.

HELEN: How dare you use that sort of language to me.

DONALD: Mr Chairman, might I suggest ...

HELEN: How dare you, you seedy little man. How dare you.

ERIC [*rising violently*]: Oh, damn it.

SOPHIE: Where are you going?

ERIC: I'm sorry ... I can't ... her sort of person ... I can't ... gets right up my ... I'm sorry. I'm going.

RAY: Now, now, Eric. Come on, lad. Calm down. We're all getting heated. Calm down.

LAWRENCE: Hear! Hear!

DONALD: Mr Chairman, might I suggest ...

HELEN: I'm sorry. I am not prepared to sit here calmly and have that sort of language used to my face. I demand an apology.

ERIC: If you think I'm apologizing to you, mate ...

RAY [*shouting*]: Now sit down, both of you. This is not a political meeting. And I won't have any politics. [*Quieter*] Right, that's it. Now sit down. [*They do.*]
Eric, I respect your views. I don't agree with them but I respect them. We must respect Helen hers. Beg to differ. And all that.

AUDREY: Boiled sweet?
[ERIC *takes one.*]

HELEN: Well, I'll tell you one thing. We're never going to get anywhere if we've got Trotskys on the committee.

ERIC: I am not a Trotskyite. If you must know I'm a Marxist.

SOPHIE: Oh golly.

HELEN: God, that's even worse isn't it? A Marxist. That's even worse. They're completely round the bend.

RAY [*roaring*]: Helen, will you bloody shut up.

HELEN: Oh right, that's it. Good night, everyone.

RAY: Now what are you doing?

HELEN: I am now being sworn at by everyone. Good night.

SOPHIE: Helen ...

HELEN: Good night. [*As she goes*] It's freezing in here anyway. Not that the Russians would notice.
[*She goes.*
A silence.

ERIC *boils*.

RAY *sinks his head in his hands with a groan*.]

DONALD: Mr Chairman ...

RAY [*sharply*]: What? [*Recovering*] Sorry, Councillor. Sorry, Donald, yes.

DONALD: I was merely going to observe that it's generally helpful we have found in our experience of committees, if all remarks are addressed through the chair. It avoids these personal confrontations.

RAY: Yes that's a very useful point that, Donald, thank you. Well, I'd better finish this, I suppose, if everyone ...

SOPHIE: Yes go on, please.

RAY: Well, there's more description of the men – I'll skip that and – er – anyway ... [*Reading*] The activities of the pair ... that's Cockle and Brunt of course – did not pass unnoticed. Indeed, the authorities were becoming disturbed by the popularity this cause espoused. On several occasions the militia had intervened in an attempt to break up their meetings but invariably they arrived too late. Yet as the movement gathered momentum so Cockle and Brunt grew bolder. Thus it was that in June of that year, a meeting was arranged in Pendon itself intended as the climax of the campaign. On the day, the protestors had chosen for their meeting the old Market Place at the lower end of the town ... That of course is the square just outside here ... As was the custom, Cockle spoke for upwards of an hour until a sufficient crowd had gathered, whereupon he beseeched them to pledge support for his cause. From the other end of the High Street the militia, until then well concealed, finally showed themselves. A company of foot soldiers, muskets primed and ready, advanced in formation towards the crowd. At the head, their commander – none other than the Earl of Dorset himself, mounted and with sword in hand. At the sight of such a show of force, the crowd swiftly dispersed and fled till the square was empty save for twelve men – among them Cockle and Brunt. This Twelve now armed themselves with rudimentary weapons and stood ready to resist. Three times the Earl called upon them to surrender and three times the men refused ... That's very good that bit. You can see that working very well in terms of a pageant ... At length, the Earl without further ado commanded his soldiers to fire. Many fell mortally wounded, including Cockle himself. Brunt, though himself injured, charged forward before the soldiers could reload and together with several of his fellows set upon the militia with fists and cudgels until, exhausted, they were overcome by sheer numbers. Some weeks later, Brunt with seven others stood trial and was executed. The bodies of the Twelve were buried outside the prison in unmarked graves. It was natural that, in time, they should come to be remembered simply as the Pendon Twelve.

SOPHIE: Hey, that's terribly sad.

LAWRENCE: Hear! Hear!

ERIC: Terrible.

DONALD: May I ask, Mr Chairman, before we go any further whether we intend forming ourselves into a Trust?

RAY: Yes, I have made inquiries about that. It is in hand. Well, that's it. That's the basis. I think we should have the makings of something quite spectacular with that. You could imagine the crowd in the Market Place with these two fellows and then the militia charging down the High Street . . .

ERIC: I hope we intend this as a tribute to these men? That we're going to take it seriously enough, that's all . . .

RAY: Oh yes. I mean, we wouldn't . . . yes.

ERIC: I mean, they were real people, after all. I mean, it's all very well a lot of middle-class businessmen and their wives dressing up for fun and prancing about the streets . . .

RAY: No, no, Eric. No. No. Not at all. I mean. Point taken.

DONALD: It is to be hoped, Mr Chairman, that we will get the full support of the ordinary working people as well.

RAY: Essential, yes.

ERIC: Well, let's just get the facts right, that's all.

LAWRENCE [*clearing his throat for a momentous announcement*]: Mr Chairman.

RAY: Lawrence.

LAWRENCE: Might be a good idea to get someone on further research, mightn't it? I mean, it's got to be accurate. There's no point otherwise, it seems to me. [*He tails away clearing his throat and muttering.*]

RAY: Yes, well, perhaps we ought to appoint someone to be in charge of that. Any offers?

SOPHIE: What about Mrs Evans?

RAY [*dubious*]: Well, I don't know if . . .

DONALD: I think that might be a very good idea, Mr Chairman. She is an avid reader and may well disinter one or two useful details which could be of use.

RAY: All right then. Splendid. Would you like to take care of that, Mrs Evans?

AUDREY: Yes?

RAY: We were wondering if you would care to do some additional research?

AUDREY: Additional research? Yes, I'm going to. Very odd.

RAY: Well, thank you. That's it then. Meeting closed. Who's for a drink?

DONALD: Might I suggest, Mr Chairman, that we arrange our next meeting date now. Some of us may have . . .

RAY: Yes, we can do that by all means. Let's see. Everybody got his diary? About a fortnight, shall we say? How about the 16th? Any good for anyone? Tuesday the 16th evening?

DONALD: Er – no. Not the 16th, Mr Chairman. We have our Church meeting on that date. It's usually the second Tuesday of every month.

RAY: Monday the 22nd then?

ERIC: Not Mondays. Youth Club.

RAY: 24th. Wednesday the 24th?

SOPHIE: Fine.

WRENCE: We're free. I am.

R ᴀᴦ 24th it is. No hang on, I can't do that. I've got a dinner.

WRENCE: What about the 25th.

RAY: Fine.

ERIC: That's O.K.

SOPHIE: Yes. I can change that.

RAY: Is 7.30 p.m. all right?

DONALD: Providing it's no earlier, Mr Chairman. We do have a rather critical meeting of the Highways and Byeways Committee. That may run on a little. We're discussing the shelving of the new ring road scheme, you see, and I could see that could run on.

RAY: Well, do your best. Right. 25th – 7.30 p.m. I'd better dig my wife out of the bar. Lawrence, are you having one?

SOPHIE: I'm dying for the loo . . .

[SOPHIE *hurries out immediately.* DONALD *buttonholes* ERIC *and under the ensuing talks to him again.*]

DONALD: You see, the trouble with these meetings is they can get out of hand. We've found this particularly lately with the Civic Society meetings. Our present Chairman, Councillor Highsmith, he's served on it for fourteen years and two of our members, Mrs Whittaker and Mrs Paxton, they've been on it for twenty-four years since it was initially founded . . .

ERIC: Oh yes.

[*They move out of earshot.*]

LAWRENCE [*meanwhile during this*]: I'll have a quick one. You see, to be perfectly frank – Charlotte and I had just the smallest tiff this evening . . .

RAY: Oh dear. [*He starts gathering his papers.*]

LAWRENCE: Over those kids of ours, actually. Nothing serious, I don't think –

RAY: Ah well.

LAWRENCE: I mean, I don't necessarily think one needs to take a strong line. Not with kids these days. [*Moving off*] See you in the bar.

AUDREY: Have we finished?

RAY: Yes, all finished. Hey, Lawrence, old son. Where's my track lighting, then?

LAWRENCE: Your what?

RAY: I ordered it from your lot a month ago. They told me a week to ten days.

LAWRENCE: I'll sort it out for you tomorrow.

RAY: I wish you would. It's pitch dark in my shop. Customers falling over themselves. [*He laughs.*]

LAWRENCE: I'll see to it, old boy.

    [LAWRENCE *goes out.*]

DONALD [*still at* ERIC]: In fact you won't believe this, in the past five weeks we've had three emergency meetings just to cope with the normal agenda. Our recent emergency meetings went on for a total of seven hours and we finished up with only half an hour for lunch.

RAY [*seeing* ERIC's *plight, trying to interrupt* DONALD's *flow*]: Excuse me a moment, Donald. Eric, you're not dashing off straightaway, are you? You'll stay for a drink?

ERIC [*moving rapidly away from* DONALD]: No, thanks.

DONALD [*determined to finish his story*]: . . . so you can imagine.

ERIC: Yes.

DONALD [*helping* AUDREY *to struggle up*]: All right, mother. Just a minute.

RAY [*putting down his papers to help*]: Hang on. I'll – er – Would you both like to stay for a drink?

    [ERIC *wanders up on to the bandstand.*]

DONALD: No, I'm afraid not. Mother wouldn't . . .

RAY: No.

AUDREY: Get a bit stiff.

RAY: Yes. There we are.

AUDREY: Thank you. Soon as I get moving. Are we staying for a drink?

DONALD: No, mother, not tonight. Mind yourself. That's it. I'll manage us from here, thank you, Mr Dixon.

RAY: Don't forget her coat.

DONALD: No, we won't.

AUDREY: We never stay for drinks.

    [DONALD *and* AUDREY *go out.*

    RAY, *following them, passes* SOPHIE *returning.*]

RAY: You staying for a drink, Sophie?

SOPHIE: No thanks, Ray. Got to get back and get the meat cut up for the morning. Helen's in the bar, by the way.

RAY: Thought so. 'Night.

SOPHIE: 'Night.

[RAY *goes out.*]

ERIC: Want a lift then?

SOPHIE: Oh heavens, I didn't see you.

ERIC: Can I give you a lift home?

SOPHIE: Well, I – well, yes please.

ERIC: O.K. Probably not up to the standard you're used to.

SOPHIE: I'm used to an eight-year-old Landrover with a broken front seat which smells of dogs. What have you got?

ERIC: Nothing as luxurious as a Landrover.

SOPHIE: Going to be fun, isn't it? The Festival.

ERIC: Possibly. On the other hand, it could be something more than that. It could really mean something. For everyone. Fantastic story, isn't it? I thought it was. Puts what it's all about into a nutshell.

SOPHIE: Are you really a Marxist?

ERIC: Yes. So?

SOPHIE: So jolly good. Hope you enjoy it.

ERIC: Well, what are you then?

SOPHIE: I'm – an agnostic.

ERIC: Oh yes.

SOPHIE: Waiting to be converted – to some worthy cause.

ERIC: Try mine.

SOPHIE: Not just now. Too intense for me.

ERIC [*smiling*]: Not all the time. You'd be surprised. Try it sometime.

SOPHIE: Not – just this actual minute, thank you. Anyway, I expect you'll be wanting to get home to your – lady.

ERIC: Yes. Right. [*He moves off.*]

SOPHIE [*indicating her shopping bag*]: Could you carry this, please?

ERIC: Ah. [*He returns and takes it.*] God! Were you going to walk home with this?

SOPHIE: It's not heavy. You don't teach sports, I take it?

ERIC: Modern history.

SOPHIE: Super.

[TIM *appears in the doorway. A man in his late forties. He wears gum boots, a sheepskin coat and a cap.*]

TIM: Ah, there you are.

SOPHIE: Hallo, Tim.

TIM: Popped down to fill her up. Save me doing it tomorrow morning.

SOPHIE: Tim, this is Eric. Collins, isn't it?

ERIC: Collins, yes.

SOPHIE: This is Tim, my brother.

TIM: How do you do.

ERIC: Hallo.

SOPHIE: Eric teaches.

TIM: Does he?

ERIC: Yes.

TIM: I see.

> [TIM *sizes* ERIC *up. He doesn't like what he sees.* ERIC *doesn't either. A silence.*]

SOPHIE [*to* ERIC]: Well. Thank you. Won't need the lift after all.

ERIC: No ... Here. [*He hands over her bag.*]

TIM [*turning*]: I think Queenie's on heat, you'll be glad to hear.

SOPHIE: About time.

TIM: Good night to you.

ERIC: 'Night.

SOPHIE: See you again ... My regards to your good lady.

TIM [*as they go*]: Whose good lady?

SOPHIE: His good lady.

TIM: What are you prattling about ...?

> [*They have gone.*
>
> ERIC *stands staring after her for a moment. Then he moves thoughtfully round the room till he arrives at the top of the table at* RAY'S *chair. He sits on it. He eyes the other chairs meaningfully. He stands.*]

ERIC [*in a low vibrant voice*]: Brothers – I –

> [*The lights go out.*]

Oh, damn it. [*As he crashes his way off*] Lights. Blast you. Oh, damn it – damn it ...

ACT ONE
SCENE TWO

RAY *enters. He is followed by* LAWRENCE *who carries a festive carrier bag and a half-finished whisky.*

RAY: In here, Lawrence. We're a bit early, nobody's due to arrive for a bit.

LAWRENCE: Thanks.

[*He puts down his carrier bag and paces about nervously.* RAY *watches him.*]

RAY: What seems to be the trouble, Lawrence? Something worrying you about the way things are going?

LAWRENCE: No, no – er – it's nothing to do with the committee, nothing at all. It's – er – about – er – Charlotte – and I. You see, the fact is – we're breaking up . . .

RAY: Oh, I see.

LAWRENCE: Yes.

RAY: Oh. I am sorry, Lawrence, I really am . . .

LAWRENCE: Yes, it's a – very sad business. I think things haven't been going frightfully well in any direction lately. I had a few business worries. Of course the present state of the country tends to hit we smaller firms.

RAY: Yes, I quite see.

LAWRENCE: So we're splitting. Charlotte's got a bit of a health thing as well. That doesn't help. The point is – if you'd like us to stay on the committee, we will.

RAY: Wouldn't that be a bit awkward for you?

LAWRENCE: No, you see what we thought was – we could do sort of alternate stints. I'd come to this meeting and she'd come to the next one. And so forth.

RAY [*dubiously*]: Well, I suppose so – yes – I suppose it –

LAWRENCE: The point is, frankly – a thing like this fête thing – it's a bit different. It's probably the only thing that's going to keep us both sane at the moment, if you want the truth. Take us out of ourselves a bit. If you follow . . .

RAY: Ah yes.

LAWRENCE: Of course, Charlotte used to have the amateur dramatics to fall back on. But she hasn't done a lot of that lately. There don't seem to be any good parts for her these days. They're not writing them for some reason. Sad about Noël Coward, wasn't it?

RAY: Yes.

LAWRENCE: Anyway, keep this under your hat. It's not common knowledge yet.

RAY: Yes, of course. As long as you're both sure you're up to it. I mean, committee work can be ...

[HELEN *enters*.]

HELEN: Oh sorry. Were you ... ?

LAWRENCE: No, no, Helen, no. Finished now. Expect Ray'll tell you, so I won't keep you. I'll just get a refill. Be straight back. [*Seeing carrier bag*] Oh, dump this in the Cloaks. Presents. For the girls. They're with the in-laws. By the way, I'm chasing up those lights you ordered, Ray. Any day now. Gave them a terrific balling out this morning. Excuse me. [*As he moves away, his carrier clinks with the sound of bottles.*]

[LAWRENCE *goes out.*

RAY *has started correcting some roneod sheets.*]

HELEN: What are you doing?

RAY: I'm just correcting the typing errors in the Chairman's report. Otherwise we'll have to wait while Donald Evans points them out.

HELEN: Well, I still think making him Hon. Secretary was a terrible mistake. None of us will get a word in now.

RAY: Oh well ...

HELEN: What was that all about just now with Lawrence?

RAY: He and Charlotte are splitting up.

HELEN: Oh well, we all knew that. Is he resigning?

RAY: No, he wants to stay on.

HELEN: What about her?

RAY: She wants to stay on too, apparently. They're going to attend alternate meetings.

HELEN: Oh, that's ridiculous.

RAY: Going to be a bit tricky.

HELEN: Oh, they'll both have to go. That's ridiculous. They're a dead loss anyway. He's incoherent and she keeps falling asleep. Have you seen those things she's on? About fifteen a day. She sucks them like cough sweets. And she's going potty.

RAY: Well, we'll see how it works out.

HELEN: I can tell you that now.

RAY: I'll get rid of them if we have to. I just think it would be rather heartless to do it at this moment.

HELEN: Oh well. I hear he's going bankrupt anyway. [*She wanders.*] I do wish they'd cheer this place up a bit. I had to leave the bar. The local branch of the Red Army marched in with guess-who of course.

RAY: Sophie?

HELEN: Tim's getting very worried about her, you know.

RAY: Yes, you said.

HELEN: You know he phoned me.

RAY: That's right.

HELEN: I mean, they're sitting in the bar holding hands.

RAY: Oh well ...

HELEN: I mean, you can see Tim's point. She's made one mess of her life. He doesn't want to see it happen again.

RAY: It may not. Wait and see.

HELEN: But don't you see, she's doing precisely the same thing as she did the last time she ... Mind you, Tim's very odd really. I admire him but he's certainly peculiar.

RAY: Well, he's a – he's all right is Captain Barton.

HELEN: I heard a rumour. I don't know if it's true. He sleeps with a loaded revolver under his pillow, you know. He shot a cat one night.

RAY: Well ...

HELEN: Mrs Mason's. In error.

[DONALD *and* AUDREY *enter.*]

DONALD: Good evening.

HELEN: Hallo there.

RAY: Good evening, Donald.

DONALD: And, I suppose, festive greetings are in order. We're in here as usual, I take it?

AUDREY: Good evening.

HELEN: Hallo, Mrs Evans. How are you?

DONALD [*sitting* AUDREY *down*]: There we are, mother. She was giving a piano lesson. So we're a little bit late, I'm afraid.

HELEN: No, dead on time. As usual.

DONALD [*seeing* RAY's *report*]: Ah, you've been correcting those, have you, Mr Chairman? I was going to point those out to you at the meeting.

RAY [*laughing*]: Well, I thought I'd get in first, Donald.

DONALD: Yes, I see.

HELEN: How's your research going, Mrs Evans?

AUDREY: My research? Oh, nothing much so far. We'll keep looking.

HELEN: Nothing to report yet?

AUDREY: No, not yet.

HELEN: Oh dear. As long as we get it before the Festival.

AUDREY: Oh yes, you'll get it before the Festival.

DONALD: She's been reading avidly. Burning the midnight oil. I only wish I had her eyesight. I'm afraid I get my eyesight from my father's side, unfortunately ...

[ERIC *and* SOPHIE *enter.*
They are no longer holding hands but they are very much together. ERIC *has a file of papers.* LAWRENCE *wanders in behind them. He carries a large drink.*]

Good evening.

SOPHIE: Hallo.

ERIC: Evening.

LAWRENCE: Back again.

AUDREY: Good evening. Happy Christmas.

[HELEN *eyes* SOPHIE *and* ERIC. *Everyone sits.*]

RAY [*over this*]: They still haven't managed to do very much to the heating, I'm afraid. The manager tells me it's something to do with an air-lock in the system. Anyway, welcome again. I think we can make this, our third meeting, a fairly brief one. More in the nature of a progress report. Right. Apologies for absence, Councillor Evans?

DONALD: Yes, Mr Chairman. We have firstly very sincere regrets from Mr Lorne-Messiter, who had hoped very much to be here tonight but was unexpectedly called away, but wishes us to be assured of his continuing interest, so his wife informed me when I telephoned her this evening. Apologies also from Mrs Adamson.

LAWRENCE: Indisposed, Mr Chairman.

RAY: Right. Yes. We must take the Minutes as read, I think, as Mrs Evans is probably still working on those, so Item 3 Chairman's Report. Well, there is a copy of that you should all have. You'll see the main point is that the Leisure and Amenities Committee couldn't see their way to offering us any financial support this year.

DONALD: Yes, if I could interrupt one moment, Mr Chairman ...

[SOPHIE *and* ERIC *whisper together during this next.* HELEN *glares at them.*]

I was at that particular meeting and fought our case vociferously. Regrettably the committee did feel that whilst they viewed what we were doing with extreme interest and favour, they were unable to recommend a grant for this year owing to the slightly unusual financial situation in which we find ourselves as a Council at this particular moment in time.

RAY: Thank you, Mr Evans.

HELEN: Did you catch that all right, Sophie?

SOPHIE: What? Oh yes.

HELEN: Oh, I thought you might have missed it.

SOPHIE: No.

RAY: Yes. So it's up to us to do a little bit of digging in our own pockets, I suppose ...

    [LAWRENCE *clears his throat*.]

    ... when we can and continue to think of other ways such as jumble sales and coffee mornings to come up with what we need.

AUDREY [*to* LAWRENCE]: Where's your wife?

LAWRENCE: I beg your pardon?

AUDREY: Where's your nice wife? Isn't she here tonight?

LAWRENCE [*muttering*]: No, she's – er – indisposed.

AUDREY: She's what?

RAY: She's indisposed, Mrs Evans.

AUDREY: Indisposed? Oh dear. Something the matter with her?

    [LAWRENCE *smiles weakly.* HELEN *gives a dry laugh*.]

ERIC [*with urgency*]: Mr Chairman, I assume we're now on Item Four.

RAY: Yes, I think we will be. Yes.

ERIC: Which is the preliminary report of the action group which was set up at the last meeting ...

HELEN: Which you set up at the last meeting ...

ERIC: Headed by Miss Barton and myself. Well, we've already made some feasibility studies on this and, in accordance with the brief we were given, we've co-opted one or two outside members on to the group who we feel could be useful. Now then ...

HELEN: Excuse me, Mr Chairman, could we ask Mr Collins who these members are? Whom he's co-opted on without our knowledge.

ERIC: Certainly. We have Mr Raymond Snaithe, who is a lecturer in Sociology at the Polytechnic. He has also agreed to help us find volunteers to take part in the Pageant. We have Mr Platt who's an Art Teacher from the Catherine Stoker school. Mr Ron Sowerby who works at Foxton's Engineering ...

DONALD: Mr Sowerby? I don't think I know him at all. I know most of the staff at Foxton's.

ERIC: I can assure you he's been employed there several years and also serves as a shop steward.

DONALD: Oh I see.

HELEN: My God.

ERIC: And finally Miss Sally Prince and Mr Max Kirkov both, at the moment, full-time students.

HELEN: Mr who?

ERIC: Mr Kirkov.

HELEN: You see, now we have got the Russians.

ERIC: Mr Kirkov is actually Jewish and was born, I believe, in Slough,

Buckinghamshire. He is in fact a keen athlete and I feel will be very suitable to take the part of William Brunt in the Pageant. He incidentally has a beard.

RAY: Oh well that's splendid, isn't it?

ERIC: The technical college, whom I've approached, have also expressed willingness to loan us their printing machinery free of charge to help our publicity.

RAY: Well, that's first rate. Thank you very much, Mr Collins. You've obviously been very busy.

HELEN: Yes.

ERIC: Mr Chairman, I wonder if at this point I can make a suggestion to the committee. It seems to me that the organization of this rally could best be tackled if we divide the organizational responsibility.

RAY: No, I don't quite follow you there, Mr Collins.

ERIC: Well, it appears to me we have within the rally itself two distinct factions ...

HELEN: I do wish he'd stop calling it a rally.

ERIC: I'm sorry.

HELEN: It's not a rally. It's a pageant.

ERIC: All right. A pageant, if you prefer. What's the difference?

HELEN: My dear boy, there's a great deal of difference between a pageant and a rally and if you don't ...

ERIC: Listen, madam, if you want to discuss semantic niceties perhaps you'd care to do that afterwards ...

HELEN: I'm sure you're far too busy to do anything afterwards.

RAY: Now, just a minute please. You're out of order, Helen, that'll do.

HELEN: What do you mean, I'm out of order? Don't you speak to me like that.

RAY [*placatingly*]: Would you let Mr Collins continue, Helen. Please.

HELEN [*quietly*]: I will not be brow-beaten and shouted down by you or anybody. Ever since I made you chairman, you've behaved like a petty little dictator ...

RAY: When the chairman asks you to stop talking, you must stop. I've told you that. Otherwise ...

HELEN [*muttering*]: Oh well, if you're going to side with him ...

RAY [*embarrassed, aware of the others*]: Mr Collins? Divide the functions, you were saying?

ERIC: Thank you, Mr Chairman. Divide the factions. The pageant naturally divides into two factions. On the one hand, the military faction and on the other, the proletarian faction represented by the Twelve.

RAY: Yes.

ERIC: Owing to the amount of organization involved, I would be happy to take the responsibility for recruiting and rehearsing the Twelve and the entire Market Square faction if someone else could deal primarily with the military side.

RAY: Oh, I see. You mean like two team leaders.

ERIC: That's it, Mr Chairman. Obviously both working in close co-operation ...

RAY: I think that sounds a very sensible idea.

DONALD: Yes. Yes ...

LAWRENCE: Hear! Hear!

HELEN: Well, I think it sounds a terrible idea.

RAY: What's wrong now?

HELEN: Dividing it up? This whole thing is a group effort. We're all mucking in together. We don't want them going off here and us going off there into little huddles ...

RAY: It's only for organizational purposes.

HELEN: It's not for organizational purposes. It's for his purposes. And it will absolutely suit him down to the ground. That's how they work. That's the way they gain their power. By dividing people up.

SOPHIE: Oh Helen, really, you do talk rubbish ...

HELEN: Well, look at him. He's already formed his own committee with half the card-carrying rabble from the district ...

ERIC: Now, wait a minute. Wait a minute. What basis do you have for that allegation?

HELEN: It's patently obvious. We, as a committee, are being used by this man for extremely sinister purposes.

ERIC [*thrusting out a sheet of paper*]: All right, all right. Here's the list of my working group. You tell me which of these names you object to and why.

HELEN: Though God knows what he's hoping to gain by it.

ERIC [*stabbing his finger at his sheet of paper*]: Which of these names do you object to and why?

DONALD: Mr Chairman ...

HELEN: Somebody tell me what this man's hoping to achieve by taking over a committee whose sole function is to bring gaiety and light into the town.

ERIC [*thrusting his piece of paper right under her nose*]: Which of these names you object to and why?

HELEN [*swotting the paper away*]: And will you kindly stop prodding me with that piece of paper.

DONALD: Mr Chairman ...

RAY: Order! Order! ORDER!

[*Silence.*]

Thank you. Now then. Mr Collins.

ERIC [*quietly*]: Could I ask, Mr Chairman, which of these names Mrs Dixon objects to and why?

RAY: Helen?

HELEN: What?

RAY: Which of those names do you object to and why?

HELEN: Well. I don't know. I mean. Well, what about that shop steward from Foxton's? He sounds a very fishy character. What's he doing there?

ERIC: He's interested. Any reason why an engineer shouldn't be interested?

HELEN: Well. He should be busy making engines. Or whatever he does. Well, he's an engineer. Nothing to do with the Arts. Nonsense. Totally unsuitable.

ERIC: Might I suggest, Mr Chairman, to avoid further conflict we put it to the vote? Does the committee feel that the division of the pageant into two separately organized but mutually linked groups is a good idea?

DONALD: I was about to suggest that myself, Mr Chairman.

RAY: Yes, that seems a good idea. So we'll vote on that, shall we? Does the committee feel ... and so on. All those in favour of dividing responsibilities?

    [DONALD, LAWRENCE, ERIC and SOPHIE *raise their hands.*]

Those against?

    [HELEN *raises her hand.*]

Motion carried then.

HELEN: Just a minute, Mrs Evans hasn't voted.

DONALD: I think she may have missed some of the arguments.

RAY: It wouldn't have altered things.

HELEN: Well, I've done what I can. On your own heads be it.

LAWRENCE [*clearing his throat*]: Er –

RAY: Mr Adamson.

LAWRENCE: Mr Chairman, I don't often have occasion to speak at these things – because I feel people should be allowed to get on with it. However, I do feel that someone ought to say a few words in defence of Mrs – er – Dixon's arguments which I felt were heartfelt and extremely moving and – from the heart.

    [ERIC *slides down in his chair.*

    LAWRENCE *sees him.*]

Now you can slide down in your chair if you like, young man. Just let me have my say. You've had plenty of say already. You see, it's very rare in these days of cynicism and a generally diminishing of personal idealism and — so on, for someone to come out and say what they feel. It does seem to me that a lot of what's wrong with the country today comes about because we've lost what we used to hold most dear. You can include in that our concept of family and home life which has been eroded by all these pressures. I'm a business man who's felt the effects of those as much as anyone. It's also inevitable that it does creep regrettably into one's own personal life, which I won't bore you with here, except to say I admire Mrs Dixon. I admire her for what she stands for. I admire her as a woman. I admire her as a person ...

HELEN [*out of the side of her mouth*]: What's he talking about?

LAWRENCE: Well, that's all. My life's a mess but that's my fault. Nobody else's. You can't blame Governments if your own home comes crashing round your ears. I wish to God one could. I do. Thank you.

> [LAWRENCE *sits down*.
> *A stunned silence*.]

RAY [*eventually*]: Yes. Thank you, Mr Adamson. I think we can all learn something from that.

DONALD: Hear. Hear.

AUDREY: It's a lot warmer in here tonight, don't you think?

RAY: Right. So we've decided to divide responsibility. Now, Mr Collins has agreed to run the Market Square group. Do we have anyone who'd care to organize the military? [*Silence*] Anyone?

HELEN: Yes. I volunteer.

RAY: Oh. Are you sure now, Helen? I mean, it's quite a task.

HELEN: I'll manage. I can get help. Like Mr Collins.

RAY: Well, if you're sure.

HELEN: My main problem, I think, will be on the costume side. The military uniforms and so on. We are going to have to borrow or steal those from somewhere. I wonder, Mr Chairman, would it be in order to have someone co-opted on to this committee to assist me?

RAY: No, I don't think anyone would have any objection to that. Would anyone?

> [*General headshaking*.
> ERIC *looks suspicious*.]

Perhaps Mrs Pakenham would ...

HELEN: No, it's all right. I'll find somebody suitable.

RAY: Right. Splendid. Well, we seem to be making progress.

HELEN: May I just add, Mr Chairman, that from the military side — we'll do everything in our power to make sure the pageant is a resounding success.

ERIC: May I add, so will we, Mr Chairman.
DONALD: Bravo.
RAY: Yes. That's really very reassuring. Thank you, both. Any other business. No? Good. A happy Christmas everyone. Shall we adjourn?

ACT ONE
SCENE THREE

SOPHIE *enters. She carries a box file marked PERSONNEL. She puts it on the table. After a moment,* TIM *enters and stands in the doorway. He is dressed as before. He studies her.*

TIM: Look, Sophie ...

SOPHIE [*looking up*]: Oh, now what?

TIM: I'm not leaving it at that, Sophie. Now, what the devil's going on? What are you playing at?

SOPHIE [*busying herself*]: How do you mean?

TIM: You know perfectly well. Apart from anything else, you're never home. The kennels are all to cock. You've abandoned me and a damned sight more important you're neglecting the dogs.

SOPHIE: I said I'm busy. I have a lot of work to do on this committee.

TIM: But surely you ...

[*From the floor above, sounds of hammering.*]

What on earth's that?

SOPHIE [*removing her coat*]: I don't know. Workmen, I suppose. [*She is wearing a* JONATHAN COCKLE *tee-shirt. On the front is a picture presumably of Cockle looking remarkably like* ERIC, *with letters* JOHN COCKLE. *On the back of the shirt are the words:* BACK TO BRUNT.]

TIM: What the hell are you wearing?

SOPHIE: It's our Pendon Twelve tee-shirt. Do you like it? We're selling them. The tech did them for us.

TIM: Isn't that – that fellow on the front?

SOPHIE: Jonathan Cockle.

TIM: No, the one you're – working with ...

SOPHIE: Eric Collins? Yes, a bit. We based it on him. There aren't any existing pictures of Cockle. So we decided since Eric was playing him ...

TIM: And I don't like that either. I've said it before ...

[*Another burst of hammering. He pauses till it stops.*]

And I'll say it again. I don't like him from what I've heard. And I don't like your associating with him.

SOPHIE: Too bad.

TIM: He's got a wife or some such, hasn't he? For one thing?

SOPHIE: Yes.

TIM: Well, then.

SOPHIE: Philippa and I happen to be very good friends. I like her. Now.

TIM: Yes, that may be – but don't you see, Sophie, sooner or later ...

    [*A burst of hammering. He pauses till it stops.*]

    Sooner or later, you're going to get hurt again. As soon as he's had what he wants from you, he'll leave you high and dry. Like Patrick.

SOPHIE: Patrick was totally selfish and self-centred. He never intended leaving his wife for me for one minute. He was far too middle class and cosy.

TIM: Well, does this fellow Eric intend to?

SOPHIE: No. But then he's never said he would. He loves Philippa anyway.

TIM: But –

SOPHIE: There's room for both of us.

TIM: But I – I – I –

    [*More hammering.*
    He paces about till it stops.]

    Well, what about her? What's she got to say about it?

SOPHIE: Philippa? She's seems happy enough. Now look, Tim, I do have things to do before the meeting. I'm sorry.

TIM: Well, I don't know. I don't know at all. I only hope to God you know what you're doing, Sophie. I'll come and pick you up afterwards.

SOPHIE: No, there's no need.

TIM: Save you walking.

SOPHIE: I may work on. It depends what Eric wants to do.

TIM: I see. I'll look in anyway. Just in case.

    [TIM *turns to go. He nearly collides with* PHILIPPA *who enters carrying several rustic-type jerkins and her sewing kit. She is an amiable casual girl, inclined to be extremely shy. When she speaks, particularly in the company of strangers, she is often completely inaudible.*]

    [*Raising his hat as he nearly collides with her*] Oh, I do beg your pardon.

PHILIPPA [*softly*]: That's all right.

    [TIM *goes out.*

    PHILIPPA *dumps her sewing down by* SOPHIE.]

SOPHIE [*looking up*]: Oh, Philippa. Hallo.

PHILIPPA: Hallo.

    [PHILIPPA *takes off her coat to reveal another* JOHN COCKLE *tee-shirt. Another burst of hammering as she does this.* PHILIPPA *looks up.*]

SOPHIE: Dreadful din, isn't it? I think they're laying carpets. [*Indicating*

list] I'm just checking this for duplicates. So far, we've got over eighty
names if they all turn up.

PHILIPPA: Good.

> [PHILIPPA *sits*.
> *They both start working*.
> PHILIPPA *starts humming the* JOHN COCKLE SONG *quietly to
> herself. After a bit,* SOPHIE *joins in.*]

SOPHIE: Terribly catchy, isn't it? [*Starting singing*] John Cockle, John
Cockle ...

BOTH: Who feared not what they say,
John Cockle, John Cockle, who spake out come what may.
The man who brought the sun to shine so others could make hay.
John Cockle comes alive, my friends, in Pendon Town today.
John Cockle, John Cockle ...

> [HELEN *enters under this last.*]

HELEN: Oh my God. Sorry to interrupt the dirge. Philippa dear.

PHILIPPA: Yes.

HELEN: Have you started on my uniforms yet?

PHILIPPA [*shaking her head*]: Sorry.

HELEN: Well, what on earth are you – ? [*Seeing* PHILIPPA's *work*] Oh
no. You're not still on these bodkins. How many bodkins
are you making, for heaven's sake?

SOPHIE: She's got a lot to do, Helen. There's dozens of them.

HELEN: It's only the Pendon Twelve, you know. Not the feeding of the
Five Thousand.

SOPHIE: There's the crowd too.

HELEN: I mean, it's all very well. You've only got twelve to worry about.
I've got a whole company of soldiers. And an Earl. I really think this
very selfish. I mean, I got Philippa on this committee to help me ...

SOPHIE: We know why you got Philippa on this committee.

HELEN: And I do wish you'd take off those frightful shirts. You're turning
the whole thing into a Pop Festival.

SOPHIE [*swinging a little*]: John Cockle ... John Cockle ...

HELEN [*moving to the door*]: Well, I'm going to raise this at the meeting.
I've got a whole load of bones to pick with someone.

> [DONALD *and* AUDREY *enter*]
> [*Sweeping past them*] Good evening. Excuse me.
> [HELEN *goes out*.
> *A burst of hammering.*]

DONALD ⎫ [*after her*]: Good evening.
AUDREY ⎭

AUDREY: They've taken all the carpets up.

DONALD [*helping her to the table*]: Yes, I think they're laying some new ones, mother.

AUDREY: About time.

DONALD: Ah, good evening, ladies.

PHILIPPA:⎫
SOPHIE:　⎭ Good evening.

DONALD: Here we are, mother.

AUDREY: Good evening. You look like groupies. Don't they?

DONALD: Like what, mother?

AUDREY: I said they look like groupies.

DONALD: Groupies. No, I don't think we know that word, mother.

SOPHIE: Groupies, yes. That's right, Mrs Evans.

DONALD: And how are our military uniforms coming along, young lady? Have you started on those yet?

PHILIPPA [*shaking her head*]: No.

DONALD: Oh dear, oh dear. Only three more weeks. I understand Mrs Dixon took my tip and obtained several from the Pendon Players. They're a very fine group. I was actually with the Pendon Players for a brief while.

SOPHIE [*not frightfully interested*]: Oh, were you?

DONALD: In a backstage capacity. I did the thunder for them one year. Do you remember that, mother? My doing the thunder?

AUDREY: Thunder? Yes, that was *Moby Dick*.

DONALD: That's right. *Moby Dick*.

SOPHIE: The Pendon Players did *Moby Dick*?

DONALD: Yes, the one about the whale. It was very successful. In fact, many people preferred it to the film.

[*Heavy hammering from above.* RAY *and* HELEN *enter.*]

RAY: Good evening, everyone.

['*Good evenings*' *from all.*

ERIC *follows them in. He, too, is wearing his* JOHN COCKLE *tee-shirt. He carries more files and papers than before.*]

ERIC [*nodding briskly*]: Evening.

[ERIC *sits between* PHILIPPA *and* SOPHIE.]

AUDREY: More groupies.

ERIC: Beg your pardon?

[*The banging continues unabated.*]

RAY [*over this*]: Sorry about the noise. I've had a word with the manager. Apparently they're having to lay new carpeting and, being a hotel, they have to do it at ungodly hours to suit the guests. He has assured me though that they'll keep the noise down as much as possible. Now, is everyone here? No, we seem to have one Adamson missing. Which one is it tonight, Donald?

DONALD: Tonight is the turn of Mrs Adamson, Mr Chairman.

HELEN: Oh lord, I don't know which is worse ...

DONALD: Apologies have been received from Mr Adamson as usual. [*In more of an undertone*] And of course – er ...

RAY: Oh yes. A piece of sad news, I'm afraid. I have just received the following communication from Mr Lorne-Messiter. Thank you, Mr Secretary. [*Reading*] Dear Mr Dixon, Of late, pressure of work has prevented me from attending as many meetings of your admirable and well-intentioned Trust as I would have wished ...

HELEN: He hasn't been to one.

RAY: Well, he's a busy man. He may have overlooked that. [*Continuing reading*] As matters stand, it seems unlikely that I shall be in a position to attend many more.

   [*The banging recommences.*]

Under the circumstances – God, I wish they'd stop that – may I crave the indulgence of you and your fellow members and request that you accept my resignation from the committee. I enclose a small donation towards your pageant which I hope will in some way compensate for my absence. With best wishes for a successful Festival, Yours sincerely, Bernard Lorne-Messiter.

ERIC: How much did he send?

RAY: Er – five pounds.

ERIC: I got more than that from a whip round at Foxton's factory canteen at lunchtime.

HELEN: They've probably got more money than Bernard Lorne-Messiter.

RAY [*swiftly*]: Yes. Well. While the banging's stopped, let's proceed, shall we? We won't wait for Mrs Adamson. Apologies – we've had those – minutes of the last – well, we're still a bit behindhand with those, no matter – Chairman's Report. Right. Now. As agreed, I've arranged that the eighteenth-century banquet will be held in this room on the evening of the day of the pageant. The Swan Hotel have promised to lay it on at very reasonable cost. Tickets will be on sale shortly – those are in hand – and they tell me they will serve, among other things, roast venison or something approximating to that ...

HELEN: I can imagine.

RAY: Now, I've also rented this room for the entire day because obviously it's very conveniently situated right on the Market Square out there. You'll recall, we've had to abandon the proposed Charge down the High Street because of the present one-way traffic scheme. This, I may add, despite Councillor Evans's plea on our behalf to both the Police ...

DONALD: I did my very best, Mr Chairman, but they did feel that to make one exception ...

RAY: Yes, quite understood, as is his subsequent appeal on our behalf to the Highways and Byeways Committee.

DONALD: Who took a similar view, I'm afraid.

RAY: So ...

[*Loud hammering from above.*]

Oh lord, damn it.

[*Hammering stops.*]

So, instead of the original charge down the main street, the soldiers will be concealed at various vantage points around the Square – in which case this room is obviously ideal as a Headquarters and changing room. Those crash doors there, of course, leading directly on to the Market Place. I think that's it. Now. Reports from Group Leaders ...

DONALD: Mr Chairman, before you proceed. On the matter of the banquet ...

RAY: Yes, Councillor.

DONALD: I am wondering how the committee would react to the idea of Mrs Evans, my mother, providing some musical interlude during the course of the evening. You'll note that there is already a piano there. As you may know, she is a trained pianist and has expressed a great willingness to do so.

[*A slight pause.*]

HELEN: Oh.

RAY: Ah. Well, that's a very nice gesture by Mrs Evans, Councillor ...

HELEN: Yes, but won't she want to eat with the rest of us? She can hardly have her venison at the keyboard.

DONALD: Actually, mother is not a great eater. I think you'll find she won't particularly want to join in too many of the gourmet proceedings.

ERIC: Do we need music?

RAY: Well – er –

DONALD: I think it might be a nice additional touch, Mr Chairman. Of course, if the committee feel ...

RAY: No, no. We're more than grateful. I think we're agreed then. Mrs Evans will provide a musical interlude during the banquet. Something suitable, no doubt ... ?

DONALD: Oh yes, she has a very sizeable repertoire.

RAY: Right. Agreed. Now. Reports from Group Leaders. Helen?

HELEN: Well, I have one or two very serious matters to raise. Firstly, the costumes. Now, I co-opted on to this committee Philippa to assist me – my group – with the military uniform and some ladies' dresses. She has now been with us two months and she has done nothing but stitch up these bodkins. Half of which aren't necessary anyway.

RAY: Well, you could have asked Mrs Pakenham like I suggested. She's been standing by, needle in hand. Why didn't you ask her?

HELEN: Because I don't want Mrs Pakenham. I don't happen to like Mrs Pakenham. I don't get on with her. Not at all. I asked for Philippa and I don't see why I can't have Philippa.

SOPHIE: Philippa's got an awful lot to do, Helen.

HELEN: And that's another thing ...

RAY: Just a minute. Just a minute. I take it, you really do have your work cut out, do you, Philippa?

PHILIPPA [*totally inaudibly*]: I do have quite a bit to do. I still have the sleeves on these to finish and then I have to do all the binding around the necks.

RAY [*straining forward to hear*]: I beg your pardon?
 [*A burst of banging.*]

PHILIPPA [*a little louder but drowned by this*]: Binding around the necks and the cuffs mostly.

RAY: I'm sorry, love, I can't quite ... It's this banging as well, it ...

HELEN: Oh do speak up, Philippa. I know you're shy and we're all very sympathetic but nobody's going to eat you, for heaven's sake.

RAY: Now, don't start on her, Helen ...

HELEN: Well I mean, she's supposed to be a teacher, isn't she? What on earth does she do when she gets among her infants. They can't have learnt a thing.

ERIC: Philippa happens to be very good with children.

HELEN: Presumably why she lives with you.

ERIC: Some of us just prefer quiet women.

RAY: Now, now.

PHILIPPA [*inaudibly*]: I'm not really all that shy.

ERIC: Sorry, what's that, love?

AUDREY: She says she's not really all that shy.

PHILIPPA [*to* AUDREY]: Thank you.

RAY: Right. Group Leaders' Reports. What about you, Eric?

HELEN: Just a minute. I haven't finished. Secondly. I want to know this. Just how many of these bodkins does she intend making?

SOPHIE: They're jerkins.

HELEN: Well, whatever they are. I mean, the point is there's only supposed to be twelve of them.

ERIC: There's got to be a crowd as well.

HELEN: Whereas I'm supposed to have a whole company of soldiers to clothe. And their ladies. And the Earl of Dorset. And his horse. I mean, we're supposed to look splendid. They can wear any old clothes, it doesn't matter.

RAY: All right then. Now, let's try and sort it out. How many people have you got needing costumes, Helen?

HELEN: That's my next point. Practically no one. I had planned originally on at least thirty soldiers. I mean, we need a minimum of that to make it look believable but every time I recruit someone, I find he's been lured over to the other side.

ERIC: Mr Chairman, I resent that.

RAY: Yes, well. I know we've discussed this privately, love. I mean, you don't know that for certain, do you?

DONALD: Lured, Mr Chairman? How exactly does Mrs Dixon mean lured?

HELEN: I'll tell you. By extremely underhand tactics. For instance, yesterday evening I had arranged a costume fitting for twelve very nice sixth form boys from the High School. And only two turned up. And they weren't interested. The rest had been lured away by promises of free beer and garish tee-shirts.

ERIC: There is no proof of this, Mr Chairman.

HELEN: Oh yes, there is. Look at you, you're all wearing them.

ERIC: This is part of our publicity campaign. Why don't you wear one?

HELEN: I wouldn't be seen dead ...

RAY: Now, look, look, look. Let's sort this one out. You obviously need some help with the Personnel side to start with, Helen. Now, how many people have you actually got so far?

HELEN: Well. You, me – Mr Adamson if he arrives, Mrs Adamson if she turns up and Councillor Evans.

[*A silence, punctuated by a burst of hammering.*]

RAY: Is that all?

HELEN [*very near to tears of frustration*]: Yes. That's what I'm saying.

RAY [*soothingly*]: All right, love, all right.

HELEN: It's not fair. It really isn't. I've been working my heart out. You should see my dress. I've been working on it for weeks ...

RAY: Yes, I have. I've seen your dress, love. It's very nice.

HELEN [*weeping*]: I mean, all those trimmings are hand sewn. I've gone to endless trouble.

RAY: Yes, all right, all right.

[*Hammering.*]

Shut up.

[*Hammering stops.*]

Is there any way your group might be able to help Helen, Eric?

ERIC: I'm very sorry, Mr Chairman. We are working to capacity.

RAY: Oh well. You've got the Earl of Dorset's horse, anyway. I managed to borrow that.

DONALD: Ah, Mr Chairman ...

RAY: Just a moment, Councillor. Who were you thinking of, Helen, as the Earl of Dorset?

HELEN: Well. Mr Adamson, I suppose ...

RAY: Mr Adamson? Yes. Do you feel that Mr Adamson on a horse would be all that safe? I mean, no disrespect to him ...

HELEN: Who else is there? We can't ask Councillor Evans.

DONALD: Oh no, no.

HELEN: And you're not riding one. It's far too dangerous.

DONALD: Mr Chairman ...

RAY: Councillor?

DONALD: There is yet another piece of bad news, I'm afraid. I hate always to be the harbinger of bad tidings but ... during my meeting with the Police on the other matter, I did have occasion to speak with the Chief Inspector concerning your proposed plan to have a horse ridden through the Market Place. Their feeling was that on a Saturday, with possibly many elderly shoppers, an untrained horse ridden by perhaps an untrained rider could constitute a hazard.

HELEN: What do you mean? You mean, I can't have my horse?

DONALD: I'm afraid the Police do feel ...

HELEN: But the only thing I've got is a horse.

DONALD: Well.

RAY: Oh dear.

ERIC: Perhaps he can ride a bicycle.

HELEN: Oh, don't be ridiculous. Well, that's it, isn't it? That's that. We might as well call it off. All off. Cancel everything.

RAY: Now, just a minute, just a minute.

HELEN: Well, the man can't walk, can he? He's the Earl of Dorset, for heaven's sake ...

RAY: We could find an alternative means of transport.

ERIC: That's what I'm saying. A bicycle.

HELEN: Oh, just you shut up.

DONALD: Mr Chairman, if I might suggest, perhaps some more stylized form of horse might be acceptable.

HELEN: What the hell does a stylized horse look like?

DONALD: Well now, if you'll let me continue. I do remember the Pendon Players did perform with great success a mummers' play in the gardens of St Mary's Church in which they made use of a type of hobby horse They may still have it for all I know. They do keep things.

HELEN: Ridiculous. We might as well have a pantomime horse and have done with it.

DONALD: That's another possibility, of course.

AUDREY: Ride a cock-horse to Banbury Cross.

RAY: Yes, the stylized horse sounds possible.

HELEN: No, it doesn't.

RAY: I mean, it's a pageant after all. We did agree at the start we weren't going in for great realism. Otherwise we'd have the Market Square strewn with bodies, wouldn't we? [*He laughs.*]

HELEN: We can but hope.

RAY: I'll put that down to investigate, anyway. I'll do that personally. Thank you, anyway, Councillor Evans, for your good offices.

DONALD: I can assure you I used my most persuasive arguments. As a matter of fact the Police were adamant about all types of livestock.

SOPHIE: It is a Market Square after all.

DONALD: The old Market Square.

RAY: Yes, right. How about the other Group? Mr Collins?

ERIC: Yes, everything seems to be proceeding ...

[*A burst of hammering.*]

[*As it stops*] ... satisfactorily, Mr Chairman. As you've heard, Philippa is working hard on the costumes. Sophie is now working exclusively on promotion and recruiting. We have a promise from the Foxton Works' Band to play before the rally. Besides these tee-shirts which you've seen, we're expecting shortly badges, car stickers and pennants. In short, we're selling the name and image of John Cockle whenever and wherever we can.

HELEN: Never mind John Cockle, what about the Earl of Dorset?

ERIC: I think he can take care of himself, don't you?

DONALD: I hope, Mr Chairman, we are not going to leave out any mention of Mr Walter Brunt ... I, myself, found him a very colourful character ...

ERIC: William Brunt was but a henchman, Mr Chairman. Mr Max Kirkov will in fact represent him but Brunt was ultimately merely the tool of Cockle's intellect. Cockle is the key, Mr Chairman. It is to John Cockle we must look for our inspiration for this pageant. For it is John Cockle who represents the ideals behind it. Cockle stood like some giant, head and shoulders above his contemporaries. A visionary if you like. A man who saw that people were of this earth and that thus people owned this earth. All people.

[*Continual hammering starts behind causing* ERIC *to get louder and louder till finally he is bellowing as if to a mass rally.*]

That it was the natural birthright of every man, woman and child to sow the land and to reap where they had sown. Without interference and without intimidation. From anyone. That land did not belong to the few but to the many. That words like landlord, tenant, ownership, land speculation would, in time, become as meaningless and empty as the capitalist philosophy which lay behind them. And ultimately, the smallest – yes, I say the smallest, most wretched of children would be able to dig his hand deep into the raw dirt at his feet, clutch it in his fist and shout 'Yes. This too belongs to me ...'

[*The banging stops.*

A silence.]

Thank you, Mr Chairman. If you'll excuse me now, we do have another meeting. Would you excuse us?

RAY: Yes – er –

ERIC: Thank you, Mr Chairman. Ready, girls?

[ERIC *marches out. The two girls just behind him.*

As they go] Good night.

SOPHIE: Good night.

PHILIPPA [*inaudibly*]: Good night.

[*Silence.*

Banging.]

RAY: Well. Meeting closed, I suppose.

HELEN: He's a megalomaniac. The man's paranoid. He's cracked.

DONALD: He's certainly very enthusiastic.

HELEN: He's raving mad.

RAY: Well, he's entering into the spirit of it, I suppose. I must say, that did seem just a little bit worrying ... I don't know, we seem to be losing a lot of the fun of this thing. I don't know. Maybe just me. Anyone for a drink?

AUDREY [*swiftly*]: A drink? Yes, please.

DONALD: Oh. Are you sure, mother? We have to ...

AUDREY: Yes, please.

[DONALD *helps her up.*]

RAY: Good. Helen?

HELEN: In a minute.

RAY: Are you coming?

HELEN: In a minute.

DONALD: Mind how you go then, mother.

[DONALD *and* AUDREY *go out.*]

RAY [*from the doorway*]: Now, you're not to worry, love. We'll all rally round you. Don't you worry about it.

HELEN: No.

[RAY *goes out.*

HELEN *sits.*
After a second, she cries a little.
TIM *enters.*]

TIM: Ah. Hallo.

HELEN [*recovering*]: Oh, hallo, Tim.

TIM: Something wrong?

HELEN: No – I –

TIM: I was just looking for Sophie.

HELEN: She's gone.

TIM: Gone? That's funny. I was waiting in the bar, I ...

HELEN: She went off with that man and his woman.

TIM: Oh lord. [*He paces about.*] Very worrying this, Helen, you know. I don't quite know what to do.

HELEN: You've got to do something, Tim. That man's as mad as a hatter.

TIM: Who? Collins?

   [*Brief banging.*]

HELEN: I need help, you see.

TIM: You do? How's that?

HELEN: I've got no soldiers, no uniforms, no horse, nothing ...

TIM: So you want a hand then?

HELEN: Oh, Tim. Would you?

TIM: Well – yes. I'd have to keep an eye on the dogs occasionally but ... All right. Say the word. I don't know if I can be of much use.

HELEN: Oh, we need you. We need you so badly. We all do. Your country needs you, Tim.

   [TIM *seems startled.*]

CURTAIN

ACT TWO
SCENE ONE

HELEN, LAWRENCE, RAY, DONALD *and* AUDREY *sit round the table. A silence. They are waiting.* LAWRENCE *is very soporific. He has his usual glass.*

RAY: I hope he's coming, Helen.

HELEN: If he says he'll come, he'll come.

RAY: I must say I feel rather guilty ... I mean, holding secret meetings like this. Without notifying half the committee.

DONALD: It's not strictly in order, Mr Chairman.

HELEN: Why not? That's what they've been doing. With their Action Group.

RAY: You think he might possibly come up with the answer, then?

LAWRENCE: He's a very strange chap. I heard a rumour that he sleeps with a sword under his pillow.

HELEN: He has plenty of ideas. And he has the advantage that he was an Army man.

RAY: Yes. Quite. A captain.

DONALD: I served myself for a brief period, Mr Chairman. But that was in the Air Force.

HELEN: Yes, well, unfortunately, we're not going to be able to bomb them so that's not much good.

DONALD: I saw no action, I'm afraid. I was ground crew.

RAY: Ah.

[TIM *marches in. He carries a rolled up plan and a rucksack.*]

TIM: Sorry I'm late. Bitch trouble, I'm afraid.

RAY: Ah, we'd nearly given you up.

TIM: Evening.

ALL: Good evening.

TIM: Sit here, shall I?

RAY: Yes, please do, Captain Barton.

TIM: Thank you.

RAY: Well, this is in the nature of an extraordinary meeting. I think it's best left unminuted ... Unminuted, Mrs Evans.

AUDREY: Unminuted. Right.

RAY: In view of the fact that we haven't notified all members. I think we can go straight into the main business. As you'll know, Captain Barton here has very generously offered us his services as adviser to aid our military department of the pageant. Which has regrettably fallen behind the rest.

HELEN: And which was not entirely my fault.

RAY: No. No. No blame is attached. On the other hand, those persons organizing the activities of the Twelve seem to have drawn rather further ahead. Perhaps under the circumstances more than some of us would feel is right. So the aim is, I think, to restore the balance as it were. I'll now ask Captain Barton whether he has anything he can immediately suggest.

TIM: Thank you, Chairman. Well now. I have, of course, already had quite lengthy talks, particularly with Mrs Dixon, so I am not entirely out of the picture. The situation it appears to me is as follows. We have one highly under-organized but basically benevolent faction and a second highly organized but undoubtedly malevolent faction. Is that the case?

RAY: Well, I think malevolent is rather a strong word to . . .

TIM: I'm sorry to contradict you but they're scum, Dixon, scum. Grubby little people with grubby little minds. And they're making use of you, make no mistake about it. Let's get that clear. They are filth. Vermin. In a wartime situation, Collins would have been hanged long ago. So we'd better start from that premise.

RAY: Ah.

TIM: Now then. How to deal with them. Well, I have here a map of the Market Square . . . [*He unrolls it.*] Excuse me . . . It's fairly up to date. Good enough for our purposes. Would you mind? Thank you.

[*During the next,* LAWRENCE *drops off to sleep.*]

Now the first thing to bear in mind is we're hardly going to win this fight through strength of numbers. We could probably get support if we had time to look for it but it's too late now to start recruiting. So it's all down to strategy. We're forced to treat everyone not involved as neutral civilians who'll run away at the first sign of trouble. And there's going to be trouble, make no mistake about that.

RAY: Don't you feel that could be avoided, Captain, if we . . .

TIM: Listen, Dixon, that lot is highly organized. I've had a snoop round for myself. I live with one of them, God help me. When she bothers to come home at all. So I know what I'm talking about. It consists of a mob of youths and louts who are spoiling for a good punch-up with you as its prime target. As soon as your three-man army starts its charge, you'll be torn to pieces.

DONALD: Oh dear.

HELEN: What did I tell you?

RAY: Are you sure? It sounds very ... But why?

TIM: Because this chap wants his meeting, this rally of his, to go uninter-
rupted, that's why. Once he gets on his soapbox, spouting his rubbish,
you'll never get him off. As your wife rightly says, he's half off his
chump. He thinks he is this chap Winkle.

HELEN: Cockle.

TIM: Cockle. And he's taking the law into his own hands. Now, I think
I can get hold of at least a dozen reliable men for that Saturday.
Probably. If they're not playing golf. I phoned round and got half-
promises. So pray for wet weather. Then half the scum won't turn up
either. This room obviously becomes H.Q. ... [*Spying* LAWRENCE] Is
that chap listening to this?

HELEN: He's fallen asleep.

TIM: Hardly officer material, is he?

DONALD: He's the Earl of Dorset.

TIM: God help the Countess. This room becomes H.Q. and this is where
we'll run things. Look at the map. We're here, you see. At the moment.
Those crash doors there are about here. So this is the first concealment
point. We can conceal further troops here in the Library. You'll recall
their Reading Room looks right out over the Square ...

DONALD: Mr Chairman, on cold days, a lot of people including older folk
make regular use of the Reading Room. You don't feel that the presence
of military uniforms in there will cause unnecessary alarm?

HELEN: What uniforms?

TIM [*answering* DONALD]: I've thought of that. They can wear macs over
their uniforms and conceal their hats till they get the signal. Then they
strip off and into action.

HELEN: Ideally, they ought to have wigs as well.

TIM: Well, that's out. We can't have a lot of chaps wandering around the
Reading Room in wigs. That will frighten people.

RAY: At the rate we're going, I don't think we need any uniforms. I mean,
this is just going to be a free-for-all.

TIM: You still need uniforms. Otherwise you're punching your own side
instead of the enemy.

DONALD: Who exactly are the enemy, Captain? How will one know them?

TIM: Anyone wearing a jerkin, clout him. Ask questions afterwards. Now.
We have other points of concealment here in this alleyway. [*Indicating
map*] Here in the bus shelter, and we could even stick a couple of chaps
here behind the War Memorial. Now I'm drawing up a detailed
timetable. That'll say when we're to take up our positions and what to
do when I give the signal. Basically, we have to get Collins who'll be

on his rostrum. Once we've nobbled the ringleader, the crowd'll lose heart. All except the hard core. And that's where the diversion comes in. Now somebody mentioned a horse. Have we still got it?

RAY: Well, I have collected a horse, yes.

TIM: Grand.

RAY: But it's not a real one.

TIM: What is it then? Stuffed?

RAY: No, it's by way of — well, it's difficult to describe. It's a stylized horse.

TIM: Ah well, that'll have to do. Something to attract attention.

DONALD: The police, you see, were very ...

TIM: You can't rely on the police. They'll be hiding in doorways along with everybody else. First sign of trouble. Who's supposed to be riding this horse?

HELEN: The Earl of Dorset.

TIM [*looking at* LAWRENCE]: What, this chap?

RAY: Yes.

TIM: Well, I suppose he'll be safer up there than he will be on the ground, by the look of him ... Anyway, he's the diversion. He goes in first. He's dispensable. Under cover of him, the rest of us make a dash for Collins.

HELEN: What can the ladies do?

TIM: Keep out of the bloody way, mostly. Pardon the language. Bathe any sore heads. Now, there's also this crisis of uniforms.

HELEN: Desperate.

TIM: Well, we'll have to sort out and make do. We don't need to look immaculate. We're not going on dress parade. Weapons? What weapons do we own?

HELEN: Muskets.

TIM: Splendid.

RAY: Wooden.

TIM: Reverse the ends and use them as clubs.

DONALD: Mr Chairman, we do appear, if you don't mind my saying, to be entering into this in a very belligerent manner. I still, myself, feel that we may have misjudged Mr Collins and the whole affair may pass off without incident.

TIM: In which case, we won't use violence. We'll do the whole thing as we planned but in the friendly spirit of the pageant. This scheme'll work both ways equally well. Peacefully, if need be, or if not ... We won't be aggressors. We'll leave them to strike the first blow but only the first one. That's what that chap on the horse is all about. We'll throw him in, see how they react. Well, if that's agreed, I'll go back, do some more work on this and then we'll meet again. How long have we got? A week?

HELEN: Six days.

TIM: Then we'd better get weaving. Now, no one's to get alarmed about this. As we say it could all pass off perfectly peacefully . . .

[*The lights go out.*]

RAY: Lights! Oy –

TIM [*bellowing in the dark*]: Get down! Everybody, get down!

[*A suppressed scream from* HELEN.
The lights come on.
AUDREY *is sitting as before.*
LAWRENCE *has woken up with a jolt and is now staring horror-struck at* TIM, *who is brandishing an Army revolver.* HELEN, RAY *and* DONALD *are in varied crouching positions.*]

LAWRENCE: Oh, my God.

HELEN [*seeing the gun*]: Oh.

DONALD: Ah.

RAY: Oh. [*Laughing feebly*] That Italian waiter must be on again.

AUDREY: Got a gun.

TIM [*slightly embarrassed, stuffing the gun back in his knapsack*]: Sorry. Didn't mean to startle you. Old war souvenir. Keep it for intruders, muggers and so on.

RAY [*trying to laugh*]: I hope you aren't intending to use that on the day, Captain Barton?

TIM [*gathering up his belongings*]: I hope it won't come to that, Dixon. I sincerely hope it won't. Good night to you.

[TIM *marches out.*]

RAY: Well, I think in the event the whole pageant will probably pass off without incident.

DONALD: I agree, Mr Chairman.

HELEN: Yes.

LAWRENCE: Hear! Hear!

AUDREY [*brightly*]: Time for a drink?

ACT TWO
SCENE TWO

The same. Festival Day.
The committee table has been separated into its original units and is scattered around the room.
SOPHIE *sits. She is dressed befittingly as a humble serving wench. She is watching* ERIC *anxiously.*
ERIC *in his simple rough Cockle costume is pacing up and down silently running through his forthcoming oration. The speech is evidently a fiery one.*
ERIC *does miniature hand movements to indicate the huge gestures he eventually intends to use. Both are very tense.*
Outside, the Foxton Works' Band is playing unsuitable melodies. Also, beyond the crash doors, the sounds of a vociferous and increasingly drunken crowd.
ERIC *finishes his speech and stops his pacing.*

SOPHIE: Are you nervous?
ERIC [*snapping*]: Of course I'm nervous.
SOPHIE: Sorry.
ERIC: Sorry. Hell ...
SOPHIE: You'll be wonderful.
ERIC: Yes. It'll do, won't it? The speech?
SOPHIE: It's super. Really super. [*Pause*] It's very powerful. [*Pause*] The way you repeat things. Something *this* and something *that* ...
ERIC: That's rhetoric.
SOPHIE: It's really effective.
ERIC: What's the time?
SOPHIE: Ten minutes to go. Ten to three. Hark at that crowd. It's a terrific size. Have you had a look?
ERIC: Yes.
SOPHIE: They're all really enjoying themselves.
ERIC: You don't think it's too big? I mean, it could get out of hand. Some of those fellows have been putting it away since eleven o'clock this morning.
SOPHIE: Oh, no. They're high spirited ...
ERIC: Max Kirkov looked pretty unsteady just now.
SOPHIE: Oh well, Max ...

ERIC: You know, he wasn't the right choice ultimately. Not for William Brunt.

SOPHIE: He looks good.

ERIC: Oh, he looks good. He looks fine. But his heart's not really in it. Basically he's far too – rugger club. He only comes along for the beer, let's face it. I mean, the last thing I need is a drunken Brunt.

SOPHIE: I'll be with you.

ERIC: Yeah.

SOPHIE: Do you want another throat sweet?

ERIC: No, I'm all right. I'm all right. Did you tell Philippa I wanted her?

SOPHIE: Yes, she's coming. She's in the Ladies helping Helen with her costume.

ERIC: Mrs Dixon all dolled up, is she?

SOPHIE: It's a lovely dress. She's done it very well. It must have taken her hours.

[PHILIPPA *enters. She is dressed as a lady's maid in slightly better style than* SOPHIE. *She carries some military uniforms and a large plumed hat.*]

PHILIPPA: Hallo.

ERIC: Ah, Philippa. Come here – here . . . Now, how many of their lot have turned up? I mean, apart from those on the committee.

PHILIPPA: Two.

ERIC: Hah! Right, listen. I have now chained and padlocked those EXIT doors. Here's the key. Sophie will hang around the foyer out there and as soon as you're all in here, she's going to lock you in. I pinched the key from Reception. And make sure it's everyone, Sophie.

SOPHIE: Yes.

ERIC: Now, Philippa, on no account let them have that key until I've finished speaking. Understand?

PHILIPPA: Yes.

ERIC: Right, put it away somewhere.

[PHILIPPA *tucks it in her dress.*]

SOPHIE: I can't see why you're bothering with all this. There's so few of them now.

ERIC: Because that mad brother of yours is plotting something. That I do know. He's not going to let me get a word out if he can help it. No, that lot are spoiling for a fight. Well, they can have it. But they can wait until I've finished speaking. I'm only going to get a chance like this once in a lifetime.

[*He pauses. The Band stops playing.*
The crowd are singing a drunken version of the COCKLE SONG.]

Is it time?

SOPHIE: Oh yes. Sorry. You must go. [*Kissing him*] Good luck, darling.

PHILIPPA [*also kissing him*]: Good luck.

ERIC [*pushing them away*]: Yes, all right, all right. [*To* SOPHIE] Lock these doors.

SOPHIE: Yes.

> [ERIC *moves to the main doors.*
>
> SOPHIE *follows him.*
>
> PHILIPPA *starts work on a pair of breeches.* TIM *enters from the hotel. He has on his hat, wig, jacket and shirt but no trousers. He is carrying his boots. He comes face to face with* ERIC. *They stare at each other a moment.*]

TIM: Would you kindly get out of here. This is a privately booked room.

ERIC: We're going.

TIM: And take your – crony with you . . .

ERIC: Come along, Sophie.

> [ERIC *goes out.*
>
> SOPHIE, *with an icy look at* TIM, *follows him.*]

TIM [*crossing to* PHILIPPA]: Now for heaven's sake, girl, where are those trousers of mine?

PHILIPPA: I'm fixing them so they'll . . .

TIM: I'm sorry, I just haven't the time.

PHILIPPA: Well, unless I finish these fastenings they won't stay up properly . . .

TIM: Give them here. [*He snatches them from her.*] Thank you. [*Struggling into them*] They're perfectly all right. What are you talking about?

> [PHILIPPA *watches anxiously*
>
> TIM, *his trousers on, sits and starts pulling on his boots.* PHILIPPA, *taking advantage of his stillness, kneels beside him and resumes her sewing in situ.*]

The others all dressed?

PHILIPPA: Yes.

TIM: What did you say?

PHILIPPA: Yes.

TIM: And how many extra soldiers turned up for costumes?

PHILIPPA: Two.

TIM: What?

PHILIPPA: Two.

TIM: Two? My God, we're on our own then. Just listen to that lot out there. Drunken scum. They may want to destroy our country but they don't mind drinking our beer when it suits them.

> [HELEN *enters. She has on a splendid dress. It may not be strictly in period but she certainly knows what suits her. The effect is slightly*

spoiled by her unsuitable shoes when visible and her handbag which she continues to carry.]

Ah, my dear lady. How resplendent.

HELEN: Thank you. All home-made. Listen to that rabble out there.

TIM: Terrible.

HELEN [*seeing* PHILIPPA *at work*]: Oh, running repairs?

TIM: I don't know what she's up to. She's been fiddling around ... [*Brushing* PHILIPPA *aside*] All right, girl, that'll do. That'll do.

PHILIPPA [*shaking her head*]: They're still not fixed.

TIM: Look they're holding up all right, aren't they? What are you on about?

PHILIPPA [*shrugging*]: All right. They're your trousers.

[PHILIPPA *goes away into a corner and starts work on the plumed hat.*]

TIM: Now then ... [*Confidentially*] Has she lost her voice or something?

HELEN: No, that's her normal volume.

TIM: Very infuriating to live with. Where are the others?

HELEN: Ray's getting the horse out of the Estate. Lawrence is in the bar, of course. Thank God they close in a minute. Donald took his uniform home last night. I think he's bringing Mrs Evans with him. She doesn't want to miss the fun.

TIM: Fun? This isn't going to be a picnic, you know. This is war.

HELEN: Well, possibly.

TIM: No, Helen, Helen ... whatever I said to the others, this is undoubtedly going to be war.

[DONALD *brings on* AUDREY.

He is dressed in his soldier's uniform. It is none too good a fit — particularly the breeches which were made for a man with very short legs and a long body so that the crutch is low slung. He walks with some difficulty. He is still wearing his glasses. Under one arm, he carries a pile of music. His other hand supports AUDREY, *dressed simply but suitably.*]

DONALD: Here we are, mother.

HELEN: Hallo there. Oh, doesn't Mrs Evans look splendid. Very nice, Mrs Evans.

AUDREY: You look nice.

HELEN: Thank you.

AUDREY: Oh, look ... [*She points at* TIM *who smiles briefly.*]

[TIM *goes out into the hotel under the next.*]

DONALD: If it's all right with everyone, mother felt she might take the opportunity before the pageant actually gets under way, of practising her interlude for this evening.

HELEN: Oh, what a good idea.

DONALD: Yes, I felt it was a good idea. I brought her music, you see. Up we go, mother.

[DONALD *helps* AUDREY *up on to the stage and to the piano stool.*]

AUDREY: More steps.

DONALD: Yes . . .

HELEN: Philippa dear, is there anything we can do about Councillor Evans's trousers? He seems to be having difficulty.

[PHILIPPA *advances on* DONALD *with a needle.*]

DONALD [*as* PHILIPPA *tugs at him*]: Oh hallo, there. Can I help at all?

PHILIPPA: It's all right, I'm just . . .

[TIM *returns from the hotel with a sackcloth bundle.*]

TIM: Nearly forgot these. Weapons. [*He drops them on the floor.*]

HELEN: The jackets have been very successful but we've been badly let down on the trousers.

[DONALD *helps* AUDREY *sort out her music.*]

TIM: I've just had a squint through the curtains in the Lounge. It's growing into quite a nasty mob out there. They're cheerful enough at the moment but as soon as the pubs close, they're going to turn very ugly.

HELEN: Is that big Russian with the beard still out there? The one who's supposed to be William Brunt?

TIM: Oh yes, large as life.

HELEN: Terrifying.

TIM: Russian, is he?

HELEN: Well, they claim he was born in Slough. He doesn't look like anyone from Slough I've ever met.

TIM: Yes, he's strong, drunk and dangerous, that one. I think we'll make our charge when he's the other side of the Square. Got your weapon, Councillor?

DONALD: I'm being sewn into my trousers apparently.

TIM: Yes. She's got a thing about stitching people into breeches, that one. Don't know where she gets that from.

HELEN: Listen . . .

[*The crowd outside has grown quieter. In the distance, we hear* ERIC'S *voice. The words are indistinguishable but he is speaking with great fire and conviction.*]

TIM: Right, they've started. Let's get organized. Break out the armoury.

[TIM *starts unwrapping the weapons.* AUDREY *starts playing. Mainly a selection of light operetta with the odd saucy 1920s popular number thrown in. She evidently could once play quite well. But age has told.*]

What the blazes . . . ? [*He straightens up and stares at* AUDREY.]

[AUDREY *favours them with one dazzling smile, then turns and concen-*

trates on her playing, which she continues under all the ensuing, oblivious of what occurs.]

Does she intend to play that thing now?

HELEN: She's rehearsing.

TIM: How very inappropriate. Never mind. Might help to frighten the enemy. [*Pulling out from the bundle a very unconvincing silver painted stage musket*] Grief. Is this the best we can muster?

HELEN: I'm afraid so.

TIM: Courtesy of the Pendon Players, I presume?

HELEN: Yes.

TIM: Never liked them. Ropy crew. Completely ruined *Private Lives*. Here, Councillor, cop hold of this.

[TIM *tosses a musket which* DONALD *manages, with difficulty, to catch.* PHILIPPA *continues her work on* DONALD'S *trousers.* DONALD *holds his musket in a normal amateurish musket-holding position.*]

DONALD: How does that look?

TIM: No, no, not like that. Hold it by the other end.

DONALD [*doing so*]: Like this, you mean?

TIM: That's it. Now swing it round your head.

DONALD [*doing so uncertainly*]: Like this?

TIM: That's the ticket.

DONALD: Surely a little bit dangerous.

TIM: Yes.

[RAY *enters astride his horse.*
He wears his soldier's uniform.
The horse is a four-wheeled animal which the rider is meant to sit astride and walk along with his feet, as RAY *is doing now. The creature has been decked out in some regalia hurriedly pinned on by* HELEN. *It has a proud tail and glassy staring eyes, protruding from a head which has swivelled through 45 degrees as if it is trying to look over its shoulder.*]

RAY: Hallo there.

TIM: Oh, my God.

HELEN: It's the best we could do in the time, I'm afraid.

TIM: Well, that ought to create a diversion, I suppose.

RAY: I felt a bit of a fool riding this through the foyer.

HELEN: What's happened to its head? It wasn't like that this morning.

RAY: I think I bashed it getting it out of the car. It won't twist round again, I've tried.

HELEN: What a shame. It spoils the whole look of it.

TIM: Right come along, then. Get weaving. Wheel it down there by the crash doors.

RAY: Righto.

[*He pushes it across.*

TIM *sorts out the weapons.*]

HELEN [*as* RAY *passes her*]: Your trousers seem all right.

RAY: They're fine. I can't lift my arms though. This jacket's very tight. That's very pleasant, Mrs Evans.

HELEN: She can't hear.

DONALD: She does play very well, doesn't she? [*To* PHILIPPA *still at work*] Have you nearly finished, dear?

PHILIPPA: Yes, practically.

DONALD: Time to go, you see.

TIM: Dixon? Musket for you. [*He tosses him one.*]

RAY: Ta.

TIM: One for me. Now, where's our diversion? Where's our damned diversion gone to?

HELEN: All right. Here he comes.

[LAWRENCE *walks in very stiffly.*

He wears a very dandified outfit which somehow manages to hang off him. He is evidently someone's idea of what the then Earl of Dorset looked like.

PHILIPPA, *seeing* LAWRENCE, *finishes with* DONALD *and goes to fetch* LAWRENCE's *hat. From outside, chanting in unison is heard.*]

LAWRENCE: Sorry, everyone, sorry. Called away.

TIM: Right, get him on his horse. Get him on. It's 15.05.

RAY [*still near the crash doors*]: It sounds as if they're barracking young Eric out there.

TIM: Never mind them. There's some in every crowd. Probably the Chinese mob. Get him on his horse.

[DONALD *and* TIM *steer* LAWRENCE *towards the horse.* RAY *steadies it.*]

LAWRENCE: I'll tell you – a rather tragic thing's just happened – rather upset me.

[*They help him on to his horse.*

PHILIPPA *following on with* LAWRENCE's *hat, slaps it on his head, then commences running repairs on the horse itself.*]

[*During this*] I don't know if you remember me telling you that there was just this faint chance that my wife Charlotte and I would be getting back together. Well, she phoned me this morning and it's off. She doesn't want to come back. Not at all.

HELEN: Now, are you comfy, Lawrence?

LAWRENCE: It won't throw me, will it? [*He laughs.*] No, you see, seriously, it was the last hope really. Last hope.

TIM [*under this last*]: Right. Open those crash doors, Dixon. We're launching the diversion. Stand by, everyone.

RAY: They appear to be shut.

TIM: Shut?

RAY: They're padlocked.

TIM: My God, it's them. The swine. Typical Marxist trick. Right. We're not beaten. We'll take him out the front doors. Wheel him out the front.

[TIM *and* RAY *turn* LAWRENCE *round.*]

HELEN: Be careful with him.

[RAY *and* TIM *wheel* LAWRENCE *at speed across to the other doors.* DONALD *hurries ahead of them.*]

LAWRENCE: Whoa there, my beauty.

TIM: Get those doors open, Councillor.

DONALD: I regret to say these appear to be locked as well.

HELEN: Oh no, we're trapped.

RAY: Oh.

HELEN: Help! Help!

TIM: Don't panic, just a minute. Don't panic, for the love of mike. Right bring him back over here. Follow me.

[TIM *hurries back towards the crash doors, fumbling in his jacket pocket.*

DONALD *and* RAY *push* LAWRENCE *back across.* PHILIPPA *is still in tow, stitching at the horse.*]

LAWRENCE: Tally ho!

DONALD: I'm afraid these trousers are still very difficult to run in.

TIM [*producing his gun*]: Stand back! I'm going to shoot the lock.

RAY: Now, you said you weren't going to bring that, Captain ...

TIM: Stand back!

[*A loud explosion. He shoots the lock.*]

That's done the trick. Right, hold the doors, you two. When I give the word, shove them open.

[RAY *and* DONALD *each take a crash door.*]

[*Running round the back of* LAWRENCE] Stand back, girl.

[PHILIPPA *retreats.*]

Right. Open up! [*Slapping the horse's rump*] Off you go, my beauty!

[*He stands back.*

LAWRENCE, *overcome finally by drink, does the slowest possible sideways fall, emitting a low groan as he does so.*]

LAWRENCE: Oooooooooooooooooohhhhh!

[*He finishes up on his side underneath the horse.*]

[*Apologetically*] Sorry. It threw me.

HELEN: Oh dear.

TIM: Right. Forget the Earl of Dorset. It's up to us now. Muskets ready.

HELEN: Are you going to leave him there?

TIM: No time now. [*To* DONALD] Glasses off, man, glasses off.

DONALD: Oh, I couldn't do that. I'm unable to see a thing.

TIM: One knock in the face and you're blinded, man ...

DONALD: I'm as blind as a bat without them, anyway.

TIM [*snatching them from his face*]: Here, get them off. Hold these for him.

    [*He thrusts the glasses at* HELEN *who puts them down on the bandstand.*]

DONALD: Oh dear.

RAY: That big Brunt fellow was outside there a minute ago.

TIM: Dodge him then. Right. Ready? Charge!

    [TIM *and* RAY *rush out.*

    DONALD *gropes after them.*

    PHILIPPA *helps* LAWRENCE *to the bandstand where he sits for the next section, gradually starting to sing along with the piano.*

    HELEN *stands by the crash doors watching the action.*]

HELEN [*getting shriller and shriller as she urges on her heroes*]: Go on, men ... Go on, Ray ... Come on, get in there. Go on ... That's it ... Let him have it ... Well done ... Look out ... Hit him, Councillor, hit him ... That's it ... Come on ... Come on, you cowards, come on ... Kill, kill ... That's better. That's what I want to see ... [*etc.*]

    [*Behind her, a crash as the hotel doors are broken open. Only* PHILIPPA *turns. A very powerful looking man, a mop of black hair standing on end, a thick black beard, wearing a torn jerkin, sweating heavily and panting, appears. He leers round. It is Max Brunt Kirkov. He spies* HELEN *doing her war dance and begins to advance on her.*]

PHILIPPA [*running to* HELEN *to warn her*]: Excuse me, it's Brunt. Brunt. Brunt's coming ...

HELEN [*irritably*]: What is it, girl? Do, for heaven's sake, speak up for yourself ...

    [PHILIPPA *points frantically.*

    HELEN *turns too late.*]

    [*Faced with* BRUNT] Oh no ... Oh my God, it's the Russians.

    [BRUNT, *with a roar, swoops and picks her up easily.*

    HELEN *screams to no avail.*

    BRUNT *bears her off through the hotel doors, singing the* COCKLE SONG *drunkenly.*]

    [*As she goes*] Heeeeelp ...

    [PHILIPPA *taps* AUDREY *on the shoulder to attract her attention.*]

AUDREY [*to her clearly*]: It's a very jolly tune this one, isn't it?

LAWRENCE: Very, very jolly.

[RAY *appears through the crash doors, bloody and battered, still clutching his musket.*]

RAY: It's no good. It's split right up the back, love. I knew it would. First time I lifted my arms over my head, you see.

PHILIPPA: Oh dear ...

[*She gets out her needle and cotton.*]

RAY: Where's Helen got to?

PHILIPPA: She's been carried off.

RAY [*not hearing her*]: Oh, I see. Just wondered. Could you just put a stitch in this, love, temporarily?

[PHILIPPA *goes round the back of* RAY *and starts sewing. She continues this for some time.*

TIM *appears briefly through the crash doors.*]

TIM: Come on, man. We nearly got to Collins that time. Once we've got Winkle, we've as good as won.

RAY: Just coming, Captain Barton, coming ...

[TIM *has gone.*

DONALD *blunders in from the hotel entrance whirling his musket round his head.*]

DONALD: I'm afraid I've no idea where I am now. I'm completely lost.

RAY [*giving him a shove in the direction of the crash doors*]: That way, Councillor Evans.

DONALD: Oh, thank you, Mr Chairman ...

[DONALD *whirls out.*]

AUDREY: The old songs are the best, aren't they?

LAWRENCE: True, true.

RAY: Quite right, Mrs Evans.

LAWRENCE: They took trouble with the left hand, you see ...

[*Pistol shots off.*]

RAY: What the hell's that? [*Shouting through the crash doors*] Captain Barton!

[*A scream.*

ERIC *rushes in and fumbles with the crash doors trying to close them.*]

ERIC [*yelling*]: Stop him! Stop him! He's gone barmy! The stupid fascist loony!

[TIM *appears round the door – gun drawn – inches away from* ERIC'S *nose.* ERIC *retreats.*]

TIM: Come back here, you weasel, Winkle. Come here and be shot like a dog!

RAY: Now, Tim, that's enough, call it a day ...

TIM: Come on, then. [*He brandishes the gun.*]

ERIC [*making a panic dash for the bandstand*]: Somebody stop him.

[TIM *fires.*
ERIC *cries out, clutches his leg and falls behind the piano.*]

RAY: Oh, my God.

[PHILIPPA *rushes to* ERIC.
ERIC *pushes her away.*
She sits by him, on the bandstand, waiting patiently.]

TIM [*foaming slightly*]: Any more for the same? I have more shells in this chamber. [*He laughs.*]

RAY: For heaven's sake, Captain Barton ...

[*A whirling musket appears round the crash doors.*
It catches TIM, *who is still in the doorway, on the back of his head.* TIM *staggers a couple of paces, collapses, firing his gun in the air as he falls.*]

DONALD [*emerging on the end of the offending musket*]: Oh, I'm terribly sorry. Was that somebody's head?

RAY: All right, all right, Councillor. I'll see to him.

[RAY *looks to* TIM.]

DONALD: Could somebody pass me my glasses, please? I'd feel a lot safer.

RAY [*to* PHILIPPA]: Could you pass the Councillor his glasses, love. They're on there.

[PHILIPPA *does so.*]

I think we'd better get the Captain out to the Lounge. He can lie down there. He's had a nasty crack ...

[RAY *helps* TIM *up.*]

DONALD: Here, I'll give you a hand, Mr Chairman.

[DONALD *and* RAY *support* TIM *towards the hotel entrance and exit.*
ERIC, *trying to stand, levers himself up on the piano, moaning. He appears over the top, face to face with* AUDREY.]

ERIC: Aaaaaah – aaaah – aah ...

AUDREY [*looking up*]: What's the matter? Don't you know the words?

ERIC: Aaaaah ...

[AUDREY *sings a little to help him out.*
SOPHIE *rushes in through the crash doors.*]

SOPHIE: Eric, Eric. Are you all right? I couldn't get to you, darling. I couldn't get to you. The police are everywhere. How are you?

ERIC [*brushing her and* PHILIPPA *aside*]: I'm all right. I'm all right. Just leave me alone. They always do it. Tory fascist wreckers. They always manage to stifle the people's voice.

SOPHIE: Look, darling, you ...

ERIC [*snarling*]: Get away from me. Both of you. Leave me alone. You pair of bourgeois, middle class ... housewives. They haven't won yet. They haven't heard the last of Jonathan Cockle.

[*He limps out through the crash doors.*

SOPHIE *stands, disillusioned.*]

PHILIPPA [*gathering up her belongings*]: I'll go with him. He'll be all right in a minute.

[PHILIPPA *follows* ERIC *out.*

SOPHIE *stands, thoughtful.*

HELEN *crawls in through the hotel doors.*

She is grimy. Her dress is torn.]

SOPHIE: Helen ...

HELEN: Oh, dear God ...

SOPHIE: What's happened?

HELEN [*giggling hysterically*]: William Brunt has just thrown me into the air.

SOPHIE: Max did? Did you fall? Did you hurt yourself?

HELEN: It's what happened after I fell that worries me ...

[HELEN *giggles.*

SOPHIE *starts to cry softly.*]

Did we win? Our side?

SOPHIE: No, I don't think anyone did, really.

[RAY *enters from the hotel.*]

RAY: I think I'll have to ... [*Seeing* HELEN] Oh no, what's happened to you, love?

HELEN: It doesn't matter. Just take me home, please.

RAY [*supporting her*]: Yes, I will, love, I will. I've just got one or two things to do here. Sophie, your brother's doctor. Do you know who it is? It's just he might have mild concussion.

SOPHIE: Oh, it's Dr Gray. Shall I ... ?

RAY: Oh, it's Gray, is it?

SOPHIE: Shall I go to him?

RAY: No, there's no need. He's more or less unconscious at the moment. And besides there's a lot of policemen standing round him. He's all right, though.

[DONALD *enters.*]

Oh, Donald, would you help Helen to the car, please? It's just in the car park there. The red Estate, you know the one. Here's the key.

DONALD: Certainly, certainly.

RAY: And tell the police it's Dr Gray.

DONALD: Right, certainly. Ready, Mrs Dixon?

HELEN: Yes, I'm sorry. I know I ought to stay but ...

RAY: That's quite all right, love.

HELEN: I feel I've given quite enough for this country this afternoon already.

[DONALD *takes her out.*

AUDREY *finishes her recital with a flourish.*]

AUDREY: There. How did that sound?

RAY: Oh, very good indeed, Mrs Evans.

AUDREY: Quite a nice selection. Do you think it's varied enough? [*Seeing* LAWRENCE *is still singing*] All finished now, Mr Adamson. No more.

LAWRENCE: Oh dear. Time to go home then?

RAY: That's right, Mr Adamson. Off you go.

LAWRENCE: If you can call it a home. There's only me there. Nobody else. No wife. No kids, just me ... nobody else, you know.

[LAWRENCE *goes out through the hotel.*]

AUDREY: Horse has fallen over.

RAY: Oh yes, we'll pick it up.

AUDREY: Just gather my music.

RAY: Yes. I hope we get as good a turn out for the eighteenth-century banquet tonight.

[AUDREY *gathers her music together.*
Sound of police car departing.]

All right, Sophie?

SOPHIE: Yes.

RAY: Your friend Eric seems to have gone off.

SOPHIE: Yes.

RAY: With Philippa.

SOPHIE: Yes.

RAY: I saw them talking to the police.

SOPHIE: Oh.

RAY: You not going to join them?

SOPHIE: No. No, I don't think so ...

[SOPHIE *moves towards the hotel doors.*]

RAY: Ah. Where are you off to then?

SOPHIE: I think I'd better go and feed the dogs. Till something else turns up. 'Bye.

RAY: Good-bye, then.

[SOPHIE *goes out.*
RAY *turns and sees* AUDREY *struggling to gather her music together.*]

Just a minute, Mrs Evans, I'll give you a hand with that.

AUDREY: Oh, thank you so much. If you wouldn't mind.

[RAY *moves to her.*]

When does the pageant start?

RAY: Oh, I'm afraid that's over, Mrs Evans. All over.

AUDREY: All over? Oh dear. I must have lost track of the time. Once I start playing ... I've missed it then?

RAY: I'm afraid so.

AUDREY: Oh dear. What a pity. I'd like to have seen the horse. Did it all go satisfactorily?

RAY: For a first one, yes. Not bad for a first one.

AUDREY: Will you be holding another?

RAY: Possibly, possibly. If we get the support.

AUDREY: Oh, by the way — next year — if you do have one, I wouldn't have this Cockle and Brunt thing again.

RAY: No, I don't think we will.

AUDREY: You see, I can't find anything about them at all. I've even had my friend with the British Museum ticket, she's been having a look for me. Nothing at all. I've a feeling Elizabeth Arnott Hutchings made the whole thing up. Isn't that naughty?

RAY [*helping her down the stairs*]: Oh dear, really?

AUDREY: Very naughty. Though I did discover one interesting thing, though. While I was researching. Did you know, when the Romans first arrived in Britain, they met a very strong pocket of resistance round here. From the Britons. Just on the edge of Pendon.

RAY [*walking her across to the hotel doors, interested*]: Really? Did they?

AUDREY [*as they go out*]: A very bloody battle.

RAY: That sounds very interesting. Romans, you say?

AUDREY: Romans, yes. And Ancient Britons . . .

[*They have gone.*]

CURTAIN

JOKING APART

First produced at the Stephen Joseph Theatre-in-the-Round, Scarborough, on 11 January 1978 and subsequently by Michael Codron at the Globe Theatre, London, on 7 March 1979 with the following cast:

RICHARD	*Christopher Cazenove*
ANTHEA	*Alison Steadman*
HUGH	*Julian Fellowes*
LOUISE	*Marcia Warner*
SVEN	*Robert Austin*
OLIVE	*Jennifer Piercey*
BRIAN	*John Price*
MELODY	
MANDY	*Diane Bull*
MO	
DEBBIE	

Directed by Alan Ayckbourn
Designed by Alan Tagg

ACT ONE

Scene One: Twelve years ago, 5 November, 7.15 p.m.
Scene Two: Eight years ago, July morning, Sunday

ACT TWO

Scene One: Four years ago, Boxing Day, 3 p.m.
Scene Two: This year, August evening, Friday

ACT ONE
SCENE ONE

A garden, in which we see part of a tennis court, which although in disrepair underfoot, has solid enough fencing and the door is in working order. The rest of the court extends offstage. A bench alongside the court. At the other side a small summerhouse/pavilion, very weathered. Rough grass underfoot. Bushes and trees. A wonderful garden for children – slightly more hazardous for adults. At present it is dark. About 7.15 p.m. on 5 November, twelve years ago. A fine clear night with a little moon. From the other end of the tennis court the sound of three children's (aged between four and six) excited shrieks and yelps.

RICHARD, a man in his late twenties, enters from the far end of the tennis court. He has on suitable bonfire gear, scarf, coat, old trousers and gumboots, thick gloves and possibly a hat. He carries a battery lantern.

RICHARD [*shouting to the children behind him*]: Now, the first one of you to touch those fireworks goes up on the bonfire instead of the Guy, all right? Now, Debbie, you're the oldest. I'm leaving you in charge, young lady.

ANTHEA [*off from the house*]: Are we all ready?

RICHARD: Oh, come on, you lot. We've been waiting out here for hours.

ANTHEA: Coming.

RICHARD: Have you brought the matches?

ANTHEA: Brian's bringing them.

[ANTHEA *appears, a year or two younger than* RICHARD. *Cheerful, disarmingly frank, attractive but not beautiful.*]

God, this place is treacherous in the dark. [*Extending her hand to someone behind her*] Do be careful, Mrs – er – Emerson. Can you see?

[ANTHEA *waves the small pocket torch she's carrying ineffectually.*]

RICHARD [*bounding forward with his larger lantern*]: Here, let me . . .

[*We see now that* ANTHEA *is leading the* EMERSONS. LOUISE, *a pale, rather tense woman of twenty-four and* HUGH, *her husband, a young clergyman, two years older. Shy, rather nervous but with an air of quiet determination.*]

LOUISE: That's fine, thank you. I can manage.

RICHARD: All right back there?

HUGH: Yes, thank you, Mr Clarke.

ANTHEA [*moving towards the summerhouse*]: We're going to watch from over here, darling, if that's all right?

RICHARD: You're a bit far away. You won't see much from there.

ANTHEA: No, this is fine.

RICHARD: Come in the tennis court.

ANTHEA: No. Mrs Emerson doesn't like the bangs, darling.

RICHARD: We haven't got many bangs. She wouldn't let me buy many bangs. Bangs are the best bit.

ANTHEA: No, we're happy. Mrs Emerson and I will be perfect here.

LOUISE: Please do call me Louise.

ANTHEA: Oh fine. In that case, I'm Anthea. This is Richard.

RICHARD: How do you do?

HUGH: Hugh.

RICHARD: I beg your pardon?

HUGH: I'm Hugh.

RICHARD: You're what? Oh Hugh, I see. Hallo. Right. I'll set things going. Where's Brian with the matches?

ANTHEA [*calling*]: Brian!

RICHARD: Brian!

ANTHEA: Brian!

RICHARD: We're not waiting for the Holmensons, are we?

ANTHEA: No, they're obviously going to be late.

RICHARD: Late? Late? Sven is never late. You must know that by now. Everyone else has got to be early. [*Shouting*] Brian!

[RICHARD *goes off towards the house.*]

ANTHEA [*laughing*]: This is my husband's partner and his wife. Sven and Olive Holmenson. Sven is terribly solemn, terribly Scandinavian, a sweet person but never, ever wrong.

LOUISE: Really?

HUGH: How awfully convenient.

LOUISE: I can't believe that. I mean, nobody ...

ANTHEA: Well, he never admits he's wrong. Let's put it that way. I mean, you could go up to him and say – Excuse me, Sven, I'm afraid you're on fire. Your jacket is alight and blazing. And he'll say – No, no, I'm not, and that's the end of it. No point in arguing.

LOUISE: When was this?

ANTHEA: What?

LOUISE: The ...

ANTHEA: Oh, no, sorry. I've got fire on the brain with this bonfire. That was just a sort of example. I mean, that sort of thing.

HUGH: He wasn't really on fire, dear.

LOUISE: Oh. That's a relief.

ANTHEA: No, you'll have to get used to me. I chat away sixteen to the dozen. Nobody knows what I'm talking about, least of all myself. Not that anybody cares. Most of the time nobody's listening anyway.

HUGH: It's really very kind of you to ask us.

ANTHEA: Well, you'll be feeling a bit stranded, won't you? I mean, how long have you been moved in? A couple of days, isn't it?

LOUISE: Yes, two days. Literally.

[*During the following,* HUGH *sidles away from them and down the side of the tennis court to check on his offspring.*]

ANTHEA: You got everything straight yet?

LOUISE: No, I'm afraid not. It's a terrible mess. I'm glad to be able to shut the door on it for ten minutes.

ANTHEA: Well, we've been here six months and our place is just chaos.

LOUISE: Of course you're in a very big house, aren't you.

ANTHEA: Enormous.

HUGH [*crouching down and talking through the wire mesh*]: All right, Christopher? Now, be a good boy. Play nicely with the little girl and boy, won't you?

[*During this* RICHARD *returns with the matches.*]

ANTHEA: Got them?

RICHARD: Yes.

LOUISE: Is he all right, dear?

HUGH: Yes. He's getting a tiny bit over-excited, I think.

RICHARD [*calling*]: All right, kids, just a second.

ANTHEA: Aren't Brian and thingy coming out?

RICHARD: I don't know. [*Pulling a face*] Things are a bit tense in there.

ANTHEA: Oh.

RICHARD: I thought I'd better leave them. [*Moving into tennis court*] Now then, you 'orrible lot. What's been going on behind here?

ANTHEA [*to* HUGH *and* LOUISE]: Brian, whom you met, and girlfriend whom you haven't. Going through agonies all weekend.

LOUISE: Oh dear.

ANTHEA: Ah well, that's love. I suppose.

HUGH: Yes, yes.

LOUISE: It's very good for our Christopher to have some other children to play with.

ANTHEA: Didn't he have any friends before?

LOUISE: No, there weren't any his own age where we were.

ANTHEA: Oh dear. How old is he?

LOUISE: Four and a half.

ANTHEA: Oh well, he's just between ours. Debbie's, what, nearly six and Giles was four last Thursday.

RICHARD [off]: Here we go then. Ready?

ANTHEA: Right.

LOUISE [covering her ears and shutting her eyes]: Oh.

    [Blaze of firework.]

ANTHEA: Whee! Isn't that pretty?

HUGH [trying to make his wife hear him]: It's all right, Louise, it's all right.

ANTHEA [amused]: Is she all right?

HUGH: She doesn't like the bangs.

ANTHEA: There aren't any bangs. Tell her we haven't got any bangs.

HUGH [shouting]: They haven't got any bangers, Louise.

    [A second different-coloured firework. Cries from the children off.]

ANTHEA: Darling? Richard?

RICHARD: Hallo?

ANTHEA: If you're going to light a bang, could you give us some warning so it doesn't frighten Louise?

RICHARD [off]: I'll try.

ANTHEA: We're bringing some food out later on when we've lit the bonfire.

HUGH: Lighting it in the middle of the tennis court, is that a good idea? I mean, it won't do it a lot of good, will it?

ANTHEA: No, well with that court, it doesn't matter that much.

    [Another firework.

    LOUISE, who has emerged temporarily from her shell, goes back into it again.]

It's in a terrible state. We're going to have to have it re-done sometime. I don't think the previous owners ever used it. Do you play, either of you? [Looking towards LOUISE] Oh. [She sees she'll get no answer from that quarter.]

HUGH [answering for them both]: I do a little. But I don't think Louise does.

ANTHEA: Well, I'm hopeless. We must learn together.

HUGH: Good idea.

    [Firework light goes out.]

LOUISE [emerging]: All clear?

ANTHEA: Yes, all clear now.

    [A big bang. LOUISE screams and covers her ears.]

RICHARD [off]: Sorry. That was a banger.

ANTHEA: Thank you, darling.

    [HUGH has moved back down the side of the tennis court to check on his offspring.]

HUGH [*crouching down by the side of the wire*]: Christopher? Keep your balaclava on, there's a good boy. You keep your little hat on, there's a good boy.

LOUISE: I am sorry. They just make me jump, I can't . . .

ANTHEA: That's all right. It was frightfully loud. No, what I was going to say was, our house of course, was the original vicarage. Did you know that . . .

> [*A firework screams overhead.*
> LOUISE *ducks*.]

And then, of course, they built – oh lord . . . [*Calling*] Richard, have you got any quieter ones? Poor Louise is cowering away here.

RICHARD [*off*]: Sorry.

HUGH [*hurrying back*]: Yes, I'm sorry. She shouldn't really have come. She's absolutely terrified of bangers.

ANTHEA: Would you like to wait in the house?

RICHARD [*off to one of the kids*]: Oy, oy, oy. Hands off.

> [HUGH *hurries back that way to investigate*.]

LOUISE: No, I'm fine, fine.

HUGH: Is Christopher being a nuisance – er – Richard? Shall I take him?

RICHARD [*off*]: No, he's all right. Just a bit overexcited – [*Suddenly, fiercely*] Giles, that is still alight. Now put it down.

HUGH: Now, Christopher, quieten down. Quieten down, dear.

> [*During this,* BRIAN, *a man in his late twenties, has appeared from the house. He stands moodily apart*.]

ANTHEA [*spotting him now*]: Oh come on, Brian, you're missing it all. Is Melody coming out?

BRIAN: I have no idea whatsoever.

ANTHEA: Where is she?

BRIAN: In the kitchen, I think, heating the soup.

> [*Another brilliantly coloured firework*.]

ANTHEA: Oh, good for her. [*Taking in firework*] I say, what a gorgeous colour. What's this one called, darling?

RICHARD [*off*]: I haven't the faintest idea.

ANTHEA [*calling*]: Giles, look at the colours . . . Giles? . . . Honestly, the kid's half-witted. He's looking in the wrong direction. Turn him round, Debbie, so he can see.

> [BRIAN *has wandered away and is gazing morosely at the display without enjoyment*. HUGH *sidles after him*.]

Brian's working for my husband. Just temporarily. He's working in the retail shop. We import a lot of household stuff. Glassware – furniture – fabrics and so on. From Scandinavia.

LOUISE: Ah.

HUGH [*to* BRIAN]: Mild enough, anyway.

BRIAN: Yeah.

[*A silence between them.*]

ANTHEA: Are you glad you're here? I mean, is this the sort of parish you wanted?

LOUISE: Well, yes. Of course, it is only our first proper parish. We were very lucky to get it at all. I'm delighted. I think Hugh wanted more of an urban area but I love the country, you see. I was brought up in the country ...

[*A firework blazes.*
She blocks her ears.
ANTHEA *absent-mindedly follows suit.*]

[*Continuing loudly*] It'll be a challenge. Our predecessor, the Reverend Armthwaite, he was here for fifteen years. He was very popular.

ANTHEA [*unhearing*]: Yes, yes.

LOUISE: So we have a lot to live up to, I'm afraid.

ANTHEA: No, no, quite.

[*A swoosh of a rocket.*]

Oh look, a rocket.

RICHARD [*off*]: Rocket just gone up.

ANTHEA: Yes.

HUGH [*to* BRIAN]: Rocket.

BRIAN: Yes.

HUGH: Do you live locally?

BRIAN: No.

HUGH: Ah.

BRIAN: I'm just here for the weekend.

HUGH: I see. Friend of the family?

BRIAN: Something like that.

ANTHEA: Watch the rocket, children. See? No, up, Giles. Up. It's up there, you fool. Honestly.

LOUISE: Of course, in a way, I mean, I know your house is much more historical and interesting but I think, in some ways, I prefer our little new house. I mean, as far as day to day running is concerned.

ANTHEA: Oh gosh, yes, yours any day.

LOUISE: I mean, it should be very easy to keep up. I don't normally like red-brick that much but I don't find, in this case, it's obtrusive at all. And as for keeping it clean ...

ANTHEA: Oh, there's no comparison. None at all. Modern houses are wonderful for that. I mean, we only got this place because it was going for absolutely nothing. And we happened to know the previous owner, that sort of thing. We wouldn't have bought it otherwise.

LOUISE: It must be very difficult to keep clean.

ANTHEA: It must be. I never tried. The place is a tip. Fortunately none of my family seems to mind. They're a totally squalid bunch.

LOUISE: Oh.

RICHARD [*off*]: This is an Arctic Snowstorm.

ANTHEA: What?

RICHARD [*off*]: It's called an ARCTIC SNOWSTORM.

ANTHEA: Lovely. Darling, can you make sure Giles sees this one? I mean, you've set fire to a fortune out there and he's seen absolutely none of it. Debbie, don't pick noses with gloves on, please.

LOUISE: No, I think we're going to find this job a very stimulating and challenging one. I'm really looking forward to it. And Hugh's full of good ideas. He's absolutely bursting with them. What he wants to do –

ANTHEA: Golly! Sorry to interrupt you but just look at this. Isn't it lovely?

LOUISE [*covering her ears*]: Oh yes.

RICHARD [*off*]: What about that?

ANTHEA: It's almost like daylight. It's – good God! What on earth is your little boy doing by the fireworks? Richard, Richard, stop him.

RICHARD [*off*]: Oh, my God ...

HUGH: Christopher. Christopher, you naughty boy. Stop that.

LOUISE [*simultaneously*]: Christopher, Christopher, you little beast. Hugh, stop him.

RICHARD [*simultaneously*]: Oy, oy, oy.

HUGH: You naughty boy. You naughty, naughty boy.

[HUGH *goes into the court and disappears.*]

LOUISE [*following him*]: Right, Christopher, I'm taking you straight home. I'm taking you straight home this minute. I'm taking him home, Hugh.

HUGH [*off*]: You hear that, Christopher. Mummy's taking you home.

[*During this,* BRIAN *goes back towards the house.*

RICHARD *comes into sight in the tennis court, abandoning the* EMERSONS *to their offspring, and shrugs towards* ANTHEA.]

ANTHEA: Yes, that's right, Giles. Christopher did a wee-wee in the fireworks. Wasn't that funny? Giles thinks it's a hoot.

RICHARD: Oh well, on to the bonfire.

ANTHEA [*calling*]: It's all right, Debbie, don't cry now. Daddy's going to light the bonfire.

HUGH [*off*]: Naughty boy ...

LOUISE [*off*]: Naughty, naughty boy ...

RICHARD: Don't worry, Hugh, don't worry about it.

HUGH [*reappearing*]: I am so sorry. I don't know what to say.

RICHARD: No need.

ANTHEA: Light the bonfire, darling.

RICHARD: Coming up. [*He goes.*]

HUGH [*approaching* ANTHEA]: I am absolutely mortified. I don't know how to apologize.

ANTHEA: It's just the excitement.

HUGH: He's suddenly started behaving like this. It's most weird.

ANTHEA: Does he do a lot of that sort of thing?

HUGH: No, not that particularly. But he suddenly gets these furious rages.

[LOUISE *appears momentarily on the tennis court.*]

LOUISE: I'm taking him home.

HUGH: All right. I'll follow you.

LOUISE: Don't be too long. He won't go to sleep unless you're there.

HUGH: All right. Five minutes, I promise.

LOUISE [*to* ANTHEA]: May I go back this way?

ANTHEA: Yes, do. Just squeeze through the gap. [*Calling*] Richard. Could you hold the fence for them so they can get through the gap?

[LOUISE *goes.*]

RICHARD [*off*]: Right.

LOUISE [*off*]: Come along, you naughty little boy.

ANTHEA: By the way, it goes without saying, I hope, but do feel free, any of you, or your friends to use this garden when you want to.

HUGH: That's really most . . .

ANTHEA: They've been a bit stingy with your garden, haven't they? You haven't got much, have you?

HUGH: No, not – er . . .

ANTHEA: They just pinched enough of this garden to build your house and left it at that. Still, you've got nothing to mow or cut or prune – I suppose you can look on the bright side . . .

HUGH: I still don't know how to apologize.

[BRIAN *returns. He carries a tray with soup mugs and a dish of hot sausages.*

MELODY, *a woman of about* BRIAN'S *age, follows him.*]

BRIAN: Soup.

ANTHEA: Oh, well done. Hallo, Melody.

MELODY: Hallo.

BRIAN: Sausages.

ANTHEA: Melody, this is Hugh.

MELODY: Hallo.

ANTHEA: Hugh's our new vicar. Just moved into the house at the bottom of the garden. Melody's from Canada. She's a friend of Brian's.

MELODY: You want soup?

HUGH: Oh, thank you.

MELODY: You're welcome.

BRIAN: Shall I take some round to Richard?

HUGH: Oh no, let me please. Let me do something to make up.

MELODY [*has poured a mug of soup and hands it to* HUGH]: That's yours.

HUGH: Thank you.

ANTHEA: Have a sausage as well.

HUGH: Oh well, wouldn't say no.

MELODY [*handing* HUGH *a second cup*]: That's for Richard.

HUGH: Oh, thank you.

MELODY: You're welcome.

> [HUGH *moves away, laden with sausages and two mugs of soup. He goes into the tennis court.*]

> [*Pouring another cup*] That's yours.

ANTHEA: Thank you.

MELODY: You want some, lover boy?

BRIAN: Yes.

> [*The bonfire crackles alight with a roar.*]

RICHARD [*off*]: There she goes. Watch yourself, Hugh.

ANTHEA: Hooray! [*Tasting soup*] This has turned out quite well.

MELODY: The sausages are there. [*She stomps off towards the bonfire.*]

ANTHEA: Where are you going?

MELODY: I don't want to be in the way.

BRIAN: Oh God.

ANTHEA: Did I say something I shouldn't?

BRIAN: Oh forget it, forget it.

ANTHEA: What?

BRIAN: Forget it. Forget her. I'm sorry for bringing her down. I might have known.

ANTHEA: She was very jolly yesterday.

BRIAN: Oh, she can be if it suits her.

ANTHEA: Oh Brian, try not to argue all weekend, there's a love. I mean, we adore you coming down here, but you always seem to bring down some girl you loathe the sight of and then shout at her all weekend.

BRIAN: And why do you think that is?

ANTHEA: Well, can't you find one you like?

> [BRIAN *gives a bitter laugh.*]

RICHARD [*off*]: There goes the guy.

ANTHEA: Oh, super. Hooray! [*Sotto again*] What do you mean?

BRIAN: Are you that naïve?

ANTHEA: What?

BRIAN: Do you really think that because you're living with Richard my feelings for you have changed one iota? Do you?

ANTHEA: Oh Brian, come on.

BRIAN [*gripping her arm*]: Well, do you?

ANTHEA: Oh, for heaven's sake ...

[MELODY *is watching them amused.*]

MELODY: Go ahead.

ANTHEA [*pulling away*]: Oh, don't be ridiculous. Do be your age, Brian.

[ANTHEA *goes down the side of the tennis court and disappears.*]

BRIAN [*glaring at* MELODY]: Enjoying yourself?

MELODY: Get lost.

BRIAN [*going towards the house*]: Don't stand too close to the fire, you'll melt.

MELODY [*screaming after him*]: Aw, screw you, brother! Screw you!

[BRIAN *has gone.*

Simultaneously HUGH *appears round the other side of the bonfire. He stands next to* MELODY.]

HUGH [*conversationally*]: Warm enough here. [*Pause*] Of course, you won't have Guy Fawkes' Day in Canada, will you? [*Pause*] No. It's very beautiful, I understand. So I've read. Of course in the south, you have the great lakes and, of course, the Niagara Falls. Then you have the big wheat-growing districts. Alberta. Manitoba. Saskatchewan. And then further north, you have the North-West Territories, of course. And a whole mass of lakes. Not forgetting good old Baffin Island.

MELODY: Why are you telling me this?

HUGH: I beg your pardon?

MELODY: I don't want to hear all this. I know all this. I come from the goddammed place.

HUGH: Ah.

MELODY: I don't want to hear about it. Why do you think I'm here?

HUGH: Ah.

MELODY: Because I hated the place.

HUGH: I'm sorry, I was ... [*He moves away unhappily.*]

MELODY [*calling after him*]: Reverend?

HUGH: Mmm?

MELODY: I'm sorry. That was rude. That was churlish. That was ungracious. Will you accept my apology?

HUGH: Er, well. Yes.

MELODY: I think I would like you to understand. You see that dummy? That thing burning up there? That poor little helpless, half-charred rag doll?

HUGH: The guy.

MELODY: The guy? You call that the guy? Well, I'm like that guy, Reverend. Do you understand that? Someone is trying to burn me alive.

HUGH: Metaphorically, I take it?

MELODY: Metaphorically. Any other phorically. You name it. He uses me like a pawn in some game he's playing with that woman. My God, he has tried to take away my dignity. How dare he take away my dignity. Jesus Christ. I'm sorry, I'm sorry. God bless you, Reverend, God bless you and keep you. Why should you care about my problems?

[*She hurries off towards the house.*

HUGH *stands perplexed.*]

RICHARD [*coming round the other side of the bonfire*]: Watch Giles, Debbie, just for a minute. Don't let him get any closer. Now then, Hugh, are you being looked after?

HUGH: Oh, yes ...

RICHARD: Where is everyone?

HUGH: Well, I'm not ... I think ...

RICHARD [*calling*]: Anthea. Antie.

ANTHEA [*off, beyond the tennis court*]: Hallo.

RICHARD: Now, what can I get you? More soup?

HUGH: I really ought to be getting back.

RICHARD: Oh, go on, please. Sven hasn't turned up, we've got far too much. What have we got here? Aha, sausages. Have some of these.

HUGH: Thank you ... [*He helps himself to one.*]

RICHARD: Go on, go on. Take a handful.

HUGH [*complying*]: Well ...

RICHARD [*as he pours soup for them*]: No, though I say it myself, when it comes to soups, Anthea takes a lot of beating.

HUGH: Yes. I don't actually usually drink it but this is really quite ...

RICHARD: Oh, she knows her soups.

HUGH [*taking his mug*]: Thank you. Yes, I must say I rather envy you. I – er – Louise doesn't claim to be anything of a cook so I'm not being disloyal. She really doesn't see eye to eye with a stove at all.

RICHARD: Oh dear. What about you?

HUGH: Me?

RICHARD: Do you cook?

HUGH: No. Not at all.

RICHARD: You should learn. Highly satisfying. I always cook at the weekends. It's very relaxing.

[ANTHEA *returns.*]

ANTHEA: They're having a wonderful display over in the distance there. Dozens of rockets. Are the kids all right?

RICHARD: I'm going back. I'm just feeding up Hugh. He claims his wife starves him.

ANTHEA: No.

HUGH: No, I didn't say that. I . . .

ANTHEA: Grief. He's eating sausages by the fistful.

HUGH: I'm sorry.

ANTHEA: No, please do, there's masses. I'm joking. Please. [*She smiles dazzlingly at* HUGH *who manages to smile limply back.*]

RICHARD [*who has been surveying the bonfire*]: That's burning really well this year. I think I've found the knack of building them . . .

HUGH: Wonderful.

ANTHEA: I've just been having a snoop up at the end there. You know, Richard, it wouldn't be a huge job to widen the gap in their fence and put a sort of gate there. And then Hugh and Louise could use the garden whenever they wanted.

RICHARD: Why don't we knock the whole fence down altogether and have done with it? Ridiculous putting a fence there anyway. Not even well-designed. If we took it down, they could look out at the garden instead of a fence.

ANTHEA: What a marvellous idea. [*To* HUGH] Don't you agree?

HUGH: Well, it's – yes – I mean . . .

ANTHEA: Come on, let's knock it down.

RICHARD: I'll do it now. Why not?

HUGH: Now?

RICHARD: Burn it on the bonfire. Best way . . . [*He moves off.*]

HUGH: Well, I . . .

ANTHEA: There you are. No sooner said than done. [*Yelling*] Check the kids.

RICHARD [*off*]: Right.

HUGH: Well, I hope Louise is agreeable.

ANTHEA: Heavens, she'd far sooner look at trees than a fence. Besides this was your garden originally.

HUGH: Well, yes.

[*She smiles at him again. He smiles back.*]

ANTHEA: Look, we're not actually church-going people or anything, you know – either of us – but if there's anything we can do to help – you know, organizing or just fetching and carrying, do ask us, won't you? We'd be only too pleased.

HUGH: Well, that is kind. Thank you.

ANTHEA: We're always here.

[*A distant splintering of timber.*]

Heavens, what is he doing?

[*A gleeful yell from* RICHARD.]

HUGH: Yes. Well, we might actually call on you sooner than you ...

[ANTHEA *offers him another sausage.*]

Thank you ... sooner than you think. I think, especially early on, we're going to need all the help we can get. I mean, I really intend to get involved in as many different spheres as possible. My predecessor was, well, fairly ancient and – understandably, I think – he let things slide a bit. I noticed the other Sunday when I visited, there were very few young people in evidence. I'm hoping to remedy that ...

[*Another splintering crash.*]

I hope your husband knows what he's doing. He'll stop when he gets to our house, will he? That's not to say that I want to discourage older people. Of course not. But it's a bit depressing if most of your congregation are in the churchyard instead of the church. [*He laughs.*]

[RICHARD *enters brandishing a piece of timber.*]

RICHARD: Piece of cake. The most pathetic fence I've ever come across.

ANTHEA: Don't go too mad, darling.

RICHARD: Trust me. [*He goes.*]

HUGH: I must say, when your husband does a job, he certainly ...

ANTHEA: Hugh, I'm going to have to correct you on one thing.

HUGH: Yes?

ANTHEA: I'm afraid Richard's not my husband. We're not married.

HUGH: Oh.

ANTHEA: Oh gosh. You're not shocked, are you? You're not going to go all Church Militant on me?

HUGH: No, no, not at all. Not these days, no. Are the children –?

ANTHEA: They're my children. They're not Richard's. I'm divorced from my first husband whose children they are. Richard is separated from his first wife who has no children.

HUGH: I see. I see. Are you known as Mrs Clarke?

ANTHEA: I couldn't honestly care less. Everyone calls me Anthea. But Mrs Clarke if you like or even Mrs Watkins or if you really insist, Miss Braddlestone. Though I'm not too fond of that one, which is why I got married.

HUGH: Ah well. If you ever want to ... – if you're ever in a position to make it official, I'd be glad if you came to us first.

ANTHEA [*offering him a sausage*]: But we'd be divorced. Doesn't that ... ?

HUGH [*accepting*]: Oh, we're not so fussy these days. Glad of the trade. I'm sorry, I'm eating all these.

ANTHEA: Go ahead.

HUGH: Not so much the Church Militant as the Church Ravenous. [*He laughs awkwardly.*]

LOUISE [*off, distant*]: Hugh. Hugh.

    [HUGH *stops laughing.*]

ANTHEA: Was that someone?

LOUISE [*off*]: Hugh, where are you?

HUGH: It's Louise.

ANTHEA: Oh.

    [LOUISE *enters from the house direction.*]

LOUISE: Hugh? What are you doing?

HUGH: What?

LOUISE: Where have you been?

HUGH: Here. I've been here.

LOUISE: But I thought you said ...

ANTHEA: Is anything wrong?

LOUISE: There's someone round the back of the house breaking down our fence. They're just ripping it down. I looked out of the bathroom window. They're kicking at it. Pulling it away in chunks.

HUGH: Ah yes, well. That'll be Richard.

LOUISE: Who?

HUGH: Mr Clarke. Richard — he's ...

ANTHEA: Oh dear —

LOUISE: Richard? You mean, Mr —? Richard? Why is he doing it?

HUGH: Well, I said he could.

LOUISE: You said he could knock down our fence?

HUGH: We thought it might be nicer.

LOUISE: Why?

HUGH: Er ...

ANTHEA: I think it's probably my fault — well, our fault. We thought it'd be rather nice for you to use the whole garden, that's all.

LOUISE: But this is your garden.

ANTHEA: Well, yes but ...

LOUISE: Our garden was on the other side of that fence.

ANTHEA: Yes.

LOUISE: When there was a fence. Now we haven't got a fence so we haven't got a garden at all.

HUGH: Well, we've got this garden.

LOUISE: No, this is their garden. I'm talking about our garden. I don't want their garden. I want our garden.

    [*An ear-splitting crash.*]

RICHARD [*off distant*]: Whey-hey!

HUGH: I'm sorry – I ...

ANTHEA [*calling*]: Richard! Richard, could you stop a minute, darling?

RICHARD: What's that?

ANTHEA: I said, could you stop ... [*She moves off towards him.*]

RICHARD [*distant, off*]: Yes, all right. All finished now.

ANTHEA: Richard.

[ANTHEA *goes off past the tennis court.*]

HUGH [*smiling faintly*]: Have you left Christopher?

LOUISE: Yes, he's in bed.

HUGH: Right. I'll ... [*He takes a swig of his soup.*]

LOUISE: What's that you're drinking?

HUGH: Oh. Just soup. Some homemade soup.

LOUISE: You don't like soup.

HUGH: Well, not usually.

LOUISE: How come you suddenly like soup?

HUGH: Yes, well, we better just say good night and – um ...

LOUISE: I think it's terrible. Just pulling down somebody's fence like that. Without even asking them. I mean, it wasn't even their fence. It was our fence. I don't feel secure without that fence. Anybody could walk into that garden. Anyone could look in through the windows.

HUGH: Well, I'll get another. I'm sorry.

[RICHARD *creeps on, rather sheepish.*]

Oh, good night, Richard.

RICHARD: I hear we might have been a bit premature.

HUGH: Yes.

RICHARD: Sorry.

LOUISE: You coming, Hugh?

HUGH: Yes.

LOUISE: Hurry up then. He won't go to sleep without you.

[LOUISE *goes out via the house.*]

HUGH: I'm sorry. This was my fault.

ANTHEA [*creeping on behind*]: Is she frightfully upset?

HUGH: She'll be all right. She has these little tempers. But they're nothing ...

ANTHEA: Would you like to take her some soup?

HUGH: No. No, thank you. Anyway, I've had a very pleasant evening and I'm so pleased we're neighbours and – er – so on. I look forward to seeing a lot of you. Good night.

SVEN [*off*]: Hallo? Where is everyone? Hallo?

ANTHEA: It's Sven! You must meet Sven and Olive, Hugh.

RICHARD [*calling*]: Sven.

HUGH: Well, I ...

[SVEN *enters. He is thirty, already trying hard to be fifty. There is a great sense of importance about him.*]

ANTHEA: Sven.

SVEN: Anthea, my darling, my darling. [*He holds out his arms.*]

ANTHEA: Oh Sven. [*They embrace.*]

[OLIVE, *twenty-eight – already rather staid – follows.*]

OLIVE: Hallo, Richard.

RICHARD: How's lovely Olive?

ANTHEA: This is ridiculous. It's as if we haven't seen them for months.

SVEN: Six weeks ... Hallo, Richard. How are you? Six weeks we've been away.

ANTHEA: Hallo, Olive.

OLIVE: Oh, Anthea, I really could kill you. I could throttle you, girl, look at you. You've got thinner.

ANTHEA: I haven't.

OLIVE: How dare you get thinner? It isn't fair. It really isn't. I wouldn't mind, but she never stops eating.

RICHARD: Olive, Sven. Can we introduce Hugh? The Reverend Hugh Emerson. He's now living at the cottage at the bottom there.

OLIVE: What, the little red-brick Wendy house? That's nice.

RICHARD: This is Olive Holmenson.

OLIVE: How do you do?

HUGH: How do you do?

RICHARD: And Sven Holmenson.

HUGH: How do you do?

SVEN: So? You've chosen to live next door to these crazy people, eh?

HUGH: Yes, yes ...

SVEN: God help you. But in your case, he probably will. Now then, where are these fireworks?

ANTHEA: We've had them.

SVEN: Had them?

RICHARD [*gesticulating to* ANTHEA]: Kids.

[RICHARD *moves back behind bonfire.*]

ANTHEA: You're an hour late.

SVEN: Late? Who's late? [*Holding out his watch.*] Look at this. Half past eight. Dead on time.

ANTHEA: We said half-past seven. We wouldn't have said ...

SVEN: Anthea, Anthea. Half-past eight. Believe me, that's what you said. Half-past eight.

ANTHEA: Oh well, it doesn't matter. Let's take you in.

OLIVE: Yes, I must have a wash.

SVEN: If you had said half-past seven, my darling, I would have been here at half-past seven.

ANTHEA [*calling to* RICHARD]: Are they O.K.?

SVEN: But as you said half-past eight, we've come at half-past eight.

ANTHEA: Oh Sven, you really are impossible.

OLIVE: He's never wrong about times. Sven's never wrong where time's concerned.

SVEN: It's true. Never about times.

ANTHEA: Can I take that for you, Olive?

OLIVE: Oh, it's not heavy. I've got a couple of little things for the kiddies. And I've brought some of that Danish chocolate you like.

ANTHEA: Oh, you shouldn't. You staying for a drink, Hugh?

HUGH: Oh, no, no . . .

ANTHEA: Good night then.

HUGH: Good night.

OLIVE [*now far in the distance*]: Good night.

[ANTHEA *goes off after* OLIVE.]

HUGH [*calling to* RICHARD *on the far side of the tennis court*]: Good night, Richard.

RICHARD [*appearing briefly*]: Oh, good night, Hugh. See you soon.

HUGH: Yes.

RICHARD [*disappearing*]: Now then, you two. That's it. All over.

SVEN: I think we've missed a splendid bonfire.

HUGH: Yes, indeed.

SVEN: Yes. Yes. You've just moved here, have you?

HUGH: That's right.

SVEN: But you've known Anthea and Richard some time?

HUGH: No. We actually only met tonight.

SVEN: Uh-huh. Uh-huh.

HUGH: Delightful people.

SVEN [*neither agreeing nor disagreeing*]: Yes. Yes. Yes.

HUGH: Well, that's certainly my impression.

SVEN: May I say just one thing? As friends, be careful of them.

HUGH: How do you mean?

SVEN: No. I'll say nothing more. Be careful. Beware. That's all. Good night to you.

[SVEN *goes into the house.*

HUGH *stands for a moment, distinctly puzzled. Then follows in that direction.*]

ACT ONE
SCENE TWO

The same. Summer, four years later. Sunday morning, very sunny. A game of tennis is in progress. From our restricted viewpoint we see BRIAN *now and then, bobbing about on the base line and receiving service as he and* RICHARD *play out the final few points of a 'friendly'.* RICHARD'S *voice is heard off from time to time, from the other end of the court. Both are dressed for tennis, but casually. Seated on the grass is* MANDY, BRIAN'S *current girlfriend. At first glance, she is strikingly like* MELODY. *She is younger though and pays very little attention to this world. She is sketching on a sketch block, totally absorbed in her task through most of the scene. Unlike the others, who have made, in their attire, some concession to sunshine, she is draped in shawls, long dresses and a large hat.*

SVEN *enters, taking the air in his Scandinavian lightweight summer suit and Polaroid sunglasses. He nods approvingly at nature as he walks. A ball clangs into the back fencing of the court.*

BRIAN: ... shot ... [*He recovers the ball.*]
RICHARD [*off*]: Fluke, I'm afraid. What's that? Thirty love?
BRIAN [*flinging back the ball*]: Forty love.
RICHARD: Really? Oh.
 [SVEN *watches.* BRIAN *prepares to receive.* RICHARD *serves again.* BRIAN *lets it go. A fault.* BRIAN *prepares to receive.* RICHARD *serves again.* BRIAN *runs into the net and returns. We don't see the rest of that rally. It culminates off in a despairing grunt of vain effort from* RICHARD.]
RICHARD [*off*]: Shot.
 [BRIAN *returns to our end, looking like a man who's pulled back a point.*]
SVEN: Good shot. Good shot. Well played, good shot.
RICHARD [*off*]: Forty fifteen then.
 [SVEN *wanders over behind* MANDY *who ignores him.*]
SVEN [*looking at her picture*]: Good. Good ... Coming along, coming along.
 [*The ball hits the back fencing.*]
RICHARD [*off*]: Damn.
 [BRIAN *runs in to meet the second service.*]

SVEN: I would like you to think about this. Art is a lie which makes us realize the truth. Do you know who said that? It was Picasso who said that.

RICHARD [*off*]: Oh, lovely. Forty thirty.

[BRIAN *returns to receive service*.]

SVEN: I think in some ways you are trying to be too truthful. The result being, at the moment, that your picture has no truth. Think about that.

[RICHARD's *service hits the back fencing*.]

RICHARD [*off*]: Was that in?

BRIAN: Yes.

RICHARD: You sure? Looked out from here.

BRIAN [*gathering up his sweater from the court*]: It was in.

RICHARD [*off*]: Play it again if you like.

BRIAN [*snarling*]: It was in.

SVEN: No, it was in. It was definitely in, Richard, I could see from here. It was in. Not a difficult service to return, provided you remember you also have a backhand.

[BRIAN *considers killing* SVEN *but resists it*.]

RICHARD [*coming into view*]: You going to have a game this weekend, Sven?

SVEN: Not this weekend, no. This weekend I want to talk to you, Richard. When is this possible?

RICHARD: Well, I'm going to change and do the lunch now.

SVEN: This is business, Richard. It's important.

RICHARD: O.K. After lunch then?

SVEN: Yes, but we must leave at four.

RICHARD: O.K. [*He picks up* BRIAN's *racket*.] Oh no, you weren't playing with this, were you? It's amazing you got a point. Sorry, I meant to throw this away. Mandy, I must ask you. Do you like courgettes?

MANDY: Yes, thank you.

RICHARD: Right.

[RICHARD *goes. A silence.*

SVEN *stands.* BRIAN *sits a little apart from* MANDY *on the grass.* SVEN *wanders and inspects the court from the outside*.]

SVEN: I think the surface of this court is still not absolutely right. It's too slow. It makes it difficult to play a natural game.

[*Silence*.]

Yes.

[*He wanders off past the tennis court*.]

BRIAN: Are you going to be doing that all day?

MANDY: Mmm?

BRIAN: What's it meant to be?

MANDY [*imitating* SVEN]: Truth.

BRIAN: Oh.

MANDY [*still sketching*]: Who won?

    [BRIAN *does not reply.*]

Is he a good player?

BRIAN: Richard? No. He's rotten. He's the worst player in the world.

MANDY: Then why didn't you win?

BRIAN: Because when you're playing Richard, there's no satisfaction in beating him. He's more pleased if you win than if he does. At least if he wins he's apologetic about it. I mean. There's got to be some satisfaction in winning. Otherwise what's the point? He's the only person I know who enjoys genuine loser satisfaction.

MANDY: He's very attractive.

BRIAN: Attractive?

MANDY: As a personality. Very warm.

BRIAN: Fancy him, do you?

MANDY: No, I didn't say that.

BRIAN: Huh.

MANDY: That's not what I said. [*Pause*] Anyway, you're a fine one to talk.

BRIAN: How do you mean?

MANDY: The way you behave.

BRIAN: What?

MANDY: With her.

BRIAN [*guilty*]: What do you mean?

MANDY: You know.

BRIAN: Who?

MANDY: Anthea.

BRIAN: Rubbish.

MANDY: I don't mind.

BRIAN: I said rubbish.

MANDY: It doesn't worry me.

BRIAN: Bloody rubbish.

    [ANTHEA *and* OLIVE *enter,* ANTHEA *with the Sunday papers.*]

ANTHEA: Did you win?

BRIAN [*storming past her*]: No.

    [*He goes.*]

ANTHEA: I think he lost. Hallo, Mandy. Quite happy?

MANDY: Hallo.

OLIVE: Oh, she's drawing. [*Moving behind her*] What's she drawing? What are you drawing, dear?

MANDY: I'm just drawing.

OLIVE: Oh, that's nice. She's drawing a lovely picture.

ANTHEA [*settling in the summerhouse*]: Want to read one of these?

OLIVE: No, dear. I never read the papers. I haven't read a paper since I married. I rely on Sven to tell me if there's a war broken out. No, I think there's far too much going on already without reading about it as well. Oh, look at you. I hate you, Anthea, I simply loathe you.

ANTHEA: What?

OLIVE: Look at you. You eat and eat and eat and stay exactly the same. If there was any justice in this world, you would be like a barrel.

ANTHEA: I'm just lucky, that's all.

OLIVE: Yes. I can't eat anything. Nothing. Not a thing. It's not fair. It really isn't. I could kill you.

[*A pause.* ANTHEA *reads.* MANDY *draws.* OLIVE *fidgets.*]

Lovely day for drawing, isn't it? I say, it's a lovely day for drawing.

MANDY: Mmm.

OLIVE: Oh, I wish I could draw. I've always wanted to draw. I'd've given my right arm to be able to draw. It must be very relaxing.

ANTHEA: Why don't you have a go?

OLIVE: Oh, no, no, no. Too late now. I leave things like that to Sven. Sven can draw quite well, you know. He might have been an artist at one time. Only there's not a lot of future in it. Oh, look at that girl. Look at her. Look at that figure. I could kill her.

[SVEN *reappears.*]

SVEN: Now, now, Olive. You mustn't disturb our little artist.

OLIVE: Oh, there you are.

SVEN: Very pleasant. Very pleasant indeed.

ANTHEA: We'll have drinks when the Emersons arrive. Unless you fancy one now.

SVEN: No, no. Too early, too early. Yes, I presume Hugh Emerson will be somewhere in the middle of his sermon by now.

ANTHEA: Yes, I suppose so.

SVEN: Well. For me one visit was enough. I'm certainly glad we're not there today.

OLIVE: Oh dear, yes.

ANTHEA: Well, he does try his best.

SVEN: No, no, Anthea. It was the most appalling rubbish. The man was not only inarticulate but he was often totally inaccurate. He managed to bore you, mystify you and misinform you all in one breath.

ANTHEA: Yes, but he does sort of mean it, doesn't he? I mean, he's very sincere.

SVEN: A couple of hundred years ago they would simply have burnt him for heresy.

ANTHEA: He is a bit of a waffler I must say. He's not going down awfully well, poor love.

OLIVE: No. We noticed when we were there.

ANTHEA: I think he's a bit radical for this village. I mean, all the congregation are four times his age. They see him as a sort of teenage tearaway. Richard and I give him all the support we can, but I think we're fighting a losing battle.

SVEN: Now, Anthea. Has Richard mentioned our present problems to you?

ANTHEA: What about? The business?

SVEN: Yes, indeed.

ANTHEA: Oh. He didn't say there were any problems.

SVEN: Well, I'm afraid there are.

ANTHEA: Oh dear. Serious?

SVEN: They could become so if we don't discuss them together. Now, it is a fact there are four directors of The Scandinavian Craftware Co. Ltd. Richard, myself, you and Olive. Though naturally you and Olive are not strictly active partners. None the less, in the case of Richard and myself, we are equal partners and it is vital that we discuss everything together. Not, as Richard has been doing, acting on his own individual whims. Making unilateral decisions which could quite easily have bankrupted the firm.

ANTHEA: Has he done that?

SVEN: Thank heavens, no. More through luck than good judgement, he has actually lost us very little. In fact, to be strictly accurate, he has made us a little. In fact, he has made us quite a nice little sum and he has incidentally found us a new outlet for Swedish glassware. Nevertheless, these decisions were irrational, made without reference to known trading conditions, the present state of the world market or, more important, to me.

OLIVE: Sven's very worried.

ANTHEA: I should talk to Richard.

SVEN: I have been trying to talk to Richard. If I can get his attention for five minutes, I will talk to him with pleasure.

OLIVE: Sven's quite serious about this, Anthea. He's quite serious.

ANTHEA: Yes, yes.

OLIVE: I mean, Sven wouldn't say this unless he was very worried. I know Sven.

SVEN: Not unless I was very, very, very worried I wouldn't say this.

ANTHEA: Well, I'm sure Richard will see your point of view. He's never difficult.

SVEN: Anthea, I'm not saying he is difficult. I have endless respect for

Richard. Endless respect. But he must be made to understand that I cannot remain in partnership with a man who doesn't totally trust me.

[BRIAN *enters with a croquet mallet.*]

BRIAN [*to* ANTHEA]: Excuse me. The kids say you promised them a game of croquet before lunch.

ANTHEA: Did I? Oh lord, yes, I think I did.

OLIVE: Now, don't you go jumping up, Anthea. You spoil them.

ANTHEA: No, I promised.

BRIAN: It's you and Debbie against Giles and me. Penny a hoop.

ANTHEA: Oh no.

BRIAN: And they're also saying that if Christopher Emerson is coming to lunch, they're going to hide all their toys.

ANTHEA: Oh dear. They don't like Christopher at all. He's quite nice now.

BRIAN: He's awful.

ANTHEA: Well, fairly awful. [*Going*] All right, all right, I bags be blue.

[BRIAN *and* ANTHEA *go.*]

OLIVE: Debbie's growing up, isn't she?

SVEN: Mmm.

OLIVE: She's, what, nearly ten. Well, they're adults by that age these days, aren't they? Are you going to play tennis today?

SVEN: Not today, my darling, no.

OLIVE: Every time we come down here, I pack all your stuff. Your rackets and your gym shoes. You never use them.

SVEN: Not today, darling. There are other problems.

OLIVE: She shouldn't spoil those children like she does, though. Everything they ask for, they get. It isn't right. They'll grow up with a false sense of values.

SVEN: No. Nobody should have everything they want. Not even you, my darling. [*He kisses her.*]

[LOUISE *comes from the tennis court direction.*
She is in her church clothes but is somewhat flustered.]

LOUISE: I know we're late. It can't be helped.

OLIVE: Late?

LOUISE: Hallo, Olive. Hallo, Sven.

SVEN: Dear Louise, hallo.

LOUISE: It can't be helped. He's just being absolutely impossible. The little brute, he just screamed and yelled. I had to leave him to Hugh. He's getting too strong for me now. He's eight years old and when he punches you, it really hurts.

OLIVE: Is this Christopher?

LOUISE: Yes. So anyway, I'm afraid we're late. And Hugh will be even later.

OLIVE: You're not late.

LOUISE: Oh. I thought we were supposed to be ...

SVEN: After four years of living next door to these people, you still expect their meals to be on time? Time is nothing in this house.

LOUISE: Oh well.

OLIVE: Sit down, Louise. Get your breath. That's a lovely outfit.

LOUISE: Oh, do you think so? I – um – I've got a great bruise here. [*Pulling up her sleeve*] Look ... [*She sees* MANDY.] Oh ...

OLIVE: Oh, you wouldn't have met Mandy. This is Brian's new friend, Mandy. She's down for the weekend.

MANDY: Hallo.

LOUISE: How do you do?

OLIVE: This is Mrs Emerson, Mandy. Louise.

LOUISE: What's she doing?

OLIVE: She's drawing a picture. It's very good. [*In an undertone*] She's an art student but quite pleasant.

LOUISE: Oh.

OLIVE: And how was your service?

LOUISE: My what?

OLIVE: Isn't that what you've been doing? Your Morning Service?

LOUISE: Oh yes. Oh, very good. Disappointing turn-out but I think it's the time of the year too. A lot of people are on holiday.

OLIVE: Your husband preached the sermon, did he?

LOUISE: Yes, yes.

OLIVE: A good one, was it?

LOUISE: Er – yes – yes, not – quite – very good, yes. He – er – well, to be honest, he's getting better of course, but I don't think his sermon's his strongest point. He admits that. He goes over them with me in bed – I mean, you know, when we're alone – and they're quite marvellous. You know he's speaking just for you and you can see his eyes and that he really means everything he says and it's awfully important ... but, directly he gets up there, in front of all those people, he seems to get all tense. You know, and you can't see his eyes because he tends to keep them closed and then he speaks so fast, it's difficult to hear what he's saying sometimes. Particularly for a lot of the people there because they're quite elderly. And someone shouted at him to speak up the other day and that really did upset him because he does try awfully hard. Really.

OLIVE: We found him very good indeed.

LOUISE: Did you? Oh, that's nice. That is nice to hear. I'll tell him that. People don't say a lot, you know, except to criticize. And you wonder ... I had to leave him to deal with Christopher. He's going to get Mrs Gregson to sit in.

OLIVE: We would have come to church only we overslept, I'm afraid.

LOUISE: Oh. That's all right.

OLIVE: Our one day off.

LOUISE: Yes.

> [*A scream from* ANTHEA *off.*
> *A blue croquet ball rolls on.*]

ANTHEA [*off*]: Oh, you brute, Giles, you little brute. [ANTHEA *enters with croquet mallet.*] Oh no, look. I'm right down here. Oh hallo, Louise. You've arrived. Splendid.

LOUISE: Hallo.

ANTHEA: Before you go, remind me to give you those envelopes. I've done them all.

LOUISE: Oh, wonderful. You needn't have ...

ANTHEA: Is Hugh with you?

LOUISE: He's coming. He's just seeing to Christopher.

ANTHEA: Isn't Christopher coming?

LOUISE: No. He's not feeling on top form. Hugh's getting Mrs Gregson to sit with him.

ANTHEA: Oh dear. Sad. [*Shouting*] Debbie! Debbie darling, will you ask Daddy to give you the drinks to bring out ... Quickly, darling. No, we'll wait for you. We won't play without you. Promise. [*To the others*] We're playing this absurd game of croquet. Every time I get near a hoop, Giles bashes me to kingdom come. Look at me. I can't even see the lawn. Anyone else want a swing?

SVEN: No, no. I think to win this game, you need inside knowledge of the local conditions.

ANTHEA: When are we going to see you on the tennis court, Sven?

SVEN: I think not today.

ANTHEA: Oh, come on. I don't believe all this talk about you being a great player.

SVEN: Now, be fair, Anthea, be fair. You never heard me say I was a great player.

ANTHEA: We've been hearing it for years. Every time you come down.

SVEN: If I may correct you, what I said was that I was a good player. Not a great player.

OLIVE: He was a champion.

SVEN: No, my darling. I must correct you too. I was a junior champion.

OLIVE: Junior champion.

SVEN: For three years running.

LOUISE: This was for all of Sweden, was it?

SVEN: No. It was not for all of Sweden. I come from Finland.

LOUISE: You were champion of all Finland?

SVEN: Well. Nearly all Finland. There were some parts of Finland that didn't compete. Let us say, most of Finland.

ANTHEA: Well, I'll believe it when I see it.

SVEN: One day. One day. You wait . . .

[RICHARD *enters, now dressed for cooking, carrying a tray with a jug of fruit cup and some glasses.*]

RICHARD: Morning all. Mind your backs.

ANTHEA: Why didn't you get Debbie to carry them?

RICHARD: Because she nearly dropped them. Can you help yourselves everyone? I'm in the midst. Lunch in ten minutes. Louise, do you like courgettes?

LOUISE: Yes, I think so.

RICHARD: Good. You've got them. Right.

[*He moves back towards the house and shifts the croquet ball to a better position.*]

I'll have you know Giles has been cheating. I saw him. I'd cheat as well if I were you.

[RICHARD *sprints off.*]

OLIVE: Well – er – shall I pour? I don't know what it is.

ANTHEA: It looks like his fruit cup.

OLIVE: Oh. It smells nice. Louise?

LOUISE: Thank you. A little.

ANTHEA [*looking over* MANDY's *shoulder*]: I like that.

MANDY: Thank you.

OLIVE: Anthea? [*She proffers a glass.*]

ANTHEA: Please. [*She takes one.*]

OLIVE: Some for – um – Mandy?

MANDY: What?

OLIVE: Do you want some of this?

MANDY: No, thanks.

ANTHEA: She's immensely sensible, this girl. She doesn't drink.

OLIVE: Oh, how wise.

LOUISE: Very sensible.

[BRIAN *enters with a croquet mallet.*]

BRIAN: Anthea, it's your go.

ANTHEA: Oh, all right. [*Handing* BRIAN *her glass*] Hold that, will you?

BRIAN: We're going to have to stop in a minute. He wants the kids in to help serve up.

ANTHEA: Right. [*Calling*] All right, Giles, I'm coming to get you. [*She hits the ball. To* BRIAN] We'll stop after the next hoop.

    [ANTHEA *goes out.*]

OLIVE: Brian, would you like a glass?

BRIAN: I'll be back in a second. Thanks.

    [BRIAN *goes off.*]

LOUISE: Is Brian still working for you?

SVEN: Yes, yes. He's working for Richard and me. In the office. He's very good. Quite bright. Not very forthcoming but he does a good job.

LOUISE: I find him a funny person, really. He never seems to want – [*She looks over at* MANDY.] – Yes, anyway . . .

SVEN: Yes, well, enough said. Cheers.

    [*They drink.*]

OLIVE: Oh, it's really very pleasant.

LOUISE: Oh, yes it is. It's very nice, yes.

OLIVE: Refreshing.

LOUISE: Yes.

OLIVE: What do you think, Sven?

SVEN [*tasting it carefully*]: Yes. Yes. It's pleasant. A little bit . . .

OLIVE: Yes. Yes.

SVEN: Bland. A little bland, perhaps.

OLIVE: Yes, I suppose it's a little bit bland.

LOUISE: Yes, I know what you mean.

SVEN: It is in danger of becoming watery.

LOUISE: Watery.

SVEN: In my opinion.

OLIVE: Yes, it is a bit watery. I could have done with a bit more taste.

LOUISE: Yes, I wouldn't want too much of it.

OLIVE: No.

SVEN: No.

LOUISE: No.

    [*A pause.*]

OLIVE: I hope your husband's not going to miss his lunch.

LOUISE: Oh, he'll be along.

OLIVE: Mind you, from what I know of him, I can't see him missing a square meal. He's certainly got an appetite.

LOUISE: Yes.

OLIVE: I like a man to have an appetite.

LOUISE: Yes, he certainly has when he comes here.

OLIVE: Oh. Doesn't he at home? Eat, I mean?

LOUISE: No, not overmuch.

OLIVE: Well, that's disappointing for you. I mean, if you go to all that trouble.

LOUISE: Yes, it is sometimes.

OLIVE: Mind you, this one's a devil. Over his food. Aren't you? You're a devil.

SVEN: No, darling, not a devil. I just like first-rate food, beautifully cooked. Like you cook it, most of the time.

OLIVE: Oh, get on.

SVEN: She's jealous because I'm a better cook than she is. I can't help that. That's the way it is.

OLIVE: Oh yes, he's a wonderful cook.

LOUISE: Is he?

OLIVE: Oh, wonderful. With Finnish things, of course.

SVEN: Well, of course with Finnish things. I'm Finnish. I'm not going to cook steak and kidney Yorkshire puddings or whatever.

OLIVE [*laughing*]: Steak and kidney Yorkshire puddings. Get on.

LOUISE [*rising and moving to behind* MANDY]: I'm sorry, I can't resist it. I must just peep and see what she's ... [*She studies* MANDY's *picture.*] Oh yes, that's very ... very good indeed. Yes, that is nice. What's this down here, dear? Down here? This?

MANDY: That's grass there.

LOUISE: Grass. Oh yes. No, I meant this thing here. This thing.

MANDY: That's a snake.

LOUISE: A snake?

MANDY: Yes.

LOUISE: A grass snake?

MANDY: No, just a snake in the grass.

LOUISE: Oh. Unusual. [*She withdraws.*] She's drawing snakes.

OLIVE: Snakes, ugh.

SVEN: Well, perhaps the girl sees snakes. Who knows?

OLIVE: Good job she hasn't drunk this stuff.

LOUISE [*laughing*]: Yes ...

> [HUGH *enters from behind the tennis court.*
> *He has his hand bandaged with a handkerchief.*]

HUGH: Hallo. Sorry, everyone. You're all waiting for me, no doubt. I'm sorry.

OLIVE: No, no. You're just right. Just in time.

HUGH: Oh, splendid.

OLIVE: Will you have a glass of this?

HUGH: Er – oh, is it er ... ?

SVEN: I should think the alcoholic content is non-existent.

HUGH: Oh well, fair enough. I don't want to be hung over for Evensong.

LOUISE [*sotto*]: How is he?

HUGH: He's all right. Mrs Gregson's with him.

LOUISE: What happened to your hand?

HUGH: Oh, he was being – very difficult, very stubborn . . .

LOUISE: Are you all right?

HUGH: He bit me. It's not serious. He didn't know what he was doing. He just bit without thinking. [*Taking a glass proffered by* OLIVE] Thank you very much. Good health.

    [ANTHEA *enters with her glass.*]

ANTHEA: I think this is absolutely delicious and I am going to have some more. Hugh, you're here. [*She kisses him on the cheek.*] I love Hugh on Sundays. He's all pink and shiny.

HUGH [*embarrassed*]: I don't think I'm any more . . .

LOUISE: Do you want to sit down, Anthea?

ANTHEA: No, I've only come for a refill. Then I'm going to help. [*Refilling her glass*] Now, has everyone been asked if they like courgettes? Hugh?

HUGH: Oh yes, rather.

ANTHEA: Because you can have sprouts.

HUGH: No. Courgettes are fine.

LOUISE: They wouldn't be fine if I offered them to you.

HUGH: You've never offered them to me.

LOUISE: No, because I know what you'd say if I did.

HUGH: Yes, well . . .

    [BRIAN *enters.*]

ANTHEA [*on her way again*]: Help yourself, Brian.

BRIAN: Right.

ANTHEA: We'll give you a yell, folks.

    [ANTHEA *goes.*]

OLIVE [*proffering a glass*]: Brian.

BRIAN: Thank you.

    [*Pause.*]

OLIVE: Well, I must say, I do enjoy my weekends down here. We always enjoy them, don't we, Sven?

SVEN: Yes, yes.

BRIAN: Very peaceful.

LOUISE: Yes, it's a lovely spot.

HUGH: Yes.

    [*Pause.*]

OLIVE: It's a pity your little Christopher couldn't come to lunch.

HUGH: Yes, he's . . .

LOUISE: I was saying, he's a little under the weather.

HUGH: Yes.

OLIVE: Poor little mite. How old is he now?

LOUISE: Eight. Eight and a half.

OLIVE: Oh. Young Debbie's shot up, hasn't she?

LOUISE: Oh yes.

OLIVE: Quite the young lady now. Little Giles is growing.

HUGH: Yes.

BRIAN: Yes.

LOUISE: They're very lucky.

OLIVE: Oh yes.

LOUISE: I mean, there's no reason why they should necessarily have turned out such nice children.

OLIVE: There's no law, no.

HUGH: Well, I suppose they're very pleasant parents, so . . .

LOUISE: That doesn't always follow.

HUGH: Well . . .

SVEN: No, no, she's right. It doesn't always follow. But there it is. Richard and Anthea are some of the lucky ones. They accept it without question. If you like, they take it for granted.

OLIVE: Yes, they do rather, don't they?

LOUISE: What?

OLIVE: Take things for granted a little bit. I mean, they've been very lucky.

LOUISE: Well, yes. Good luck to them.

OLIVE: Oh, quite. But, well, with the children . . . I mean, they take very little trouble with them as far as I can see. They let them do very much what they want.

LOUISE: Yes, they do. They do. I mean, we could never let Christopher run wild.

OLIVE: Oh, and I could kill her for that figure of hers.

SVEN: Now, the woman can't help her figure, darling.

OLIVE: She eats like a horse, too.

LOUISE: Well, I think they eat too much, frankly. I mean, as soon as you arrive here it's food, drink, food, drink.

HUGH: Oh, I don't know.

OLIVE: Well, as you say, good luck to them.

LOUISE: Yes, good luck to them.

SVEN: I think I must disagree. I think I would go a little further than luck, you know. It's not just luck.

OLIVE: Oh no. They know what they want.

LOUISE: Oh yes.

OLIVE: Richard's got his head screwed on.

SVEN: Oh yes. Don't be fooled by Richard. He's nobody's fool. He works quietly at it and gets what he wants.

BRIAN: True.

SVEN: You agree with me?

BRIAN: Oh yes, he usually gets what he wants.

OLIVE: Well, so does she.

LOUISE: Yes, well, she's certainly taken us over. I mean, it started with just a helping hand but now they're running everything.

HUGH: Oh no, I don't know that ...

LOUISE: The first day we were here, they burnt our fence down.

HUGH: Well, yes ...

LOUISE: Let's face it, what are we doing here now, Hugh? I mean, I don't mind being here but would we be here but for them? No, we would be getting on with our own lives like we should be. I mean, we spend more time here than we do in our own home.

HUGH: Well, yes, but ...

SVEN: Remember the first time we met? Remember I said to you, beware.

HUGH: Yes, yes.

SVEN: They are nice people but they are insidious people. They have to take people over. And why? Because eventually they want to own people.

OLIVE: Yes, that is true. That is very true.

BRIAN: Yes, yes.

SVEN: And they do it in this very pleasant way. In this friendly way. But the motive itself is that most selfish of human motives, the desire for power over other people. I know this. I am in business with him.

OLIVE: And that business would collapse without Sven.

BRIAN: I'd say that was certainly true of Richard.

LOUISE: Well, I'm sorry. I know this is a dreadful thing to say but I have never trusted her one inch.

HUGH: Well ...

LOUISE: I'm sorry, Hugh. Not one inch.

OLIVE: I'm afraid as far as I'm concerned that goes for both of them. I mean, I love them dearly but ...

SVEN: I think your instincts, unfortunately, are probably right.

BRIAN: Probably, yes.

HUGH: Well ... yes. Well ...

[*Slight pause.*

ANTHEA *enters.*]

ANTHEA: Grub up, everyone.

OLIVE: Oh goody, I'm starving.

ANTHEA: Sorry we're late. You can't hurry the chef when he's being creative. Could you bring your glasses with you in case you want wine? We're sparing the washers–up.

    [RICHARD *appears behind her.*]

RICHARD: Could they bring their glasses?

ANTHEA: I've just asked them, darling.

RICHARD: Oh, splendid.

SVEN: Wait, wait, wait. A drink for the chef.

OLIVE: Oh yes. For the chef.

RICHARD: Well, thank you. But if I don't get back to the kitchen, it'll be – [*Taking glass*] Thank you. God bless. Bon appetit. [*He takes a hasty swill.*] It'll be stone cold. Follow me.

    [RICHARD *goes out.*

    OLIVE *and* LOUISE *follow first.*]

OLIVE: Nothing but eat, drink and be merry. Isn't it wonderful?

ANTHEA: Coming, Hugh?

HUGH: Yes, yes . . .

ANTHEA: Cheer up. We love you.

HUGH: Yes . . . Right.

    [*He goes.*]

ANTHEA: Sven?

SVEN: You go on, my darling. I'm going to be supremely helpful and bring the tray.

ANTHEA: Sven, you're tremendous.

    [ANTHEA *goes.*]

BRIAN [*to* MANDY]: Are you coming?

MANDY: In a minute.

BRIAN: O.K. Suit yourself.

    [BRIAN *goes out.*

    SVEN *picks up the tray, moves towards the house and stops to look over* MANDY's *shoulder.*]

SVEN [*studying the picture*]: Yes, yes. That is an improvement. That is a great improvement. That is now a good picture. You see? You can do it. Good. Clever girl.

    [SVEN *goes out.*

    MANDY *finishes with her drawing, holds it at arm's length to study it, closes one eye, then the other. Scowls and, without ceremony, tears the picture into pieces and goes in for lunch.*]

CURTAIN

ACT TWO
SCENE ONE

Boxing Day. Four years later. A rainy, grey afternoon. Activity on the tennis court. An eccentric, rather drunken game is in progress. At this end, ANTHEA, in plastic rain hat, tennis gear and gumboots partnering RICHARD, dressed in more conventional tennis kit except for a long scarf wrapped round several times and gloves. At the other end, BRIAN and MO, his latest girlfriend, at present both out of sight. A lot of shrieks and yells. A ball hits the back fencing.

MO [*off*]: Yahoo!

ANTHEA [*who has vainly tried to intercept it*]: Aaah! It's these boots. I can't run in these boots.

RICHARD: Fancy playing in boots.

ANTHEA: I'm not playing in shoes, it's soaking wet. Soaking.

BRIAN [*off*]: Our service.

RICHARD: You're not still scoring?

BRIAN [*off*]: Five three. Second set.

MO [*off*]: To us.

RICHARD: This ball's so wet, it won't even bounce.

ANTHEA: It's stopped raining.

RICHARD: You wouldn't know it.

BRIAN [*off*]: Ready?

RICHARD: Ready. What a ridiculous way to spend Christmas.

BRIAN [*off*]: Right.

RICHARD: Anthea, yours.

   [*The ball again hits the back fencing.*]

ANTHEA [*chasing, breathless*]: Oh, I'm too old. I'm too old.

MO [*off*]: Old. Who's old?

RICHARD: She's very, very old. [*Mock sotto*] Thirty-four.

MO [*loudly, off*]: Thirty-four?

RICHARD [*even louder*]: Thirty-four.

ANTHEA [*attacking RICHARD with her racket*]: Shut up, shut up, shut up.

BRIAN [*off*]: Right ... Whoops.

ANTHEA: Where did that go?

MO [*off*]: Oh, well served. Well served, partner.

BRIAN [*off*]: Somebody in this court is drunk and it's not me.

RICHARD: Second service. [*To* ANTHEA] It's no use standing back there, dear. He can hardly get the ball over the net as it is.

BRIAN [*off*]: Coming up.

ANTHEA [*rushing in to meet the serve, whirling her racket*]: Wheee!
[*The game continues.*
ANTHEA *and* RICHARD *bound into view occasionally but most of it is sounds off, the ball rarely reaching the back of the court.*
SVEN *enters, unsteadily. He is supported by* OLIVE. *At thirty-eight and thirty-six respectively, they have both put on a bit of weight.* SVEN *is looking rather green.* OLIVE *still wears her paper hat.*]

OLIVE: Breathe in. Get some air in you. Take deep breaths.

SVEN: I'm all right, my darling. I am perfectly all right. You don't have to propel me round the garden.

ANTHEA [*entering and gathering up a ball at the back of the court*]: Hallo. Have you revived?

OLIVE: Yes.

ANTHEA: You were both fast asleep on the sofa. We left you.

SVEN: A little too much of your plum pudding.

OLIVE: Too much booze ...

SVEN: No, darling. I had very little booze indeed. Very little.

ANTHEA: Have a walk round. It's cleared up, anyway. We'll have some tea and Christmas cake in a minute. [*She goes.*]

SVEN: Oh, my God. That woman never stops producing food. She's obsessed with food.

OLIVE: And look at her. Just look at her. Like a stick. When I think I spend fifty-one weeks a year on a diet – oh, I could throttle her. Feeling better?

SVEN: Fine, my darling. I am feeling perfectly rosy.

OLIVE: You don't look it. You've been very peaky lately. Can't we have a proper holiday sometime?

SVEN: Well, there's nothing to stop us certainly.

OLIVE: Do us both good.

SVEN: The way the firm is going, I could probably take a year off, no one would notice the difference.

OLIVE: Hardly.

SVEN: It's perfectly true, my darling. Over the past few years, I have been reduced to nothing more than a piece of glorified office furniture.

OLIVE: Oh, I'm not listening to this.

SVEN: It's absolutely true.

OLIVE: Rubbish.

SVEN: This firm now runs completely without my help. Let's face it. Let us face it.

OLIVE: Ssh. Ssh.

RICHARD [*appearing momentarily to pick up a ball*]: Hallo.

SVEN: Hallo.

OLIVE: Hallo.

[RICHARD *goes.*]

SVEN: That man there, my excellent partner, runs the whole business in his sleep. He's never in the office. He neglects to turn up for important meetings. He fails to read anything that's sent to him. And even if he does, he doesn't reply. And yet, yet, he thinks he knows more about the whole thing than we do who are there in the office working seven days a week. And the ironical thing, my darling, is that he does. Every damn decision he makes is invariably right. People like Brian there, me, we are the pen-pushers. Totally dispensable, believe me.

OLIVE [*rather tearful*]: I wish you wouldn't go on like this. You know I don't like it when you go on like this.

SVEN: I'm sorry, my darling, I'm sorry.

OLIVE: It's not like you to run yourself down.

SVEN: But I am always objective. I am first and foremost objective.

OLIVE: I'm going in.

SVEN: Yes, go in, go in. Please go in. And take off that ridiculous hat.

OLIVE [*taking it off*]: Oh, I forgot I had it on. I must ... I wish you wouldn't, Sven.

[OLIVE *goes in.*]

BRIAN [*off*]: Game.

RICHARD [*coming into view*]: Well played, well played.

ANTHEA [*also coming into sight*]: Is it over? Thank God.

[ANTHEA *pauses to put on her mac which has been hanging up in the tennis court.*

MO *bounds into view. She has rolled-up jeans, unsuitable shoes, striped socks, a tee shirt and a combat hat.*]

MO: We won, we won, we won.

SVEN: What are you ridiculous lot playing at?

ANTHEA: Underwater tennis. It's very difficult.

SVEN: Your children are the only sane people in this house. Sitting in the dry in front of the fire, watching the television.

BRIAN [*coming into sight*]: You going to have a game, Sven?

RICHARD: I don't think Sven looks in form this afternoon.

SVEN: No, no. Don't be too sure, Richard. Don't be too sure.

RICHARD: Sorry. I thought you looked a bit ...

SVEN: I'm rosy. I'm rosy.

RICHARD: Good. Good.

SVEN: In fact, maybe I will have a game, yes.

RICHARD: Are you sure? It will be dark in a minute.

SVEN: No, no. I'll have you a game, Richard. We'll see. Who knows? Maybe in tennis I can still teach you something, eh?

RICHARD [*without a trace of acrimony*]: O.K.

ANTHEA: Ah-ha. Lessons from the Finnish Junior Champion, Richard.

SVEN: Now, now, now. You can laugh, Anthea my darling, you can laugh.

ANTHEA: No, Sven, I . . .

SVEN: We shall see. Maybe the laughter will stop.

RICHARD: Sven, she didn't mean . . .

SVEN: We shall see, Mrs Clever, we shall see. Now, I shall change. Wait for me.

[SVEN *goes.*]

BRIAN: What was that about?

ANTHEA: Darling, do you think he ought to play?

RICHARD: Why not?

ANTHEA: Well, he's had a bit to drink.

RICHARD: So have I.

ANTHEA: Yes, but for Sven . . . You know he gets fighting drunk on Vichy water.

MO [*approaching*]: What was the matter with him?

ANTHEA: We were just wondering whether Sven ought to play. Actually, Olive hinted that he has been drinking lately. I mean, she didn't say that because Olive would never say a word against Sven but she sort of hinted.

RICHARD: Oh. I hadn't noticed.

MO: What are we doing now?

RICHARD: Well – er – I think I'm about to play another game of tennis.

MO: I'll play you then.

RICHARD: No, I'm playing Sven.

MO: No, you're not. You're playing with me. Come on, you play with me. [*She clutches on to* RICHARD.]

RICHARD: Hang on.

ANTHEA [*amused*]: Mo, don't. He's playing with Sven.

MO: You mind your own business, you. He's playing with me, aren't you?

RICHARD: No, I'm . . .

BRIAN [*embarrassed*]: Mo, come on. [*He takes hold of her.*]

MO: Oh, get off.

BRIAN: Come on, Mo.

MO: Get off.

ANTHEA [*also grabbing* MO]: Come on, Mo. Let go.

MO: I'm playing with him.

RICHARD [*disentangling himself*]: I'll change into some dry things. [*He flees towards the house.*]

ANTHEA [*still rather amused*]: Yes, do, darling ... Come on, Mo – Mo ...

MO: Let go. You let go.

BRIAN: Mo! Mo! Look leave her to me, Anthea, will you? Leave her to me.

ANTHEA: Pleasure. Let her sit for a minute till she's calmed down.

MO: Yes, you bugger off.

ANTHEA: Certainly, yes. Fine, good-bye. [*As she goes*] My God.

BRIAN [*still clutching* MO]: Are you going to sit still?

MO: Yes.

BRIAN: Promise.

MO: Yes.

BRIAN: Promise then.

MO: I promise.

BRIAN [*releasing her*]: All right. Sit still.

MO: Oh, I feel ill. It's all that food.

BRIAN: What do you expect? You ate like a pig.

MO: I am a pig.

BRIAN: What did you behave like that for?

MO: When?

BRIAN: Just now.

MO: Felt like it.

BRIAN: Why?

MO: You wouldn't understand if I told you.

BRIAN: Why not?

MO: You're too old.

BRIAN: Too old?

MO: You're over thirty.

BRIAN: What's that got to do with it?

MO: If you're over thirty, then you're too old. You've forgotten what it's like.

BRIAN: What what's like?

MO: To be under thirty.

BRIAN: Oh, great.

MO: Oh, I feel terrible.

BRIAN: Serve you right.

MO: You known these people long?

BRIAN: Yes. I've known Anthea for – ten years ...

MO: Oh.

BRIAN: I knew her before she met Richard. I met her when she was married before. She's not married to Richard, you see.

MO [*not very interested*]: Oh.

BRIAN: She was married before and then – she broke up with him. She was very unhappy then. And she had the two kids and nowhere much to go. I had a couple of rooms at that time in Gloucester Road and she rang me, she must have been desperate, because I'd met her briefly through her husband Matthew. And she said, did I know of anywhere? And I said, well, there's here. I mean, you can muck in here for a few weeks – no obligations. And so she came. It was mad, really mad. I mean, four of us in two rooms and the kids wouldn't sleep and we both sat up and talked all night and ... she was magic. Just a magic lady. And we went on like that for weeks. I used to drive a mini-cab in those days. And I'd come home and there she'd be with Debbie and Giles and it was the happiest time I've ever had in my life. Then Richard came and that was that. I never told her, you see. What I felt. Because I'd promised at the beginning there'd be no obligations. So I said nothing to her at all. Not until it was too late. I think I sort of hoped she'd guess what I felt, but she couldn't have done, and she went with Richard and that was that.

[*A silence.*]

MO: Oh, I've got a pain in me guts.

BRIAN: O.K., come on. I'll get you in. I'll get you indoors.

MO: Oooh.

[BRIAN *steers her towards the house.*
They pass ANTHEA *coming out.*]

ANTHEA: Better?

BRIAN: She'll be all right. Come on.

MO: I'm coming.

ANTHEA: Richard's left his jacket.

[BRIAN *and* MO *go out.*

ANTHEA *goes into the tennis court and collects* RICHARD's *jacket. As she does so,* HUGH *and* LOUISE *enter from the side of the tennis court, off on their Boxing Day walk.*]

HUGH: 'Scuse us. Just cutting through.

ANTHEA: Off on a walk?

LOUISE: Just a quick one.

ANTHEA: Have a nice Christmas?

HUGH: Yes, yes. Not too bad. We have Louise's mother with us so we've been quite busy.

ANTHEA: How is she?

LOUISE: Oh, very well. We left her playing chess with Christopher.

ANTHEA: Does he play chess? How impressive. Ours can only just manage four letter scrabble.

HUGH: Oh, Christopher's really very good. Too good for me now, I'm afraid. I think he's got a talent quite definitely.

ANTHEA: Marvellous.

LOUISE: It takes a certain sort of mind.

ANTHEA: Yes. Not mine, I'm afraid.

HUGH: Did we hear you playing tennis earlier?

ANTHEA: Oh yes, sorry. Were we very rowdy?

HUGH: No, no. It just seemed very energetic for Boxing Day.

LOUISE [anxious to move on]: Yes, well we must ...

HUGH: Yes.

ANTHEA: Mind you, if you stick around, you might witness a classic encounter.

HUGH: What's that?

ANTHEA: Sven is about to make his début on the tennis court.

HUGH: Really?

ANTHEA: At long last. Sven v. Richard.

LOUISE: It's a bit wet for tennis, isn't it?

ANTHEA: Not for Finnish tennis.

HUGH: I say, perhaps we ought to stay and see them.

LOUISE: I thought we were going for a walk.

HUGH: We will.

LOUISE: It'll be dark soon.

ANTHEA: Well, don't ruin your day. It's not that important.

[OLIVE comes from the house, agitated.]

OLIVE: Anthea, I don't know what's got into you and Richard, I really don't.

ANTHEA: Sorry?

OLIVE: Encouraging Sven to play tennis.

ANTHEA: Me?

OLIVE: He's in no condition. He's in no fit state.

ANTHEA: I haven't said a thing.

OLIVE: He'd never have agreed to it without encouragement.

ANTHEA: Well, I don't see how I ...

OLIVE: He hasn't taken any exercise for ten years. What'll this do to him?

ANTHEA: Well, I'll try and stop it then if you like.

OLIVE: You'd better. It'll kill him.

HUGH: Perhaps he ought to be a little careful.

OLIVE: Of course he should. He's thirty-eight, you know. Thirty-eight. That's the age they have to watch it.

HUGH: Oh really?

[SVEN *enters in borrowed tennis gear, made for a man a trifle slimmer.*]

SVEN: All right, all right. Where's the opposition?

ANTHEA: Oh gosh. Is that the best we could find for you?

SVEN: These are perfectly adequate, Anthea. Provided I do no sudden arm movements.

OLIVE: Oh, Sven.

SVEN: Where is he, then? I'm ready for him.

OLIVE: Please, Sven, do be careful.

SVEN: What's the woman talking about? I'm going to play a game of tennis, my darling, that's all. You would think I was going out for a gunfight.

ANTHEA: I don't think you should play for too long, Sven. If it's your first for some time.

SVEN: It won't be for too long. Don't worry. A few love games, it'll all be over. Good afternoon, Louise. Good afternoon, Hugh.

HUGH: Hallo.

LOUISE: Hallo.

HUGH: You look – ready for action . . .

SVEN: I'm ready, yes.

[SVEN *goes into the court and starts a few knee bends.*]

OLIVE: He shouldn't be playing. He really shouldn't.

LOUISE: Are you coming?

HUGH: I thought we might watch.

LOUISE: No, I want to go for a walk.

HUGH: In a moment.

LOUISE: I want to deliver these envelopes round the Crescent anyway.

ANTHEA: Oh, you can leave those here if you like. I'll do them when I do the others.

LOUISE: No, I'll do them.

ANTHEA: Well, I'm delivering the others first thing tomorrow, I'll –

LOUISE: I'll do them. I'm not totally incapable, you know, Anthea.

ANTHEA: No, of course not.

HUGH: She was only offering, dear.

OLIVE: The first time I haven't packed his tennis gear and he decides to play.

[BRIAN *is dragged from the house by* MO.]

MO: Come on, then. Come on.

BRIAN: All right, all right. I'm coming.

ANTHEA: She's recovered.

BRIAN [*sourly*]: She's recovered.

SVEN: Ah, Brian. Good. Just the man we need. An umpire, please.

BRIAN: Oh come on, Sven.

SVEN: No, seriously. We need an umpire. This game must be played properly. Fair play must be seen to be done.

BRIAN: You don't need me.

MO: Go on.

SVEN: Come on. Come, come, come.

BRIAN: All right, all right.

> [*He goes into the court.*
> MO *loiters outside.*]

ANTHEA: Are the kids coming out?

MO: No. They're watching some boring old love film in black and white.

ANTHEA: Oh, well.

SVEN: Come on. Where's the opposition? I'm getting chilly out here.

ANTHEA: He had to change, Sven. He was soaked through from the last game.

SVEN: Well, I can't wait all day.

ANTHEA: He's taking this awfully seriously.

OLIVE: That's the trouble. I think he is serious.

LOUISE: Well, I'm going to walk on up and deliver these.

HUGH: Oh, all right then.

LOUISE: No, you stay and watch if you want. I'll be all right on my own. I'll see you back home.

HUGH: I could follow on and meet you.

LOUISE: If you want to. Good-bye.

ANTHEA: You off, Louise?

LOUISE: I'd better deliver these before it gets dark. It's not well lit in the Crescent.

SVEN: Louise, you're not staying to see the great victory?

LOUISE: No. Sorry, I can't. Some of us just don't have time for playing games. Much as we might like to.

> [LOUISE *goes out.*]

MO [*chanting*]: Why are we waiting? Why are we waiting? Why are we waiting?

OLIVE: Oh, that little girl's terribly rowdy, isn't she? I don't know where Brian finds them.

ANTHEA: Well, he likes variety, I think.

OLIVE: I don't know about variety. They all look alike to me.

> [RICHARD *enters in fresh tennis kit.*]

RICHARD: Sorry.

SVEN: Ah-ha! At last!

MO: Hooray.

RICHARD: Sorry, couldn't find my old shoes.

SVEN: Come along, come along.

RICHARD: All right.

ANTHEA: Richard ...

RICHARD: Mmm?

ANTHEA: Make it a short game, please. Sven's very out of condition.

RICHARD: All right, don't worry.

SVEN: Come on, come on.

RICHARD: Make it the best of five games, shall we?

SVEN: Best of five? What are you talking about? This is a major tournament.

OLIVE: No, Sven, make it the best of five.

SVEN: No such thing.

BRIAN: Best of five. Umpire's decision.

SVEN: How can we ...

BRIAN: Umpire's decision.

RICHARD: Umpire's decision.

MO [*chanting*]: Off – off – off – off –

BRIAN: Shut up.

OLIVE [*shadowing* SVEN *outside the court fencing, anxiously*]: Now take it gently, dear, take it gently.

SVEN: I have no intention of taking anything gently, my darling.

BRIAN [*producing a coin*]: Spin for service. Call.

RICHARD: Heads.

BRIAN: Heads it is.

SVEN: I'll take this end.

RICHARD: Change after three?

SVEN: Fine with me.

OLIVE: Sven ...

RICHARD: Want a knock-up?

SVEN: Just one or two.

RICHARD [*going off to the other end*]: I warn you, the ball hardly bounces at all, so watch it.

SVEN: Right.

> [MO *moves off outside the court after* RICHARD.
> BRIAN *has moved off inside the court, presumably to stand square with the net.*]

BRIAN [*off*]: Play.

RICHARD [*off*]: Ready?

SVEN: Right. [*He runs in.*] [*Off*] My God.

RICHARD [*off*]: I warned you.

SVEN [*returning*]: It's like playing with a cannon ball.

ANTHEA: I know, it's quite impossible.

OLIVE: Be careful, Sven.

SVEN: My darling, will you please, please be quiet. [*He runs in to return a shot.*]

[OLIVE *moves after him.*]

RICHARD [*off*]: Shot.

MO [*off*]: Come on, Richard. We want Richard.

ANTHEA: We're all worrying about Sven. This is the second game Richard's played today.

HUGH: He's pretty fit, isn't he?

ANTHEA: Well, fairly.

SVEN [*off*]: All right, let's start. Can we start, please?

RICHARD: Fine.

BRIAN: O.K.

HUGH: I – er – was hoping to catch you actually. Anthea – I –

ANTHEA: Oh, they've started ...

HUGH: Yes – I –

[SVEN *is seen jigging about, preparing to receive service.*]

RICHARD [*off*]: Ready?

SVEN: Right.

BRIAN [*off*]: Play.

[SVEN *rushes in.*]

SVEN [*off*]: Ah.

BRIAN [*off*]: Fifteen love.

MO [*off*]: Hooray, hooray.

SVEN [*returning*]: I hope that girl isn't going to keep that up all afternoon.

[SVEN *crouches to receive.*

RICHARD *serves off.*

SVEN *runs in. The ball hits the back netting.*]

SVEN [*off*]: Ah.

BRIAN [*off*]: Thirty love.

MO: Hooray, hooray.

[SVEN *returns scowling.*]

RICHARD [*off*]: Sorry. A bit flukey.

ANTHEA: I'd stand a bit closer to the net, Sven, if I was you. The ball's so wet it hardly travels.

SVEN: Thank you, Anthea, I know what I'm doing, thank you.

[SVEN *crouches.*

He runs in.]

SVEN [*off*]: Ah-ha!

BRIAN: Thirty fifteen.

MO [*off*]: Boo.

RICHARD [*off*]: Good shot.

[SVEN *returns pleased.*
Crouches to receive. Runs in.
The ball hits the back netting.]

HUGH: Anthea, I – could I – have a word ...

SVEN [*off*]: Ah.

BRIAN [*off*]: Forty fifteen.

MO [*off*]: Hooray, hooray.

SVEN: Oh, shut up, you rowdy little girl.

MO: Boo.

SVEN [*returning indignant*]: How can I concentrate with that – that ...

OLIVE: Be quiet.

BRIAN [*off*]: Shut up, Mo.

[MO *shuts up.*
SVEN *runs in to meet the service.*]

SVEN [*off*]: Oh, damn to hell.

RICHARD [*off*]: Bad luck.

BRIAN [*off*]: Game to Richard. One love.

[SVEN *returns into sight, dejected.*
OLIVE *follows him from outside the court.*]

OLIVE: How are you feeling, dear?

SVEN: Olive, you are sorely trying my patience. [*Shouting down to*
RICHARD] Ready?

RICHARD [*off*]: Yes.

SVEN [*stepping towards the base line for a mighty serve*]: Right.

[*A grunt as* SVEN *serves, almost immediately the ball flies back hitting*
the back netting.]

BRIAN [*off*]: Love fifteen.

ANTHEA: Oh, good shot.

HUGH: Anthea, I think I have to say this now ...

ANTHEA: Oh yes?

[SVEN *serves again.*]

RICHARD [*off*]: Nice one.

BRIAN [*off*]: Fifteen all.

ANTHEA: Well served. [*To* HUGH] Is it about the Famine Relief
envelopes? Because most of those are being done by the W.I.'s. I had
a word with their chairman, Molly Maintrap, and she's farmed them
out to volunteers.

[SVEN *has served successfully again.*]

BRIAN [*off*]: Thirty fifteen.

OLIVE: Well played, dear.

ANTHEA: Bravo.

HUGH: No, it's more than that, you see ...

ANTHEA [*calling across to* OLIVE]: He's got a jolly good service, hasn't he?

SVEN [*appearing in view momentarily*]: Of course I have a jolly good service.

> [*He turns, runs in and serves.*
> *The ball comes hurtling back.*]

BRIAN [*off*]: Thirty all.

SVEN [*returning to gather the ball, sourly*]: Good shot, good shot.

HUGH [*urgently*]: Anthea, please.

ANTHEA: Hang on, Hugh love. This is getting very exciting.

> [SVEN *serves.*]

RICHARD [*off*]: Hey. No chance ...

BRIAN [*off*]: Forty thirty.

MO [*off*]: Come on, Richard.

OLIVE: Come on, Sven.

ANTHEA: Come on, Sven.

> [SVEN *serves.*
> RICHARD *returns.*
> SVEN *wins.*]

BRIAN [*off*]: Game to Sven. One all.

ANTHEA: Well done. Well played. You're looking awfully hangdog, Hugh. Are you all right?

HUGH: No, I'm not all right. That's why I want to talk to you.

ANTHEA: Are you ill?

HUGH: I think I am, in a sense.

SVEN [*off*]: Ah.

BRIAN [*off*]: Fifteen love.

RICHARD [*off*]: Were you ready?

SVEN [*off*]: Yes, yes, yes.

HUGH: You see, the point is – I – well – you see the –

BRIAN [*off*]: Fifteen all.

ANTHEA: Hugh, what are you talking about?

HUGH: Do we have to talk here?

ANTHEA: Well, I'm watching the game.

HUGH: Yes but – I was going to talk to you in the New Year but ...

RICHARD [*off*]: Good shot.

BRIAN [*off*]: Fifteen thirty.

ANTHEA: Come in and have some tea with us afterwards and –

HUGH: No, no.

SVEN [*off*]: Ah-ha!

BRIAN [*off*]: Fifteen forty.

MO [*off*]: Come on, Richard.

ANTHEA: Come on, Richard. Poor Hugh, have you had a miserable Christmas?

HUGH: Well – fairly –

ANTHEA: Was Christopher playing up?

HUGH: No, he's really much better. He's grown into a very quiet boy. Almost secretive, I suppose. Very contained. I don't think he loves either of us very much . . .

BRIAN: Thirty forty.

MO: Hooray.

HUGH: Still things have definitely turned a corner.

ANTHEA: Good shot. And Louise is looking better.

HUGH: Yes, well that's very largely thanks to you, Anthea. I mean, you've taken practically all her worries off her shoulders . . .

ANTHEA: Oh, rubbish. I've rattled a few collecting tins, that's all.

HUGH: And all those leaflets.

ANTHEA: Five minute job.

HUGH: And the jumble sales.

ANTHEA: They're enormous fun.

[*The ball hits the netting.*]

SVEN [*following it*]: That was out.

RICHARD [*off*]: Oh, well played.

BRIAN [*off*]: Game to Sven. Sven leads two one.

SVEN: We're really getting warmed up now.

[RICHARD *arrives beside him.*]

[*Startled*] What are you doing?

RICHARD: Aren't we changing ends?

SVEN: Oh yes. You want to go straight on?

RICHARD: Might as well before it gets dark.

SVEN: Right. Fit, fit, fit.

[SVEN *sprints off up the other end.*

ANTHEA *laughs.*]

RICHARD [*to her*]: There's no stopping him. On we go.

[RICHARD *positions himself at this end of the court.*

The game continues under the next with SVEN *serving from the other end.*

Eight points in all. The majority of the action offstage.]

OLIVE [*moving away from the court towards the house*]: I think I'll fetch him a glass of water. He's looking very hot.

ANTHEA: Oh, fine. You know where . . .

OLIVE: Yes. I do hope he wins. I dread to think what he'll be like to live with if he doesn't.

ANTHEA: It's all right. Don't worry. Don't worry.

[OLIVE *goes off worried.*]

HUGH: Anthea.

ANTHEA: Now, Hugh. Come on then, tell me all about it. Is it another crisis of faith?

HUGH: No, no. Well, not really.

ANTHEA: Oh good. Because you know, I'm not good at those. We've solved some pretty knotty ones though, haven't we?

HUGH: Yes. Well, the point is, Anthea, I don't know whether half the problems I have come to you with are genuine or not. It's not the problems so much as the ... This is not the easiest thing to say at the best of times. Particularly not coming from someone in my position. It's something I shouldn't say. And yet, if I don't say it, maybe the very fact of my not saying it will be just as bad in the long run as if I had said it.

ANTHEA: Said what?

BRIAN [off]: Fifteen love.

HUGH: I am in love with you.

   [A pause.]

ANTHEA [blankly]: What?

HUGH: I am in love with you. It happened a very long time ago actually. I think at first, it was just a general sort of love for both of you. You and Richard – as people. I don't know if you're aware of it but you're both very good people. At least I feel you are.

BRIAN [off]: Fifteen all.

HUGH: And I think it was that very goodness that I fell in love with. Your unselfishness, your generosity ... You were in a way everything I wanted to be but couldn't be. I almost envied you.

ANTHEA: But Hugh ...

HUGH: Please. Let me say it all first.

BRIAN [off]: Thirty fifteen.

HUGH: You can imagine if this has been happening over eight years, then it's pretty permanent as far as I am concerned. In fact it's taken me over completely. It's killed what little there was between Louise and me. It was unfortunate in the first place, marrying a woman I realize I cared for hardly at all. But at least the lack of feeling is mutual at any rate. Whereas my love for you ... I promise you I've tried desperately hard to stop this feeling for you from growing. Or at any rate, tried to channel it into more conventional Christian love ...

BRIAN [under this]: Forty fifteen.

HUGH [continuing but closing his eyes and beginning to speak faster and faster]: But whenever we are together, I feel overwhelmed with a desire for you, a longing for you – not just a spiritual longing, I'm afraid. I pray God it were just a spiritual longing but it's not. It's good old fully

fledged carnal longing as well. For you and your body. For all of you.
And I want you and I need you . . .

BRIAN [*off*]: Forty thirty.

HUGH [*continuing remorselessly*]: And I'm sorry, I'm sorry, forgive me. I
am a middle-aged clergyman who's making a fool of himself and ought
to know better but I love you, Anthea, I love you. For ever and ever
and ever. World without end.

BRIAN [*off*]: Deuce.

ANTHEA [*after a pause, in a strangled voice*]: Oh, dear God.

HUGH: Dear God indeed.

ANTHEA: Oh, Hugh . . .

　　[*The ball hits the back fence.*]

RICHARD [*following it up*]: That was in.

BRIAN [*off*]: Game and set to Sven.

RICHARD: Congratulations, Sven mate. Well played.

OLIVE [*entering with a glass of water*]: What happened? Is he all right?

RICHARD: All right? He won.

OLIVE: He won?

SVEN [*appearing*]: Of course I won.

OLIVE: Oh, well done. Well done. [*To* ANTHEA] He won.

ANTHEA: Oh, good.

SVEN: Well now, who's for another game?

RICHARD: Not at the moment, thank you.

SVEN: So perish all enemies of the Finnish Junior Champion.

OLIVE: He hasn't played for ten years either.

BRIAN [*coming out of the court and patting* SVEN'S *shoulder*]: Very good.
Well played.

SVEN: Yes, I think we must play some more, eh?

RICHARD: The court's there. Any time.

MO [*coming round the side of the court to* RICHARD]: You bloody twit.

RICHARD: What?

MO: Why'n't you beat him?

RICHARD: They're too good, these Finnish Junior Champions.

MO: Rubbish. He's a rubbish player. You can beat him . . .

SVEN [*coolly ignoring this*]: Coming in, my darling? It's a little chilly.

OLIVE: Yes, you mustn't catch a chill.

MO [*to* RICHARD]: Why didn't you play with your proper hand then?

RICHARD: What?

MO: Why?

RICHARD: Don't know what you mean.

MO: You know.

SVEN: What is she talking about?

MO: I am asking him why he played you left-handed, when he was right-handed when he played with us.

SVEN: You were playing left-handed?

RICHARD: Well.

SVEN: Against me?

RICHARD: Um ...

SVEN: But you're right-handed.

ANTHEA: He wasn't, he ...

MO: He was. I watched him. That's why he lost.

SVEN: You were playing with me left-handed?

RICHARD: Well, some of the time. Thought I'd ring the changes.

SVEN: I see. I see. At least you paid me the compliment of not hopping on one leg as well. Let's go in.

[SVEN *goes off with* OLIVE.]

ANTHEA [*after a pause*]: I don't think that was awfully clever.

RICHARD: Well – he – I thought he needed to win.

ANTHEA: Yes, but couldn't you have lost right-handed?

RICHARD: Yes, I – oh hell. Too late now, isn't it? Sorry.

[RICHARD *goes in dejected*.]

MO [*muttering*]: Twit.

BRIAN: Your husband's going to get himself murdered one of these days.

[BRIAN *and* MO *go in*.

ANTHEA *finds herself alone with* HUGH.]

ANTHEA: Oh Hugh ...

[HUGH *smiles weakly*.]

Have you ever mentioned this to Louise?

HUGH: No, no.

ANTHEA: Well, please never do.

HUGH: Oh no – never, never. I wouldn't – it would ... no.

ANTHEA: Oh Hugh.

HUGH: I love you.

ANTHEA: Go home.

HUGH: Yes. Quite right. Good night.

ANTHEA: Good night.

[HUGH *goes*.

ANTHEA, *after a moment, goes in too*.]

ACT TWO
SCENE TWO

Four years later. A summer evening about 7 p.m. BRIAN *and* RICHARD *are busy running sound and lights out to the tennis court.* RICHARD *is in the tennis court up a stepladder clamping a floodlight to the rail. Visible at one corner of the court, a loudspeaker with wires running away presumably to the amplifier at the other end. A mains lead running from the court into the house.* BRIAN *enters, carrying a twin loudspeaker, from the house and takes it into the tennis court.*

SVEN *is sitting in the summer-house watching them at work. Despite the fine evening, he wears a light coat.*

SVEN [*as* BRIAN *appears*]: My word, my word. More and more.

RICHARD: Won't be a minute, Sven. This is the last one.

BRIAN [*with loudspeaker*]: You want this one in the other corner?

RICHARD: I think so, don't you? The lead should reach all right.

[BRIAN *goes off to the far end of the court.*]

SVEN: And all this for little Debbie.

RICHARD [*wrestling with the lamp*]: Yeah.

SVEN: A very lucky young lady.

RICHARD: Oh well, eighteenth birthday. Quite a milestone.

SVEN: Eighteen, my goodness.

RICHARD: Are you all right there? Do you want anything?

SVEN: No, no, no. Olive is fetching me my drink.

BRIAN [*appearing*]: Shall I tie those leads against the wire? People are going to trip on them otherwise.

RICHARD: Yes, not too securely. The first sign of rain I've got to whip this lot in. It's rather expensive this gear.

[BRIAN *has gone.*]

SVEN: You'll have to hope she has well-behaved friends, young Debbie.

RICHARD: Oh, they're not too bad, the ones we've met. I mean, they scare the life out of me to look at but they're not too badly behaved.

SVEN: How many are you expecting?

RICHARD: God knows. It started at thirty. I think it's gone up to fifty now. We set the limit at fifty so we're expecting about seventy-five.

BRIAN [*off*]: You want me to test this?

RICHARD: Would you? And could you plug the floods in for a second, too?

BRIAN [*off*]: O.K.

RICHARD [*coming down the steps and heading towards the house*]: Hang on, I'll switch it on at the other end.

BRIAN [*off*]: Righto.

RICHARD [*nearly colliding with* OLIVE *coming from the house*]: Sorry.

OLIVE: It's like a madhouse here.

RICHARD: We'll be straight in a minute.

OLIVE: I nearly fell over that wire back there.

RICHARD: I'm fixing it down, my love.
   [RICHARD *goes.*]

OLIVE [*handing* SVEN *a medicinal concoction*]: Here we are. Like a madhouse back there.

SVEN: Is that anything unusual?

OLIVE: Do you want me to bring the car rug to wrap round you?

SVEN: No, I'm perfectly capable. Don't treat me like a two-year-old, darling.

OLIVE [*looking at the tennis court*]: What are they doing?

SVEN: They're going to have dancing in the tennis court. There's the lights and the music, you see. Which Brian's fixing.

OLIVE: Oh, I see.
   [RICHARD *returns.*]

RICHARD [*calling to* BRIAN]: Anything?

BRIAN [*off*]: Not yet.

RICHARD: See that switch on the plug is on ... No, the one that end. [*Turning to the others*] You looking after him, Olive?

SVEN: She's looking after me far too much. I'm being ridiculously spoilt.

OLIVE: He won't let me look after him half the time.

RICHARD: You seem better.

OLIVE: If he's sensible and does as he's told, he'll never have any trouble again. That is a fact. The thing about a heart condition is, provided you're sensible, it needn't be a worry.

SVEN: I'm being perfectly sensible. I'm doing absolutely nothing. What less could I do?
   [*The floodlights come on momentarily.*]

RICHARD: They're working fine.

BRIAN [*off*]: Is that one on by me?

RICHARD: Yes. [*To the others*] It's good you came.

OLIVE: Well, we couldn't miss Debbie's eighteenth, could we? I mean, that's the really important one these days, isn't it? I mean, in our youth it used to be your twenty-first but ...

SVEN: Of course the whole legal position has changed now since the voting age was reduced. This has made ...

OLIVE: Of course, we've known Debbie since she was, what, three?

SVEN: This has made – [*He gives up.*]

OLIVE: Is Giles here?

RICHARD: No, he's keeping well away. Staying with a schoolfriend. He has a very low opinion of Debbie's associates.

OLIVE: Oh dear.

RICHARD: He says they're frivolous. Very serious young man is Giles. Not awfully bright but very serious.

SVEN: Well, he's of an age. Of an age. Don't you remember –
[*A blast of loud music from the speakers causes him to jump.*]
Oh, my God.

OLIVE [*rushing to* SVEN's *side*]: Oh heavens.

RICHARD [*simultaneously calling to* BRIAN]: Hey, hey.
[*The music stops.*]

BRIAN [*off*]: Sorry.

OLIVE: Are you all right?

SVEN: Yes, yes. Just about. Oh dear, oh dear.

RICHARD: Sorry about that.

OLIVE: You're sure you're all right, dear?

SVEN: This man is obviously trying to kill me. He takes over the business. He practically sees me into a wheelchair, now he's trying to kill me.

RICHARD: Hardly.

OLIVE: Calm down, now, calm down.

SVEN: No, I'm joking. I'm joking. But you must understand, Richard, that I won't be as active as I was for some time. You understand that?

OLIVE: Yes, he understands that.

RICHARD: You'd better hurry up. The place can't run without you, you know.

SVEN: No, Richard, please, don't start kindnesses, please. I'm old enough now to see for myself my strength and my weaknesses. If that hasn't happened to a man by the time he's forty-two years old, then heaven help him. Despite what my darling Olive may say to the contrary, I'm a man of only average ability. An average ability only. Before I reached this shattering conclusion, I once made the mistake, Richard, of trying to compete with you. You responded to my challenge with a gesture of supreme disdain. Playing with me left-handed. Not only in tennis but also in business.

RICHARD: I don't think I did that.

SVEN: Oh, Richard ... The fact is, when it comes down to it, you have the one advantage over me that matters. You have flair, Richard. That's something that can't be learnt. It's handed out at birth, along with all those other unfair advantages like physical beauty, under a most monstrously devised random system. And as always happens in these cases, it's always given to the very people who in my opinion do least to earn it. It's taken me forty-two years to think of that and I'm very depressed.

OLIVE [*getting tearful*]: He goes on like that these days for hours. I don't know. I don't listen.

RICHARD: I don't quite see what I'm supposed to do. Sorry, I –

SVEN: Nothing, Richard. Nothing more than usual. Kindly continue to support us all in the style to which we are accustomed, that's all.

RICHARD [*smiling*]: I'll do my best.

[ANTHEA *enters with a tray of drinks. It's another concoction in a jug.*]

ANTHEA: Here we are. I thought we'd sample this. Debbie and I concocted it for the party. We can drink her health.

RICHARD: I'd be very wary of that if I were you.

ANTHEA: Are the lights working?

RICHARD: Yes.

ANTHEA: Do they look all right?

RICHARD: Well, yes. A bit like a prisoner-of-war camp but not bad. I've put some colours in. It's made it a little more tasteful.

ANTHEA: Well, don't ruin those lamps. They want them back for *White Horse Inn* next week. [*Pouring out a glass*] Sven won't, will he?

OLIVE: No.

ANTHEA: You will?

OLIVE: Well, a little one. I'm driving.

ANTHEA: Oh lord, so you are. Is it a hell of a hike?

OLIVE: Not too bad.

SVEN: No, once we get on to the motorway ...

ANTHEA: What's the latest you can leave?

OLIVE: We ought to be away by eight. It's an hour's drive.

SVEN: Yes, but once we get on to the motorway ...

ANTHEA: Well, you'll have time for a quick snack anyway. [*Calling to* BRIAN] Brian, do you want some of this?

SVEN [*muttering*]: ... it'll be plain sailing.

OLIVE: What's that, dear?

SVEN: Nothing, my darling.

BRIAN: Yes, ta. Leave it there for me. Richard, I'll loop these leads up out of the way.

RICHARD: Fine.

BRIAN [*holding up wire*]: Can I use this wire?

RICHARD: Go ahead.

ANTHEA: I'll leave it here.

OLIVE: Where's Debbie then?

ANTHEA: Very, very slowly getting out of the bath, when I last saw her. It's lovely you managed to break your journey. Thank you. She really does appreciate it.

OLIVE: Oh, well ...

ANTHEA: Well, I think she does anyway ...

OLIVE: How do you mean?

ANTHEA: Oh, it's always awkward to know what to do when they get to that age and they're still living at home. I mean, to be truthful, she'd be far happier if we weren't here at all but seeing as it's our house, too bad. So we said to her, right. Ten minutes of boring old us – happy birthday from the older generation and so on and then we'll vanish ...

SVEN: Older generation. Now, we're the older generation.

OLIVE: We're not in the grave yet.

SVEN: You hear that, Richard? Older generation?

RICHARD [*moving to* BRIAN]: Yes ... Be careful of that speaker wire. It's caught round the net post.

BRIAN [*off*]: Oh yeah.

[RICHARD *goes into the court and disappears.*]

ANTHEA: She'll be down in a minute.

OLIVE: Are the – er – are the Emersons coming round?

ANTHEA: Ah. Thereby hangs a tale. Possibly. I've asked them.

OLIVE: Oh, are they ... ?

ANTHEA: Oh dear. Well, Louise has been – you know, peculiar again. And Hugh had to get her mother in to look after her and then Hugh and her mother had a row and – oh gosh, yes. If they do come, don't whatever you do ask after Christopher.

OLIVE: Something wrong?

ANTHEA: With Christopher? No, he's fine. In fact he's brilliant. I mean, he got this public school scholarship, of course, and now he's got a University Open Scholarship and he's only seventeen. I mean, he's got to be Prime Minister or something, hasn't he?

OLIVE: I should think they're very proud.

ANTHEA: They would be. Only he won't speak to them, that's the trouble. He really is a weird youth when you meet him. You can almost hear this brain going round as he stares at you. Quite spooky. He's completely cut off from Louise and Hugh. He's quite gentle with them. He treats them like a couple of deaf-mute family retainers.

OLIVE: Oh dear.

ANTHEA: It's one of the reasons for Louise's condition, of course. She has her high days and low days, a bit like the church. It depends what miracle drug the doctor's currently got her on. She can be anything from soporific to suicidal. We haven't seen them for yonks. We asked them today of course. Well, it wouldn't be the same without them, would it?

RICHARD [*off*]: That's it. Pull the whole thing this way a bit.

BRIAN [*off*]: O.K.

SVEN [*who has been watching the men during this last, muttering*]: No, no, no. You'll never do it if you pull it that way. You'll never do it . . .

RICHARD [*off*]: That's it. That's done it.

BRIAN: Thank you. Brilliant.

SVEN [*muttering*]: Oh well, I don't know . . .

ANTHEA: Have you got a nice hotel?

OLIVE: Yes. Well, it looks nice in the pictures. It's a . . .

SVEN: Four star. English catering. Hard beds. No air conditioning. If you put your shoes outside to be cleaned, they're stolen in the night. It'll be hell on earth. But who cares, we're on holiday.

OLIVE: It looked very nice.

ANTHEA: You should have stayed here.

[RICHARD *wanders back from the tennis court.*]

OLIVE: Oh no.

ANTHEA: We'd've looked after you.

SVEN: No, no, no.

ANTHEA: Wouldn't we, Richard? They should have stayed here with us. We'd've built you up.

OLIVE: Oh yes. We can do without that. It's all right for you. Look at you.

ANTHEA: Look, I can call now and cancel.

OLIVE: Oh no, it's . . .

SVEN: No, Anthea. Please.

ANTHEA: Well, it's silly. You can have all the rest in the world here. Don't you agree, Richard?

RICHARD: No, Antie.

ANTHEA: But it's stupid.

RICHARD: Antie, I think they want to go to the hotel.

ANTHEA: But it makes no sense.

RICHARD: Antie, don't push them, darling.

ANTHEA: I'm not, I – oh, well, super. Fine. I mean, suit yourself.

OLIVE: Be best.

[HUGH *and* LOUISE *appear round the side of the tennis court.* HUGH, *pale and drawn.* LOUISE, *bright, like a painted doll. Smiling incessantly, but unnaturally, as one under the influence of drugs. She is, in fact, under the influence of drugs.*]

RICHARD: Hallo, there.

ANTHEA: Oh, splendid. Welcome. Come on.

HUGH: Hallo.

LOUISE [*chirpily*]: Hallo.

OLIVE: Hallo. Lovely to see you both. Been a long time.

LOUISE: Hallo.

HUGH: Yes, yes. Over a year, I think, at least.

LOUISE [*to* SVEN]: Hallo.

OLIVE: It must be. Of course, Sven's illness has meant ...

HUGH: Yes, of course. How are you, Sven? Are you better? You look good.

SVEN: Yes, I'm well mended now, Hugh.

HUGH: You look good.

SVEN: Yes, I'm well mended.

HUGH: Yes, you look good.

SVEN: Yes.

HUGH: Good, good.

LOUISE: Hallo, Richard.

SVEN: Excuse me, Louise, if I don't bound up to greet you in my customary manner but I'm not allowed too much violent exercise.

HUGH: No more games of tennis then, eh?

SVEN: No, no. No more games of tennis.

[*A pause.*]

LOUISE [*seeing* BRIAN]: Hallo.

BRIAN [*off*]: Hallo.

ANTHEA: You're looking very bright, Louise.

LOUISE: Yes, yes.

HUGH: She's on these new stimulants. I think they're rather stronger than she's used to. But we're giving them a try.

LOUISE: Yes.

RICHARD: Is she allowed a glass of – [*He indicates tray.*]

LOUISE: Oh, super.

HUGH: No, not with these particular pills. They would react, dear.

RICHARD: Oh dear. A small glass for you?

HUGH: Thank you, Richard. A very small glass.

[RICHARD *hands him a glass.*]

HUGH: Yes, well, good health. And – um – where's the girl of the moment.

ANTHEA: She's coming down. She takes hours over everything these days. She's been getting ready since this morning.

HUGH: Oh well, after all, that's ... that's – er ... that's – er ... that's ...

RICHARD: Youth.

HUGH: Yes. Youth, yes.

[*A pause.*]

LOUISE [*laughing suddenly*]: This is fun, isn't it?

ANTHEA: Yes, yes.

[*A pause.*]

HUGH [*confidentially*]: Er, I thought we'd check first – er – we didn't quite know what to give her ...

ANTHEA: Oh no, no. For heaven's sake, don't give her anything. She's most horribly spoilt.

HUGH [*producing a small, badly wrapped parcel*]: Yes, well – it's a bit – a bit obvious but – I wondered if she'd like this ... if not, I could probably get her something else – but – er – you see – quickly, have a look. [*Showing* ANTHEA] It's a cross, you see. It belonged to my grandmother, actually.

ANTHEA: Oh, Hugh, it's lovely.

HUGH: It's not at all valuable or anything.

ANTHEA: It's beautiful. Look, Richard.

RICHARD [*approving*]: Lovely.

HUGH: Do you think she might ...

ANTHEA: Oh, she'd adore it. She loves anything like this, doesn't she, Richard?

RICHARD: Are you sure you want to give it away, Hugh?

HUGH: Oh yes, yes.

RICHARD: I mean, wouldn't Louise like it?

HUGH: No, Louise wanted her to have it.

LOUISE: Yes, she must have it. She must have it. Debbie must have it.

ANTHEA: Well, it's glorious. She'll love it.

[*Slight pause.*]

Sven and Olive gave her a record token.

HUGH: Ah-ha.

OLIVE: It was quite a big record token.

HUGH: Yes. Well, that's probably something much nearer to her heart if we did but know it.

[*Another pause.*]

LOUISE [*laughing again*]: Really fun, isn't it?

ANTHEA: Look, I'm going to see where Debbie's got to. Her friends are going to start arriving soon and Sven and Olive have got a journey and, well, we've all got things to do, haven't we? Won't be a sec.

[ANTHEA *goes.*

A silence.]

RICHARD: Brian, come and have a glass of this.

BRIAN [*coming out of the tennis court*]: All right, thanks. [*Sensing the atmosphere*] Thank you. [*He takes his glass.*]

HUGH [*indicating tennis court*]: And that's where it's all happening, is it?

BRIAN: Oh yes, yes. Just been rigging up the sound.

RICHARD: Now, remember, if it gets too much for you, let us know. We won't let them go on too late.

HUGH: Oh, a little bit of music ... do us good, eh? [*Smiles at* LOUISE.]

LOUISE: Yes.

RICHARD: I'll cut them off at the mains if it gets too much.

HUGH: Well, don't worry on our account.

SVEN: Young people, eh?

HUGH: Yes.

SVEN: If you have children, you must expect to pay the penalty.

HUGH [*clouding*]: Yes ... yes ...

   [*A pause.*]

SVEN: Yes, yes, yes. [*To* OLIVE] Remember that hotel? They actually stole my shoes.

OLIVE: Yes, dear.

HUGH: Oh.

   [*A pause.*
   LOUISE *starts singing softly.* TEDDY BEARS PICNIC
   HUGH *looks apprehensive but before anyone can really react,* ANTHEA *enters, ushering in* DEBBIE, *her eighteen-year-old daughter. A pleasantly 'normal' girl with a great deal of* ANTHEA's *straightforwardness about her. Although (being younger) in older company she is at present understandably shy.*]

ANTHEA: Eureka.

RICHARD: Oh, I don't believe it.

OLIVE: Ah, here she is.

LOUISE: Hallo, Debbie.

SVEN: Debbie, my dear.

HUGH: Hallo.

SVEN: Look at the child. Look at the dear child, how she grows.

DEBBIE: Hallo.

BRIAN [*offering a drink*]: Debbie, will you?

DEBBIE: Thank you, Uncle Brian ... [*Confused*] I mean, Brian. I'm sorry.

BRIAN [*embarrassed*]: I made her promise not to call me Uncle Brian now she's eighteen.

OLIVE: Yes, well. Makes you feel your age.

SVEN: I'm sorry I can't bound up to greet you, Debbie, in my customary fashion but, you know, we old men, eh?

DEBBIE: Thank you very much for the token.

SVEN: Well ...

OLIVE: A little something.

[*Pause.*]

ANTHEA: Well, look, darling, we're not going to embarrass you any more. Heaven knows why we're doing this really. I suppose it's because we're all people who are very fond of you and we wanted, on your birthday, to say it to you personally. Just quickly. So, you know I'm awful at speeches, but I'm sorry if we're being a drag for you. Happy birthday, darling, that's all. And may you have many happy ones to come.

LOUISE: Hear, hear.

BRIAN: Hear, hear.

ALL

RICHARD [*raising his glass*]: To you, Debbie. Happy birthday.

   [*They are about to drink.*]

SVEN: Sorry, Anthea ... May I just? Excuse me, Richard ... Debbie, I just wanted to add a word, if I may. I wish you success, Debbie. I know you will have success because you come from a family which knows nothing but success. There are some lucky ones among us who we refer to as being born with a silver spoon in their mouths. You, Debbie, have been born with a whole canteen of cutlery. May I, on behalf of life's losers, those of us without a lousy plastic teaspoon to our name, ask you, please to accept humble greetings from one middle-aged mediocrity ...

   [OLIVE *starts crying.*]

Shut up, Olive ... who has fought and lost. Remember if you will, Debbie, this saying: The tragedy of life is not that man loses but that he almost wins.

   [*A silence except for* OLIVE's *sobs.*
   SVEN *shrugs, a man exhausted. His chin drops on his chest.*]

DEBBIE [*totally stunned*]: Thank you.

ANTHEA [*softly*]: Olive, dear.

   [LOUISE *laughs for no good reason.*]

HUGH [*moving forward tentatively*]: Debbie, we thought perhaps you'd care to ... We thought perhaps you might like ...

   [HUGH *offers the present.*
   DEBBIE *accepts.*]

DEBBIE: Oh, thank you. [*She holds it.*] Thank you very much.

LOUISE: Open it up, Debbie.

ANTHEA [*prompting*]: Open it.

DEBBIE: All right.

   [DEBBIE *opens the present.*]

LOUISE: Isn't it gorgeous?

DEBBIE: Yes. Thank you. Very much.

ANTHEA: Aren't you lucky?

HUGH [*clearing his throat*]: We felt that that little gift, Debbie, would help to remind you in the days ahead ... when you walk in the paths, that ... nevertheless, in that, you will find a reminder of all the good things in life. That are important. I think they're important anyway and I'm sure you do. And that you will remember and treasure it always in your heart. I think, Debbie, that you could do a lot worse than hold up your mother ... in your eyes, as it were, as someone very much to live by, as is your father too, in a different way. I think, knowing these wonderful people as I do, you should be very proud.

[*He steps back.*]

ANTHEA: Thank you, Hugh.

[DEBBIE *looks totally baffled.*]

DEBBIE: Thank you.

[LOUISE *starts to sing a hymn.*
They stare at her.
She invites them to join in.]

HUGH: Louise ...

RICHARD [*briskly*]: Well, I think that's as good a cue as any for us all to buzz off and leave you to your party, Debbie.

ANTHEA: Yes, quite right. Look at the time. We've got to feed them all and put them on the road. Olive, would you ...

OLIVE [*blowing her nose and helping* SVEN *to rise*]: Yes.

[LOUISE *sings on.*]

ANTHEA: Hugh?

HUGH [*apologetically*]: I am sorry. She's ... we're changing the prescription on Monday.

ANTHEA: That's quite all right. I think it's rather jolly.

HUGH: It is in short bursts, but she can go on indefinitely. She falls asleep singing.

ANTHEA: It's like Christmas.

HUGH: Anthea, I must talk to you urgently.

ANTHEA: Yes, all right, Hugh. Later, later. In you go.

[*She ushers them along.*
SVEN *and* OLIVE *are on the path to the house.*]

OLIVE [*passing* DEBBIE, *gripping her arm*]: God bless you, Debbie.

DEBBIE: Thank you.

SVEN: I won't wish you good luck, Debbie. It's people like us who need good luck.

[SVEN *and* OLIVE *go out.*]

LOUISE: Bye bye, Debbie.

DEBBIE: Good-bye.

HUGH: Good-bye, Debbie.

DEBBIE: Thank you. Good-bye.

LOUISE: Bye bye.

[HUGH *and* LOUISE *go out.*]

BRIAN: Shall I switch things on, now?

RICHARD: Oh, would you, Brian? Thanks. We'll set everything working for you, Debbie.

BRIAN [*going into the court*]: Shall I put on some music?

RICHARD: Yes, not too loud. Not till the Holmensons are on their way.

[RICHARD *gathers up the glasses.*

BRIAN *goes out of sight.*

ANTHEA *moves towards the house.*

She stops by DEBBIE.]

ANTHEA: Well done, darling. You coped very well with all that. Very tactful.

DEBBIE: Haven't you got any normal friends at all?

ANTHEA: What on earth do you mean?

DEBBIE: Well, they're sort of lost-looking.

ANTHEA: I don't think you could call them ... not really. You see, I've always said this to you, Debbie, some of us are very lucky. We have everything we want. We've got enough money. We've got people we love round us all the time and it's easy enough to forget those who haven't. But I think it really is up to us who have, to help the others a little bit.

RICHARD: You think it might be worth opening that champagne?

ANTHEA: There's a thought.

RICHARD: Might just cheer things up a bit.

ANTHEA: Well, I could do with it.

RICHARD: Right.

[*He moves towards the house.*]

ANTHEA: Don't forget the pie.

RICHARD: Under control.

ANTHEA: And there's some fresh baked bread on the top.

RICHARD: Right. [*Kissing* DEBBIE *in passing*] Happy birthday, darling.

DEBBIE: Thank you. [*She kisses him.*]

RICHARD [*going*]: Be good.

[RICHARD *goes into the house.*

Soft music from the speakers in the tennis court.]

RICHARD [*off as he goes*]: That sounds good.

ANTHEA: Lovely. Are you going to do the lights, Brian?

BRIAN [*off*]: Yes.

ANTHEA [*confidentially to* DEBBIE]: Darling ...

DEBBIE: Mmm?

ANTHEA: Could you try and be specially nice to Brian while he's here this time?

DEBBIE: How do you mean?

ANTHEA: Well, don't tease him about his age like you do. I mean, Daddy and I don't mind but Brian's rather sensitive.

DEBBIE: Oh well, he asks for it. He dyes his hair, did you know?

ANTHEA: Well, he's got no one at the moment and so he's rather lonely.

DEBBIE: What are you suggesting? I'm not getting that close. He's terribly creepy.

ANTHEA: Now, Debbie, he's perfectly harmless.

DEBBIE: He is not harmless.

ANTHEA: Nonsense, of course he is.

DEBBIE: What about all these girls he brings down?

ANTHEA: Ssh.

DEBBIE: Well.

ANTHEA: He never does anything with them. [*The lights go on.*] Oh, lovely!

DEBBIE: How do you know?

ANTHEA: Because I know Brian. My God, darling, I was only just a bit older than you when I shared a room with him for three months. Nothing happened. Nothing.

DEBBIE: Gosh. Do you think he's . . .

ANTHEA: No, he's a nothing. He's a neutral. All I'm saying is be pleasant.
     [BRIAN *emerges from the tennis court.*]
     Doesn't that all look splendid? I must see to people. Have a lovely party, darling. [*She kisses* DEBBIE.]

DEBBIE: Thank you. [*She kisses* ANTHEA.]

ANTHEA [*as she goes*]: If you're still dancing at dawn, I'll join you.
     [BRIAN *and* DEBBIE *stand.*]

BRIAN: Well. Anything else I can do?

DEBBIE: No. [*Pause*] No, I can't think of anything.

BRIAN: Right. Well, have a good party.

DEBBIE: Thank you.

BRIAN [*about to say something else*]: Well, I'll – go in . . .

DEBBIE: Yes.
     [BRIAN *moves towards the house.*]
     Er . . .

BRIAN [*stopping and turning*]: Yes?

DEBBIE: Oh, nothing. Good night.

BRIAN: 'Night.
     [BRIAN *goes into the house.*

DEBBIE *watches him go.*]
DEBBIE [*to herself, wrinkling her face in disgust*]: Uggh. Sorry. Not even
for Mummy.
[*She dances by herself to the music while waiting for her guests to arrive.*]

CURTAIN

SISTERLY FEELINGS

First produced at the Stephen Joseph Theatre-in-the-Round, Scarborough, on 10 January 1979 and subsequently at The National Theatre in the Olivier Theatre, London, on 3 June 1980 with the following cast:

RALPH	*Andrew Cruickshank*
ABIGAIL	*Penelope Wilton*
DORCAS	*Anna Carteret*
MELVYN	*Greg Hicks*
LEN	*Michael Bryant*
RITA	*Susan Williamson*
PATRICK	*Michael Gambon*
BRENDA	*Selina Cadell*
SIMON	*Stephen Moore*
STAFFORD	*Simon Callow*
MURPHY	*Michael Fenner*
MAJOR LIDGETT	*Gordon Whiting*

Directed by Alan Ayckbourn and Christopher Morahan
Designed by Alan Tagg

ACT ONE
Scene One: February, Thursday afternoon
Scene Two: June, Sunday afternoon

ACT TWO
Scene One: September, Saturday afternoon
Scene Two: November, Saturday afternoon

ACT ONE
SCENE ONE

Prologue

A section of Pendon Common. A steep grassy bank with planked steps cut into it allows access to the top and, presumably, the view over the rest of the Common beyond. At the foot of this bank, a grassy area flat and lush like a meadow. There is the odd patch of bramble about, perhaps the occasional small tree. Three quarters of the way up the bank, a plain one-plank bench set in a concrete plinth.

It is at present late February. A cold, damp day, about 2.30 p.m. An occasional bird is heard perhaps, maybe the distant rumble of traffic on the main Pendon to Reading road. Incongruously, the meadow area is occupied by ten figures all in black or dark clothes. Clearly a funeral party.

First, DR RALPH MATTHEWS, *a robust man of seventy. Next to him, his brother-in-law,* LEN COKER, *Det. Insp. in the local force. A sallow fifty-year-old, awkward in his unaccustomed best dark suit. With* LEN, *his wife* RITA, *a woman of forty-five with the air of one persecuted by fate. Next, the eldest of* RALPH'S *three children,* ABIGAIL, *aged twenty-six. Like her brother and sister, she has a somewhat naïve air and her impetuosity has only been slightly dulled by two years of marriage to* PATRICK SMYTHE, *her husband, aged thirty.*

DORCAS, ABIGAIL'S *sister, twenty-four. There is at first glance a superficial resemblance between the two women.* DORCAS *stands with her current 'attachment',* STAFFORD WILKINS, *also aged about twenty-four. He is a thin, unkempt young man who gives the impression of having inner fires that have been dampened by ceaseless disappointment. He is dressed or perhaps he has been dressed to suit the occasion but it is evidently from a limited wardrobe.*

The youngest of RALPH'S *children is* MELVYN, *twenty years old and, although at present subdued by the recent funeral, still very much young, confident and greatly in love. The object of his affections, his fiancée,* BRENDA, *nineteen years old, clings to his arm. A pleasant if rather deadpan girl. Beside them, finally, standing slightly apart as befits a comparative stranger to the group,* SIMON GRIMSHAW, BRENDA'S *older brother — a good looking, well-built man of twenty-eight. He is distinguished further by an unEnglish tan.*

The group stand now silent and respectful. RALPH *has apparently said*

*something recently and has now paused reflectively. The others wait for him
to continue.*

RALPH [*eventually*]: Yes . . .

RITA [*agreeing*]: Mmm. Mmm.

LEN: Fancy.

RALPH: That was twenty-eight years ago, mark you. I'm going back a
bit now.

RITA: Oh yes. You're going back twenty-eight years.

LEN: Nearly thirty years, yes.

RALPH: There used to be a bench, you see. You know what I mean by
a bench? A public bench? It was around here somewhere. Gone now.

ABIGAIL: There's a bench over there, father.

RITA: Oh yes, look, there's one over there.

RALPH [*slightly irritable*]: No, no, no. This was a different bench. Totally
different. It wasn't that one. That bench is recent. That's only been
here a matter of, what . . . ?

LEN: They have to replace those benches every three or four years, you
know. I mean, once the vandals get at them . . .

RALPH: Four or five years. Five years at the most.

LEN: I mean, it used to be three or four years but the way things are going
now it's probably nearer every year. These days.

RITA: These days. Yes.

LEN: I mean, we in the Police Force, we do what we can but there's
nothing we can do, you see. We're powerless. I mean, the time was
you'd catch your vandal on the job, over your knee and wallop. No hard
feelings. But nowadays, legislation favours the vandal . . .

RITA: The Police are powerless. Len's powerless.

RALPH [*who hasn't been listening*]: Yes, yes . . .

LEN: Anyway, that's where your benches go, if you want to know.

PATRICK: Time's getting on, Ralph, if you want to . . .

RALPH: Yes. I just wanted to . . . I just wanted to show everybody
something . . .

ABIGAIL: Does it have to be today, Pa?

RALPH: It's only at the top there. Just a few steps.

PATRICK [*to himself*]: Oh, my God. [*He looks at his watch.*]

RALPH: You remember this place, Dorcas? Abi? You remember us all
coming out here?

DORCAS: Yes, Pa, for picnics.

RALPH: Picnics, yes. I think you were too young, weren't you, Melvyn?

MELVYN: No, I remember.

RALPH [*riding over this as he has a habit of doing, to* LEN *and* RITA]:

He'd've been too young, you see. He was an after-thought, that boy. Amy and I'd forgotten all about it by the time we had him. Wonderful picnics we had, Len. Your sister and I.

[BRENDA *snuggles up to* MELVYN.]

MELVYN: You cold?

BRENDA: No, I'm fine.

RALPH: Now, follow on, everyone. I insist that you see this view. If you haven't seen it, it's really ... well, it's a marvellous view right over the Common.

[RITA *has begun struggling up the slope semi-assisted by* LEN.]

Can you manage, Rita?

RITA: Yes. Yes, it's just this ...

LEN: Here, lean on me properly. You'll be all right.

[RALPH *moves fairly nimbly up the slope.* MELVYN, BRENDA *and* SIMON *move forward to follow.* LEN *struggles with* RITA.]

DORCAS [*watching this*]: Oh dear. Why does he always choose days like this ...

LEN [*seeing* MELVYN *and* BRENDA *are trying to get past*]: Let the young ones through, Rita.

RITA: Oh yes, let them get past.

MELVYN: Thank you.

[RALPH *has vanished momentarily over the top of the hill.* MELVYN *and* BRENDA *have slipped past the struggling* RITA *and followed* RALPH. SIMON *lingers wondering whether to help.*]

ABIGAIL [*to* PATRICK]: O.K.?

PATRICK: Perfect.

SIMON [*tentatively to* LEN *and* RITA]: Could I ... ?

RITA [*offering a hand*]: Oh, would you?

SIMON: Certainly.

LEN: Careful.

ABIGAIL: Are you coming up?

PATRICK: No. I think I'd prefer to stand here and watch the last of my thirty-guinea shoes sinking slowly into the mud.

LEN: Careful, careful.

RITA: Ooh.

SIMON [*who's been too hearty with her*]: Sorry.

RITA: It's my knee, you see.

ABIGAIL: Well, why do you keep standing there, darling? Why don't you stand on firm ground?

PATRICK: Because there is none, my sweet. There is no firm ground. We are standing in a marsh.

LEN: Has it locked?

RITA: I think it has.

SIMON: I'm most awfully sorry.

PATRICK: You see, we all somewhat foolishly came dressed for a funeral. We steeled ourselves to face perhaps some light breezes; maybe a little rain round the graveside; the odd bit of churchyard gravel underfoot. We came prepared for that. But your father, in his wisdom, has decided instead to lead us all into a bloody swamp.

[RALPH *has reappeared at the top.*]

DORCAS: Patrick ...

RALPH: What's your husband rabbiting about down there, Abi?

ABIGAIL: Nothing.

[LEN *and* SIMON *are lowering* RITA *on to the bench.*]

LEN: Down you go, down you go.

RITA: Yes, yes, that's it.

LEN: I think you'll have to have another look at Rita's knee again, Ralph, if you would.

RALPH: Nothing I can do for that knee – delightful though it is. She needs an operation. I've told her that.

RITA: I'm not having an operation. I'd sooner have the knee.

PATRICK: Ralph, could I briefly remind you that I had arranged to deliver you back home by 2.45?

RALPH [*to* RITA]: Then you'll have to put up with it, won't you? You know, Len, I think this was the bench.

RITA: Next thing I know, they'll have my leg off.

PATRICK [*without conviction*]: 2.45, Ralph. I do have a meeting ... [*To himself*] As if that matters a damn to anyone.

ABIGAIL: I'll remind him.

PATRICK: Please do or I shall go without you.

ABIGAIL: Patrick ... !

PATRICK: Five minutes. Then I'm off.

[PATRICK *goes back to the car.*]

ABIGAIL [*calling vainly after him*]: We can't all get home in one car ... Oh, God.

DORCAS: He won't go.

ABIGAIL: Don't you believe it ...

[ABIGAIL *goes off after* PATRICK.]

LEN [*to* RITA]: Right, are you fit?

RITA [*struggling to her feet*]: Yes, yes.

RALPH [*returning to them*]: Come and look at this view. It's absolutely stunning.

SIMON [*offering to help* LEN]: Can I ... ?

LEN: No, no.

RITA: No, no, no.

LEN: Leave her to me.

[LEN *and* RITA *slowly disappear over the brow of the hill.*]

RALPH [*as they go*]: You'd be better off with a wooden leg, anyway, Rita. Drop of linseed oil, that's all you'd ever need.

RITA: Oh, don't say things like that.

[LEN *and* RITA *exit.*]

RALPH: Dorcas, you coming up?

DORCAS: No, we'll wait here, Pa, if you don't mind. We're not dressed for mountaineering. Besides we have seen it.

RALPH [*seeing* STAFFORD]: What about thing? Young thing there.

[STAFFORD *who is crouching studying blades of grass intently, doesn't hear.*]

DORCAS: Stafford?

STAFFORD: Eh?

RALPH: Come up here, boy, have a look at the view. You look as if you need the exercise.

DORCAS [*gently*]: Go on.

STAFFORD [*reluctantly*]: All right.

[*He starts slowly up the slope pulling out a cigarette as he does so.*]

RALPH [*meanwhile*]: You know, Dorcas, I think this was the bench, you know. It's the very same one I proposed to your mother on. Isn't that extraordinary?

DORCAS: Good heavens.

RALPH [*as* STAFFORD *draws close to him*]: And don't light that. You don't need a cigarette. You want some air. You keep smoking those things, you'll get full of soot. [*Calling*] I'm telling him, Dorcas, if he keeps smoking these, you'll have to have him swept.

DORCAS: Nothing to do with me.

STAFFORD [*disappearing over the hill*]: Oh, Jesus . . .

RALPH: We really must have a picnic again, you know. As soon as the weather's better. One Sunday. When you're home.

DORCAS: Lovely.

RALPH: Great fun. What's the matter with that boy?

DORCAS: How do you mean?

RALPH: He's always miserable. I've never seen him smile. Does he ever smile at you?

DORCAS: Sometimes.

RALPH: A woman needs to be smiled at, you know. Good for them. What is it? His stomach?

DORCAS: No. His principles.

RALPH: Oh, God help him. No cure for those.

[ABIGAIL *returns holding* RALPH's *scarf.*]

ABIGAIL: Pa, if you're going to gallivant around like this, for heaven's sake put your scarf on, will you?

RALPH: We were just wondering how we could cheer up Dorcas's thing.

ABIGAIL: Stafford? Oh, I wouldn't bother. Here. [*She holds out the scarf.*]

[RALPH *comes down the slope slightly to take it.*]

How are you feeling, Pa?

RALPH: Oh, I'm perfectly fine.

ABIGAIL: Are you?

RALPH: I'm sad your mother's gone. I mean, it wasn't a surprise. We all knew it was going to happen sooner or later but all the same, it's ... sad. [*Pause*] I'll say this though, now we're alone. If you get one quarter the happiness out of your marriages – or your relationships or what have you ... if you get one quarter what your mother and I had, then I'll envy you.

DORCAS: You can never guarantee it.

RALPH: It entirely depends what you both put into it.

DORCAS: Aha.

ABIGAIL [*dry*]: With strong emphasis on the 'both'.

[MELVYN *appears at the top.* BRENDA *is still in tow.*]

MELVYN: Dad, is that St Mary's Church spire or Pendon Church?

RALPH [*to the girls*]: You take a tip from that one. He knows what he's about. Don't you?

MELVYN: What?

RALPH [*reclimbing the slope*]: Where's Pendon Church supposed to be?

MELVYN: Over there behind us.

RALPH: Not unless it's been moved. You ought to know that. You're looking north-west that way. Pendon'll be over there.

[RALPH, MELVYN *and* BRENDA *go off.*

ABIGAIL *and* DORCAS *are alone.*]

ABIGAIL: Was this really where we came for picnics? I suppose it was. I remember it as much bigger.

[*An impatient car horn.*]

ABIGAIL [*calling*]: All right. My husband is at his worst today. It is my mother's funeral and all he can think about is his bloody meeting. I don't know how long I can cope. I honestly don't. [*Indicating* RALPH] It's all right for him and his 'what you put into it'. I've flung the lot in and it's disappeared without trace.

DORCAS: You shouldn't have given up your job.

ABIGAIL: We can't have Mrs Smythe working, can we? That won't do.

DORCAS: We're going to have to sort Pa out, you know.

ABIGAIL [*abstracted*]: Oh yes.

DORCAS: I mean, if in the long run we consider it best that I come home and look after him . . .

ABIGAIL: Well, we'll see, shall we?

DORCAS: I hastily add I don't want to. I love him. But not that much. It's taken me a hell of a long time to get where I am and unless I have to . . .

ABIGAIL: No, well, don't.

DORCAS: I mean, I've got my own programme now, you know.

ABIGAIL: Yes.

DORCAS: Twice a week.

ABIGAIL: Yes.

DORCAS: Half an hour.

ABIGAIL: Super.

DORCAS: Well . . .

ABIGAIL: Do people listen? I mean . . .

DORCAS [*flaring*]: Yes, they do listen. Thousands of people listen. Do you have any idea of the daytime listening figures for local radio?

ABIGAIL: O.K. O.K.

DORCAS: Well, it's a lot of people. A lot of people listen to radio. I know you don't.

ABIGAIL: I don't. Well, I can never find anything on our radio. Except cricket or German stations. Mind you, ours is so complicated. You press buttons and all sorts of lights flash on and off and then Germans start talking in the bathroom . . .[*Slight pause*] Don't worry about Pa. We'll keep an eye on him. I'll keep an eye on him.

DORCAS: That's right. We used to toboggan down this slope. It all comes back to me now.

ABIGAIL: Stafford seems his usual jolly self.

DORCAS: Oh yes. There are problems. I think I've found a way to use him on my programme anyway. That'll help. You know, book reviewing and the odd interview. Could help his confidence. Mind you, he's not at his best today. He doesn't approve of all this, you see.

ABIGAIL: What, you mean the funeral?

DORCAS: No. He came along but he deliberately refused to go into the church for the service.

ABIGAIL: Didn't he come in? I never noticed.

DORCAS: No, I don't think anyone noticed. Except me. That's why he's upset really. I mean, what's the point of standing outside in a freezing churchyard for hours on end if no one notices. I suppose God might have done.

ABIGAIL: And mother.

DORCAS: She'll have laughed.

ABIGAIL: So would God, I should think. Are you going to marry this Stafford man?

DORCAS: No.

ABIGAIL: Thank goodness.

DORCAS: He doesn't believe in marriage either.

[PATRICK *returns*.]

PATRICK [*genially*]: Just to say quickly – sorry to interrupt – just to say cheerio, love, see you later on tonight.

ABIGAIL: What are you doing?

PATRICK: I'm going. I said 2.45. It is now 2.50. We're in injury time and I'm off.

ABIGAIL: Patrick, you cannot leave us here.

PATRICK: Sorry. I did say.

ABIGAIL: You realize people are going to have to walk home?

PATRICK: Sorry.

[PATRICK *has gone*.]

ABIGAIL: Patrick! God, the bastard. Patrick! The b – a – s – t ... Now what are we going to do?

DORCAS: Walk, I suppose. [*Calling*] Pa! Pa, we're going ...

ABIGAIL: I'll see if I can stop him.

[ABIGAIL *goes out after* PATRICK.]

DORCAS [*calling*]: Pa.

[SIMON *appears at the top of the hill*.]

SIMON: Hallo. Want some help?

DORCAS: No, it's all right. Could you just hurry them up, please.

SIMON [*coming down the slope*]: Right. They're just coming. Been a slight mishap.

DORCAS: What's happened?

SIMON: Nothing much. Your aunt's fallen down a hole, actually.

DORCAS: God.

SIMON: Quite a small one. She's a bit shaken up, that's all. [*Waving car keys*] I said I'd get her boot from the stick. Or rather her stick from the boot. Excuse me.

[*As he turns, he nearly collides with* ABIGAIL *returning*.]

Excuse me. Just getting the ... [*He waves the keys and goes off.*]

ABIGAIL: Well, Pat's gone. He's driven off, nearly running me over in the process. In films, if the wife jumps out in front of the car waving her arms, the husband generally pulls up with a scream of brakes. Patrick accelerates and drives straight at me.

DORCAS: How many does Len's car hold? Five at a pinch, I reckon. That's Len, Auntie Rita, Pa and two others. The rest of us can walk.

ABIGAIL: I'm not walking. Not in these shoes. It's miles.

DORCAS: Well, all right. You and Brenda go. We'll start walking and Len can come back for us.

ABIGAIL: That's if we can prise Brenda away from Melvyn for that long. God, she's a dreary girl. I tried to talk to her in the car. Everything I said – [*Imitating* BRENDA] Gneeer.

DORCAS [*similarly*]: Gneeer.

ABIGAIL: She'll have to go. I mean, Melvyn is not getting stuck with that.

DORCAS: The main worry is she's stopped him doing any work. If he doesn't get his exams this summer, they'll sling him out of Medical School.

ABIGAIL: She'll have to go.

DORCAS: Gneeer.

[STAFFORD *comes stamping down the slope.*]
Are they coming?

STAFFORD: Stupid old bag's fallen down a hole.

ABIGAIL: Who has?

DORCAS: Rita. She's O.K.

STAFFORD: My shoes are leaking.

DORCAS: Good, it'll wash your feet. Did you push her?

STAFFORD: Who?

DORCAS: Auntie Rita.

STAFFORD: No, her fascist husband, wasn't it?

ABIGAIL: Len pushed her?

STAFFORD: The fascist.

DORCAS: Well, I've got some wonderful news for you. You're going to have to walk home now.

STAFFORD [*appalled*]: Walk?

ABIGAIL: Yes. That other great fascist, my husband, has gone off in his car.

STAFFORD [*stamping off*]: Oh, Jesus.
[*He nearly collides with* SIMON *who is on his way back with* RITA'S *walking stick.*]

SIMON: Whoops, sorry, old boy.

DORCAS: You're very athletic.

SIMON: I'm very out of training. Your husband's car's gone, did you know?

ABIGAIL: Yes, thank you.

SIMON: Oh. Oh well. Walk'll do us good, won't it? Shan't be a tick.
[SIMON *bounds up the slope with great ease and is gone.*]

ABIGAIL: Well, say what you like about Brenda ...

DORCAS: Gneeer.

ABIGAIL: Her brother's a bit of all right, isn't he? Where did she find him? I didn't even know she had a brother.

DORCAS: Apparently he's been abroad till recently. Africa.

ABIGAIL: What is he? An oilman?

DORCAS: No. Machinery, I think he said.

ABIGAIL: Oh. Married, of course?

DORCAS: No. Divorced, apparently.

ABIGAIL: Oh.

DORCAS: He's quite nice, isn't he? I mean, he tends to call you 'old bean' a bit. I suppose that comes of living in Africa.

ABIGAIL: How come you know him and I don't?

DORCAS: Well, he's a great friend of Mel's and ... um ... you don't get invited to Christmas dances at the rugger club, do you?

ABIGAIL: What, with Patrick? He faints at the sight of a goal post. Does Simon play?

DORCAS: Yes. Wing forward.

ABIGAIL: Is that good?

DORCAS: Tough.

ABIGAIL: God. No wonder Stafford's sulking.

DORCAS: How do you mean?

ABIGAIL: If he thinks he's competing with that.

DORCAS: Rubbish.

ABIGAIL: How do you mean?

DORCAS: What I say. Mind your own business. Rubbish.

ABIGAIL: What have I said?

DORCAS: Keep your nose out.

[ABIGAIL *looks at her.*]

ABIGAIL: Oooo-hoooo-hoooo.[*Slyly*] Toss you for him then.

DORCAS: Don't be childish, Abigail, be your age.

ABIGAIL: Oooo-hoooo-hoooo.

DORCAS [*a little hot and embarrassed*]: I'm going to find Stafford.

[DORCAS *goes towards the car.* ABIGAIL *pulls a face. In a second,* SIMON *appears at the top of the slope.*]

SIMON [*smiling at* ABIGAIL]: Hallo.

ABIGAIL [*with new charm*]: Hallo.

SIMON: They're all coming. She's able to walk.

ABIGAIL: Oh, good.

[RALPH *appears with* RITA *and* LEN *following behind.*]

RALPH: What's that Patrick doing, driving off like that?

ABIGAIL: I'm sorry, Pa, he couldn't wait.

RALPH: Well, someone's going to have to walk and it won't be me. [*Descending the slope*] Rita's fallen down again.

ABIGAIL: Yes, I heard she had.

RALPH: I think she drinks, you know.

ABIGAIL: No, she doesn't. It's your fault, Pa, you shouldn't take her up hills.

RALPH [*ignoring this*]: Anyway, the first fine day we have this year and there probably won't be more than one anyway, we're going to have a picnic. That's settled.

RITA [*descending the slope*]: Carefully, now, carefully.

LEN: All right. Let me take the weight, let me take the weight.

RALPH: How many can your car hold, Len?

LEN: Four. Not more than four. The springs won't take it.

RALPH: How many of us are there, then?

ABIGAIL: Nine. There must be nine of us now Patrick's gone.

LEN: He's a big help, he is.

SIMON: I've said I don't mind walking at all.

RALPH: Splendid. That makes eight, then.

LEN: You're going to have to take another look at this knee, Ralph.

RALPH: Yes, with the greatest of pleasure but not in the middle of a field.

[MELVYN *and* BRENDA *emerge from the top of the slope and start down. Simultaneously,* DORCAS *returns from the direction of the road.*]

DORCAS: Stafford's not waiting. He's gone. He's going to hitch back to the village.

RALPH: Splendid. Now we're seven. Any more volunteers?

MELVYN: We'll walk.

RALPH: Good lad.

MELVYN: You don't mind walking, do you, Bren?

BRENDA: No.

ABIGAIL [*sotto*]: Gneeer.

LEN: They shouldn't be there, those holes up there, you know. I think they've been dug maliciously. I'm going to have a quiet word about this in the right ear. I mean, if Rita had fallen badly, this would have been very serious.

[LEN *and* RITA *have gone to the car.*]

RALPH [*making to follow them*]: We'll be waiting in the car, you lot. You sort it out between you. One spare seat going. That's all. You used to toboggan down that slope, you know, Dorcas. Do you remember that?

DORCAS: Yes, Pa.

RALPH: Yes. [*He gazes at the slope.*] I'm glad we stopped, you know. I couldn't have come home straight away.

[RALPH *leaves. Slight pause.*]

MELVYN: Well, we'll be starting off then.

ABIGAIL: Yes, yes. We'll catch you up.

DORCAS: No, Abi, you're going in the car.

ABIGAIL: No, no, you go.

DORCAS: Don't be silly.

ABIGAIL: No, please.

DORCAS: But you said just now ...

ABIGAIL: No – no – please. You go.

[*Slight pause.*]

MELVYN: Well, see you there.

ABIGAIL: Yes.

DORCAS: Yes.

SIMON: Cheers, Mel. Bren.

[MELVYN *and* BRENDA *go.*]

Well ...

DORCAS: Now, for goodness sake, this is stupid. Abi, please ...

ABIGAIL: No, honestly.

DORCAS [*getting meaner*]: Abi.

ABIGAIL: What?

DORCAS: Simon, tell her to go in the car.

SIMON: Well ...

DORCAS: Simon ...

SIMON: Er ... [*Slight pause.*]

DORCAS: Oh, this is stupid. I mean, it's just stupid. There is no point
in the three of us walking. I mean, it's miles. It's stupid. It'll take
hours.

ABIGAIL: Quite.

SIMON: Well, why don't I go in the car? [*He laughs.*]

[DORCAS *and* ABIGAIL *look at him unamused.*
He stops laughing.
A distant car horn.]

SIMON: Well ... Tell you what, why don't you toss for it?

ABIGAIL: Why not?

DORCAS [*reluctantly*]: All right.

SIMON: O.K. [*Producing a coin*] Easy solution. Call. [*He tosses.*]

ABIGAIL: Heads.

[SIMON *has tossed in the manner of all good sporting referees. The coin
lands in the grass. The women move to examine it. They look at each
other. Depending on the result, either prearranged but preferably
random, one of them moves towards the car.*]

ABIGAIL:

or   O.K. See you back there, then.

DORCAS:

SIMON: Yes, right. See you. 'Bye. Think of us.

[*One sister leaves. A pause.* SIMON *scoops up the coin. The sound of a car starting up and departing.*]

Right. Here we go. Best foot forward, eh?

ABIGAIL:
or   Yes ...
DORCAS:

[*They go out.*
The lights fade.]

End of Act One Scene One

If Abigail leaves with Simon, Act One Scene Two A follows. If Dorcas leaves with him, the reader should turn to Act One Scene Two D (p. 269).

ABIGAIL: ACT ONE
SCENE TWO A

The scene break has been very swift. We return to the same but it is now a bright, sunny Sunday afternoon in June. STAFFORD *enters carrying a car rug and the Sunday papers. He throws the rug down, sits on it and starts to read.* DORCAS *enters, after a moment, bearing picnic baskets and paraphernalia.*

DORCAS: God, I wish there was a way we could park nearer. That car's overheating. [*She dumps down the gear.*] Stafford, you have carried precisely nothing.

STAFFORD [*swatting about him*]: Bloody wasps.

DORCAS: You're useless, Stafford. What are you? You're useless. I have to do everything, don't I?

STAFFORD [*unmoved by this*]: You're bigger than me.

DORCAS: No sign of the others. Stafford ...

STAFFORD [*reading*]: Uh?

DORCAS: You're going to have to try and join in a bit today.

STAFFORD [*looking up*]: Join in?

DORCAS: When the others arrive, when the picnic starts.

STAFFORD [*alarmed*]: Join in what?

DORCAS: Conversation, Stafford. Chitter chatter. Social niceties.

STAFFORD: God.

DORCAS: Like talking to my father. When he asks after you, you do not turn your back or bury your head and particularly you don't walk away.

STAFFORD: Walk away? When did I walk away?

DORCAS: Always. Always you're walking away. As soon as anyone says anything to you that you don't particularly like the sound of. I mean, unless there really is something wrong with you ...

STAFFORD: There's nothing wrong with me.

DORCAS: Well then.

STAFFORD: It just so happens I am that rare being, someone who doesn't automatically and egocentrically want to be the continual centre of attention.

DORCAS: Oh, cobblers.

STAFFORD: Eh?

DORCAS: Of course you do. What else do you think you want?

STAFFORD: What?

DORCAS: That's exactly what you want to be. By deliberately walking away from the centre of things, you're merely trying to draw attention to yourself, thus making yourself the centre of attention which is all you wanted in the first place.

STAFFORD: I – Oh ... God. [*He walks away.*]

DORCAS: There you go.

STAFFORD [*snarling*]: What now?

DORCAS: You're walking away.

STAFFORD [*flinging himself down*]: Oh.

DORCAS: What are you, Stafford? You're useless.

STAFFORD: Look, I'm a poet. I'm a writer. I'm not a Knightsbridge socialite.

DORCAS: Fine. Then be a poet, Stafford. Only in that case, let's at least see or hear some poetry.

STAFFORD: It's just, you know ... With you, it's fine. It's when I get among people. You know?

DORCAS: Yes, I know.

STAFFORD: I let you down, didn't I? I let you down with the BBC job. I blew it.

DORCAS: It doesn't matter.

STAFFORD: It matters to me. You gave me that chance and I blew it. You're a rock, kid. No one else has helped me like you have. I rely on you, Dorc. Do you know that?

DORCAS: Yes.

STAFFORD: Do you mind? Me relying on you?

DORCAS: No. That's all right.

STAFFORD: It's all right?

DORCAS: Only ...

STAFFORD: What?

DORCAS: Well, there are just occasions, Staff – I mean, only once in a very blue moon – when I need someone to prop me up for a change.

STAFFORD [*considering this*]: Yes. I see that, I see that. I'm getting it together. Just give me time, Dorc.

[MELVYN *and* BRENDA *enter.*
He carries the rest of the picnic gear.
She carries a stunter kite (still in its box) and the kite string separately.]

MELVYN: Here you are. I locked the car.

DORCAS: Dump them there. [*She indicates the spot where she's put the other gear.*] Any sign of the others?

MELVYN: No, not yet. If they've gone by way of the cemetery they won't be here for a bit. Not with Len driving at four miles an hour.

DORCAS: The regular weekly visit. Well, we finally made it. Perfect day. Not even Rita can complain.

MELVYN: Is Abi coming?

DORCAS: Abi probably, yes. But who with is anyone's guess.

MELVYN: Ah. [*He doesn't care to pursue that.*] Brought the kite.

DORCAS: Oh yes.

MELVYN [*taking it from* BRENDA]: Look, you see, it's a stunter.

DORCAS: Oh yes. All right, Brenda?

BRENDA: I'm all right.

DORCAS: Good. Not keeping Mel from his studies too much, are you?

BRENDA: What?

MELVYN: She's not.

DORCAS: Sure?

MELVYN: Don't keep on at her, Dorc.

DORCAS: I'm not.

MELVYN: Yes, you are.

DORCAS [*shrugging*]: All right. It's just you've got exams in a few days, haven't you?

MELVYN: Yes, all right.

[ABIGAIL *appears at the top of the slope.*]

ABIGAIL: Hallo.

DORCAS: Good lord, hallo. Where did you spring from?

ABIGAIL: Oh, I've been here some time.

DORCAS: Have you? Where did you park your car?

ABIGAIL: I didn't bring it.

DORCAS: Oh.

ABIGAIL: I cycled.

MELVYN: Cycled?

ABIGAIL: Yes.

DORCAS: You cycled?

ABIGAIL: Yes.

DORCAS: All alone?

ABIGAIL: Yes. Most of the way.

DORCAS: Ah.

ABIGAIL: Yes.

[*Slight pause.*

SIMON *appears at the top of the slope.*]

SIMON: Ah, hallo.

DORCAS [*heartily*]: Hallo.

MELVYN: Hallo.

SIMON: Smashing day.

DORCAS: Yes.

SIMON [*after a slight pause*]: What have you got there? Is it a kite?

MELVYN: Yeah. Brand new. Bought it yesterday.

SIMON: Looks a good one.

MELVYN: Have you flown this sort?

SIMON: I have done.

MELVYN: Stunters?

SIMON: Yes.

MELVYN: Great.

[*Pause.*]

ABIGAIL: My old bike's still marvellous, you know. We – I mean, I got it out of the garage and I oiled the chain and I gave it a good clean up – and things. And it's as good as new. I'm going to ache like hell tomorrow though.

DORCAS: Yes, I wouldn't be surprised.

SIMON: Well.

[*Slight pause.*
Suddenly, BRENDA *is galvanized into action.*]

BRENDA: Yeeeow – wur – wur – yow – wow – wow ...

DORCAS: What on earth's the matter?

MELVYN: It's all right, it's all right.

BRENDA: It's a wasp, it's a wasp.

MELVYN: It's gone, it's gone, it's all right.

BRENDA: Wur – wur –

MELVYN [*soothingly*]: It's all right, calm down. It's gone. [*To the others*] She doesn't like wasps.

ABIGAIL: Yes.

SIMON: Well, shall we fly it now or after tea?

MELVYN: Well, now if you like.

SIMON: There's a bit of breeze up there. They need a bit of wind you see, these stunters. It's the type with twin lines, I take it?

MELVYN: Yes, right. Are they difficult to handle?

SIMON: No, not really. I mean, only if the wind's very strong and then they're all over the place. [*Starting to climb the slope*] No, I've seen experts handling five or six at once.

MELVYN [*following with* BRENDA]: What, flying in formation?

SIMON: Right. Will you excuse us? We're just going kite flying. [*He gives* ABIGAIL *a swift one-armed hug and a kiss on the cheek.*] Won't be long.

ABIGAIL: Right.

[SIMON *goes off with* MELVYN *and* BRENDA.
ABIGAIL *attempts to meet* DORCAS'S *stare.*]

Pa gone to the cemetery first, has he?

DORCAS: Apparently.

ABIGAIL: The Sunday ritual.

DORCAS: Yes.

STAFFORD [*a suppressed snarl of rage at what he's reading*]: Gurrrr!

ABIGAIL: What's the matter with him?

DORCAS: Nothing. He's reading the Sunday papers. He always does that. Take no notice. [*Moving slightly away from* STAFFORD] Haven't seen you for a bit.

ABIGAIL: No. Well, I've been ... er ...

DORCAS: Yes.

ABIGAIL: Tell me, how does Pa seem to you these days? I mean, you see him less than I do so it's probably more noticeable to you. It's difficult for me to tell, seeing him, what, two or three times a week. He does seem to me to be getting – well – a bit odd. Do you find that?

DORCAS: He's always rather odd.

ABIGAIL: Yes. He keeps telling me he's seen mother.

DORCAS: He's told me that, too.

ABIGAIL: And sometimes, if you turn up unexpectedly, you can hear him talking to her in the other room.

DORCAS: He may be talking to himself.

ABIGAIL: No, no. The other day I heard him telling her a funny story. Roaring with laughter. Him that is. And then there's some days he refuses to wear socks and at least once a week he wants his bed moving round because of the way the earth's rotating ... I mean, he can't be senile, can he, not yet? He's not old enough. He's only just seventy. [*She reflects.*] That reminds me, it's his birthday soon.

DORCAS: I don't know why he gave up his practice. At least he met a lot of people.

ABIGAIL: Perhaps it's a good job he did. Otherwise he might have had all his patients shifting their beds about in their bare feet. Oh well, he's harmless at the moment. [*Slight pause*] How are you?

DORCAS: Not so bad.

ABIGAIL [*nodding towards* STAFFORD]: Things still all right with huh-huh?

DORCAS: Chugging on.

ABIGAIL: I see.

DORCAS: That's about all you can say. I shan't ask about you.

ABIGAIL: No.

DORCAS: You don't find it a problem?

ABIGAIL: No. [*Slight pause*] Yes. I don't know. [*A sudden outburst*] I'm sorry, Dorc, but I'm having a marvellous time. I know it sounds immature and adolescent to say it but he's just an amazing, super, wonderful, sexy, understanding man.

DORCAS: Oh, goodo.

ABIGAIL: And I'm incredibly happy.

[*Pause.*]

DORCAS: Is Patrick happy too?

ABIGAIL: Oh, don't go and spoil it by mentioning Patrick.

DORCAS: I'm sorry. I'm afraid I'm out of touch with all this. I take it Patrick knows?

ABIGAIL: I suppose he does. He's not a fool. I've never told him officially. We haven't discussed Simon. But then we don't discuss anything anyway. Unless it appears on Patrick's official breakfast-time agenda. And that consists mainly of food. Minutes of the last meal and proposals for the next.

DORCAS: Are you planning to leave him?

ABIGAIL: I might. I don't know. I honestly don't know. Simon wants me to, of course. But ...

DORCAS: You'd be giving up a lot.

ABIGAIL: Hah ...

DORCAS: Of course you would.

ABIGAIL: Perhaps. But look what I'd be getting.

DORCAS: In other words, you're still not fully committing yourself to Simon yet?

ABIGAIL: No. Not fully. [*Suspicious*] Why?

DORCAS: No reason.

[*Slight pause.*]

ABIGAIL [*happily*]: Oh, Dorc. You just don't know.

DORCAS: No. True enough.

[STAFFORD *comes across another offensive paragraph.*]

STAFFORD [*groaning*]: Gaaaarrrrrrr!

DORCAS: Still, while a girl has Stafford, things can't be all bad.

ABIGAIL: Is that permanent now?

DORCAS: No.

ABIGAIL: Why not?

DORCAS: I don't think that's practical. Not with Stafford. Unless I legally adopt him. I suppose that would make it permanent.

ABIGAIL: You don't hate me, do you? It was really only luck, wasn't it? I mean, that day. It could just as easily have been you and Simon. And if it had been the other way round, I would've ... I *would* have been. I promise. Thrilled. Delighted.

[BRENDA *enters down the slope.*]

BRENDA: It's flying, it's flying. Look.

DORCAS: Oh yes.

ABIGAIL: Wheee!

BRENDA [*going to her handbag, as she passes* STAFFORD]: It's so pretty. Look, look.

STAFFORD: Fantastic.

BRENDA: It's really lovely.

DORCAS [*to* ABIGAIL]: Well, until you've decided, please for God's sake don't let Pa hear about it.

ABIGAIL: Of course not.

DORCAS: He's very fond of you and Patrick. And I'd keep it from Uncle Len as well, unless you want it splashed all over the front of the *Police Gazette*.

BRENDA: Simon, can I have a go? Please, please. [*She runs off.*]

ABIGAIL: Now, there's a more urgent problem.

DORCAS: What?

ABIGAIL: That. [*She nods in* BRENDA's *direction.*]

DORCAS: Oh, that. Gneeer.

ABIGAIL: I mean, dear brother's more infatuated than ever. And she gets more horrific each day. Well, I've done my bit. He won't listen to me. I've tried.

DORCAS: I think it's a lost cause.

ABIGAIL: She'll trap him into marriage eventually. She's the type. Poor kid. I mean, he knows nothing. She'll destroy the boy. We can't let that happen, can we?

[SIMON *and* BRENDA *come on.*

BRENDA *holds the two control lines to an invisible kite somewhere offstage. She grips the plastic handles tied to the lines.* SIMON, *behind her, attempts to guide her actions by guiding her wrists.*]

SIMON: Now, keep it steady. Keep it steady. Now, pull on your left. Pull on your left. Left, left, left.

BRENDA [*very excited*]: I am, I am.

SIMON: This is your left. This one. Pull.

BRENDA: I'm pulling.

SIMON: Look out, it's going to hit the tree. Let me take it, let me take it.

MELVYN [*off*]: It's going to hit the tree.

BRENDA: It's terribly difficult.

SIMON: That's it, I've got it, I've got it. There she goes.

MELVYN [*off, distant*]: Well done.

ABIGAIL: Oh, look at that. Isn't that marvellous? Wheee! That's brilliant, Simon.

SIMON: Want a go?

ABIGAIL: Isn't it difficult?

SIMON: No, not at all.

BRENDA [*running off to rejoin* MELVYN]: Don't believe him. It's terribly difficult.

SIMON [*enveloping* ABIGAIL *between his arms to allow a takeover of the controls*]: Now, here. Take the lines. That's it, one in each hand. Now, you pull that and it goes that way. And that makes it go that way. With a bit of practice, you can do that.

ABIGAIL: Whee!

SIMON: That's it. Let it come back.

ABIGAIL: Fun!

SIMON: Otherwise you'll lose the wind. It's too sheltered down here, you see.

ABIGAIL: Wheeee! Look, Dorc, isn't this marvellous?

DORCAS: Yes.

ABIGAIL [*calling off*]: Look out!
        [*A distant scream from* BRENDA.]

MELVYN [*off, distant*]: Careful.

ABIGAIL: Sorry. Whoops.
        [*She moves off controlling the kite.*
        SIMON *watches with a protective eye.*
        DORCAS *studies* SIMON.
        STAFFORD *reads on doggedly.*]

STAFFORD [*hurling the Colour Supplement from him*]: Oh, Jesus. [*To* DORCAS] A two-thousand-pound bathtub.

DORCAS: What's that, love?

STAFFORD: A bath costing two thousand pounds. I hope he drowns in it, the stupid bastard.

DORCAS: Ah. [*She goes back to watching the kite.*]

SIMON: You going to have a go later?

DORCAS: No, I don't think so. I don't think it's really me somehow.

SIMON: There's nothing to it. Just a knack. Once you've got the hang of it, you're ... [*Watching the kite's manoeuvres*] Hey! How are you keeping then? Haven't seen you for a bit.

DORCAS: Oh, I've been around.

SIMON: Are you still doing your radio programme?

DORCAS: Oh yes. Tuesdays and Thursdays.

SIMON: Do you know, I've never managed to catch it. What's it about?

DORCAS: Well, it varies. Depends what I feel like. It's a sort of general arts programme and then I play records and then people phone up. Mainly to complain.

SIMON: About the records?

DORCAS: No – well – sometimes. Mostly about roads and street lighting and should the Mayor have a car or a bicycle, that sort of thing.

SIMON: Ah. Good lord, look at that! She's getting very good. [*Calling*] Well done.

DORCAS: Are you in love with her?

SIMON: Er – yes. Yes.

DORCAS: Sorry.

SIMON: No, no. Not at all, no. Yes, I do. I mean, I am. Yes.

DORCAS: So you would like it to be permanent?

SIMON: Well, from my side, yes. Naturally I can't speak for Abi, she's –

DORCAS: It's a bigger decision, isn't it? For her.

SIMON: Yes. [*He ponders.*] How do you mean?

DORCAS: Well, she'd be giving up quite a bit. Materially. Patrick's not poor. Let's be honest. It's a consideration. It has to be.

SIMON: Oh yes, yes.

DORCAS: I mean, God, we're adults. None of us are quite that naïve any more. To think we can live our lives on love. Like Melvyn.

SIMON: Or Brenda. Quite. No. I'm starting teaching again this autumn. I used to teach before I went abroad. P.E. & games, you know. Abi wants to get back to work again, too. She's been rusting away, you know. Terrible waste of a good brain.

DORCAS: Well, if that's what she wants.

SIMON: Yes. That's what she says she wants, anyway.

DORCAS: I just hope she doesn't finish up being hurt or disappointed. I mean, no criticism of you. One's seen it before, you see. When she married Patrick, she couldn't wait to give up her career. Become a home wife, a mother even – all things domestic. It was all she dreamed of. And now she wants out again.

SIMON: Yes, but isn't that typical of all of us? Wanting what we haven't got. And then once we get it ... [*Shouting*] Mind the trees ... Don't worry. She won't be hurt. Not by me, anyway. And I'll do my best not to disappoint her.

DORCAS: That's not what I meant.

SIMON: I know. I know. I'm joking ...

DORCAS: Abi's a person who expects rather a lot from life.

SIMON: Yes, yes. I do know.

DORCAS: She also expects a lot from people, too. And generally we let her down, I'm afraid. At least, she feels we have. In her eyes, that amounts to the same thing. Father, me – mother, of course. And now Patrick. I think she feels we've all failed her somehow. The point is, I don't think her image of us was one we could possibly live up to. Let's face it, most of us are just ordinary people. Average. Like you and me.

SIMON: Yes. I think she's fond of me, though.

DORCAS: I'm sure she is.

SIMON: Has she said anything to you?

DORCAS: She doesn't say much to me.

SIMON: No ... [*Looking back at* ABIGAIL] She's a marvellous person, though.

DORCAS: Oh yes. God, there's a lot to be said for idealists .. I'm not knocking them.

[ABIGAIL *bounds into view, still holding on to the kite.*]

ABIGAIL [*over her shoulder*]: Were you watching?

SIMON: Yes.

DORCAS: Well done.

ABIGAIL: It's hard work.

SIMON [*drawing further away from* ABIGAIL]: This disappointment you say she feels with her relationships. Is it general or just ...

DORCAS: Only the ones I've known, that's all.

ABIGAIL: What are you two doing?

SIMON: Just talking. [*Returning to* DORCAS] I mean, you could say that's the same with a lot of people, couldn't you? It's not that exceptional.

DORCAS: Probably not. I don't know. I'm more misanthropic, that's all. I don't expect anything much from anyone and as a result, I'm frequently quite pleasantly surprised. It probably means I'm lacking in imagination or something.

SIMON: Not at all. I'm sure you're not.

DORCAS: Well, it's nice of you to say so but I think I probably am.

SIMON: Now, you're not one of those people who continually run themselves down, are you?

DORCAS: How does it go? 'Look in thy glass and tell the face thou viewest – Now is the time that face should form another.'

SIMON: No, I don't know that one.

DORCAS: From the sonnets, I think.

SIMON: Aha, aha.

DORCAS: Well, I suppose if one gets positively no encouragement after a bit it tends to happen. Particularly for a woman.

SIMON: Oh, come on. Don't give me that. No one's ever encouraged you at all?

DORCAS: Not a lot.

ABIGAIL [*still struggling with the kite but trying to get a better look*]: Can someone take over now, please?

DORCAS: Women are very realistic, you know. We acknowledge our faults pretty early in life. We have to, to conceal them. I mean, I know I'm not beautiful in the conventional sense ...

SIMON: Now, I must stop you there. What do you mean by conventional? What is a convention? It's something man-made, surely. Literally man-made.

DORCAS: Yes, and as a man you're necessarily ruled by them, aren't you? Like all men, you're a slave to convention.

ABIGAIL: I can't hold this thing much longer. I'm going to let go.

SIMON: No, I don't accept that. That I'm conventional. I mean, I like to think of myself as something more than that.

DORCAS: All right then, stop beating about the bush, be perfectly honest. In the face of all that pre-conditioning, all that male-oriented propaganda to which you've been subjected from childhood upwards, can you honestly describe me as a beautiful ... no, that's too unfair ... I'll re-phrase that ... as an attractive woman?

ABIGAIL: Look, will somebody take this bloody kite?

SIMON [*laughing, confident now*]: Well, I'm very sorry, young woman, but I'm about to upset every preconception you've ever had. I'm sorry to shatter all your myths about men but it so happens that I do consider you to be an extremely attractive woman. No – to hell with it – a beautiful woman. And may I add by way of a bonus, quite fancy-able.

[ABIGAIL *releases the kite.*]

ABIGAIL: Right. I have let it go.

DORCAS: Thank you.

SIMON: My pleasure.

ABIGAIL [*slithering down the bank to join them*]: Hallo.

SIMON: Oh, hallo. What have you done with the kite?

ABIGAIL: I let it go.

SIMON: Oh, for God's sake, Abi, what did you do that for? Why?

DORCAS: She probably got bored with it.

MELVYN [*appearing on the brow of the hill*]: Oy, you let go of it.

ABIGAIL: Sorry.

MELVYN: It's all tangled up in the tree, now.

BRENDA [*who has arrived beside* MELVYN, *examining her bare foot*]: I've got a splinter.

ABIGAIL: Sorry. Couldn't be helped.

SIMON: I'll come and help, Mel.

MELVYN [*looking out from the vantage point of the bank*]: Hey, there's a car just arrived.

DORCAS: Oh, they're here. We'd better get things organized. Mel, can you see if they want anything carrying?

MELVYN: It's not Len's car.

ABIGAIL [*sitting up*]: Whose is it?

MELVYN: I think it's yours, Abi. Yes, it is, it must be ... [*Realizing*] Oh.

ABIGAIL [*a look of hatred at* DORCAS]: You little sod.

DORCAS: What?

[PATRICK *enters, quite at ease. Although in his Sunday gear, he still appears more formal than anyone else.*]

PATRICK: Afternoon, all.

SIMON: Ah, hallo.

PATRICK: Hallo. [*Nodding to* ABIGAIL] Hallo, dear.

ABIGAIL: Hallo, dear.

DORCAS: Did you say the kite was caught in a tree, Mel?

MELVYN [*still staring*]: Yep. [*Taking the hint*] Oh, yes, right.

DORCAS: I'll give you a ...

MELVYN: Yes, thank you, would you ... ?

DORCAS: Not at all. [*She hurries up the bank, following* MELVYN *and* BRENDA] See you in a minute.

PATRICK [*beaming at them*]: Surely.

[*He gives* STAFFORD *a glance but* STAFFORD *remains unmoving and, as far as we can tell, unaware.*]

PATRICK: Well, now, what's all this then?

SIMON [*defensive*]: What?

PATRICK: A secret picnic, is it? Everyone invited except me. That's a bit secretive, isn't it? I might have missed out. If someone hadn't told me.

ABIGAIL: Who told you?

PATRICK: A little bird.

ABIGAIL: I see. I didn't think you liked picnics.

PATRICK: Me? How little you know of me. I adore them. I never miss out on a picnic if I can possibly avoid it. Hallo, Simon, you're looking very fit. Don't you think so, Abi? You're looking marvellous. Terribly muscular. Just the sort of chap to have around in a tight picnic, eh?

[SIMON *laughs rather nervously.*]

Don't like the look of those clouds. Could be a bit of rain about later. How did you get here, Abi? Did you walk?

ABIGAIL: No, I came by bike.

PATRICK: Really? You mean, the old one in the garage? I thought that had seized up solid. Well, well. You come by car, Simon?

SIMON: By bike as well, actually.

PATRICK: Both on bikes. Coincidence. How splendidly healthy. Not the same bike, I take it?

[*He laughs.*

They don't.]

I'm ashamed to say I came in the Merc. Isn't that terrible? Perhaps I should take up cycling. It's obviously the way to meet people. Now, how do we intend to sort this one out? Any ideas?

ABIGAIL: There's nothing we can do this afternoon. Father will be arriving at any moment. Not to mention Uncle Len. Or Auntie Rita.

PATRICK: Well, something's going to have to be decided soon, darling, for all our sakes. Much as I admire this Spartan flurry of cycling and kite-flying, someone somewhere's got to give up with good grace, don't you think?

SIMON: I think it's rather up to Abi to choose who that's going to be, don't you?

PATRICK: Well, that's a point of view. She's not at her best as a decision-maker, you know. She does tend to become easily confused. Her eyes being bigger than her stomach. Or hadn't you noticed that about her?

SIMON [tense]: No, I can't say I had. She always strikes me as being perfectly capable. As a woman, she seems to me to –

ABIGAIL: Would you both mind not talking about me in the third person?

PATRICK: Sorry, darling. She gets like this sometimes.

ABIGAIL: I am warning you, Patrick . . .

PATRICK: Splendid. We'll leave it to Abi then, shall we? Can't say fairer than that.

SIMON: You're taking this very casually.

PATRICK: The point is, have I any choice? Supposing I get physical and threaten you. You'd knock me down without the slightest difficulty. Screaming my head off at you both will only weaken my case further and as Abi will tell you, I'm not much good at begging. So I'll have to be content to wait for her decision, won't I? But I'll tell you this much. If, finally, she does decide to leave me for you then I promise you I shall prove to be an extremely bad loser. No proper sporting background, you see. I shall drag you both through the most public, most vicious, expensive divorce it is possible for man to devise. I shall fight you both every inch of the way and by the time I've finished with you, you'll probably have to sell both your bicycles.

[PATRICK moves away from them.]

ABIGAIL [sotto]: What are we going to do?

SIMON: To be perfectly honest, I don't really know. At this present moment, I have a strong urge to go over there, wrap both his legs round his neck and stick his suede shoes in his mouth. But I suppose that would only be termed a temporary solution.

ABIGAIL: Yes.

SIMON: So . . .

ABIGAIL [tearful]: It's always like this. He always manages to ruin everything.

SIMON: Yes . . .

[MELVYN appears over the hill.

He carries the kite without its strings.]

MELVYN: They've just arrived.

ABIGAIL: Oh.

MELVYN [*to* ABIGAIL, *crossly*]: We had to cut the strings, you know.

[DORCAS *comes down the slope.*

BRENDA *appears behind her more slowly, still limping.*]

DORCAS [*briskly*]: All right, everyone. Now they've arrived may I remind you this is father's afternoon. It has taken six months of planning and hours of preparation so all hatchets buried, please.

PATRICK: Of course, of course.

DORCAS: You can kill each other later ... Hallo, Pa.

[RALPH *enters.*]

RALPH: At last, at last. [*Seeing* PATRICK] Ah-ha, there he is. Now, if we hadn't dropped in on him on our way to the cemetery, do you know, Abi, this fellow of yours wouldn't have known there was a picnic at all. Why didn't you tell him, you silly bundle?

ABIGAIL [*smiling limply*]: I thought he knew. I forgot.

PATRICK: We were just laughing about it.

RALPH: Scatterhead. She gets no better the older she gets, does she?

PATRICK: No.

DORCAS: Where do you want to sit, father? [*She holds one of the chairs.*]

RALPH: Just where you are, my dearest, as long as it's out of the wind. Mel, boy, see if your Uncle Len needs a hand, will you?

[MELVYN *comes down the slope.* BRENDA *limps after him.*]

And there's your girl. How's she? Good lord, she looks as if she's gone lame. You'll have to put her down, Mel.

BRENDA: I've got a splinter.

[MELVYN *goes off.*]

RALPH: Good girl, good girl. [*To* PATRICK] Going to be a fine doctor one day, that boy, if he ever gets his exams. Ah, look who's here, it's – er ...

SIMON: Simon.

RALPH: Simon. I didn't see you. This is nice. I didn't expect to see you.

SIMON: Yes.

ABIGAIL: Wasn't it extraordinary? I was cycling here and who should I run into, metaphorically, but Simon. So I said, do come. And here he is.

RALPH: And why not? I mean, he's nearly one of the family, isn't he?

ABIGAIL: I beg your pardon?

RALPH: Well, he's thingummy-tight's brother, isn't he? I mean, if she and Mel keep going on the way they are.

ABIGAIL: Oh, I see.

RALPH [*to* DORCAS *who has positioned his chair*]: No, not there, lumpkin. A bit further round. I don't want it blowing down my neck, do I?

[MELVYN *returns with a fishing stool and a rug.*]

[*Sitting*] That's better. That's better. [*To* STAFFORD] Good afternoon to you.

[DORCAS *kicks* STAFFORD.]

How are you?

STAFFORD: Yes, thank you.

RALPH: Splendid. Thank you, Mel. Is Len managing?

MEL: Yeah. He's just padlocking up the hubcaps.

RALPH: I was telling them, Mel. If you keep your nose in your books and don't spend every second of every day ogling whatsername there, you'll be a very fine doctor.

MELVYN [*spreading our the rug for him and* BRENDA, *unmoved*]: Yeah.

RALPH [*without offence*]: He doesn't listen to a blasted word I say, does he? Well, this is nice, isn't it? We'd better get our tea in before the rain, that's all.

DORCAS: What rain?

RALPH: Look over there. See those clouds? Well, twenty minutes they'll be overhead.

ABIGAIL: Nonsense.

RALPH: Betcha. Seen it before.

PATRICK [*to* DORCAS]: Why's he only got one sock on?

DORCAS: God knows.

[RITA *comes on with more bags.*]

RITA: Here we are. I don't like the look of those clouds.

RALPH: Over here, Rita. We've reserved you a spot over here.

RITA: We've been locking the car.

LEN [*entering with other picnickery*]: Can't be too careful. Not these days.

RALPH: Won't do to have a copper having his car nicked, will it?

LEN: If I related to you the statistics regarding car thefts for one month in this area, it would horrify you. Horrify you. We don't release the true figures. The general public would panic.

RALPH: Yes, yes.

ABIGAIL: Hope my bike's all right.

LEN: Locked it up, have you?

ABIGAIL: No, it's just under a bush over there.

LEN: It is quite within bounds that by the time you get back to it, they'll have stripped it of everything. Bell, gears, lights, back and front, wheels, rear reflectors, both sets of brakes and the saddle. And if it's a lady's bike and you're out of luck, they'll be lying in wait to rape you as well.

ABIGAIL: Oh terrific, thanks.

LEN: Just a warning.

SIMON [*gallantly*]: Don't worry, I'll – er ... I'll ...

PATRICK: What's that?

SIMON: Nothing.

RALPH: What's he saying?

SIMON: I'll – er – I'll be able to keep an eye on the bikes from here.

PATRICK: Jolly good.

RALPH: Splendid. What's he talking about? [*To* BRENDA] Have you got that thing out of your foot yet?

BRENDA: No.

RALPH: Well, put your hoof in your mouth and suck it. Can you suck your foot?

BRENDA: No.

RALPH: Dear oh dear. [*To* LEN] She can't be much fun, can she?

DORCAS: He's going completely mad.

RALPH [*sitting back, basking*]: Now, isn't this the perfect spot? Didn't I tell you? What could be nicer.

LEN: It's all right now in broad daylight but I wouldn't care to be sitting up here like this in the middle of the night.

ABIGAIL: Why?

LEN: Let us just say it is a favourite haunt.

RITA: Haunted?

LEN: No, not haunted. I'm saying it is a haunt for certain undesirables who wish to practise unnatural practices.

MELVYN: Unnatural practices?

LEN: I'm saying no more.

MELVYN: What unnatural practices?

LEN: I think I've said enough on that subject. We shall catch up with them and then ...

MELVYN [*to* BRENDA]: We must come up here at night.

LEN: Now, don't be young, lad, don't be young. Be your age.

RALPH: Come on, then. Let's eat before the rain.

DORCAS: It's not going to rain.

RALPH: Wait and see. Wait and see.

RITA: Are you all right on that stool, Len?

LEN: Oh yes. Many an hour I've spent on this stool, watching the rod.

RITA [*sorting out the bags*]: Now then.

RALPH: Still fish, do you, Len?

LEN: Not as much as I did. Not as much as I'd like to.

RITA: He's no time, have you?

LEN: Not any more.

RITA: Now, what have we got in here?

DORCAS: All right, now. Nobody jump about. Rita and I will organize this. Everyone just sit down.

RALPH: Do you hear that everybody? Leave it to Dorcas. In this family, you know, Simon, when it comes to organization we all leave it to Dorcas.

SIMON: Ah.

ABIGAIL [*muttering*]: It's only because she won't let anyone else help.

RITA [*finding a polythene box*]: Ah now, these are Stafford's specials.

ABIGAIL: Even if they wanted to.

DORCAS [*putting four sandwiches out of the box on to a paper plate*]: Those are Stafford's specials.

   [*N.B.: All sandwiches referred to are half rounds.*]

RALPH: What's this? Who's getting special treatment?

DORCAS: These are nut sandwiches for Stafford.

RALPH: Nut?

DORCAS: He's a vegetarian.

RALPH: Poor chap.

DORCAS: There you are, Stafford.

STAFFORD: Right.

DORCAS [*handing* SIMON *eight cardboard plates*]: Simon, could you dish those out, please?

SIMON: Certainly.

   [SIMON *hands out the eight cardboard plates, including one for himself. When he gets to* LEN, *he runs out.*]

RALPH [*watching* DORCAS]: Len, who does she remind you of now? Dorcas? Who is it she's like now?

RITA: Amy, isn't it?

LEN: Amy?

RALPH: Amy. Look at her. Once she gets set on anything. You see, Abi's like me. We're the fly-by-nights. Hopping about from this to that. [*To* ABIGAIL] Aren't you?

ABIGAIL: That's absolutely untrue.

PATRICK: I'm saying nothing.

DORCAS: Ham sandwich, everyone.

   [*She starts to take them round, eight of them, avoiding* STAFFORD. *By the time she gets to* LEN, *she's run out.* SIMON *has just discovered the shortage of plates.*]

SIMON: Oh.

LEN: What, no plate for me?

SIMON: We seem to be a plate short.

DORCAS: Oh hell, are we?

RITA: Ah well, we'll be one extra, won't we?

ABIGAIL [*looking at* PATRICK]: Yes, we will.

PATRICK: All right, I'll go. I'll go.

RITA: No, no, it's not Patrick who's extra, it's – er – Simon, there. We didn't expect him, did we?

RALPH: Ah-ha, an extra body.

PATRICK: Better hand in your plate, old son.

SIMON: Yes, well. Right. There. [*He offers* LEN *his plate.*] I don't mind.

ABIGAIL [*restraining him*]: Oh, don't be stupid. We must have a spare plate somewhere.

DORCAS: Yes, there is.

PATRICK: No, no. Look. Here. Have half of mine. [*He tears his plate in half.*] Share and share alike.

[SIMON *glares at him, his fists bunching.*]

ABIGAIL [*springing up*]: Oh, for heaven's sake. If we go on at this rate, no one's going to get anything to eat at all. For the love of mike, let me help.

DORCAS: Abi, please.

[ABIGAIL *snatches up* STAFFORD'S *plate of sandwiches.*]

ABIGAIL: Right. Come along, take one.

STAFFORD: Er ...

ABIGAIL: Oh come along, Stafford, for heaven's sake. Before it rains.

STAFFORD: Yeah, I think those are ...

ABIGAIL: There you are, one for you ... [*She takes the sandwich off the plate and plonks it on to the rug.*]

DORCAS [*who is still handing out ham sandwiches*]: Abigail, please don't. You'll only muddle things up.

ABIGAIL: We can't sit around any longer, darling, we're all starving.

[LEN *has risen momentarily and moved to look at the car.*

DORCAS *finishes handing out the ham sandwiches.*]

DORCAS: I think there will be enough to go round, Rita.

RITA [*who has been unpacking the cheese and tomato sandwiches (8)*]: I think we made a few extra. [*To* LEN] What are you doing, love?

LEN: Just checking the car.

[ABIGAIL *has handed* STAFFORD'S *remaining three sandwiches to* PATRICK, BRENDA *and* MELVYN.]

RITA: Could you hand out these cheese and tomato, please, Simon?

SIMON: A pleasure.

[SIMON *goes round handing out the cheese and tomato.* STAFFORD, *who has only one sandwich left, takes one.* SIMON *thus runs out early, omitting* RITA *and* LEN. ABIGAIL *has dumped* STAFFORD'S *empty sandwich plate on the grass and has found some cardboard cups which she is unpacking.* DORCAS *is undoing thermos flasks, one with orange and one with tea.* RITA *is opening the egg and tomato.*]

LEN [*returning meanwhile, to* SIMON]: Rumour has it, you're an athlete, young man.

SIMON [*serving cheese and tomato*]: Well, used to be.

LEN: Were you a runner, by any chance?

RALPH: Careful how you answer that question, Simon.

SIMON: Well, yes, I used to run a bit.

ABIGAIL [*taking the egg and tomato from* RITA]: What are these?

SIMON: I'm certainly not a sprinter.

RITA: Egg and tomato, those are.

ABIGAIL: Right.

LEN: Cross country at all?

ABIGAIL: One for you. [*She slaps an egg and tomato on the rug next to* STAFFORD.]

SIMON: Well, a bit. Not recently.

RALPH: Ah-ha. Ah-ha.

[ABIGAIL *is now handing out egg and tomato to everyone else. She runs out as she gets to* RITA *and* LEN.]

SIMON: Why are you asking? Were you a runner?

LEN: Years ago. Years ago.

RALPH: He was very good.

RITA: He ran for the Police.

DORCAS: Right, how are we doing?

ABIGAIL: We're doing fine.

DORCAS [*muttering*]: I wish she'd leave things alone.

RITA [*handing her the final batch of sandwiches*]: Sardine and cucumber.

[DORCAS *distributes these.*]

LEN: No, I organize the local cross-country derby once a year. It's a light-hearted jaunt but we usually get quite a good field.

RALPH: Light-hearted, he says.

LEN: We run it around here.

SIMON: Sounds fun.

LEN: I might persuade you to enter, then?

ABIGAIL: Right. Anything else?

SIMON: Well . . .

DORCAS: No, thank you so much, Abi. Sit down.

SIMON: I'll see.

RALPH: You know, Len, I'd fancy him against Murphy, you know.

LEN: Oh no, no. Nobody beats Murphy.

SIMON: Murphy?

RALPH: Young Constable Murphy. Finest runner I've seen for some time

RITA: Len's brought him on from nothing.

LEN: No, he won't touch Murphy. Promise you that.

ABIGAIL: What about drinks?

RITA: It's all right, Abi. I'll do those.

LEN: Well, it's not till September the 8th. You've plenty of time.

SIMON: I might just be fit by then, I suppose.

RITA: Now, hands up for tea. And who wants orange squash?

[*Everyone puts up their hand.*]

RITA: That's one, two ...

MELVYN: Are we putting our hands up for tea or orange squash?

RITA: This is for tea.

MELVYN: Oh no, I don't want tea.

RITA: Well, if you want orange squash – don't put your hand up. Put your hand down.

[MELVYN *and* BRENDA *put their hands down.*]

PATRICK: I'm sorry, what are we putting our hands up for then?

DORCAS: Up for tea, down for orange squash.

RALPH: I'm completely lost, I'll have both.

DORCAS [*who has been pouring tea*]: You have tea, Pa. Here you are.

RALPH: Ah-ha.

LEN: Look, I don't want to spoil anything but I've got nothing at all.

DORCAS: You must have. Where's your plate gone?

LEN: I've never had a plate.

ABIGAIL: Come on, here you are. Here's a plate. [*She picks up* DORCAS's *plate from the rug, tipping off the contents.*]

DORCAS: Abi, don't do that.

ABIGAIL: Here. [*She thrusts the plate at* LEN.]

LEN: Thank you.

DORCAS: Those are mine. Now they're full of grass.

ABIGAIL: All this fuss over a plate.

PATRICK [*picking up* STAFFORD's *old plate*]: There's another plate here.

DORCAS: Well, where did that come from?

PATRICK: No idea.

LEN: Right, I now have a plate. Is there anything to put on it?

DORCAS: Look, this is ridiculous. If you'd only ... Why has nobody given Uncle Len anything?

RALPH: Well, I'm all right. [*He starts to eat.*]

DORCAS: Someone's got more than they should have.

RITA [*taking over the tea duties*]: Stafford, orange or tea?

STAFFORD: Er – orange.

[RITA *serves everyone with drinks. By the finish,* LEN, RITA, RALPH, ABIGAIL *and* PATRICK *have tea.* SIMON, BRENDA, MELVYN, DORCAS *and* STAFFORD *all have orange squash.*]

BRENDA: It's a funny sandwich, this.

RALPH: What's that, my beautiful?

BRENDA: It's all sort of gritty this sandwich.

RALPH: Gritty, is it? Never mind, it's probably been dropped somewhere. It's good for you, grit. They give it to hens.

BRENDA: Uggh. [*She looks inside the sandwich.*]

DORCAS [*interrupting her count*]: Just a minute. Brenda, what are you eating there?

STAFFORD: I think that's one of mine.

DORCAS: Is that a nut sandwich?

MELVYN: Yes, it looks like nut.

BRENDA: Nut, yes.

DORCAS: Then what are you doing eating nut? That's supposed to be for Stafford.

BRENDA: Well, I didn't know. Someone gave it to me.

DORCAS: Oh, this is ridiculous. If you'd only all listened – if we'd only done this properly ...

RALPH: Now, come on, old lumpkin. It's all right.

DORCAS: It is not all right. It happens every bloody time we have a picnic.

PATRICK: All right, own up. Who's eating Stafford's nuts? Come on.

LEN: I'm not eating anything. I've only got a plate.

DORCAS: All right, all right. We'll have to go round. Everybody stop eating, please. Just for one minute. Now, Stafford, what have you got?

STAFFORD: Er ... [DORCAS *snatches his sandwiches from him.*]

DORCAS: You've got a nut. That's a nut one. Good. [*She hands that back to him.*] A cheese and tomato and an egg and tomato. I don't know what you're doing with these.

   [DORCAS *holds on to the egg and tomato and the cheese and tomato.*] Right, next. Simon?

SIMON: Er – I've got a ham, an egg and tomato, a cheese and tomato, and a cucumber and something.

DORCAS [*who has been checking her own sandwiches*]: Cucumber and sardine. That is correct. Good. That is what I've got.

PATRICK [*to* SIMON]: Well done.

DORCAS: Next. Abi?

ABIGAIL: Ditto.

DORCAS: Are you sure?

ABIGAIL: I said, yes. Ditto.

DORCAS: This is all your fault, you know. If you hadn't ...

ABIGAIL: My God, if we'd waited till you ...

PATRICK [*riding over this*]: Now then, I have a very interesting selection here. It could qualify me for a major prize. I have a ham, a half-eaten cheese and tomato, a totally eaten egg and tomato that you'd better take

my word for, a sardine and cucumber that I don't much like the look
of and a nut one that I don't want at any price.

DORCAS: Right. Give me the nut one, please.

PATRICK: It's all yours.

DORCAS: Thank you. Melvyn?

MELVYN: Cheese and tom., egg and tom., cuc. and sard., one ham, one
nut.

DORCAS: Give me the nut.

MELVYN: What do I get instead?

DORCAS: Nothing. Brenda?

BRENDA: The same as Melvyn.

DORCAS: Right, give me the nut one, please.

BRENDA: I can't

DORCAS: Why not?

BRENDA: I've eaten most of it.

DORCAS: Oh God, why the hell did you eat it? Here you are, Staff, here's
two more.

STAFFORD: Right.

DORCAS: Pa, are you happy?

RALPH: Perfectly. I've come out of it very well. The God of sandwiches
has smiled upon me.

RITA: Yes, I only seem to have two but . . .

DORCAS [*handing her the couple she has taken from* STAFFORD]: That's all
right. You have these two. And then I think we're all right. Is everybody
happy now?

LEN: No. I still have nothing to eat whatsoever.

DORCAS [*snatching up her own sandwiches*]: All right, all right. Have
these . . .

LEN: No, those are yours. I can't . . .

DORCAS: Please, I insist. Have them. [*She thrusts the sandwiches at* LEN.]

LEN: Now, what are you going to . . . ?

DORCAS: Eat them.

   [DORCAS *goes and sits on the rug. A slight pause.*]
   [*Muttering*]: This is the last time, this is positively the last time . . .
   [*Pause.*]

RALPH: Well, we've beaten the rain.

RITA: Yes, they're coming closer.

RALPH: Told you so. Well, just to say thank you all for coming along and
humouring me. I'm sure you've all got other things you'd far sooner
be doing.

PATRICK: No, I'm sure we haven't. Have we?

ABIGAIL: No.

RALPH: I must say when I told Amy on Wednesday, she was very, very touched. She wanted me to thank you.

LEN: Ah.

RITA: Oh.

DORCAS: Good.

  [*Pause.*]

RALPH: And what's been happening to Stratford these days?

ABIGAIL: Where?

DORCAS: Stafford, father. He's called Stafford.

RALPH: Stafford. I beg his pardon. I'm always getting him wrong, aren't I? I know he's a railway station. What did I call him once? Stoke, Staleybridge, something like that. How are things going? Still working for Dorcas?

STAFFORD: No.

DORCAS: No, unfortunately it didn't work out.

RALPH: Why not?

DORCAS: Well, actually, he got sacked.

RALPH: Good lord, sacked? Did she sack you, this girl?

DORCAS: No, of course I didn't. Vernon did.

RALPH: Vernon?

DORCAS: Vernon Bradshaw, the station manager. It's a long story.

MELVYN: Were you sacked because of your politics, Staff?

STAFFORD: Yeah.

DORCAS: No, he wasn't. You weren't.

MELVYN: If they fired him because of his politics ...

DORCAS: They didn't. If you must know, he started a fight in the B.B.C. canteen over the price of salads. And he finished up punching a vision mixer from the Sports Unit. The man was off work for three days and Vernon has banned Stafford from the studios pending an inquiry. That's all there was to it.

RALPH: Good lord. The things they get up to in the B.B.C., eh?

LEN: Nothing would surprise me where the media are concerned.

RALPH: Ah.

  [*Slight pause.*

  MEL *kisses* BRENDA.]

STAFFORD: You see, it's ...

RALPH: She'll get terrible indigestion, Mel, if you do that to her while she's eating.

ABIGAIL: Come on, Mel, knock it off.

MELVYN: All right.

PATRICK: Otherwise we'll all start.

STAFFORD [*speaking softly and nervously*]: It's – er – to do basically with more than just that ...

DORCAS: What are you saying, Staff? [*She signals for him to speak up.*]

[STAFFORD *speaks again a little louder but not loud enough for* RALPH, *who drowns him out with his own reminiscences.*]

STAFFORD: It's to do with more than that, you see. It's the whole repressive attitude of the entire organization wherein they are pre-conditioned into thinking along establishment lines that have been laid down by a privileged class which has had no contact or serious regard for the working person. Or indeed to that person's basic predicament in a capitalist controlled bourgeois run system. So that the working artist's voice is ultimately stifled ...

RALPH: [*over all this*]: Do you know, Amy and I discovered this spot years ago. I don't think anybody else had even heard about it. Of course, now it's all been opened up. I'm talking about what – thirty-eight years ago – before most of this lot were born. Do you know, we had it practically to ourselves. And I'll tell you something interesting. You see, up there where that bench is now, that's where I proposed to her. Just up there.

DORCAS: Pa, I think Stafford is trying to say something.

[RALPH *stops speaking.*

So does STAFFORD.]

Sorry. I think he was saying something.

RALPH: Was he? I do beg his pardon. You must excuse me. I have a little bit of difficulty hearing on this side. Now, what was it you were saying, old man? Sing it out.

STAFFORD [*unhappily*]: I – er ... It was just ... I – [*All the eyes upon him are too much for him. He rolls on to his back.*] Oh, shit.

[RALPH *nods sagely and gazes at the sky, lost in his memories. Pause.*]

RITA [*swatting*]: The wasps have smelt the orange squash.

LEN [*swatting too*]: Yes ... yes ...

[*The wasp flies to* ABIGAIL.

She swats it away.

It flies around for a bit, finally landing on BRENDA's *hair.*

She doesn't notice.]

MELVYN [*seeing it*]: Just a sec, love.

BRENDA: What?

MELVYN: Nothing, keep still, it's a wasp. I'll just ... [*He goes to knock the insect from* BRENDA's *hair but before he can do so, she leaps into demented action.*]

BRENDA: Waaah. ... ooh ... waah – eeeeee – woooh ...

[*She is on her feet dancing among the picnickers. The wasp follows her*

*as wasps tend to do. An elaborate dance follows as other people come to
their feet, either to avoid being trampled by* BRENDA *or to protect their
food from being ground underfoot or to catch the wasp or, as in*
PATRICK'S *case, because she has kicked a drink over him.*]

DORCAS [*during this*]: Don't dance about. You'll only get it angry. Sit
down, you silly girl.

LEN [*simultaneously*]: A wasp will never sting you unless it's provoked. It's
a popular fallacy, you know, that wasps sting for no reason...

RITA [*simultaneously*]: Keep it away from me, keep it away from me. Keep
it away.

ABIGAIL [*simultaneously*]: If she'd only sit down, it'd go away. It's only
after the orange squash ...

SIMON [*simultaneously*]: Keep still, why don't you keep still? If you'll all
keep still, I'll catch it.

MELVYN [*simultaneously*]: Don't be so daft, it's only a wasp. What are you
panicking about?

PATRICK [*simultaneously*]: God help us, that's all we need. An hysterical
female with St Vitus's Dance.

[STAFFORD *sits huddled and isolated on the rug, unaffected by the chaos
– or relatively so.* RALPH *views the proceedings benignly, waving his hat
idly as if conducting a country dance.*]

RALPH [*conversationally during this*]: Such a lot of fuss over a little insect.
Good lord, what a lot of fuss.

DORCAS [*finally topping it all*]: It's all right. It's all right. Simon's got it.
He's got it. Panic over. Simon's killed it.

RITA: Oh, he's killed it.

LEN: He's killed it.

[*People settle down.*]

MELVYN: What did you kill it with?

SIMON: Just with my hands. It's a trick. I learnt it in Africa, actually.
Depends how fast you clap, you see. You do it like that, you see, [*He
does so.*] and you don't notice you've – um ... [*Examining his hand*] You
don't – um ...

ABIGAIL: You all right?

SIMON: Yes, fine.

DORCAS: Let me see.

SIMON: No, I'm all right. It usually works ... [*He sits, staring at his palm.*]

RALPH: Well done, that man.

PATRICK: I bet you put the fear of God into ants.

SIMON: Yes. And I have been known, very occasionally, to do it to human
beings as well.

PATRICK: How do you mean? You clap your hands at them, do you?

SIMON: Mind you, they have to keep asking for it.

PATRICK: What? Yes, please. That sort of thing?

SIMON: Like you're doing now.

ABIGAIL: Simon, please don't.

SIMON: Because I don't mind saying, for the past half hour, to put it bluntly, you have been getting right up my nose.

ABIGAIL: Will you please stop it.

RALPH: Hallo, hallo.

PATRICK: Well, isn't that altogether just too unfortunate?

DORCAS: Patrick.

SIMON: Yes, isn't it?

PATRICK: To coin a phrase, I think you're going to have to sniff and bear it, old boy.

SIMON [*rising*]: Is that right?

PATRICK: Right on, old African bush-whacker.

[PATRICK *too, has risen.*

ABIGAIL *has started crying.*]

DORCAS: Now chaps, fellas ... Please. Don't start, please. She's not that worth it, believe me.

ABIGAIL [*sharply*]: What did you say?

RALPH: I think there's going to be a fight.

[*The rain comes down suddenly.*]

RITA: Oh, here's the rain.

RALPH: Told you so. Didn't I tell you?

BRENDA: Oooh.

MELVYN [*to her, handing her some stuff*]: Take that and run. I'll bring the rug.

[*In a matter of seconds, the stage has emptied as they flee the sudden, very violent downpour. RALPH runs with his chair over his head as an improvised umbrella. LEN grabs one bag, his stool and RITA's chair. RITA clutches another bag. On her way out, assisted by LEN, she falls over. ABIGAIL, who is gathering things up, gives LEN a hand to drag the limping RITA out. PATRICK gathers up one or two things but disappears very swiftly to the car. The rain is very loud and the voices are barely audible. STAFFORD plunges out, enveloped in one of the rugs. DORCAS remains to gather things up, looking angrily after STAFFORD for not staying to help. BRENDA runs out with the kite and personal bits. MELVYN stays to help DORCAS gather up the rest. SIMON has gone off the other way for the bicycles. MELVYN and DORCAS are the last to leave the scene. As they hurry off, they pass ABIGAIL, now very wet, returning having helped RITA to the car. ABIGAIL stands, alone, looking for SIMON. SIMON returns*] *wheeling two bicycles. One,* ABIGAIL's *old machine, and a newer racing version of his own. He and both machines are also very wet.*]

ABIGAIL [*yelling above the rain*]: We can't cycle in this.

SIMON: What?

ABIGAIL: I said, we can't cycle in this.

SIMON: Well, come under the tree there. We'll soon dry out.

ABIGAIL [*unconvinced and miserably undecided*]: Oh God . . .

[*For a second, she stands uncommitted, getting wetter.*]

SIMON: Come on.

[PATRICK *enters from the car, dry under an umbrella.*]

PATRICK: I say, can I give you a lift anywhere?

[ABIGAIL *looks from one to the other.*

She decides.

When she has gone one way or the other, with one man or the other, DORCAS *emerges now also very wet to check the picnic site for forgotten items. She happily accepts either the offer of a dry umbrella or the prospect of a wet bicycle ride.*

They go out.]

End of Act One Scene Two A

Should Abigail have chosen to stay with Simon, Act Two Scene One A follows. If, however, Abigail opts to go with Patrick, the reader should turn to Act Two Scene One D (p.296).

ABIGAIL: ACT TWO
SCENE ONE A

The same. Early September. Saturday early evening at about 7.30 p.m. A warm, pleasant evening at nearly sunset. LEN enters from the road. He has the air of a man surveying the land. He looks about him, worried. He whistles, obviously to a dog. No response. He climbs the bank, whistling again.

LEN: Trixie! Come on, Trixie girl. [*No response. After a swift glance around him, in a high unnatural falsetto*] Trix – Trix–Trix–Trix–Trix . . .
    [MELVYN *and* BRENDA *enter from the road.*
    He carries a newly-made home built glider.
    LEN *stops calling abruptly.*]
MELVYN: Good evening, Uncle Len.
LEN: What are you doing here?
MELVYN: Lost Trixie, have you?
LEN: Yes. She'll have smelt rabbit. Rabbit scent. Probably.
    [MELVYN *whistles.*]
  No, she'll be away. She never lets the scent go. Never.
MELVYN: Right.
LEN: What have you got there, then? An aeroplane?
MELVYN: Supposed to be.
LEN: I see. [*He looks at it without favour.*]
BRENDA [*softly*]: We made it.
LEN [*sharply*]: What's that?
BRENDA: I said, we made it.
LEN: Uh-huh. How did you get here?
MELVYN: On the bus.
LEN: I see. Well, I'll give you a tip. Just a friendly tip from me. If I were you, I wouldn't hang around here after dark on a Saturday night. All right?
MELVYN: Why not?
LEN: Because. That's why. Take her home and watch the football, that's my advice.
MELVYN [*a suspicion of sarcasm*]: All right if we fly this, is it?
LEN: Suit yourself, it's a free country. You're free to do as you please.
  Don't behave in any manner so as to cause annoyance or inconvenience

to other people, don't cause any undue or wanton damage to property, and if that thing is on a control line, [*He nods at the plane.*] don't fly it above 200 feet, or you'll have the Air Ministry to answer to.

> [*He laughs at this as it amuses him.*
>
> MELVYN *and* BRENDA *just stare.*]

[*Getting more aggressive*] Have you got nothing better to do than that?

MELVYN: How do you mean?

LEN: I thought you'd have been sitting at home, racking your brains as to what went wrong.

MELVYN: What with?

LEN: With your exams, boy. All these medical exams your father spent money on for you to take. What happened?

MELVYN: I failed them.

LEN: Yes. You made a right Mafeking of it, didn't you? Broken your father's heart.

MELVYN: Dad doesn't care.

LEN: How do you know?

MELVYN: He said so. I went to tell him. He said, how did the exams turn out, Mel? And I said, I failed, I'm afraid. And he said, oh well, fair enough. Better luck next time. And I said, I'm not taking them next time. And he said, oh well, fair enough then.

LEN [*digesting this*]: Yes, well he's a ... He's not been himself. He was a fine doctor. Very little he couldn't put right when he set his mind to it. Rita's knee got the better of him, though.

MELVYN: Yep. See you, then.

> [MELVYN *and* BRENDA *go up the slope.*]

LEN [*beckoning* MELVYN *back*]: Here.

MELVYN [*coming to him*]: Yes?

LEN: Try and cheer her up a bit, will you?

MELVYN: Why?

LEN: Because she's like a mourner peeling onions, that's why. What's the matter with her?

MELVYN [*moving off*]: She's all right.

> [MELVYN *joins* BRENDA *at the top of the slope.*
>
> *They disappear.*]

LEN [*after them*]: Remember what I said? Not too late. [*He consults his watch. Then, resuming his search, whistling*] Trix-Trix-Trix-Trix-Trix.

> [PATRICK *enters from the road.*]

PATRICK [*surprised to see* LEN]: Oh. Good evening, Len.

LEN: Ah, good evening.

PATRICK: Very mild.

LEN: Yes ... Yes ...

PATRICK: Have you lost the dog?

LEN: No, no. She'll be after rabbit. It's rabbit she'll have scented.

PATRICK: Ah.

LEN: Once she gets the scent.

PATRICK: Yes.

LEN: Taking a stroll, are you?

PATRICK: In a way. In a way. Well. A stroll in the car, if you follow me.

LEN: Ah.

PATRICK: I find walking on the whole upsets me, you know.

LEN: Oh yes.

PATRICK: I mean, taken in any large quantities that is. Anything over, say, a hundred consecutive paces plays absolute havoc with my nervous system.

LEN: Oh yes.

PATRICK: Ever since my firm moved to a larger building it's posed endless problems for me.

LEN: Uh-huh. Uh-huh.

PATRICK: My secretary has to carry me everywhere.

LEN [*gravely*]: Yes. Yes. [*Realizing the joke*] Ah. Ha-ha. Yes. Yes. Yes. [*A pause.*] Yes.

PATRICK: Actually I was looking for my wife. Have you seen her at all?

LEN: Abi? Abigail? No, no. Gone missing, has she?

PATRICK: In a way. She was on her bike, you see, wobbling along some B road. I was following in the car a few yards behind her. Then all of a sudden, she's gone. Pedalled off like mad down a footpath. Turned left and vanished. No hand signal, nothing.

LEN: Dear, dear, dear.

PATRICK: So.

LEN: You were unable to follow?

PATRICK: I was in the Merc, not a tractor.

LEN: Yes, yes, quite. Pardon my asking, why were you following her in the first place?

PATRICK: Well, I think it's a good thing for a husband and wife to get out together in the evening sometimes.

LEN: What, her on a bicycle and you in the car?

PATRICK: Well, each to his own.

LEN: It sounds very peculiar to me.

PATRICK: I had the sunshine roof open, for heaven's sake. We weren't being that unfriendly. I kept shouting encouragement to her. You know, 'keep going'. Rather like a rowing coach on a river bank.

LEN [*giving all this up*]: Ah.

PATRICK: Anyway, I dare say she'll turn up.

LEN: Got lights front and rear, has she? On her bike?

PATRICK: Oh yes, rather.

LEN: She'll be all right then.

PATRICK: Are you on a walk or ... ?

LEN: Not really.

PATRICK: Oh. Business, eh?

LEN: Yes. Yes.

PATRICK: Oh. Well, enough said. I'm not interrupting a full-scale police manhunt, am I? You're not on the point of swooping, are you?

LEN: Beg your pardon?

PATRICK: Is there at present a police operation in progress which I as a member of the general public am hindering?

LEN: No.

PATRICK: Good.

LEN: The facts are, we are keeping just a little bit of a vigil, that's all.

PATRICK: I see.

LEN: There have been incidents on this common. Vandalism. Youths have been seen. Unnatural practices have been reported.

PATRICK: Unnatural practices?

LEN: Eye-witness reports.

PATRICK: But who is it who's been practising? Youths?

LEN: I wish I could say it was merely youths. If my suspicions are correct, it goes a lot higher than that.

PATRICK: Really?

LEN: That's a personal theory, you understand?

PATRICK: Good heavens. When you say higher, how high do you mean?

LEN: You name it. The sky's the limit, isn't it?

PATRICK: I mean – what? – Town Hall level, for example? That high?

LEN [*reacting sharply*]: What have you been hearing?

PATRICK: Nothing.

LEN: You can keep that under your hat to start with.

PATRICK: What?

LEN: You'll know exactly who I'm talking about, then.

PATRICK: Who?

LEN: I think you know. You'll know. We all know.

PATRICK: But what sort of things are being practised?

LEN: Well. Let's just say the Vicar is also concerned.

PATRICK: You mean, he's involved?

LEN: No, no, he's concerned. He's worried. [*Confidentially*] You've heard of a coven, I take it?

PATRICK: A coven? You mean, witches, all that?

LEN: That's what I think we're on to.

PATRICK: Good gracious.

LEN: Nude dancing and dead poultry, all that sort of palaver. Sacrifices, you know.

PATRICK: And you're hoping to catch them at it, are you?

LEN: Saturday night. A popular time we reckon. Tomorrow is Sunday, you see.

PATRICK: Well yes, they'd need a lie-in after all that, wouldn't they? Is this a big operation you're mounting then?

LEN: Well, it was originally intended as such but there have been administrative problems. A shortage of men. I sent a request to Slough requesting further assistance but they finally came through with a no. Their idea of concrete evidence and mine obviously differs.

PATRICK: Oh dear.

LEN: It's the big dance as well tonight, you see. Divisional police dance.

PATRICK: Oh, is it? Aren't you and Rita going?

LEN: It wouldn't be a lot of fun with her knee, would it? No.

PATRICK: How is she?

LEN: Middling to fair, middling to fair. [*Not wishing to dwell on this topic*] Anyway, so the operation is now down to what you might call, jokingly, a token force.

PATRICK: How many's that?

LEN: Me, a constable and the dog.

PATRICK: Ah.

LEN: Mind you, having said that, as the Army always has it, you can sometimes achieve more with a fistful of specially hand-picked men than you can with a whole regiment of recruits.

PATRICK: That sounds logical.

LEN: So.

PATRICK: All the same, between you, him and the police dog, you're going to have your work cut out, aren't you?

LEN: No, it's not a Police dog. It's my dog. It's little Trix. She'll scent anyone long before we do. She's got a good nose on her. Could save us a lot of leg work. Excuse me. [*He whistles.*]

PATRICK: She must be still chewing rabbits.

LEN: Yes. [*Calling normally*] Trixie. [*High*] Trix-Trix-Trix-Trix-Trix.
[PATRICK *looks at him, startled.*]
I have to do that. She's getting on, you see, and her hearing's going just a little. In the lower registers, that is. It's the deep voices she can't hear,

you see. Men's voices particularly. I mean, she'll always go running to Rita but if I talk to her normally, she won't hear me at all. [*Calling falsetto again*] Trix-Trix-Trix-Trix-Trix. She'll have heard that, you see.

PATRICK: She's not coming though.

LEN: No, well, she'll make her own way. She's getting on. Still a good guard dog. She hears an intruder, she barks the house down.

PATRICK: Providing they're women, eh?

LEN [*mildly amused*]: Yes, yes. Well ...

PATRICK: Yes, I think my wife's gone after a rabbit, too. Good luck.

LEN: Thank you – ah ...

[MURPHY *enters.*
A well-built young man in an anorak and heavy-duty trousers tucked into boots. He carries a loudhailer.
He looks ready for combat.]

LEN: There you are, Murphy, good lad. [*Seeing the loudhailer and taking it from him*] Ah, thank you for bringing that. This is Police Constable Murphy. This is Mr Smythe.

PATRICK: How do you do?

[MURPHY *nods.*]

LEN: You may have heard of this young man by reputation.

PATRICK: Oh yes?

LEN: He's made quite a name for himself in recent times. As a runner. He was the outright winner of the Pendon Cross-Country last year. And next weekend he's going to win it again, aren't you? And break the record if I have anything to do with it.

PATRICK: Jolly good.

LEN: That's what I mean by handpicked, you see. There's nothing on two legs will escape this lad. He moves across this sort of terrain like a bloody whippet. [*To* MURPHY] All right, lad, lead on. We've got work to do. [*Quietly to* PATRICK] He's thick enough to start a timber yard but he moves like the clappers.

PATRICK: I think I'll take advantage of police protection and just scan the horizon with you. In case there's a lone female cyclist.

LEN [*calling*]: Trix-Trix-Trix-Trix-Trix. I think she's run home, you know. I wouldn't be surprised. She's done it before. Oh well, she'll keep Rita company anyway. She's only sitting there at home with her leg up.

[*As they reach the brow of the hill, they meet* MELVYN *and* BRENDA *coming back, carrying the plane.*]

LEN [*to* MELVYN]: Did it fly, then?

MELVYN [*examining the plane*]: No, it's broken.

LEN: Hah.

PATRICK: Good evening.

MELVYN [*faintly surprised to see him*]: Oh. Hallo.

[PATRICK *and* LEN *go over the hill after* MURPHY.

BRENDA *and* MELVYN *come down into the meadow.*]

BRENDA: Are you sure it's broken?

MELVYN: Yes, it's a strut. Look, there.

BRENDA: Oh yes.

[*They examine the plane closely. We see them alone together for the first time. A glimpse of a very private relationship.*]

MELVYN: You see, if I reinforce it here that should strengthen it.

BRENDA: Won't that upset the balance on the nose?

MELVYN: It shouldn't do. It's slightly tail-heavy anyway, I think.

BRENDA: If we modified the nose section slightly by adding another piece across here ... Do you remember the other one we tried? That needed the same for some reason ...

MELVYN [*nodding slowly, considering*]: Yep – yep – yep ... Could do.

BRENDA [*staring at the aerodynamic problem*]: Yes ...

MELVYN: Back to the drawing board ...

BRENDA: Yes.

[ABIGAIL *arrives from across country pushing her bike.*]

ABIGAIL [*seeing them*]: Oh ...

MELVYN [*offhand*]: Hallo.

ABIGAIL: What are you doing here?

MELVYN: Mending this ...

ABIGAIL: It's past your bedtime.

MELVYN [*looking up to consider her*]: What are you doing?

ABIGAIL: Having a bicycle ride, aren't I? Obviously.

MELVYN: Funny place to ride it.

ABIGAIL [*irritably*]: I've stopped now, for heaven's sake, haven't I? I've got off it.

MELVYN: So you have.

ABIGAIL: I thought you'd be at home looking through the Situations Vacant. Not flying – aeroplanes. I mean, really, Mel. I mean, honestly. What are you playing at?

[MELVYN *keeps his head down examining the plane.*]

Mel?

BRENDA [*softly*]: Don't keep on at him.

ABIGAIL: What?

BRENDA: I said, don't keep on at him.

ABIGAIL [*coolly*]: I'm having a conversation with Mel on a family matter. I'm sorry. I don't think it has anything to do with you.

BRENDA: Oh yes, it has.

ABIGAIL [*startled*]: What?

MELVYN [*quietly, not wanting trouble*]: Bren ...

BRENDA: Anything to do with Mel is to do with me.

ABIGAIL: I don't know how you work that out. All that's happened to Mel since you met him is he's stopped his studies completely and has just thrown away an extremely promising career. Reverting now, as far as I can see, to second childhood, playing with toys all day ... Frankly, and I'll be absolutely blunt with you, I think your influence on Mel has been disastrous and the sooner he sees the back of you the better.

BRENDA [*evenly*]: I see.

ABIGAIL: Sorry, but it's best said, isn't it?

[*Slight pause*]

Well, at least we know where we stand. That's one thing.

MELVYN [*who hasn't looked up from his plane*]: I think it's this extra strut we put in that's doing it, you know ...

ABIGAIL [*more muted*]: I'm sorry, it's just he's – our brother and we're fond of him and we want the best for him. I suppose. I'm his sister, I'm concerned, that's all. All right, I can see I'm making no impression at all on either of you. I'll say no more. I promise. Forget I spoke ...

BRENDA: I see. I don't think it would be a very good idea for me to leave Mel now.

ABIGAIL: I can't see why not.

BRENDA [*deliberately*]: Well, with the baby coming ...

[*A pause.* MELVYN *looks to see how* ABIGAIL *has taken this. He then resumes inspection of the plane. Suspicion of a suppressed laugh from him.*]

ABIGAIL [*is silent, aghast*]: Oh my God. You're not –? Mel? She's not ...? Oh, dear God. Oh no. Oh, this is ... Oh heavens! Oh, for the love of ... Well, I don't know what to say. I am absolutely speechless. I am sorry but for once I am absolutely lost for words. I just do not know what to say. What do you want me to say? I mean, I'm sorry I just cannot find the words. For the first time in my life I have to admit it, I am completely and utterly speechless.

[*A pause.*]

What made you do it, Mel? What made you both do it?

MELVYN: Well, it's the result of a rather complicated chain of partly muscular, partly chemical changes that occur in the human body, particularly in the ...

ABIGAIL: You know what I'm talking about. There's no need for it these days. You're both old enough to know that surely?

BRENDA: We wanted a baby.

ABIGAIL: Wanted one?

BRENDA: Yes.

ABIGAIL: But he hasn't got a job.

BRENDA: Then he'll have more time with the baby, won't he?

ABIGAIL: Oh, dear God.

MELVYN: It's all right, Abi, don't fret. We've got things lined up.

ABIGAIL: What doing? Flying toy aeroplanes?

MELVYN: That's a nice idea ...

[PATRICK *appears on the top of the hill.*]

PATRICK: Well ...

ABIGAIL: Oh no.

PATRICK: I wondered where you were.

ABIGAIL [*to* MELVYN]: Why didn't you tell me he was here?

MELVYN: I thought you knew he was here.

PATRICK [*indicating the bicycle*]: I see you've dismounted your old grey mare.

ABIGAIL: Only temporarily.

PATRICK: What's she doing there? Turned her out to pasture, have you?

[ABIGAIL *laughs tinnily.*

A pause.

PATRICK *looks at* MELVYN *and* BRENDA.]

How are you two getting home?

MELVYN: Bus.

PATRICK: Want a lift in a minute?

MELVYN: Oh, yes. Ta.

PATRICK [*tossing* MELVYN *his car keys*]: Here, hop in then.

MELVYN [*taking the hint*]: Oh, yes, right ...

PATRICK: Only please – Mel – do not tinker with my electric aerial, windows, sunroof, cigar lighter, air conditioning or interior lights.

MELVYN: Can we play the cassette?

PATRICK: Yes, all right.

MELVYN: Have you still only got Mozart?

PATRICK: Yes.

MELVYN: Why don't you get something decent?

PATRICK: Because Mozart is decent. He's the only music there is.

MELVYN [*shaking his head sorrowfully*]: Oh dear, oh dear.

[MELVYN *and* BRENDA *go off with the aeroplane to the car.*]

PATRICK: Now then ...

ABIGAIL [*sharply*]: Leave me alone. Please. [*She starts to pick up the bike.*]

PATRICK: You off again?

ABIGAIL: Oh, go away, Patrick.

[PATRICK *sighs, suddenly tired.*

He walks a little bit away from her.]

PATRICK [*at length*]: It's getting awfully difficult this, Abi. It really is. I mean, I'm doing my best, honestly ...

ABIGAIL: What does that mean?

PATRICK: I'm trying to understand. You've plunged into this thing with Simon. I mean, you're not exactly being discreet about it, are you? It won't be long before everyone knows and quite frankly, it's all making me look a bit of an idiot. I don't mind that. I really don't. As long as I know. But I would like to know. Is this simply a summer frolic or the big new love of your life?

ABIGAIL: I'm – I've ... I've had a bit to drink, actually.

PATRICK: Ah, I see.

ABIGAIL: Not a lot. I stopped at the pub. On my own. I was on my own.

PATRICK: All right. Well. How long is this going on? How long do you plan to continue pedalling drunkenly round the countryside on a bicycle with a decidedly flat rear tyre?

ABIGAIL: Is it? Oh ... I don't know. I do not know. I love him. I do. I love him awfully. He's everything you're not. He opens doors for you. And he shoves you into chairs and things.

PATRICK: Oh, I see. Well ...

ABIGAIL: I mean, it's probably only because he didn't go to a smart public school like you did. And he's got lovely – well, he's got lovely manners in bed, too. If you want to know.

PATRICK: In bed?

ABIGAIL: Yes. He's – considerate ...

PATRICK: Shares the hot water bottle, that sort of thing, does he?

ABIGAIL [*supremely irritated*]: Oh, Patrick, go away. Please. Just go away. Now. Please.

PATRICK: I can't leave you sitting here, rolling drunk in the middle of a field.

ABIGAIL: Please.

PATRICK: How are you going to get home?

ABIGAIL: I shall cycle.

PATRICK: Abi, you can't ride the damn thing properly when you're sober.

ABIGAIL [*loud*]: Go away.

PATRICK: Are you meeting him?

ABIGAIL: What?

PATRICK: Lover boy. Is this a tryst?

ABIGAIL: Don't be silly.

PATRICK: I see. What are you planning to do? Meet up and pedal off together to a youth hostel? Better be careful which one you choose. Some of them don't like to see their young guests getting up to that sort of thing, you know. Or is it some small hotel you've discovered? That sounds more possible, though I think you'll have trouble getting into the dining room dressed like that. Unless you have an evening dress rolled up in your saddle bag. Is that it?

ABIGAIL: Piss off.

PATRICK: Oh, tremendous. Right, good night. If you do come home at dawn, as you have been known to, creep to bed quietly, will you? I have to be up early tomorrow. I want to oil the garage door.

ABIGAIL: Patrick ...

PATRICK: Yes.

ABIGAIL: Don't be mean. Try and understand.

PATRICK: I am doing, I've already said that.

ABIGAIL [*with difficulty*]: You see ... oh, I don't know. It's all so muddled. I need all this. I need this adventure, this excitement. I couldn't simply go on running your little castle. I was getting so boring. I know, we had wonderful times, occasionally, but we always met the same people. And we'd started getting into the same routines. We watched this programme on Monday and we went to the pub on Saturdays. I thought, God, I'll be old and I'll have done nothing. I'll be like all those other dreadful women with their shopping baskets on wheels having coffee in the back of the delicatessen. And I'm worth more than that. A bloody sight more than that.

PATRICK: Dearest girl, if you'd wanted to be Amy Johnson, you should have taken flying lessons. Now. You have your affair and you ring me up when it's all over and I'll come and pick you up.

ABIGAIL [*soft*]: And if it doesn't finish?

PATRICK [*solemn*]: Then we'll have to – sort something else out, won't we? O.K.? [*Rising suddenly*] My God, I'm being absolutely marvellous about all this, you know. I am simply beside myself with admiration for the way I'm behaving.

ABIGAIL: Oh, Patrick, I am sorry. I'm an awful person.

PATRICK: Yes, we knew that, don't worry. Go on, go to your hotel. Gobble up your pre-heated dinner, charge straight up to bed, you should get in a few hours' hard grind. Before they knock you up by mistake at 6 a.m. with the man next door's breakfast. Do you travel as Mr and Mrs or And Friend?

ABIGAIL: We don't do things like that. You're making it sound very, very sordid and it isn't like that. There's nothing underhand. I have been totally honest with you. You may have behaved well but so have I. I've never lied to you.

PATRICK: Only because you lie about as well as a ball-bearing in a bunker.

ABIGAIL: I have no idea what that means so I shall ignore it. I can see what you're trying to do. Don't worry. I see through you. You always were crafty. Like the way you persuaded me to marry you in the first place.

PATRICK [*wearily*]: What? What are you talking about now?

ABIGAIL: And now you're being so deeply wonderful, aren't you? You're making me sick. I wish to God you'd savage me. At least I'd know where I was. There's so much forgiveness flying around, it's like being married to the Pope.

PATRICK: Tell you what, I'll savage your bicycle, how's that?

ABIGAIL [*snarling*]: You leave my bicycle alone. Go on, go away. And for your information, there is more to Simon's and my relationship than physical sex. We have things in common, things to talk about. He's witty, amusing, he's done things. He's seen things in Africa and places. God, he's exciting. Beside him, you're – you're like Coquilles St Jacques and Brown Windsor soup.

PATRICK: Which of us is which?

ABIGAIL [*savagely*]: You are the soup, mate. You sure as hell aren't the coquilles. And we're not going to a hotel or a youth hostel tonight, so there.

PATRICK: You aren't?

ABIGAIL: Nope.

PATRICK: No?

ABIGAIL: No. We are not tonight, as it happens, actually going to bed together at all. In the true sense of the term.

PATRICK [*intrigued*]: Really?

ABIGAIL: Promise. So work that out. Good-bye.

PATRICK: You're going round to his place then?

ABIGAIL: What, with Brenda and his mother? Ha ha. You haven't met their mother.

PATRICK [*baffled*]: Well ...

[MELVYN *returns from the car.*]

MELVYN: How do you get those cassettes out of your tape machine when they've finished?

PATRICK: You press the button marked Eject.

MELVYN: Ah yes, but is there an override mechanism if that doesn't work?

PATRICK: Oh no.

MELVYN: It's only Mozart. [*Humming a bit of Symphony No. 41*] ... diddle-oo, diddle-oo diddle-oo-doo ...

PATRICK: I'm coming, I'm coming.

MELVYN: O.K.

[MELVYN *goes back to the car.*]

ABIGAIL: Good-bye, then.

PATRICK: Yes.

ABIGAIL: Well, go on. Or you'll miss something on television. Or down the pub. Old Stan in the snug will wonder what's happened to Mr Patrick. Usually buys me a pint, does Mr Pat, on a Saturday.

PATRICK: Oh, lay off, Abi, there's a love. It's not as dreary as all that, it really isn't.

ABIGAIL: Just seems it.

PATRICK: I don't think there's anything more we can usefully say, is there?

ABIGAIL: No.

PATRICK: I love you. Is that any good?

ABIGAIL: Not just at the moment, no.

PATRICK: Ah.

[*He sits on the slope.*

ABIGAIL *is still in the middle of the meadow.*]

ABIGAIL: Are you sitting there all night?

PATRICK: Maybe.

[*A silence.*

Both in their thoughts. Then, a jingling sound approaching. They both sit up and listen, trying to locate the source. SIMON *comes on from cross country. He is laden. He carries a plastic water container, full. A small tent, a rucksack, jingling with cutlery, plates and supplies of food plus his overnight necessities. He also has a small gas camping fire, the sort that packs up with its own built-in saucepans, two rolled sleeping bags, a plastic washing bowl and a flashlamp, the type that has a red warning attachment.*]

SIMON: Sorry, darling, the chain came off the bike and I had to – [*He sees* PATRICK.] Ah.

[PATRICK *stares at him.*

SIMON *stands awkwardly laden.*]

[*At length to* PATRICK] Hallo.

PATRICK: Hallo, there.

SIMON: I'm just . . . [*He searches his mind.*] I'm just . . . carrying a few things.

PATRICK: Yes, so I see.

SIMON: Bits and pieces, that's all . . .

PATRICK: Looks as if you're going camping. [*He laughs.*]

SIMON: Yes. Doesn't it? [*He laughs very heartily.*]

[ABIGAIL *sits in the middle of them getting hot and angry.*]

PATRICK: Well, I'll be off.

SIMON: Oh, right. Must you? Yes, righto.

PATRICK: I think Abi's staying though.

SIMON: Oh, is she? Is she? Good. Splendid.

PATRICK: So you won't get lonely. Sorry I have to dash. Cheerio.

SIMON: Yes.

[*Distantly is heard the sound of* LEN's *falsetto call.*]

LEN [*off, distant*]: Trix-Trix-Trix-Trix-Trix.

SIMON: What on earth's that?

PATRICK: I don't know. Some woman calling her dog, wasn't it?

SIMON: Oh yes. Probably.

PATRICK: Good night to you.

SIMON: 'Night.

[PATRICK *goes.*

A silence until he is well clear.]

Oh lord.

ABIGAIL: You didn't handle that very well, did you?

SIMON: Well, I could hardly –

ABIGAIL: Didn't you see the car?

SIMON: No, I came the other way. So I wouldn't be seen.

ABIGAIL: Well, you were.

SIMON: What are we going to do now?

ABIGAIL: It doesn't matter.

SIMON: But he's seen us.

ABIGAIL: So what, who cares?

SIMON: Well, surely he ... I don't understand all this, I really don't. I mean, does he know?

ABIGAIL: Yes.

SIMON: Then he's behaving very peculiarly, isn't he?

ABIGAIL: He's a very peculiar man. That's why I'm with you, Simon.

SIMON [*not altogether convinced*]: Yes. O.K. Well. Gloss over that. As long as he doesn't want to sleep between us, I suppose, we'll have to accept the status quo. I'll stick your bike under the bush, shall I?

ABIGAIL: Thanks. [*Stopping him as he does so*] Oh, hang on. [*She opens the saddle bag and produces a bottle of red wine.*] My contribution.

SIMON: Is that all you've brought?

ABIGAIL: Ah. [*Returning to the saddle bag*] Toothbrush. [*She produces it.*]

SIMON: No night things?

ABIGAIL: Simon, I am not wearing night things. This whole evening's supposed to be natural and free.

SIMON [*wheeling off her bike*]: Yes, super. O.K. Won't be a tick.

[ABIGAIL, *alone, dubiously examines the equipment he has brought.*]

[*Off*] 'Way! Go 'way! Shoo, shoo.

[SIMON *returns.*]

ABIGAIL: What's going on?

SIMON: There was a repulsive fat old dog just about to pee over my bike.

ABIGAIL: Shoo it away.

SIMON: I did. It didn't appear to hear me. Anyway. Now ... [*He looks about him.*] Tent first, I think.

ABIGAIL: We don't need a tent, do we?

SIMON: You'll be glad of it at six o'clock in the morning when you wake up covered in dew.

ABIGAIL: Dew. Oh, that's wonderful. When did we last see dew?

SIMON: Don't know. It's not all that hot.

[SIMON *picks up the tent packed very small.*]

ABIGAIL: We can't sleep in that, it's minute.

SIMON [*starting to unpack the tent*]: Hang on. It does get somewhat bigger.

ABIGAIL: I want this to be a natural experience.

[*During the following* SIMON *unpacks, lays out and finally erects the tent at the foot of the slope. It is a small, modest affair just large enough for two. It has the door at one end (facing away from the slope) and a small ventilator window.*]

SIMON: It's a family heirloom, this is. Bren and I used to go camping in it at the bottom of our garden. That was when we were still young enough to be able to share tents together. It's just big enough for two to sleep in. I mean, you can get tents now, of course, with hot and cold in all rooms, french windows and a musical cocktail cabinet but that does seem to be losing the point, doesn't it, somewhat?

ABIGAIL: I'd get claustrophobia if I tried to sleep in this. I tell you.

SIMON: Surely not. Weren't you in the Girl Guides, for heaven's sake?

ABIGAIL: No, I was not. Dorcas was. But then Dorcas was in everything that was going.

SIMON: Good for her.

ABIGAIL: My first memories of Dorcas are of a very small, round girl dressed entirely in brown, eternally in search of silver paper. [*Back to the tent*] We'll never get both of us to fit into this.

SIMON: Hang on, hang on. You'll see. [*He struggles on with his task.*] It'll soon be dark, won't it?

ABIGAIL [*ferreting about*]: What's this thing?

SIMON: Oh that, that's a camping stove. Gas. Rather neat, isn't it?

ABIGAIL: A gas stove?

SIMON: Yes.

ABIGAIL: Aren't we going to light a fire?

SIMON: Yes, if you like.

ABIGAIL: We have to have a fire, a camp fire. It's not very romantic sitting round a gas stove, is it?

SIMON: Probably not. But they're damned useful when it comes to brewing early morning tea.

ABIGAIL: Early morning tea?

SIMON: Yes.

ABIGAIL: You're joking, surely?

SIMON: What?

ABIGAIL: You are, aren't you? You're joking.

SIMON: How do you mean?

ABIGAIL: Oh come on, Simon. This is an adventure. I mean, the next thing you'll have me doing the washing up.

SIMON [*laughing*]: Well, I brought the bowl there, you see.

    [ABIGAIL *looks at him dangerously.*]

SIMON: No, that's mainly for washing. You've no objections to us washing, have you? I mean, it's not too unnatural, is it?

ABIGAIL: No. As long as it's just for washing.

    [SIMON *continues to work on the tent.*]

SIMON [*after a pause*]: Abi.

ABIGAIL: Mm?

SIMON: Look – er – how many people is it that know? About us two, I mean.

ABIGAIL: How do you mean?

SIMON: Well, Patrick knows. And Dorcas knows. And Brenda and Mel know. Does your father know, for instance?

ABIGAIL: He most certainly does not.

SIMON: Oh good. And what about all these other people? Len and Rita, people like that?

ABIGAIL: Not on your life. Of course not. What's wrong?

SIMON: Well, I'm starting this teaching job in a week or two and I don't think this particular school would look too kindly on all this.

ABIGAIL: Look, I'm not telling people. I don't know if you are. If Uncle Len knew, it would be disaster. And Pa would be very upset. He adores Patrick.

SIMON: And there's no chance of any sudden whirlwind divorce, is there?

ABIGAIL: No.

SIMON: Just so long as I'm prepared.

ABIGAIL: No. Patrick wouldn't do that. He'll do what I want. He always does in the end. Anyway. Poor old Pa. I'm afraid he's gone completely dotty now. He set fire to all his shoes the other day.

SIMON: Ah. [*Standing back and presenting the tent*] There you are. What about that?

ABIGAIL [*looking at it without enthusiasm*]: Well ... You can sleep in it, I'm not.

SIMON [*easily*]: We'll see. Fancy a cup of tea, then?

ABIGAIL: No, I don't. God, you've suddenly got this obsession with cups of tea. I can't think of anything more boring. I mean, when you were out in the bush in Africa, you didn't all sit round drinking cups of tea, did you?

SIMON: I never went out in the bush. I was thousands of miles away from any bush, actually. I never even saw a bush.

ABIGAIL: Where did you live?

SIMON: In a flat.

ABIGAIL: How awfully dull.

SIMON: It had a roof garden. That got pretty wild in the rainy season. That was about it. I did see a locust once. A dead one.

ABIGAIL: Well, this is all one hell of an anti-climax, I don't mind saying. [*The midges have arrived.*

They unconsciously swat at them as they speak.]

I thought we were going to rough it. I don't call this roughing it. Tents and continual cups of tea. We might as well be sitting on our carpet in the lounge.

SIMON [*getting needled*]: Well, what do you want? For heaven's sake? There's no point in our being uncomfortable just for the sheer hell of it, is there? I mean, even the chaps who go up Everest have been known to take the odd tent, you know. And I think some of them have actually been known to wear gloves. There's a distinct difference between roughing it and sheer suicidal lunacy.

ABIGAIL: Yes, all right, all right.

SIMON: Well, just don't keep on. I've done my best. I've been crawling about in the roof of our garage for most of the day, banging my head trying to sort this lot out. I expected a bit of thanks.

ABIGAIL: Now, don't start blaming me. You're the one who started all this hearty nonsense. You dragged me into it, not the other way round, may I remind you. You started all this bicycle riding. Don't start complaining if I want to do things properly.

SIMON: I don't know what the hell you're on about, doing things properly.

ABIGAIL: Well, look at it all.

SIMON: All what? One tent with groundsheet. Two sleeping bags. One rucksack, containing two knives, two forks, two plates, two spoons, one teaspoon, one tin opener, two tin mugs, one packet of teabags ...

ABIGAIL [*scornfully*]: Teabags.

SIMON: Half a pound of bacon, two eggs, salt, pepper, one small loaf, bit of butter, tin of milk, one tin beans, one bar milk chocolate ...

ABIGAIL: That'll do.

SIMON [*relentlessly*]: One plastic bowl for washing purposes only, one camping gas stove with pans attached, one towel, one torch and one spare battery and that's your lot. We're hardly equipped on a Himalayan scale, are we?

ABIGAIL [*pointing to the water container*]: What's that then?

SIMON: That's water. Fresh water.

ABIGAIL: Well, that's unnecessary.

SIMON: What do we do then? Sit round and wait for it to rain?

ABIGAIL: No. We could have got our water from the Trickle.

SIMON: From the what?

ABIGAIL: The little stream just down there. It's called the Pendon Trickle.

SIMON: Oh, is it? Well, have you looked in your Trickle lately because it's full of scrap iron. [*Indicating his water bottle*] Personally, I'm drinking from this. If you want to drink from the Trickle and risk swallowing bits of rusty refrigerator, you're welcome.

ABIGAIL: Well ...

SIMON: I am now going to make up the sleeping bags in the tent and then, whether you like it or not, I'm going to get that stove going and have a nice cup of tea.

ABIGAIL: What about my fire?

SIMON: We'll see about your fire. It very much depends if you behave yourself from now on.

[SIMON *starts to move the sleeping bags towards the tent.*]

ABIGAIL: You can leave my bag out here, please.

SIMON: Suit yourself.

[SIMON *crawls into the tent, taking one sleeping bag with him.*]

ABIGAIL [*moving her sleeping bag to another part of the field*]: I'm putting mine here. Where I can see the stars, when they come out. [*She unrolls her sleeping bag and sits on it.*] Oh, it's so peaceful here. Wonderful.

> So, we'll go no more a-roving
> So late into the night,
> Though the heart be still as loving,
> And the moon be still as bright.

[*Trying to remember*] Who's that? Byron, is it? Or was it Shelley?

SIMON [*from within the tent with conviction*]: Shelley.

ABIGAIL: Shelley, is it?

SIMON: Uh-huh.

ABIGAIL: No, it's not. It's Byron. It's Byron, not Shelley.

SIMON: Is it? I was never too hot on Byron.

[ABIGAIL *sits.*
From within the tent, disturbing her peace, is the sound of a great deal of grunting and effortful sounds as SIMON *arranges his sleeping bag in the confined space.*]

[*From within the tent*] Heeeup – hup ... Hey – hup ... ay.

ABIGAIL: What are you doing in there, for goodness' sake?

SIMON: I'm trying to – hup – get this – round the tent – hup – post – that's it.

ABIGAIL [*curious, moving to the tent*]: What's it like in there?

SIMON: Very cosy. Come in.

[ABIGAIL *crawls cautiously half through the door.*]

ABIGAIL: Oh yes ...

SIMON: We can have a bit of fun in here.

ABIGAIL: It smells awful. It smells of old socks. You can't sleep in there. No one could possibly sleep in there. [*She comes out into the fresh air.*]

SIMON: I told you it's been in the garage for years. It'll air through.

ABIGAIL: It's quite off-putting. Ugh.

SIMON: It'll be O.K. Look, I'll open the window. [*He undoes the ventilator flap from the outside.*] There you are. See.

ABIGAIL: Oh yes, that'll make a tremendous difference.

SIMON [*still within the tent*]: You'd better watch yourself or I'll come out there and get at you with a tent pole.

ABIGAIL [*to herself*]: Oh, lucky old me.

[*Suddenly she giggles. Snatching up the stove, she runs up the slope with it. She throws it from her, presumably into the undergrowth. She returns, pleased with herself.*]

SIMON: What are you doing out there?

ABIGAIL: Nothing.

SIMON: Right, that's settled. What next?

[*He emerges from the tent, standing thoughtfully.*]

You know, just occurred to me. It's an odd time to think of it, I know, but in just a week today ...

ABIGAIL: What?

SIMON: I'll be running the big race, won't I?

ABIGAIL: Oh, that.

SIMON: Yes. Straight through here. Pitting my skills against those of the redoubtable Constable Murphy.

ABIGAIL: Oh yes. Uncle Len's home-grown champion.

SIMON: I've seen him. He's quite good, you know. I think I can beat him providing I think out my ... [*Noticing the absence of the stove*] All right. What have you done with it?

ABIGAIL: Mmm?

SIMON: My gas stove. Where is it?

ABIGAIL: Now, you'll have to light a proper fire, won't you?

SIMON: What have you done with my stove?

[ABIGAIL *points up the slope.*]

Oh my God.

[*He snatches up the torch.*]

Where the hell is it?

[*He climbs to the top of the slope.*]

ABIGAIL: Somewhere in the bracken. You'll never find it in the dark.

SIMON: Oh, you ...

ABIGAIL: Find it in the morning.

SIMON: Oh, you stupid – prat.

[ABIGAIL *laughs.*]

You stupid – daft – half-witted – prat. Now we can't have any tea at all.

ABIGAIL: Light a fire.

SIMON [*stamping down the slope*]: No, really I'm bloody angry over that. I really am. [*He bangs down his lamp on the ground and stands undecided.*] I mean, that's just a really prattish thing to do.

ABIGAIL [*softening*]: Simon, I'm sorry. Sorry. [*Cooing*] Won't you light me a fire, please?

SIMON: No.

ABIGAIL: Oh Simon, I'll boil you some tea if you make the fire. I promise.

SIMON: You can't boil me some tea.

ABIGAIL: Yes, I can.

SIMON: No, you can't.

ABIGAIL: Why not?

SIMON: Because you threw our saucepans away with the stove.

ABIGAIL: I did?

SIMON: Yes.

ABIGAIL: Well, can we still have a fire?

SIMON: No, we can't because that stove was self-lighting.

ABIGAIL: And you didn't bring any matches?

SIMON: Yes, I did bring some matches but in order to keep them safe and dry, I packed them inside one of the saucepans which you may recall you threw away with the stove. So, that's that.

ABIGAIL: Oh.

SIMON: So. You wanted to rough it, now we're going to rough it. Unless you prefer to go home.

ABIGAIL: Of course I don't. [*Penitent*] Oh, you're right. I am a prat. Whatever that is.

SIMON: I'd better get the rest of this stuff inside the tent before you throw that away. [*He moves the rucksack inside the tent.*]

[ABIGAIL *has been playing with the flash lamp, the red section of which begins to flash on and off.*]

ABIGAIL: Why does this thing flash on and off like this?

SIMON: It's a distress signal.

ABIGAIL: What for?

SIMON: For people who've had their stoves unexpectedly chucked away.
   [*He disappears into the tent.*]
   [LEN's *voice is heard again in the distance, calling his dog.*]
LEN [*off, distant, falsetto*]: Trix-Trix-Trix-Trix-Trix.
ABIGAIL [*switching off the lamp*]: What is that noise? We heard it before.
SIMON [*sticking his head out of the tent to listen*]: I don't know. It's a bit
   odd, isn't it?
LEN [*off, distant*]: Trix-Trix-Trix-Trix-Trix.
SIMON [*bounding up the bank*]: I'll have a look. [*He does so.*]
ABIGAIL: Anyone?
SIMON: No, it's too dark now.
ABIGAIL: Eerie. I'm glad you're here.
   [SIMON *comes down the bank.*]
   Perhaps it's part of these peculiar goings-on we keep hearing rumours
   about.
SIMON: What are those?
ABIGAIL: You know. One's always reading dark hints in the local rag.
   Strange goings-on on the Common.
SIMON: Oh yes, right. You mean, the witches and so on.
ABIGAIL: Yes. The funny Councillor Whatsisname, he's something to do
   with it. Councillor Polegrave.
SIMON: Is he? Is he the one with the eyebrows?
ABIGAIL: Yes, he was nearly had up some years back but they hushed it
   up. He was seen one night chasing plump, white Town Hall typists in
   and out of the bushes in the Municipal Gardens.
SIMON: How do you know all these things, for heaven's sake?
ABIGAIL: Because I have coffee with Mrs Barnsley, the Chief Executive's
   wife every Thursday in the delicatessen. I hear all the scandal from her.
   She's wonderful, she knows everything.
SIMON [*putting the washbowl in the tent*]: You know, you're right. It is
   rather small in there. Well. What do we do now? Sit and look at each
   other?
ABIGAIL: That's no good. I can't even see you – [*Swatting*] Bloody midges
   – come over here.
SIMON: O.K.
   [SIMON *sits by her on her sleeping bag.*]
ABIGAIL: It's still being fun, isn't it?
SIMON: Um.
ABIGAIL: Go on. You've got to admit this is fun.
SIMON [*catching midges vaguely*]: Be a lot nicer with a cup of tea.
ABIGAIL: I bet you haven't even got a bottle opener, either.

SIMON: Oh yes, I have.

ABIGAIL: Well, then, we can have wine.

SIMON: Good idea. [*He produces a knife with many attachments and eventually finds a corkscrew.*] I think this will work. I've used it as a screwdriver, a bradawl, a miniature axe, a stone remover, a tin opener and a bottle opener, but I think I'm christening it as a corkscrew. [*Fetching the bottle*] Hey, this is very nice. Where did you get this?

ABIGAIL: Oh, it's one of Patrick's.

SIMON: It's a damned good claret. Does he mind?

ABIGAIL: I didn't ask him, did I?

SIMON: Crikey. Do you think we ought to?

ABIGAIL: Go on.

SIMON: But it's a '62 Latour.

[SIMON *opens the bottle.*

[ABIGAIL *sits watching him. She starts to hum to herself.*]

[*Struggling with the bottle*] Ah ha, that's significant.

ABIGAIL: What is?

SIMON: When you start doing that. Humming like that.

ABIGAIL: Was I?

SIMON [*slyly*]: Ah ha. [*He opens the bottle.*] There you go. Just a tick. [*He goes to the tent and returns with the mugs he has unpacked.*] Here we are.

ABIGAIL: Oh, surely we can ...

SIMON: No.

ABIGAIL: What?

SIMON: I'm not drinking a '62 Latour straight from the bottle. Sorry. There are limits.

ABIGAIL: It's a good one, is it?

SIMON: It should be. [*He pours.*]

ABIGAIL: Have you had it before?

SIMON: No. I've dreamt about it sometimes. It's about twenty quid a bottle this stuff.

ABIGAIL: Twenty quid!

SIMON: At least.

ABIGAIL: God, that bastard.

SIMON: What?

ABIGAIL: You know, he won't even let me stock up on ginger ale. Twenty quid. That's immoral. You know, he puts the cheap bottles by the door. He thinks I can't be bothered to go right into that cellar. But I've got wise to that one.

SIMON: Cheers then.

ABIGAIL: Cheers. [*She tastes it.*] Mm. It's strong. Nice, isn't it?

SIMON: Yes, it should have been left to breathe a little. Never mind. Good health.

ABIGAIL: To us.

SIMON: Yes.

> [*They drink.*
> *A pause.*]

How's Dorcas these days?

ABIGAIL: Dorcas? Oh, she's all right.

SIMON: Still with her poet?

ABIGAIL: Stafford? Yes. I can't imagine why. She claims she's slowly renovating him but there's no outward signs of improvement as far as I can see.

SIMON: Knowing her though, I think she'll probably achieve it. If she sets her heart on it. She's quite a determined character, isn't she?

ABIGAIL: Yes, yes ... Why are we talking about her?

SIMON: Sorry.

ABIGAIL: Talk about me, please, immediately.

SIMON: O.K. Bit of a limited subject. [*He laughs.*]

ABIGAIL: You'd be surprised. What did you mean just then?

SIMON: When?

ABIGAIL: About me singing. You said it meant something. Ah ha, you said ...

SIMON: Ah, well ...

ABIGAIL: What?

SIMON: Well. It's just that you do sing.

ABIGAIL: When do I sing?

SIMON: When you're – when we're making love.

ABIGAIL: Do I?

SIMON: Didn't you know you were doing it?

ABIGAIL: No.

SIMON: Oh, yes.

ABIGAIL: What do I sing about?

SIMON: No, you don't have any words. You just make sort of musical noises.

ABIGAIL [*amused and embarrassed*]: Well. I never knew that. [*She thinks about it.*] I don't.

SIMON: Yes, you do. You start off sort of, [*Demonstrating*] hmmm ... hmmm ... hmmm in the early stages as it were and then as things really get underway, it's sort of more [*Demonstrating again*] la-la-la-la-la-la.

ABIGAIL [*incredulous*]: I don't.

SIMON: You do.

ABIGAIL: Patrick's never mentioned it.

SIMON: Perhaps he's tone deaf. [*He laughs.*]

ABIGAIL: God, how awful. How awfully embarrassing.

SIMON: Oh, I don't know. It's rather nice really. Not so good in small hotel rooms ...

ABIGAIL: So that's why you wanted to get me into a tent ...

SIMON: Ah-ah. Now, now. You wanted the tent. I could see some of the advantages, of course ...

ABIGAIL [*laughing*]: La-la-la-la-la-la.

SIMON: Yes, something like that. Only much louder.

    [*They sit, drinking.*]

ABIGAIL: Very dark now.

SIMON: Yes. Moon coming up though.

ABIGAIL: Yes. Oh, this is more like it.

SIMON: Good.

    [*He swats another midge.*]

ABIGAIL: What are you thinking about?

SIMON: Oh, nothing that would interest you.

ABIGAIL: Everything about you interests me. Tell me.

SIMON: I was just thinking about the race next week.

ABIGAIL: Oh no, not the race again.

SIMON: I told you you wouldn't be interested.

ABIGAIL: You're with me in a field under the stars raring to go. And you're thinking about running races.

SIMON: Sorry.

    [ABIGAIL *kisses him.*
    SIMON *goes to kiss her in return.*
    ABIGAIL *lies back but is immediately in great discomfort.*]

ABIGAIL: Ur –

SIMON: Mm?

ABIGAIL: Just a tick. I'm lying on something. [*She investigates.*] Oh, it's the mallet.

    [*She moves it.* SIMON *is thinking again.*]

SIMON: You see, the point about this chap Murphy ...

ABIGAIL: Who?

SIMON: Murphy. This fellow I'm running against. His strength's in his start. He's got a damn good start. His finish, however, is suspect.

ABIGAIL: Well, we won't ask him to tea, will we?

SIMON: But I'm going to have to plan my strategy well in advance.

ABIGAIL [*dreamily*]: I dearly want to remember tonight. I want to make it something memorable. Oh Simon, let's go mad. Tell you what, you think of something to do and then I'll think of something to do and then we'll both think of something to do.

SIMON [*none too sure of this*]: Yes, O.K.

ABIGAIL: What are you going to do first?

SIMON: Well, I'm going to zip the sleeping bags together for a kick off.

ABIGAIL: Brilliant.

> [SIMON *moves her sleeping bag to the tent.*
>
> ABIGAIL *watches him dreamily. She starts to hum gently, something she continues to do from here on in.*]

[*Watching him*] You're all man, Simon.

SIMON: I hope so, yes.

ABIGAIL: I'll tell you what I'm going to do now. For your delectation. I'm going to dance for you. I shall take off all my clothes and dance for you.

SIMON: Hang on. I'm not Councillor Polegrave, you know.

ABIGAIL: By the light of the fire.

SIMON: What fire?

ABIGAIL [*shouting angrily*]: Oh come on, Simon, use your imagination.

SIMON [*still working on the sleeping bags*]: Sorry, I'll get into it in a minute. [*He emerges from the tent.*]

ABIGAIL: You're about as romantic as a piece of knotted string, aren't you?

SIMON: Oh come on, Abi. We've been sitting out here getting bitten to death by midges. We could've been in the tent, behind the insect net, having the time of our lives.

> [ABIGAIL *has marched down. She now switches on the torch so that it starts to flash red, and plonks it on the ground.*]

ABIGAIL: There. That'll do for a fire. All right?

> [*She starts to hum again, accompanying herself rhythmically as she dances.*]

Bom ... bom ... der .... Watch closely.

SIMON: Yes, I will. I can't quite make you out. Can you get a bit closer to the lamp?

ABIGAIL: Bom ... bom ... der ... bom.

> [*She unbuttons her shirt in the manner of a stripper, eventually tossing it to the ground.* SIMON, *sipping his Latour, begins to enjoy this.*]

ABIGAIL: More?

SIMON: Yes, please. More. Goes well with the Latour.

ABIGAIL: Your turn, then.

SIMON: Eh?

ABIGAIL: To remove something. Come on.

SIMON: Oh God, Abi.

ABIGAIL: Come on, get it off. [*She starts to unbutton his shirt.*]

Bom ... bom ... der ... bom.

SIMON: God, we'll get eaten alive.

ABIGAIL [*throwing* SIMON's *shirt to the ground*]: That's better. Here we go. My turn.

> [ABIGAIL *continues to dance, removing her jeans. This turns out to be a difficult operation to do gracefully.*]

Bom ... bom ... der ... bom ... Oh bugger these things, they always get ...

> [*She sits on the ground and struggles.*]

Don't look. You're not to look at this bit. [*Removing her trousers finally*] Right, you can look again now. Bom ... bom ... der ... bom. Voilà, feast your eyes. Right.

SIMON: My turn again, is it?

ABIGAIL: Yes, your turn.

SIMON: Yes, I was afraid it was.

ABIGAIL: Get 'em off.

SIMON [*reluctantly removing his trousers*]: We're very near the main road here, you know, Abi.

ABIGAIL: Bom ... bom ... der ... bom.

> [*Distantly a dog barks.*]

SIMON: What was that?

ABIGAIL: What?

SIMON: Sounded like a dog.

ABIGAIL: Never mind the dog. My turn. Don't miss this whatever you do. Bom ... bom ... der ... bom.

> [*She reaches to unfasten her bra.* SIMON, *despite his unease, is distinctly fascinated. Suddenly, the proceedings are further lit by two powerful torches. One from the direction of the road and one held by a figure standing on top of the bank. The comparatively deafening sound of the loudhailer cuts through the proceedings.* LEN's *voice is heard, greatly amplified and distorted.*]

LEN [*through the loudhailer*]: This is the Police. We have reason to believe you are at present indulging in unnatural practices. You are advised to stay exactly where you are. This is the Police. We have you totally surrounded.

ABIGAIL: Oh, my God. [*She stands horrified.*]

SIMON [*urgently*]: Run for it. [*Feverishly he begins to gather up his discarded clothes.*]

LEN: Stop them. Stop them.

> [ABIGAIL *screams and starts a frenzied search for her own clothes unsuccessfully.*]

Get him, Murphy, get him, lad.

SIMON: Come on, run like hell.

[LEN *appears by the entrance to the road.* MURPHY *hurtles down the slope. His charge causes* ABIGAIL *to squawk in alarm, abandon her search for clothes and plunge for refuge in the tent.* SIMON, *who has now found his clothes, runs round the other side of the tent and up the bank avoiding* MURPHY, *who grabs at him vainly.*]

LEN: Go get him, boy. Go get him.

[MURPHY *launches like a bullet after* SIMON. SIMON *disappears over the hill with* MURPHY *in pursuit.* LEN, *eager not to miss the chase, runs up the hill after them.*]

[*Through his loudhailer*] There is no point in trying to escape. I repeat, there is no point in trying to escape. The policeman now pursuing you is a championship runner ... Go on, lad, go.

[ABIGAIL's *head comes nervously out of the tent. Her clothes seem too far away for a safe dash. Unseen by* LEN, *a figure comes hurtling on from the road doubled up. It is* PATRICK.]

ABIGAIL: Aah!

PATRICK [*pushing her back into the tent*]: Get in.

ABIGAIL: Patrick, what are you —

PATRICK: Shut up and get in.

[PATRICK *and* ABIGAIL *disappear inside the tent.*]

LEN [*during this*]: Come on, Murphy, you can do better than that. Run lad. [*He comes down the slope.*] He'll get him, he'll get him. [*To the tent*] All right, come out of there. Let's have you. Come on. Out you come.

[PATRICK *emerges, furious.*]

PATRICK: What the hell is the meaning of this? My wife and I are — Ah. Hallo, Len.

LEN: Ah.

PATRICK: I'm sorry.

LEN: What are you doing here?

PATRICK: Well, believe it or not, we've been trying to get a peaceful night. Only we've been half-terrified by naked madmen dancing round the tent.

LEN: Ah, you saw him then.

PATRICK: We did indeed.

LEN: And her.

PATRICK: Yes.

LEN: We're giving chase. Did they do anything? You know, unnatural at all?

PATRICK: No, fortunately you arrived in the nick of time.

LEN: Well, he's taken his clothes. [*Picking up the remaining garments*] Unless these are ...

PATRICK: No, no, those look like Abi's. She was – well, we were, you know ... [*He winks.*]

LEN [*understanding*]: Yes, yes, well ...

PATRICK [*offering to take the clothes*]: May I?

LEN [*handing them over*]: Of course.

PATRICK: Thank you.

LEN [*shouting at the tent*]: Evening, Abigail.

ABIGAIL [*sticking her head out*]: Oh good evening, Uncle Len.

LEN: I must say, I didn't realize this was your sort of thing. Tenting ...

PATRICK: Well, it was a spur of the moment thing, you know. We were sitting at home and we suddenly both became aware that our lives were getting into a rut, you know, always watching the same programmes on Mondays, off to the pub every Saturday ...

LEN: I know, I know, I see that. Well, you had fair warning there might be trouble round here, didn't you?

PATRICK: I'll listen next time, I promise you that.

LEN: Anyway, we'll soon catch this little flasher. He won't bother you again.

PATRICK: Much obliged.

LEN: We won't be going home completely empty-handed.

> [MURPHY *appears at the top of the slope. He is utterly exhausted. He clasps his side and bends double with the effort.*]

Ah, Murphy ... Murphy? What's happened? Where is he?

> [MURPHY *shakes his head.*]

You don't mean he got away?

> [MURPHY *nods.*]

How the hell did he get away?

> [MURPHY *shakes his head.*]

LEN [*stunned*]: Well, I don't know. I don't know at all. Well, I'm pole-axed. That's the only word. Pole-axed.

PATRICK: Anything we can do?

LEN: No, no, no. It's a Police matter. Take my advice. You keep your flap buttoned up for the rest of the night. And next time, try and pitch your tent a bit nearer civilization.

PATRICK: We will.

LEN: Good night to you.

PATRICK: Good night.

ABIGAIL: 'Night.

LEN [*to* MURPHY]: Come on, lad. Not my night really, is it? I've had my best runner beaten and lost my bloody dog. Not my night. [*Calling as he goes*] Trix-Trix-Trix-Trix-Trix.

> [LEN *and* MURPHY *go out to the road.*]

ABIGAIL: And what do you think you're doing?

PATRICK: Amongst other things, saving your reputation. And mine.

ABIGAIL: Were you watching us?

PATRICK: Only the last bit. Very good. Can I offer you a limited engage-
ment at our next office Christmas party ... All right, come on.

ABIGAIL: What?

PATRICK: Let's get home, quickly. I've had far too much fresh air already.

ABIGAIL: Did you know?

PATRICK: What?

ABIGAIL: That Uncle Len would be patrolling about out here?

PATRICK: No idea. I was just passing. I saw the big drive-in strip-tease
signs and I thought ... [*He breaks off as he finds the bottle.*] My God,
this is my '62. Did you take this? Did you take my '62? [*He sniffs the
bottle.*] Beautiful. God, that's beautiful. How could you do this to my
'62?

ABIGAIL [*handing him a mug*]: Here.

PATRICK [*shuddering*]: Ugggh! You're a barbarous creature. If I had my
way, this would be a capital offence. You should be flogged mercilessly
with cold, wet lettuce.

    [ABIGAIL *is humming to herself again.*]
Are you getting dressed?

ABIGAIL: No.

PATRICK: Are you going home like that?

ABIGAIL: Come and see inside my tent first.

PATRICK: No, thank you. Seen one tent, you've seen them all.

ABIGAIL: This one's got a window, look.

PATRICK: Oh, good. Don't fall out of it, will you?

ABIGAIL [*cooing inside the tent*]: Patrick. [*She hums.*] Patrick.

    [*A bare arm comes out of the tent doorway seductively beckoning.*]

PATRICK: Abi, what the hell are you doing?

ABIGAIL [*singing her siren's song*]: Patrick ... Patrick ... [*Her arm disappears into the tent.*]

PATRICK [*reluctantly moving to the tent and putting his head through the
doorway*]: Abi, if you don't come out of there and come home this
minute, I'm going to ... yurck ...

    [*He is yanked suddenly and violently into the tent, headfirst. He
    vanishes.*]

    [*From within the tent*]: Abi, come on now ...

    [ABIGAIL's *song is heard.*]
Abi. Abi – now, Abi ...

ABIGAIL [*laughing a very dirty laugh*]: Patrick.

PATRICK: All right, all right. That's it. All right?

ABIGAIL: All right.
PATRICK: Sure?
ABIGAIL: Mmm.
    [*In a second,* ABIGAIL'*s song gets louder.*]
  La-la-la-la-la-la . . .
    [*As* ABIGAIL *finishes her song on a high, clear, drawn-out note,*
    PATRICK'S *voice is heard joining with hers.*]

                    BLACKOUT

End of Act Two Scene One A
Please turn to Act Two Scene Two (p. 324).

DORCAS: ACT ONE
SCENE TWO D

The scene break has been very swift. We return to the same but it is now a bright, sunny Sunday afternoon in June. ABIGAIL *strolls on. It is apparent she is restless and discontent. She stands in the centre of the meadow and looks about her. Unseen by her,* STAFFORD *appears at the top of the slope. He is unkempt and crumpled. Half crouching with his back to her, he is evidently tracking someone or something invisible to us over the brow of the hill. He becomes aware of* ABIGAIL'S *presence. He stares at her, Ben Gunn-like.* ABIGAIL *herself has a feeling she is being watched.*

ABIGAIL [*turning and seeing him*]: Wuh! Oh, hallo ...
  [STAFFORD *scuttles away.*]
  Extraordinary.
  [PATRICK *enters, carrying two folding chairs, the Sunday papers and a picnic bag. He evidently considers this rather a lot to be carrying.*]
PATRICK [*surveying* ABIGAIL]: I take it this is your day for not carrying things? Is that correct? Yes, I thought it was. So long as we know. Never mind, the others can carry the rest.
  [*He dumps down the stuff and starts to put up a chair.*]
  I really must order a special year planner just for you, you know. I mean, I know women's metabolisms go round and round in cycles but you're the only one I know who has cycles within cycles. Today is your day for not carrying things. Yesterday was your refusing-to-shut-any-doors day. Monday, if I'm not mistaken, was the yearly anniversary for the start of your leaving-all-the-taps-running week. I mean, I don't mind as long as I know they're coming. But it is nice to mark these celebrations, don't you agree? Otherwise we'll miss them. Like the International Open Fridge Door Overnight Festival or the All British Leaving the Oven on Low Week or the Jubilee Celebration for –
ABIGAIL: Oh, do shut up, Patrick, for heaven's sake.
PATRICK: Right. [*Under his breath*] World Silence Day.
  [PATRICK *sits. A silence.*]
ABIGAIL: I've done all those sandwiches. Took me all morning. I hope Rita's remembered to do her half, that's all. Otherwise we won't have enough. She should remember. I've phoned her enough times. I stink

of sardines. God, the organization for one simple picnic. I don't know why Pa insists on having one. They're always disaster.

PATRICK: It won't bother me. At 4.10 precisely I must be on the motorway, steaming towards Manchester.

ABIGAIL: It's all right for you ...

PATRICK: It isn't all right for me. I didn't arrange this meeting. But since we have to charge round the country, we plain simple executives, in order to humour our Chairman's holiday arrangements ...

ABIGAIL: Yes, I'm sure. Well, you're seeing this picnic out to the bitter end.

PATRICK: Only until 4.06.

ABIGAIL: We'll see about that. You know, I thought I saw that Stafford man just now.

PATRICK: Stafford?

ABIGAIL: You know, that peculiar poet man. The one Dorcas used to go around with before she met up with her big game hunter.

PATRICK: Oh really?

ABIGAIL: I wonder what he was doing. Stafford.

PATRICK: Composing poetry? Or perhaps he's coming to the picnic.

ABIGAIL: I hope not. No, she'd hardly invite both of them ... Odd.

PATRICK: What are those two kids doing? Is that daft brother of yours playing with my car again?

ABIGAIL: I don't know. Go and see.

PATRICK: He cost me eighty quid last time when he cocked up the electric sunshine roof.

ABIGAIL: Ha ha.

PATRICK: You didn't think it was funny at the time, driving around in a raincoat for a month while they sent abroad for a part.

ABIGAIL: Did you good. The first fresh air you'd had for months.

[MELVYN and BRENDA enter.

He carries the rest of the picnic gear. She carries a stunter kite (still in its box) and the kite strings separately.]

MELVYN: Here you are. I locked the car.

PATRICK: Give me the keys immediately. Did you manage to break anything?

MELVYN: No. [Deadpan] Those electric windows always stop halfway up, don't they?

PATRICK: Keys.

ABIGAIL: Any sign of the others?

MELVYN: No, not yet. If they've gone by way of the cemetery they won't be here for a bit. Not with Len driving at four miles an hour.

ABIGAIL: The Sunday ritual. Well, let's get it over with. It's a perfect picnic day anyway. I take it Dorcas is coming with Simon, isn't she?

MELVYN: Yeah. Your brother's coming, isn't he?

BRENDA: Yes. He left home early. They were going to cycle here, I think.

ABIGAIL: Cycle?

BRENDA: Yes.

MELVYN: They cycle everywhere, didn't you know? He's the fittest man I've ever met.

ABIGAIL: Yes, but Dorcas cycling. I don't believe it. What's he done to her?

MELVYN: Dunno. Brought the kite.

ABIGAIL [*not interested*]: Oh, yes.

MELVYN [*taking it from* BRENDA]: Look, you see, it's a stunter.

PATRICK [*who is now reading the papers*]: Terrific. Don't fly it near me, will you?

MELVYN: O.K. Fair enough. [*Restless*] Well.

ABIGAIL: You've been round at Brenda's all morning, have you?

MELVYN: Yep. So?

ABIGAIL: Nothing. I just hope you're doing some studying, Mel. I mean, your exams are coming up in a few days, aren't they?

MELVYN: Yes, all right.

[DORCAS *and* SIMON *appear at the top of the slope. They stop as they see the others. They seem flushed and happy.*]

DORCAS: Hallo.

ABIGAIL: Hallo.

SIMON: Hallo.

MELVYN: Hi.

PATRICK: Good afternoon.

ABIGAIL: We hear you're being terribly healthy and cycling everywhere.

DORCAS: I can recommend it. Marvellous. You should have a go.

ABIGAIL: I think that's something I can live without.

PATRICK: Your bike's still hanging up in the garage if you want it.

ABIGAIL: It can stay there.

PATRICK: I'll oil it for you with pleasure. It'll save me a fortune in petrol bills.

SIMON: Is that the kite?

MELVYN: Yeah. Brand new. Bought it yesterday.

SIMON: Looks a good one.

MELVYN: Have you flown this sort?

SIMON: I have done.

MELVYN: Stunters?

SIMON: Yes.

MELVYN: Great.

DORCAS: Come on, let's fly it now then. I'm dying to see it.

MELVYN: Fine.

> [*Suddenly,* BRENDA *is galvanized into action.*]

BRENDA: Yeeeow – wur – wur – wur – yow – wow – wow . . .

ABIGAIL: God, what's that about?

MELVYN: It's all right, it's all right.

BRENDA: It's a wasp, it's a wasp.

MELVYN: It's gone, it's gone, it's all right.

BRENDA: Wur – wur –

MELVYN [*soothingly*]: It's all right, calm down. It's gone. [*To the others*] She doesn't like wasps.

ABIGAIL: Yes.

SIMON: Are we off then?

MELVYN: Right.

> [MELVYN *sets off up the hill with* BRENDA *in tow.*
>
> SIMON *gives* DORCAS *a quick hug and kiss.*]

SIMON [*as he does so*]: Coming?

DORCAS: You bet.

SIMON [*as they start to follow* MELVYN]: There's a bit of breeze up there. They need a bit of wind, you see, these stunters. It's the type with twin lines, I take it?

MELVYN: Yes, right. Are they difficult to handle?

SIMON: No, not really. I mean, only if the wind's very strong and then they're all over the place. [*Starting to climb the slope*] No, I've seen experts handling five or six at once.

MELVYN: What, flying in formation?

SIMON: Right.

> [SIMON, MELVYN *and* BRENDA *have gone.*]

DORCAS [*under this last, to* ABIGAIL]: You coming to watch?

ABIGAIL: – er – Dorc . . .

DORCAS: Yes.

> [DORCAS *lingers behind while the others go off.* ABIGAIL *moves to* DORCAS *in order to be a little way from* PATRICK. *Having arranged this, she seems a little lost for words.*]

DORCAS: Yes?

ABIGAIL: Well . . .

DORCAS: Yes. Pa gone to the cemetery first, has he?

ABIGAIL: Yes.

DORCAS: The regular weekly visit.

ABIGAIL: Yes.

PATRICK: Darling, this is the sort of lamp we need on that landing, you know.

ABIGAIL: Yes, just a second.

PATRICK [*going back to his reading*]: Not in this colour, of course.

ABIGAIL: If we ordered everything Patrick saw in the supplement, we wouldn't be able to get in the door. Haven't seen you for a bit.

DORCAS: No, well I've been ...

ABIGAIL: Busy.

DORCAS: Yes.

ABIGAIL: Lucky you.

DORCAS: Yes. Actually, yes.

ABIGAIL [*abruptly*]: Tell me, how does Pa seem to you these days? I mean, you see him less than I do so it's probably more noticeable to you. It's difficult for me to tell, seeing him, what, two or three times a week. He does seem to me to be getting – well – a bit odd. Do you find that?

DORCAS: He's always rather odd.

ABIGAIL: Yes. He keeps telling me he's seen mother.

DORCAS: Yes, he's told me that, too.

ABIGAIL: And sometimes, if you turn up unexpectedly, you can hear him talking to her in the other room.

DORCAS: He may be talking to himself.

ABIGAIL: No, no. The other day I heard him telling her a funny story. Roaring with laughter. Him that is. And then there's some days he refuses to wear socks and at least once a week he wants his bed moving round because of the way the earth's rotating ... I mean, he can't be senile, can he, not yet? He's not old enough. He's only just seventy. [*She reflects.*] That reminds me, it's his birthday soon.

DORCAS: I don't know why he gave up his practice. At least he met a lot of people.

ABIGAIL: Perhaps it's a good job he did. Otherwise he might have had all his patients shifting their beds about in their bare feet. Oh well, he's harmless at the moment. [*Slight pause*] You look wonderful.

DORCAS: I feel wonderful. [*Pause*] How are you?

ABIGAIL: Me?

DORCAS: And Patrick.

ABIGAIL [*only half joking*]: Don't talk about that, please.

DORCAS: All right.
    [*Pause.*]

ABIGAIL [*plunging in*]: I bet it's amazing, isn't it?

DORCAS: What?

ABIGAIL: With the big game hunter. It must be amazing. Isn't it?

DORCAS: Well. I don't know about that. Pretty good. I don't think I've been amazed though. Not yet.

ABIGAIL: You're looking marvellous.

DORCAS: Yes, you said.

ABIGAIL: It has that effect on some women. If they're getting it regularly, you know. They sparkle and shine. Everything about them suddenly sort of looks in good condition.

DORCAS: I washed my hair this morning. Maybe that's it.

ABIGAIL: Oh, you ... You're so – You're always so detached.

DORCAS: No, I'm not.

ABIGAIL: Well, aren't you happy?

DORCAS: Yes, I said so.

ABIGAIL: Yes, but really happy?

DORCAS: Abi, I have never been so happy. This may sound silly but there are some moments of the day when I literally have to stand still and hold on to something. Because I'm feeling dizzy with happiness. [*Slight pause*] O.K.?

ABIGAIL [*disconcerted*]: Yes.

DORCAS: Does that answer your question?

ABIGAIL: Yes. It's all finished with your poet, then?

DORCAS: Stafford? Yes, that's finished.

ABIGAIL: Did he ever write any poetry? Or did he just call himself a poet for something to put on his passport?

DORCAS: No, he wrote poetry. Not a lot. He burnt most of it in fits of fury. But some of the stuff was bloody good.

ABIGAIL: I only ask because I saw him just now, I think

DORCAS [*alarmed*]: Stafford?

ABIGAIL: Yes, skulking. Up there. [*She indicates the slope.*] He ran off as soon as he saw me.

DORCAS [*upset*]: Damn. Damn it!

ABIGAIL: Why?

DORCAS: He's still following us. How did he know we were here? I thought he'd gone home to Leicester. Oh damn. If Simon sees him again, he'll kill him. He's been driving us mad for weeks. How did he find out we were here?

ABIGAIL: Does he follow you everywhere?

DORCAS: Yes. He has done for months. He keeps – popping up. He was in the garden the other night. I was just drawing the curtains and there he was, crouching in the flower bed. Oh damn him, why won't he go home?

ABIGAIL: Well, perhaps he has. Perhaps he's gone now.

DORCAS: No, he hasn't. I know him. He'll be around here somewhere. [*She scans the horizon.*]

PATRICK [*still engrossed*]: What's your opinion of this bath, darling? Do you think it would look any good in the guest bathroom? [*He holds up the magazine.*]

ABIGAIL: Super, yes.

PATRICK: No, I'd have a closer look before you say that. It costs two thousand quid without the taps.

ABIGAIL [*ignoring this and returning to* DORCAS]: Do you know, I was just thinking, it was really only luck, wasn't it? I mean, that day. It could just as easily have been me and Simon. And if it had been the other way round, I wouldn't . . . I wouldn't have hesitated. Not for a second. Isn't that terrible?

    [BRENDA *enters down the slope.*]

BRENDA: It's flying, it's flying. Look.

ABIGAIL: Oh yes.

DORCAS: Terrific.

BRENDA [*going to her handbag, as she passes* PATRICK]: It's so pretty. Look, look.

PATRICK: Staggering.

BRENDA [*moving off again*]: It's really lovely. Simon, can I have a go? Please, please. [*She runs off.*]

ABIGAIL: Now there's a more urgent problem.

DORCAS: What?

ABIGAIL: That. [*She nods in* BRENDA'S *direction.*]

DORCAS: Oh, that. Gneeer.

ABIGAIL: I mean, dear brother's more infatuated than ever. And she gets more horrific each day. Well, I've done my bit. He won't listen to me. I've tried.

DORCAS: I think it's a lost cause.

ABIGAIL: She'll trap him into marriage eventually. She's the type. Poor kid. I mean, he knows nothing. She'll destroy the boy. We can't let that happen, can we?

    [SIMON *and* BRENDA *come on.*
    BRENDA *holds the two control lines to an invisible kite somewhere offstage. She grips the plastic handles tied to the lines.* SIMON, *behind her, attempts to guide her actions by guiding her wrists.*]

SIMON: Now, keep it steady. Keep it steady. Now, pull on your left. Pull on your left. Left, left, left.

BRENDA [*very excited*]: I am, I am.

SIMON: This is your left. This one. Pull.

BRENDA: I'm pulling.

SIMON: Look out, it's going to hit the tree. Let me take it, let me take it.

MELVYN [*off*]: It's going to hit the tree.

BRENDA: It's terribly difficult.

SIMON: That's it, I've got it, I've got it. There she goes.

MELVYN [*off, distant*]: Well done.

DORCAS: Hey, isn't that great? Look at it? He's brilliant.

SIMON: There she goes.

DORCAS: I want a turn, please. I want a turn.

SIMON: Sure. Come here. Take over.

DORCAS: Is it difficult?

SIMON: No, not at all.

BRENDA [*running off to rejoin* MELVYN]: Don't believe him. It's terribly difficult.

SIMON [*enveloping* DORCAS *between his arms to allow a take-over of controls*]: Now, here. Take the lines. That's it, one in each hand. Now, you pull that and it goes that way. And that makes it go that way. With a bit of practice, you can do that.

DORCAS: Hey!

SIMON: That's it. Let it come back.

DORCAS: Tremendous.

SIMON: Otherwise you'll lose the wind. It's too sheltered down here, you see.

DORCAS: Hey! Look, Abi, isn't this sensational?

ABIGAIL: Yes.

DORCAS: Whey . . .

    [*A distant scream from* BRENDA.]

MELVYN [*off, distant*]: Careful.

DORCAS: Sorry. Mind your nut.

    [*She moves off, controlling the kite.*
    SIMON *watches with a protective eye.*
    ABIGAIL *studies* SIMON.
    PATRICK *reads on.*]

PATRICK: No, I'm sorry, I was wrong. It's two thousand quid but they do throw in the taps. That's better. I was going to say . . .

ABIGAIL: Oh well, let's have three then . . .

SIMON: You going to have a go later?

ABIGAIL: No. I don't think so. It looks a bit complicated.

SIMON: There's nothing to it. Just a knack. Once you've got the hang of it, you're . . . [*Watching the kite's manoeuvres*] Hey. How are you keeping then? Haven't seen you for a bit.

ABIGAIL [*shrugging*]: Oh . . . you know.

SIMON: She's really getting the hang of that. [*Calling*] Well done.

ABIGAIL: That's Dorcas. Anything in that line.

SIMON: It's good to see her relaxing. I mean, it's marvellous this job she's got and these programmes she does are really first rate. Have you heard any of them?

ABIGAIL: No. Of course we can't really get it very well where we are ... local radio. We're on the edge of the area. Or in a dip or something.

SIMON: It really is first class. But they do expect them to work awfully hard on these local radio stations. I mean, she has to get up at dawn twice a week to read the farming news.

ABIGAIL: That must be a bit disruptive for you.

SIMON: Still, it gives us an excuse for an early night, I suppose.
    [*He laughs.*]

ABIGAIL [*somewhat cool*]: Yes.

SIMON [*immediately embarrassed*]: Oh well, holidays are over soon. I start teaching again this autumn. Of course, I used to teach before I went abroad. P.E. and games, you know.

ABIGAIL: Is that what you did in Africa?

SIMON: No, no. I was with this firm. Machine tools ...

ABIGAIL: Ah.

SIMON: Then they got taken over and nationalized and I was made redundant.

ABIGAIL: How terrible. They were sending all the Europeans packing, were they?

SIMON: No, not as far as I know. Just me. Most of the chaps seemed to be lucky.

ABIGAIL: Ah.

SIMON: Still. No regrets.

ABIGAIL: It must have been exciting, though. Africa.

SIMON: Well, different. Yes, it's an exciting place.

ABIGAIL: Makes me feel restless. There's this awful civilizing domesticating streak in us, isn't there? Urging us to curb our natural adventurous selves. To settle for the second-best.

SIMON: Don't let your husband hear you say that.

ABIGAIL: I meant within ourselves, actually.

SIMON: Oh yes. Sorry.

ABIGAIL: Though, possibly ... I don't know. I do know there's a lot more in me than I'm allowed to express.

SIMON: Well, that's true of most of us, I think ... [*Calling*] Mind the trees.

ABIGAIL: Not all of us. The lucky ones – take Dorcas, for instance – I mean, there she is totally fulfilled. She's at full stretch, doing what she wants to do. The Dorcas you see there is the the total Dorcas. That's her. No more, no less. I mean, emotionally speaking. What you see is what you get.

[DORCAS *bounds into view still holding on to the kite*.]

DORCAS [*over her shoulder*]: Were you watching?

SIMON: Yes.

ABIGAIL: Very good.

DORCAS: It's great fun.

SIMON [*drawing further away from* DORCAS]: I mean, when you say that, you're not implying she's shallow, are you? Because I can't agree with that.

ABIGAIL: Good lord, no.

DORCAS: What are you two doing?

SIMON: Watching you. [*Returning to* ABIGAIL] I still think, though, that what you're saying about her could be said about most of us.

ABIGAIL: Not everyone. I'm the reverse, I'm afraid. An incurable idealist.

SIMON: Aha.

ABIGAIL: If I could live in the clouds all day – like that thing ... [*She indicates the kite.*]

DORCAS [*momentarily losing control: to* MELVYN *and* BRENDA *off*]: Whoops, sorry, look out!

ABIGAIL: Well, perhaps not quite like that thing ... But you know what I mean.

SIMON: A dreamer, eh?

ABIGAIL: How does it go now:–

  The desire of the moth for the star

  Of the night for the morrow

  The devotion to something afar

  From the sphere of our sorrow?

That's it, isn't it?

SIMON [*unsure*]: Yes, yes.

ABIGAIL: Who is that now? Byron ...

SIMON: That's it, that's it.

ABIGAIL: No, Shelley. Of course it's Shelley.

SIMON: Shelley, yes. Sorry. I'm not too hot on Shelley.

ABIGAIL: I mean, I know, I just know that given the chance there's so much I could give, that's just at present being wasted.

SIMON: Yes, I know what you mean.

DORCAS [*still struggling with the kite but trying to get a better look*]: Does someone else want a go now?

ABIGAIL: I mean, it's not that I blame – [*Nodding in* PATRICK'S *direction*] – over there. Well, not entirely. But I know in the right circumstances – in the right hands, if you want to put it like that – I could – and of course it would be the same for him – God knows what I could.

It would be a total commitment. The sort of thing I suppose that most of us draw back from instinctively.

SIMON: Yes, well, I mean if you really are talking about total . . .

ABIGAIL: Yes, I am.

DORCAS: All right, I'm going to land it now. Mind your heads.

SIMON: I mean, let's just define what we're talking about. Are we talking spiritually or emotionally or physically . . .

ABIGAIL: Well, I would have hoped all three. Wouldn't you?

SIMON: Right, right.

ABIGAIL: My God, when I – if I give myself, and note the word 'self', as far as I'm concerned that means all of *me*. [*Indicating her body*] All this, to put it absolutely crudely.

SIMON: Good, good.

ABIGAIL: I mean, the only condition that I would ever lay down is that the other person comes prepared to take. And not sit reading the bloody Sunday papers all day, if you'll pardon the language.

DORCAS [*still at the controls*]: Whoo! Down she comes.

ABIGAIL: Still that's my problem.

SIMON [*laughing*]: Yes. Well . . .

ABIGAIL: Believe me, boy, you've made the right choice. Between us two.

SIMON: Oh, well . . .

ABIGAIL: I'm afraid I seem to have got the reputation as the one who chews men up for breakfast and then spits them out in small pieces. I think it's still considered rather unbecoming for women to have large appetites. In some quarters that is.

SIMON: Depends which quarters.

ABIGAIL: Wing three quarters, perhaps?

SIMON: Well, that's all right, I'm in the scrum.

ABIGAIL [*laughing gaily*]: Oh, that's very funny. That's very, very funny.

DORCAS [*landing the kite*]: Touch down. There.

    [*She slides down the bank to join them.*]

DORCAS: I have just given it a perfect one-point landing.

SIMON: Well done.

DORCAS: Don't ask me to try and get it up again. I can bring it down but I can't get it up again.

ABIGAIL: That's your problem, dear.

DORCAS: Don't be disgusting, Abigail. You'll have to excuse my sister, Simon. She has a depraved mind.

SIMON: Ah.

DORCAS: I am the only pure one in this family.

MELVYN [*appearing on the brow of the hill*]: That was a good landing. Are we taking it up again?

SIMON: Yes, if you like.

BRENDA [*who has arrived beside* MELVYN *examining her bare foot*]: I've got a splinter.

SIMON [*going up the bank*]: You stand by to launch it. I'll take the controls.

MELVYN: Right.

ABIGAIL [*following*]: You know, I think I'm going to have a go at this. It does look fun.

DORCAS: It's very hard work. You won't like that.

[ABIGAIL *pulls a face at* DORCAS *and goes on up the hill to where* MELVYN, BRENDA *and* SIMON *are.* MELVYN *is gathering up the control lines where* DORCAS *has laid them down.*]

MELVYN: We'd better go back this way a bit.

ABIGAIL: Remember I'm having the next go.

[*She and* MELVYN *go off.*]

SIMON [*turning back to* DORCAS *and blowing her a kiss*]: All right, darling?

DORCAS: Yes, be with you in a minute.

SIMON: O.K. [*To* BRENDA, *who is still examining the bottom of her foot.*] Come along then, Hopalong.

BRENDA: I've got an awful splinter.

[SIMON *and* BRENDA *go off.*

DORCAS *and* PATRICK *are silent for a second.*]

PATRICK: I thought kites were supposed to be quiet things. Do you want something to read?

DORCAS: No, thanks.

PATRICK [*holding out the magazine*]: What do you think of this bath?

DORCAS [*moving closer*]: Where?

PATRICK: This bath, there. What's your opinion?

DORCAS: I think it's absolutely foul.

PATRICK: Oh, do you?

DORCAS: Awful.

PATRICK: Oh. I was just coming round to liking it ... You're probably right.

[SIMON *appears over the brow of the hill. He holds a limp, unresisting* STAFFORD *by his collar.* STAFFORD *hangs from* SIMON's *grip like an old suit in need of dry-cleaning.*]

SIMON: Look what I've found, snivelling in the bushes.

DORCAS: Oh, Stafford. What are you doing here?

SIMON: I caught him tinkering with the bikes. He was on the point of letting my tyres down.

DORCAS: How did you know we were here? Who told you?

[STAFFORD *does not reply*.]

SIMON [*rattling him slightly*]: Who told you?

DORCAS: Oh, Simon, don't do that to him ...

SIMON: I'll do a damn sight more to him than this in a minute.

DORCAS: Simon!

SIMON: I'm sorry, Dorc, I'm absolutely sick to the back teeth with this little gobbit crawling around after us.

DORCAS: Well, don't do that to him, please. He's got a weak chest. If you shake him about like that, he'll cough for hours.

SIMON: Oh, damn it. [*He drops* STAFFORD *in a heap*.]

DORCAS: Now, Stafford, what do you think you're playing at? [*Silence*] Stafford? [*Silence*] Simon, would you mind?

SIMON: What?

DORCAS: Leave us for a second.

SIMON [*reluctant*]: O.K. [*To* STAFFORD, *menacingly*] You just watch yourself, Sunbeam.

[SIMON *goes up the hill*.]

DORCAS [*when they are alone*]: Staff, now listen ...

[STAFFORD *looks at* PATRICK.]

It's all right, he can't hear us. [*To* PATRICK] Can you?

PATRICK: What?

DORCAS: I'm saying you can't hear us, can you?

PATRICK: I beg your pardon?

DORCAS: Oh, shut up. Stafford, what are you doing? You will simply have to go home. Look, you can't keep creeping about in our garden at all hours. And it was you who has been sleeping in our shed, wasn't it? [*No reply*] It's over, Staff. Go home. Go home and please – have a bath.

STAFFORD: I love you.

DORCAS [*ignoring this*]: Do you need money?

STAFFORD [*doggedly*]: I love you.

DORCAS: Sssh. Have you got money for your train fare?

STAFFORD: Did you hear me? I love you.

DORCAS [*as kindly as she can*]: Yes, but I don't love you, Stafford. I'm sorry but that's the truth. You'll have to face that. I don't love you. It isn't entirely my fault and I don't know why I should be feeling guilty about it. I mean, I've tried my best to help you, Stafford. I even employed you on my programme. And what do you do? You start a fight in the B.B.C. canteen. That vision mixer is still off work, Stafford. And none of the Sports Unit will talk to me at all. It isn't true either that I gave you the job out of pity. I admire you. I do, I admire your poetry, I – well, you know what I think of your politics but I've always admired your seriousness over them. I wish I could be that serious. And most of all, I wish I was still in love with you but I'm not. I can't help it. I love Simon. I'm sorry.

STAFFORD [*calmly*]: I'm going to kill him.

DORCAS: Stafford, please. I'm sorry.

STAFFORD [*shaking his head*]: Then what's the point? [*He stands; louder*] What's the point [*Screaming as he runs off*] What's the bloody point of it all?

DORCAS [*vainly, after him*]: Stafford . . . !

PATRICK [*wincing at this added interruption*]: Oh my God.

[SIMON *is over the hill in a flash.*]

SIMON: You all right.

DORCAS: Yes.

SIMON: Sure?

DORCAS: I hope he's not going to do anything stupid.

SIMON: It's O.K., I'll keep an eye on him. If he steps out of line, I'll kill him. Simple as that.

DORCAS: Oh dear. I'd love to know who told him we were here.

SIMON: I don't know. Who could've done?

[ABIGAIL *appears breathless at the top of the hill.*]

DORCAS [*in* ABIGAIL'S *direction*]: I don't know.

ABIGAIL [*regaining her breath*]: They're here. We've just spotted the car.

[MELVYN *appears over the hill holding the kite.* BRENDA *follows on, still limping. She is finishing re-winding one of the kite strings back on to its handle.*]

[*Meanwhile coming down the slope*] I hope Rita remembered to bring the other sandwiches. [*To* PATRICK] Do try and enjoy yourself, won't you, darling?

PATRICK: Don't worry about me. I'll have a whale of a time. I'm about to leave in forty-five seconds.

ABIGAIL: Oh no, you're not, you know.

PATRICK [*unfussed*]: Oh yes, I am, you know.

ABIGAIL [*hardly heeding this last, to* DORCAS]: Was that Stafford rushing about just now?

DORCAS: Yes.

ABIGAIL: He nearly strangled himself in kite string. I hope he's not going to be trouble.

DORCAS: He won't.

[RALPH *comes on.*]

ABIGAIL: Hallo, Pa.

RALPH: At last, at last. Sorry we're late.

ABIGAIL: You're not late.

RALPH: Hallo there, Patrick. Nice to see you.

PATRICK [*shaking him by the hand*]: Hallo there, Ralph, cheerio. Sorry I couldn't stay longer. I hope you have a really nice picnic.

ABIGAIL [*hissing*]: Patrick.

PATRICK: Got the weather for it, anyway.

RALPH: Oh, you're off, are you?

PATRICK: 'Fraid so. Manchester calls.

ABIGAIL: Patrick.

RALPH: Oh well, good luck. Cheerio then.

ABIGAIL [*sweetly*]: Patrick, you cannot leave now.

PATRICK [*returning to kiss her*]: Oh my darling, of course. [*In her ear*] I told you.

ABIGAIL [*in his ear*]: You bastard.

PATRICK: 'Bye 'bye all. Darling, have a look at that bath when you've a minute. See what you think.

ABIGAIL: Yes, of course. [*Sweetly*] As long as it's deep enough to get your head under.

PATRICK: 'Bye 'bye.

[PATRICK *has gone.*]

ALL [*variously*]: 'Bye.

DORCAS [*she holds one of the chairs*]: Where do you want to sit, father?

RALPH: Just where you are, my dearest, as long as it's out of the wind. Mel, boy, see if your Uncle Len needs a hand, will you?

[MELVYN *comes down the slope.*

BRENDA *limps after him.*]

RALPH: And there's your girl. How's she? Good lord, she looks as if she's gone lame. You'll have to put her down, Mel.

BRENDA: I've got a splinter.

[MELVYN *goes off.*]

RALPH: Good girl, good girl. [*To* SIMON] Going to be a fine doctor one day, that boy, if he ever gets his exams. Ah now, and how are you – er ... young – er ...

SIMON: Simon.

RALPH: Simon. Excellent. Did Dorcas bring you?

SIMON: Yes.

RALPH: Splendid. I saw your other fellow this morning, Dorcas. The poet one. You know the chap. Strathclyde? No ...

DORCAS: Stafford.

RALPH: Stafford, that's the one. I was in the potting shed and I fell over him. I don't know what he was doing. So I asked him to the picnic. But he didn't seem very interested. Ran off shouting something. Very odd bloke, isn't he?

DORCAS: Yes, father.

SIMON [*coldly furious*]: Right, that's his lot.

RALPH: Bit of in-breeding there, I wouldn't be surprised.

SIMON: Next time I see him, that's it.

DORCAS [*moving to* SIMON, *still holding the chair*]: Simon.

RALPH [*to* DORCAS *with the chair*]: No, not there, old lumpkin. A bit further round. I don't want it blowing down my neck, do I?

[MELVYN *returns with a fishing stool and a rug.*]

RALPH [*sitting*]: That's better, that's better. Splendid. Thank you, Mel. Is Len managing?

MELVYN: Yeah. He's just padlocking up the hubcaps.

RALPH: I was telling them, Mel. If you keep your nose in your books and don't spend every second of every day ogling whatsername there, you'll be a very fine doctor.

MELVYN [*spreading out the rug for him and* BRENDA, *unmoved*]: Yeah.

RALPH [*without offence*]: He doesn't listen to a blasted word I say, does he? Well, this is nice, isn't it? We'd better get our tea in before the rain, that's all.

DORCAS: What rain?

RALPH: Look over there. See those clouds? Well, twenty minutes they'll be overhead.

ABIGAIL: Nonsense.

RALPH: Betcha. Seen it before.

SIMON [*to* DORCAS]: Why's he only got one sock on?

DORCAS: God knows.

[RITA *comes on with more bags.*]

RITA: Here we are. I see Patrick's off already.

ABIGAIL: Yes. Never mind, we'll survive.

RALPH: Over here, Rita. We've reserved you a spot over here.

RITA: We've been locking the car.

LEN [*entering with other picnickery*]: Can't be too careful. Not these days.

RALPH: Won't do to have a copper having his car nicked, will it?

LEN: If I related to you the statistics regarding car thefts for one month in this area, it would horrify you. Horrify you. We don't release the true figures. The general public would panic.

RALPH: Yes, yes.

DORCAS: Hope my bike's all right.

LEN: Locked it up, have you?

DORCAS: No, it's just under a bush over there.

LEN: It is quite within bounds that by the time you get back to it, they'll have stripped it of everything. Bell, gears, lights, back and front, wheels, rear reflectors, both sets of brakes and the saddle. And if it's a lady's bike and you're out of luck, they'll be lying in wait to rape you as well.

DORCAS: Oh, thanks a million, Uncle Len.

LEN: Just a warning.

SIMON [*grimly*]: Don't worry. Anyone comes within a yard of those bikes ...

RALPH: There you are, she's got a watchdog. She's all right. [*To* DORCAS] You're all right.

DORCAS [*strained*]: Yes.

ABIGAIL: Now, Rita, you have remembered to bring your sandwiches?

RITA [*tapping her basket*]: Yes, they're in here. Did you bring yours?

ABIGAIL: Yes, they're here.

RALPH: Well, that's all right for you two. What are the rest of us going to eat?

ABIGAIL: No, Pa. Rita and I have done half each, that's all.

RALPH: That's all right. As long as you washed your hands first, Abi. This girl, she'd never wash her hands, you know. We used to have to hold her under a tap.

ABIGAIL: All right, Pa.

RALPH: She was the grubby one, this one. [*To* BRENDA] Have you got that thing out of your foot yet?

BRENDA: No.

RALPH: Well, put your hoof in your mouth and suck it. Can you suck your foot?

BRENDA: No.

RALPH: Dear oh dear. [*To* LEN] She can't be much fun, can she?

DORCAS: He's going completely mad.

RALPH: Come on, then. Let's eat before the rain.

DORCAS: It's not going to rain.

RALPH: Wait and see. Wait and see.

RITA: Are you all right on that stool, Len?

LEN: Oh yes. Many an hour I've spent on this stool watching the rod.

RITA [*sorting out the bags*]: Now then.

RALPH: Still fish, do you, Len?

LEN: Not as much as I did. Not as much as I'd like to.

RITA: He's no time, have you?

LEN: Not any more.

RITA: Now what have we got in here?

ABIGAIL: All right, nobody move. Rita and I will do it.

DORCAS: No, Abi, let me help.

ABIGAIL: No, Dorc. Just sit down. Everyone sit down.

DORCAS: Abi, please.

ABIGAIL: Sit down. Do as you're told.

RALPH: I don't know why you don't leave it to Dorcas, Abi. We always do that in this family, Simon. When it comes to organization we leave it to Dorcas.

SIMON: Ah.

ABIGAIL: Well, she's not the only one who can organize, so there.

[RITA *unpacks the first batch of sandwiches from her own bag. Eight cheese and tomato. NB: All sandwiches referred to are half rounds.*]

RITA: Here we are.

ABIGAIL: Splendid. Now then, what are these?

RITA: Cheese and tomato, those are.

RALPH: Splendid.

ABIGAIL [*handing* SIMON *a stack of eight paper plates*]: Simon, could you hand these out, please?

SIMON: Certainly.

[SIMON *hands out the paper plates to everyone.*]

ABIGAIL [*taking the sandwiches from* RITA]: Now ... Hang on a tick, are these the ones I made?

RITA: No, those are the ones I made.

ABIGAIL: Cheese and tomato?

RITA: Yes.

ABIGAIL: You were supposed to be making egg and tomato.

RITA: No, cheese and tomato.

ABIGAIL: No, Rita. We have had phone call after phone call about this. You were supposed to be making egg and tomato. I was supposed to be making cheese and tomato. I have now made cheese and tomato.

RITA: Well, I've made cheese and tomato as well.

ABIGAIL: Oh, godfathers.

MELVYN: Hands up anyone who doesn't like cheese and tomato.

ABIGAIL: Be quiet. What else have you made, don't tell me –

RITA: Sardine and ...

ABIGAIL: Sardine and cucumber ...

RITA: Cucumber ... Yes.

ABIGAIL: Oh, dear heaven.

RALPH: Len. Who does she remind you of now? Abigail? Who is it she's like now?

ABIGAIL: I apologize everyone. I'm afraid you have the grand choice of either cheese and tomato or sardine and cucumber.

LEN: Amy?

RALPH: Amy, that's right.

ABIGAIL: And there are a great deal of those so I hope you like them.

RALPH: Once she's roused, you know, she's all Amy. Like a duchess.

ABIGAIL: Father darling, please put a sock in it. Or rather ...

DORCAS [*springing up*]: Cheese and tomato everyone.

ABIGAIL: No, I'll do them.

[ABIGAIL *takes round the sandwiches, serving first* LEN, *then her own plate, then* DORCAS *and finally* SIMON's *plate where she stops.*]

RALPH [*while she does this, to* LEN]: Abi's like me. We're the fly-by-nights. Hopping about from this to that. [*To* ABIGAIL] Aren't you?

ABIGAIL [*putting a sandwich on to* SIMON's *plate*]: Nonsense. [*Suddenly in a low voice to* DORCAS] God.

DORCAS [*low*]: What?

ABIGAIL: Don't look now, he's over there. In the bushes. Stafford. He's in the bushes.

DORCAS [*rising*]: Where?

ABIGAIL: Don't stare. In the bushes.

[DORCAS *takes the plate of sandwiches from* ABIGAIL *as a pretext for looking at* STAFFORD *unobserved. She puts a sandwich on* SIMON's *plate.*]

DORCAS: God, if Simon sees him ...

ABIGAIL [*moving away*]: Keep going, keep going.

[DORCAS, *keeping one eye on the bushes and* STAFFORD *who is at present out of view to us, having served* SIMON's *plate, then retraces* ABIGAIL's *steps serving her own, then* ABIGAIL *and finally* LEN. ABIGAIL *meantime has returned for the next batch of sandwiches which are* RITA's *sardine and cucumber.* ABIGAIL, *in a moment, will hand these to* SIMON. *She herself then concentrates on unpacking the paper cups and two thermos flasks, one of which contains tea, the other orange squash.* LEN, *at this point, has gone to check his car without going off.*]

MELVYN [*himself catching sight of* STAFFORD]: Hey look who I can see. Over ...

ABIGAIL [*drowning him*]: You going to fly your kite after tea, Mel? [*She indicates* SIMON.]

MELVYN: Oh. [*Realizing*] Yes.

DORCAS: You all right, Uncle Len?

LEN [*returning*]: Just checking the car.

SIMON [*to* MELVYN, *puzzled*]: Who can you see where?

ABIGAIL [*thrusting the sardine and cucumber at* SIMON]: Simon, could you serve these?

SIMON: Right.

[SIMON *starts to serve sardine and cucumber. First to* RITA, *then to* RALPH, *then* BRENDA *and finally* MELVYN. *At this point, he is interrupted.*]

DORCAS [*moving close to* ABIGAIL]: I think he's gone.

ABIGAIL: Thank God.

LEN [*to* SIMON]: Rumour has it, you're an athlete, young man.

SIMON [*as he serves*]: Well, used to be.

LEN: Were you a runner, by any chance?

RALPH: Careful how you answer that question, Simon.

SIMON: Well, yes, I used to run a bit.

[ABIGAIL *now catches sight of* STAFFORD *somewhere behind* MEL.]

ABIGAIL [*to* DORCAS]: My God, he's over there now. Look.

[DORCAS *looks*.]

SIMON: I'm certainly not a sprinter.

DORCAS: Where?

ABIGAIL: There.

LEN: Cross country at all?

[DORCAS *intercepts* SIMON *as he reaches* MELVYN *and is liable to catch sight of* STAFFORD.]

DORCAS [*taking the sardine and cucumber from* SIMON]: Let me do those, Si. Can you do the cups?

SIMON: Sure. [*To* LEN] Cross country? Well, a bit. Not recently.

RALPH: Ah-ha. Ah-ha.

[DORCAS, *with one eye out for* STAFFORD, *retraces* SIMON's *steps, serving* MELVYN, *then* BRENDA, RALPH *and finally* RITA.]

RITA: Here we are.

[RITA *hands* ABIGAIL *the second box of cheese and tomato made by* ABIGAIL. ABIGAIL *then serves first* LEN, *then her own plate and finally* DORCAS's *and* SIMON's *plate's.* SIMON *is going round with the cups.*]

SIMON: Why are you asking? Were you a runner?

LEN: Years ago. Years ago.

RALPH: He was very good.

RITA: He ran for the Police.

[ABIGAIL *has sighted* STAFFORD *in another direction.*]

ABIGAIL: Dorc . . .

DORCAS [*moving to her*]: Yes?

ABIGAIL: He's over there now, the little bastard.

DORCAS [*panicking slightly*]: What are we going to do?

ABIGAIL: Keep calm. He's gone again.

[DORCAS *takes the plate from* ABIGAIL *and retraces* ABIGAIL's *steps, serving* SIMON's *plate, her own plate,* ABIGAIL's *plate and finally* LEN *with cheese and tomato.*]

LEN [*meanwhile*]: No, I organize the local cross country derby once a year. It's a light-hearted jaunt but we usually get quite a good field.

[ABIGAIL *has returned and taken from* RITA *the second batch of sardine*

and cucumber. She serves these to RITA, RALPH, BRENDA *and then*
MELVYN.]

RALPH: Light-hearted, he says.

LEN: We run it around here.

SIMON: Sounds fun.

LEN: I might persuade you to enter then?

MELVYN [*as* ABIGAIL *serves him*]: He's over there now.

ABIGAIL: Yes.

SIMON: Well ...

ABIGAIL: Simon, could you serve these, please?

SIMON: Right. [*To* LEN] I'll see.

   [SIMON *serves* MELVYN, BRENDA, RALPH *and finally* RITA *under
the next.*]

RALPH: You know, Len, I'd fancy him against Murphy, you know.

LEN: Oh no, no. Nobody beats Murphy.

SIMON: Murphy?

RALPH: Young Constable Murphy. Finest runner I've seen for some time.

RITA: Len's brought him on from nothing.

LEN: No, he won't touch Murphy. Promise you that.

ABIGAIL: What about drinks?

RITA: It's all right, Abi, I'll do those.

LEN: Well, it's not till September the 8th. You've plenty of time.

SIMON: I might just be fit by then, I suppose.

RITA: Now, those who don't want tea put your hands up.

   [MELVYN *and* BRENDA, SIMON *and* DORCAS *all put their hands up.*]
  [*Starting to count*] That's one, two –

RALPH [*putting up his hand*]: Is this for tea?

RITA: No, this is not for tea.

RALPH: Ah, this is not for tea. [*He puts his hand down.*]

LEN: Not for tea? [*Putting up his hand*] No, I'm for tea. One here.

RITA: Then put your hand down. This is not for tea. Right. That's one,
two, three, four *not* for tea. Now, hands up for orange squash.

   [*The same hands go up.*]

MELVYN: It'll be the same people.

RITA: What will?

MELVYN: It'll be the same people who aren't for tea.

RITA: Who are?

MELVYN: The ones who want orange squash.

RITA: If you want orange squash, put your hand up.

MELVYN: It'll be the same. If you subtract the people who don't want tea
from the people who are here, you'll get the people who do want tea,
won't you? It's obvious the people who don't want tea must want ...

ABIGAIL: Put your hand up, Mel, and shut up.

MELVYN [*putting his hand up, muttering*]: It'll be the same.

RITA: I don't know what he's talking about, I'm sure. That's one, two, three, four for orange squash.

MELVYN [*muttering to* BRENDA]: I told her it would be the same.

   [RITA *starts to serve the drinks from the two thermos flasks. The others help ferry the cups to and fro. At the finish,* RALPH, LEN, RITA *and* ABIGAIL *have tea.* SIMON, BRENDA, MELVYN *and* DORCAS *have orange squash.*]

RALPH: Anyone any the wiser after all that?

ABIGAIL [*who has already poured one cup of tea*]: You have tea, Pa. Here you are.

RALPH: Ah-ha. Look, I'm sorry to cast a pall on the proceedings but it wouldn't be possible, would it, to have a spot more variety as regards sandwiches?

ABIGAIL: Yes, I'm sorry, I explained. Rita and I had a mix-up.

RALPH: It's just I have a sea of sardines and acres of cucumber.

ABIGAIL: You should have cheese and tomato as well.

RALPH: No. No cheese, no tomato.

LEN: Well, I have. I've got all cheese and all tomato.

MELVYN: We haven't. We've got sardine and cucumber.

DORCAS: I've got cheese and tomato.

ABIGAIL: Oh dear God. Right, hands up who've got sardines and cucumber.

   [RALPH, RITA, BRENDA, MELVYN *put up their hands.*]

ABIGAIL: Right. Now hands up who've only got cheese and tomato.

MELVYN: It'll be the people who haven't –

ABIGAIL [*shouting loudly*]: Melvyn! Cheese and tomato, please.

   [DORCAS, LEN *and* SIMON *put up their hands.*]

   And I think it'll be me as well. [*Examining her plate*] Yes.

LEN: Keep talking normally everyone.

ABIGAIL: What?

LEN: I think we're being observed.

RITA: What's the matter?

LEN: No cause for alarm. But I think we're being watched by a prowler.

SIMON: By a what? If that's who I . . .

DORCAS [*springing up*]: Right. Now let's get these sandwiches sorted out. When I give the word, I want Melvyn to give two sandwiches to Len and Len to give two sandwiches to Melvyn. Simon give two sandwiches to Rita. Rita give two sandwiches to Simon. Brenda give two sandwiches to Abi. Abi give two sandwiches to Brenda. Pa, you give me two

of yours and I'll give you two of mine. All right, everybody, thank you.
Off we go.

[*Confusion as people exchange sandwiches. Under this* STAFFORD
*appears at the top of the bank. He slithers down and hides behind the
bench.*]

Now has everybody got what they want?

RALPH: Lovely, lovely. I told you she was good at organizing.

RITA: What was this about prowlers?

LEN [*looking where* STAFFORD *was*]: I think he's gone now.

RITA: Good.

ABIGAIL [*leaning in to* DORCAS]: He's behind the bench.

DORCAS: I know. He's getting closer.

RALPH: Well, we've beaten the rain.

RITA: Yes, they're coming closer.

RALPH: Told you so. Well, just to say thank you all for coming along and
humouring me. I'm sure you've all got other things you'd far rather be
doing.

ABIGAIL: No, I'm sure we haven't. Have we?

DORCAS: No.

RALPH: I must say when I told Amy on Wednesday, she was very, very
touched. She wanted me to thank you.

LEN: Ah.

RITA: Oh.

DORCAS: Good.

[*Slight pause.*]

RALPH: It may be my imagination but I think I can see Stratford.

LEN: Stratford?

RITA: Not from here, surely.

RALPH: Behind that bench. Lying down. Do you see?

LEN: Good grief.

DORCAS: Stafford, father. His name's Stafford.

RALPH: Stafford. That's it. I'm always getting him wrong.

LEN: That's him. That's the prowler.

RITA: Oh.

DORCAS: It's all right, Uncle Len. I mean, you can't arrest someone for
lying behind a bench, can you?

LEN: Depends what he's doing behind the bench, doesn't it?

ABIGAIL: It's all right, he's – a friend.

LEN: He's known to you, is he?

SIMON [*finishing his sandwich with finality*]: He's certainly known to me.
[*Rising*] Excuse me.

DORCAS: Simon.

RALPH: Going to be a fight, is there?

SIMON: Excuse me a moment.

ABIGAIL: Simon, please.

SIMON: Won't be one moment.

[*He moves towards the bench and* STAFFORD.]

RALPH: He's quite harmless, this Stratford, Len. He spends a lot of time in our shed but he's quite harmless.

LEN [*unconvinced*]: I see.

[SIMON *reaches the bench.*

STAFFORD *lies still.*

SIMON *puts one foot up on the bench.*]

SIMON [*with his back to the others, conversationally*]: Listen, old chap, if you continue to follow Dorcas and me around for a moment longer, I shall personally pull off both your arms and stick them up your nose. And that will just be for starters. Now do us all an enormous favour, be a good chap and just bugger off.

[STAFFORD *rises, alarmed.*]

That's a good chap.

STAFFORD [*menacingly, retreating*]: Right ... right ...

[STAFFORD *goes.*]

RALPH [*as the others watch*]: He's got rid of him.

SIMON [*returning*]: That's that.

DORCAS: What did you say to him?

SIMON: Just asked him to leave.

LEN: You can't be too careful. This is a favourite spot, this is. I mean, we're all right now in broad daylight but I wouldn't care to be sitting up here like this in the middle of the night.

ABIGAIL: Why?

LEN: Let us just say it is a favourite haunt.

RITA: Haunted?

LEN: No, not haunted. I'm saying it is a haunt for certain undesirables who wish to practise unnatural practices.

MELVYN: Unnatural practices?

LEN: I'm saying no more.

MELVYN: What unnatural practices?

LEN: I think I've said enough on that subject.

DORCAS: Well, I can promise you that has nothing to do with Stafford.

LEN: I hope not, for his sake. Because we shall catch up with them and then ...

MELVYN [*to* BRENDA]: We must come up here at night.

LEN: Now, don't be young, lad, don't be young. Be your age.

[*A pause.*]

RITA [*swatting*]: The wasps have smelt the orange squash.

LEN [*swatting too*]: Yes ... Yes ...

[*The wasp flies to* ABIGAIL. *She swats it away. It flies around for a bit, finally landing on* BRENDA'S *hair. She doesn't notice.*]

MELVYN [*seeing it*]: Just a sec, love.

BRENDA: What?

MELVYN: Nothing, keep still, it's a wasp. I'll just ... [*He goes to knock the insect from* BRENDA'S *hair but before he can do so, she leaps into demented action.*]

BRENDA: Waaah – waaah ... ooh ...waah – eeeeee – woooh ... [*She is on her feet dancing among the picnickers. The wasp follows her as wasps tend to do. An elaborate dance follows as other people come to their feet, either to avoid being trampled by* BRENDA *or to protect their food from being ground underfoot or to catch the wasp or because she has knocked a drink over them.*]

DORCAS [*during this*]: Don't dance about. You'll only get it angry. Sit down, you silly girl.

LEN [*simultaneously*]: A wasp will never sting you unless it's provoked. It's a popular fallacy, you know, that wasps sting for no reason ...

RITA [*simultaneously*]: Keep it away from me, keep it away from me. Keep it away.

ABIGAIL [*simultaneously*]: If she'd only sit down, it'd go away. It's only after the orange squash...

SIMON [*simultaneously*]: Keep still, why don't you keep still? If you'll all keep still, I'll catch it.

MELVYN [*simultaneously*]: Don't be so daft, it's only a wasp. What are you panicking about?

[RALPH *views the proceedings benignly, waving his hat idly as if conducting a country dance.*]

RALPH [*conversationally during this*]: Such a lot of fuss over a little insect. Good lord, what a lot of fuss.

DORCAS [*finally topping it all*]: It's all right. Simon's got it. He's got it. Panic over. Simon's killed it.

RITA : Oh, he's killed it.

LEN: He's killed it.

[*People settle down.*]

MELVYN: What did you kill it with?

SIMON: Just with my hands. It's a trick. I learnt it in Africa, actually. Depends how fast you clap, you see. You do it like that, you see. [*He does so.*] And you don't notice you've – um ... [*Examining his hand*] You don't – um ...

ABIGAIL: You all right?

SIMON: Yes, fine.

DORCAS: Let me see.

SIMON: No, I'm all right. It usually works . . . [*He stares at his palm.*]

RALPH: Well done, that man.

ABIGAIL: Very impressive. I bet you're sensational with a charging rhino, aren't you?

SIMON: I don't know. Luckily, I never had to find out.

[STAFFORD *appears at the top of the slope astride a bicycle. He gives a bloodcurdling yell. The picnickers are frozen.*]

STAFFORD [*kicking off and plunging down the slope*]: Geronimo!

[*There are screams as people scatter.* STAFFORD *lands in the middle of them.* SIMON *grabs him. He comes off the bike. He and* SIMON *grapple.* DORCAS *is half-shouting, half-crying. The rain comes down suddenly.*]

RITA: Oh, here's the rain.

RALPH: Told you so. Didn't I tell you?

BRENDA: Ooh.

MELVYN [*to her, handing her some stuff*]: Take that and run. I'll bring the rug.

[*In a matter of seconds, the stage has emptied as they flee the sudden, very violent downpour.* RALPH *runs with his chair over his head as an improvised umbrella.* LEN *grabs one bag, his stool and* RITA'S *chair.* RITA *clutches another bag. As soon as the rain starts,* STAFFORD *darts away, escaping* SIMON'S *grip.* SIMON *thinks of following but thinks better of it. He examines the bike instead.*]

DORCAS [*to* SIMON *over the rain*]: I'll get the other bike.

SIMON [*shouting back*]: Fine.

[ABIGAIL *gathers up as many things as she can and flees to the car.* BRENDA *runs out with the kite and personal bits.* MELVYN *brings a rug and more items. On her way out, assisted by* LEN, RITA *falls over.* SIMON *bounds to help and assists* LEN *with* RITA *to the car.* DORCAS *returns pushing the other bike. She is now very wet. She starts to push it towards the road. Before she can move very far, the drenched rat-like figure of* STAFFORD *slithers out to confront her.*]

DORCAS [*shouting at him, above the elements*]: Please, Stafford, get out of my way.

STAFFORD [*shouting back*]: I love you, Dorc.

[*They stand. An impasse.*

SIMON *returns, head down, blinded by rain. He gathers up the other bicycle. Only as he straightens does he see* DORCAS *and* STAFFORD. *Even in the rain, he manages to stiffen with fury.*]

DORCAS: Stafford, please for the last time, get out of my way.

STAFFORD: You can't leave me. I love you. I need you.
DORCAS: Stafford.
SIMON: Get out of her way.
STAFFORD: You can't leave me.

> [*Impulsively,* STAFFORD *lies down on the ground in the path of her machine, face down, prostrate.* DORCAS *looks at this pathetic sight. Then at the wet figure of* SIMON, *shaking his head rather contemptuously at this craven behaviour.* DORCAS *decides whether or not to wheel her bicycle over* STAFFORD *in order to reach* SIMON. *When she has gone one way or the other, with one man or the other,* ABIGAIL *returns very wet to check that everything has been gathered up. She is stimulated by the prospect of a wet bicycle ride or resigned to dragging the prostrate* STAFFORD *to a more sheltered spot.*]

End of Act One Scene Two D

Should Dorcas have chosen to run over Stafford and go to Simon, Act Two Scene One D follows. If, however, Dorcas opts to remain with Stafford, the reader should turn to Act Two Scene One A (p. 239).

DORCAS: ACT TWO
SCENE ONE D

The same. Early September. Saturday afternoon at 2.30 p.m. A coolish day. A series of marker flags, red and blue, have been driven into the ground at occasional intervals down the slope, across the meadow and presumably leading to the road. LEN *enters immediately. He has about him a great sense of self-important urgency. It seems there is a small crisis. He is dressed in cap, top coat and boots. Round his neck, a stop watch and whistle. He carries a clipboard. Around his sleeve an armband with the words* RACE OFFICIAL *inscribed on it.*

LEN [*calling behind him*]: Right, follow me. Follow me. Quickly now.
[DORCAS, MELVYN *and* BRENDA *come on behind him, practically running to keep up. All are dressed in similar vein.* DORCAS *in a coat;* MELVYN *in a thick jersey and carrying binoculars in an old leather case;* BRENDA *in a jacket.* MELVYN *carries a home-made model glider.*]
Now then, this is Checkpoint number 7. It is the last one before the finish. We shall need a steward standing here. I'd like you to take this one over, Dorcas.

DORCAS: O.K. What do I do? Just stand here?

LEN: I'll explain to you in a minute if I may. Let me just show this lad his position. [*To* MELVYN] You follow me. I need someone at Checkpoint 5. It's just up here.
[LEN *starts up the bank and pauses to straighten a flag, forcing it further into the ground.*]
[*As he does so*] It's a crying shame this, you know. I mean normally I'd have had twenty-five volunteers from among the lads. Now half of them I discover have had their leaves cancelled. Nobody bothers to tell me.

DORCAS: Oh dear.

LEN: I mean, I'm grateful to you for stepping in but it's a crying shame.

DORCAS: Yes, yes.

LEN: There's eight of these checkpoints, you know. Every one of them needs a steward.

DORCAS: Yes, yes.

LEN: And I need six men at the finish and I'm still three men short.

MELVYN: Why has the Police leave been cancelled then?

LEN: It's this peaceful demonstration in Slough, isn't it?

DORCAS: You expecting trouble?

LEN: In our experience there's always trouble at peaceful demonstrations. Half the tearaways in the district will be there. And that is not all. I've had a dozen runners withdraw too, you know.

DORCAS: All policemen?

LEN: Well, half of them. The other half are demonstrating.

DORCAS: You've still got your star runner, I take it?

LEN: Who? Constable Murphy? Oh, yes, he's still running. I worked him a sick note. No, don't worry about Murphy. That boy-friend of yours is not going to get a walk-over, you know.

DORCAS: We'll see. Simon's trained very hard.

LEN: He'd need to.

> [MELVYN *is kissing* BRENDA.]

Right, come on, boy, stop all that monkeying.

> [MELVYN *stops.*]

Did you bring your Dad's binoculars like I asked you?

MELVYN: Yep.

LEN: Good. Because I'm wanting you to cover quite a big area. Now, straighten yourself up. What have you got there?

MELVYN: It's a glider, look . . .

LEN: You're going to have no time for gliding, lad. Where's your armband?

MELVYN: My what?

LEN: Your official armband. Your insignia. What have you done with it?

MELVYN: It's in my pocket.

LEN: Well, put it on your arm, son, put it on your arm. The Press are here today as well, you know. I want this to look good.

> [LEN *goes off over the bank.*
> MELVYN *pulls a face at the others and follows him.*
> DORCAS *and* BRENDA *stand for a moment.*]

DORCAS: Well. The rain's held off.

BRENDA: Yes.

DORCAS: I do hope Simon does well. He's been training hard enough. I've hardly seen him these past few weeks. He's run miles every day. Apparently this Murphy man is awfully good. Do you know him at all?

BRENDA: No.

DORCAS: Ah.

> [*She moves about whistling a bit.*]

I don't quite know what one does when one's stewarding, do you? I hope it's not too complicated. [*Pause*] Listen, you and Mel . . .

BRENDA: Yes?

DORCAS: Do you mind if I ask you?

BRENDA: What?

DORCAS: Well, he's my brother – my younger brother and I suppose we've always felt rather protective towards him. Perhaps over-protective sometimes. I don't know. The point is, now he's failed his exams and as far as I can make out, he refuses to take them again, this means obviously he's given up any idea of medicine as a career. Well, fair enough. Father's upset but ... Anyway, the point is, we're both – Abigail and I – we're both very worried he's going to drift aimlessly about – perhaps do something stupid – like rushing into marriage even. I think you'll agree he's got to have time to think clearly about his future. Without being affected by too many emotional considerations. He shouldn't land himself with responsibilities. Not until he's ready. Don't you agree?

[BRENDA *stares at her expressionlessly.*]

Of course you're perfectly entitled to say this is none of my business ...

BRENDA: Yes.

DORCAS: What?

BRENDA: Well, I think I am. Actually. Entitled to say that.

DORCAS: I see.

BRENDA: I mean, frankly, I don't want to be rude or anything but I don't think it has the remotest thing to do with you whatsoever.

DORCAS: Oh. Really? Well – actually, I know just now I said it didn't but I think it does. Number one, he is my brother. Number two, I don't think you're being a good influence on him. And secondly, as his sister I think I am fully entitled to say so.

BRENDA: Well, come to that, I don't think you're being an awfully good influence on my brother either. But if he wants to make a fool of himself over you that's his problem.

DORCAS: I think your brother is probably old enough to know what he's doing.

BRENDA: So's Melvyn, don't worry.

DORCAS: I'm afraid I can't agree.

BRENDA: Too bad.

DORCAS [*growing angry*]: Now, you listen to me, you ...

BRENDA: I know what you and your sister think of me. I'm not completely and utterly totally dim as it happens. I've heard what you say about me and I've seen your looks and it doesn't bother me and it doesn't bother Mel because he says you're both totally neurotic and out of touch, anyway.

DORCAS: I beg your pardon?

BRENDA: And for your further information, we shall be getting married very shortly actually because I happen to be two months pregnant. So gneeer to you too.

DORCAS [*shaken*]: Oh no. [*Pause*] Oh God. Now what's going to happen?

BRENDA: We're going to have a baby that's what's going to happen.

DORCAS: But he hasn't even got a job.

BRENDA: He'll get one, I expect.

DORCAS: I don't know what this'll do to father.

BRENDA: I can tell you that. It'll make him very happy. He already knows. Mel told him.

DORCAS: When?

BRENDA [*shrugging*]: A week ago.

DORCAS: Neither of them said anything to me.

BRENDA: I think they wanted it to be a surprise.

DORCAS: What for?

BRENDA: The wedding.

DORCAS: I don't know what's going to happen to you both.

BRENDA: We don't want much really.

DORCAS: Just as well.

BRENDA: As long as we're both happy.

[LEN *returns down the slope with* MELVYN.]

LEN: All right, have you got all that?

MELVYN [*repeating*]: Round the flag, down the dip, up the slope, through the stream, round the other flag ...

LEN: No, no. Down the dip, through the stream, up the slope, then round the flag ...

MELVYN: ... round the flag.

LEN: Now, about the third time round, some of them are sure to try it on so keep your eyes on them.

DORCAS: I thought runners were all sportsmen and totally honest.

LEN: Not this lot. They're all as bent as hell.

[MELVYN *is kissing* BRENDA.]

LEN: Blimey o'reilly, you'd think he'd been away for a week.

MELVYN: We're going to get a cup of tea.

LEN: Well, the tea van's there. But 2.50 at your positions, please.

MELVYN: Yep.

DORCAS: Mel, I'd like a word some time, please.

MELVYN: Yep. Sure.

[BRENDA *and* MELVYN *go off towards the road.*]

LEN: He's a dozy little punnet, isn't he?

DORCAS [*shrugging*]: Well

LEN: And she's no better. Oh, she's all right to look at but intellectually I don't reckon she can tell her fishcakes from her falsies quite honestly.

DORCAS: I'm sorry?

LEN: I beg your pardon.

DORCAS: In fact, I think she probably can. She's pregnant, did you know?

LEN: Yes, yes.

DORCAS: You did know?

LEN: Yes. Rita told me. I can hardly say I'm surprised. Right, now to get on . . . Checkpoint 7. [*Writing on his clipboard*] That's Dorcas. I'll mark that in. It's a crying shame all this, you know. I mean, it takes months to organize these things. I don't know if you appreciate that. I mean, as a start-off, you've got your officials, your catering, your first-aid, your toilet facilities. You've got the course to mark. A thousand things to think of, you know.

DORCAS: Yes, yes.

LEN: And now look at it. I mean, pardon me but it's a tragic fact that we're that undermanned that I've had to resort to five women.

DORCAS [*stiffly*]: Well, I expect we'll cope.

LEN: Oh, you'll cope. No disrespect but some of these fellows are big rough lads, you know.

DORCAS: Well, I'm not going to have to fight them, am I?

LEN: No, no, no. Forget I spoke. Now listen, [*speaking as to a child*] I want you to stand just here. The Start and Finish line is just through there by the road, you see. You see where my finger's pointing? This will be the last checkpoint before the finish. So it's an important one, right?

DORCAS: Oh dear.

LEN: Now, don't panic. The runners start off by the road there and they do half a mile of roadside running alongside the B481. Then before they get to the junction with the main Reading road they branch off, cross the footbridge that fords the Pendon Trickle, then they're cross country, along Durkin's Ridge, through the spinney, down through Hackett's Field, across the north-east corner of Grubb Farm and then down towards us again – this time through the Trickle, then up the other side of this slope here and then they'll be in view and down this bank here. And this is where you come in – down this bank . . . watch this, [*He demonstrates.*] around this flag here but it must be around this way because it is a red flag and a runner always goes to the left of a red flag and to the right of a blue flag . . .

DORCAS: Right of a blue flag.

LEN: Have you got that, then? He runs to the left of a red flag and to the right of a blue flag.

DORCAS [*joining in with him*]: – and to the right of a blue flag. God.

LEN [*pleased at her confusion*]: Now, you see what I mean. You see what I mean. Now then, if you see anyone going to the right of a red flag or the left of a blue flag, you will notify me or an official umpire at the finishing tape and that runner will automatically be disqualified. Just jot down his number.

DORCAS: It seems very drastic.

LEN: A matter of feet can sometimes be critical. Even in a race this length. [*Relaxing slightly*] Some of them, you know, they play crafty. They muddy up their numbers to confuse the stewards. If you see someone cheating and you can't read his number, try and get a look at his face and we'll have an identity parade afterwards. [*He laughs.*] Only joking, only joking.

DORCAS: Ah!

LEN: No, seriously, in actual fact, you should find it easier here. They'll be doing three laps, you see. Just over a mile each lap, little over five miles in all. So by the time they reach you here, they're bound to have spread out so the one thing you won't have is bunching trouble. If it runs true to form, you'll probably get Murphy first, then a ten-minute gap, then your boy-friend – then another gap, then the rest of them. All right, any questions?

DORCAS: Um. No. Left of red flag, right of blue flag.

LEN: Correct. Got your notebook and pencil to record infringements?

DORCAS [*patting her handbag*]: Yes, here.

LEN: And your armband? Where's your armband?

DORCAS: Oh. How stupid. I put it on my arm but then I put my coat on.

LEN: Well, let's have it on view, my dear, let's have it on view. Otherwise you won't be accredited. You don't want that to happen, do you? [*Looking at his watch*] We've got a few minutes now but, please, I'd like you in position by 2.50. All right?

DORCAS: All right.

LEN: We've got the loudspeaker van just along there by the start and finish so you'll be able to hear how the race is going if you're interested.

DORCAS: Oh, good.

[SIMON *comes jogging on in his tracksuit.*]

LEN: Ah-ha.

SIMON [*to* DORCAS]: There you are. I wondered where you'd vanished.

LEN: She's now officially a steward of the course so no collusion, please.

SIMON: Ah, splendid. Just time for a bit of bribery then.

DORCAS: Absolutely impossible.

SIMON [*testing her*]: And which way round the flags do we go?

DORCAS: Left of the red flag, right of the blue one.

SIMON: Very good.

LEN: All the runners arrived, have you heard?

SIMON: Well, there's quite a good number jogging around over there.

LEN: There should be twenty.

SIMON: I say, who's that very old boy who seems to be competing?

LEN: Ah, Major Lidgett has arrived, has he? I wondered if he'd make it.

SIMON: Do you think he'll cope?

LEN: Hah.

DORCAS: Is Major Lidgett running this year again?

LEN: No stopping him. Seventy-two years old, would you believe? He's been competing since it started forty-four years ago, only missing the war years.

SIMON: Has he ever won?

LEN: No, no. He's had a seventh, a twelfth and last year he was twenty-ninth in a field of thirty-four when he beat a man of twenty-three who was forty-eight years his junior. What is more, he has never failed to finish a race. Think what that means.

SIMON: Incredible.

LEN: Oh, he's got some running in him. He's got no speed now, not any more but I'll promise you this, he'll still be running when the rest of you are tucked up in bed, if need be.

SIMON: Heavens.

LEN: Having said that, I daresay you and Murphy'll lap him a couple of times. But he's a very popular competitor. He always gets a big hand from the crowd when he finishes.

DORCAS: If anyone's still up, that is, eh? [*She laughs.*]

LEN [*ignoring this cheap female joke*]: Murphy's looking fit.

SIMON: I don't think he'll last the course, will he?

LEN [*laughing*]: Last the course. [*Feeling the turf*] The going's good, you know.

SIMON: Seems firm.

LEN: Could be records today, could be records.

SIMON: I'll do my best for you.

LEN [*laughs scornfully; suddenly remembering*]: Oh, by the way, a word of warning. The Press are about, so careful what you say.

DORCAS: Why?

LEN: Well, they'll be sniffing, you know. Sniffing for tittle tattle. It's always best, we've found, to treat them with respect and kid gloves and tell them nothing except through official channels. So all interviews after the race handled officially through me, all right? We've had a bit of trouble in the past. Right, I must sort the rest out. 2.50.

DORCAS: Yes, Uncle Len.

LEN [*to* SIMON]: Don't miss the start.

SIMON: No chance.

> [LEN *goes off to the road*.]

I've been thinking. The thing with Murphy is, from what I've heard, he always goes off at a cracking start but if he's got one weak point it's his finish. If I can hang on to him for the first couple of laps, I think I might nail him.

DORCAS: Good.

SIMON: Depends if I can stick with him.

DORCAS: Look, I don't want to spoil your race but do you know what I've just heard?

SIMON: What's that?

DORCAS: Mel, my idiot brother, has succeeded in making your sister pregnant.

SIMON: Yes, that's a bore, isn't it?

DORCAS: Did you know?

SIMON: Yes, she told me.

DORCAS: Oh God.

SIMON: Actually they're taking it very calmly. I mean, in their position I think I'd ...

DORCAS: Everybody knew except me.

SIMON: Oh, I shouldn't think so.

DORCAS: It's a bit much. If Abi knows, I'll be furious. It means nobody trusts me.

SIMON [*kissing her*]: Come on.

DORCAS [*irritable*]: What?

SIMON: Come on, kiss.

> [DORCAS *kisses him very half-heartedly*.]

Oh all right, forget it. [*He moves away*.]

DORCAS: Well. It's the first time I've seen you for days, isn't it?

SIMON: Untrue. I'm the man who's sleeping with you, remember.

DORCAS: That's not much good. You're asleep then.

SIMON: Ah-ah-ah. Unfair.

DORCAS: Yes, you are. You're clapped out with all this running all day.

SIMON: And if you must work all hours of the night reading the traffic news ...

DORCAS: I shan't be doing that much longer. Not unless father improves. He's going completely crackers, I think. He was sitting in the bathroom the other morning talking to his feet.

SIMON: Oh lord. Anyway, you've always said, if I may remind you, that the reason you loved me in the first place was because I was – fit ...

DORCAS: One of the reasons.

SIMON: That's what you said to me.

DORCAS: Only one of the reasons. I mean, I didn't fall in love with you just because you were fit. That's not a reason for falling in love. I found it attractive, pleasing, yes. But I didn't fall in love with your calf muscles.

SIMON: Oh, disappointing. I thought you women went for that.

DORCAS: Hardly.

SIMON: What are all those he-man magazines doing then? I thought you all went out and bought them.

DORCAS: Those? They're not for women.

SIMON: Aren't they? Who then?

DORCAS: They're for men, aren't they?

SIMON: Men!

DORCAS: I've always assumed so. They don't interest me.

SIMON [realizing]: Really? Good lord. I never knew that. Good heavens. That's interesting.

DORCAS: Wow, you're all man, Simon. You really are.

SIMON [not hearing this]: Pardon?

DORCAS: Nothing.

SIMON: So I'm wasting my time with all this, am I?

DORCAS: How do you mean?

SIMON: Well, according to you all I can hope to do rushing about like this is excite the other runners.

DORCAS: Oh, really.

SIMON: I was only doing it for you.

DORCAS: Oh please, don't start that one.

SIMON: I was.

DORCAS: Oh, Simon, come on.

SIMON: Why else?

DORCAS: Well ...

SIMON: Why else? Eh?

DORCAS: Because – Well, because your vanity was challenged.

SIMON: Vanity? I haven't got any vanity.

DORCAS: You want to beat this man Murphy because Uncle Len says you can't.

SIMON: Don't you worry about that. I'll beat Murphy. I can beat Murphy hopping on one leg.

DORCAS: Well, that's why you're running. If you want to know. So don't blame it on me.

SIMON: I don't know what we're arguing about, I'm sure.

DORCAS: We're not arguing. I'm telling you why you're running in this ridiculous race and why I'm spending my Saturday afternoon off standing in a field wearing an armband and watching flags.

[*Off stage*, LEN's *voice is heard testing the loudspeaker equipment*.]

LEN: Testing one, two, three, four, testing ...

    [DORCAS *looks at her watch*.]

SIMON: I mean, if you'd rather I was like whatsisname ...

DORCAS: Whatsisname?

SIMON: That little squirt you were with. What's his name?

DORCAS: Stafford.

SIMON: Yes. If you'd like me like him just say the word. Lying on the sofa smoking two hundred fags a day.

DORCAS: Who?

SIMON: Isn't that what you told me he did? Damn sight less effort, I can tell you.

DORCAS: I wonder what he's doing now.

SIMON: Setting fire to someone else's sofa, I should think. Who cares.

DORCAS: You know, the last time I saw him was here at that picnic.

SIMON [*remembering him*]: Hah.

DORCAS: I'm sorry, Simon, I can't help worrying about him now and then.

SIMON: Why bother?

DORCAS: Well, he was so – hopeless.

SIMON: Very good description. Hopeless.

DORCAS [*dreamily smiling*]: The only hope for someone like me with pigeon toes is that one day, I'll be carried off feet first in a flight of my own fancy.

SIMON: Eh?

DORCAS: Poem.

SIMON: Oh. Shelley or Shakespeare?

DORCAS: Neither. It's something Staff wrote on my ceiling once. When I was feeling depressed.

SIMON: I'm not surprised if he scrawled all over your ceiling. Not even a very good poet, was he? I mean, if you're going to do things like that, you've got to make sure you're Michelangelo first. Not some offensive little erk with pigeon toes.

DORCAS [*rallying*]: Don't be so miserable.

SIMON: Miserable?

DORCAS: Well, you don't have to knock people all the time.

SIMON: Eh?

DORCAS: It's as if you're always trying to prove something.

SIMON: What?

DORCAS: Well ...

SIMON: What?

DORCAS: Well, you're always belittling people. I think in the hope that it'll make you feel taller.

SIMON: Is that another of his poems?

DORCAS: No.

SIMON: Well, it's rubbish anyway.

DORCAS: I don't think it is.

SIMON: It's an absolute load of sheep's droppings. I'm not worried about that little maggot.

DORCAS: There you go again, belittling him.

SIMON [*getting quite angry*]: I am not belittling him. He is already little. It is not possible to belittle anyone who is already as small as he is. It's like trying to insult a dwarf by calling him short. It can't be done. [*Realizing he is angry and getting angrier*] Why are you doing this to me?

DORCAS: What?

SIMON: Annoying me like this.

DORCAS: I'm sorry.

SIMON: I have a race to run in a minute.

DORCAS: I'm sorry.

SIMON: Against a flat-footed police constable with an I.Q. of ten who's . . . [*Breaking off; furiously*] All right, all right, I'm doing it again, is that it?

DORCAS: Yes.

SIMON [*shouting*]: Good. I meant to.

DORCAS: Sssh.

SIMON: My God. You are one of only two people I have ever known who could make me angry. Do you know that? The other was a salesman I worked with in Africa. I mean, you're not as bad as him but sometimes you run him pretty close, I can tell you.

DORCAS: What did he say to you? To annoy you?

SIMON: Who?

DORCAS: This salesman in Africa.

SIMON: I forget now. Nothing. I don't want to talk about it. He used to hide my briefcase. Things like that. Childish things. So-called jokes. You know.

DORCAS [*solemnly*]: I see. No, that couldn't have been much fun.

SIMON: It wasn't. That's one of the reasons I'm glad I came back.

DORCAS: You don't really like jokes much anyway, do you?

SIMON: I only like jokes if they're funny. Nothing abnormal in that, is there?

DORCAS: No. That's awfully normal, Simon.

SIMON: Oh, good. I mean, just in case you wanted to get at me some more.

DORCAS: I'm sorry. I just want everything to be perfect, I suppose. I think that's my trouble.

SIMON: I thought that was Abi who always wanted that.

DORCAS: No. Abi expects everything to be perfect. That's a bit different.

SIMON: Sounds the same to me in the long run.

[*Under the next*, LEN's *voice is heard over the loudspeaker system on the van, loud initially, then fading down under*.]

LEN: Good afternoon, ladies and gentlemen, boys and girls. Welcome once again to the Pendon cross-country event. This afternoon will be the thirty-eighth time this race has been run and will contain a field of twenty runners. The event as normal will be competed over three laps comprising a total distance of five miles, three hundred and twenty-four yards, mostly over the rough and taxing terrain of Pendon Common. Among the competitors this afternoon, we have last year's winner Police Constable John Murphy, running in this his fourth consecutive year. John Murphy, number 17. Among the other contestants, we are pleased to welcome for the thirty-seventh time, Major George Lidgett. Now, and I know he won't mind my saying this, seventy-two years of age and still running strong. Last year, Major Lidgett finished twenty-ninth in a field of thirty-four. So you can see there is still a lot of running left in him. He will be competing in the number 23 shirt. Finally, a newcomer who promises to provide a healthy challenge to the leaders, Simon Grimshaw, running in the number 8 vest. Without further ado, I'm going to ask all the entrants to gather on the starting line now, please, ready for the start. Our official starter this afternoon, as usual, will be Group Captain R. W. Brodie and the finishing judges Messrs Bradley, Townsend, Cliff and Motherwell. Would the contestants please take their places for the start? Thank you.

[*As this rumbles on interminably* –]

DORCAS: Is something happening?

SIMON [*sulky*]: Probably.

DORCAS: Well, hadn't you better be getting ready? I mean, I know you're confident but it might be as well to start with the rest of them.

SIMON: And I'll have less of that too, if you don't mind.

DORCAS: What?

SIMON: Sarcasm. I can't stand sarcasm.

DORCAS: Oh, go and run your race, for heaven's sake.

SIMON: I mean, maybe you're right. Maybe I am egocentric. I say, maybe. But if I am then I'm damn sure you are.

DORCAS: I didn't say you were egocentric.

SIMON: Building myself up at the expense of others ...

DORCAS: That isn't necessarily –

SIMON: Well, what else is it? Isn't that what you call egocentric?

DORCAS: Not entirely –

SIMON: Just answer my question, please. Are you or are you not accusing me of being egocentric?

DORCAS: You are no more egocentric than most people.

SIMON [*shouting at her*]: I don't care about other people. I'm not interested in them. I am talking about me. Do you consider me egocentric?

DORCAS [*angry now, too*]: Will you kindly not shout and scream at me?

SIMON: If you don't behave yourself, I'll do a damn sight more than shout. I'll take this flag and tan your backside with it. So there.

DORCAS: You do that and I'll put it back in the wrong place and disqualify you.

[SIMON *steps back, momentarily baffled.* MURPHY *enters, jogging. He is a powerfully built young man with the grim dedication of a serious runner. He wears a running vest with the number 17 pinned back and front. He still wears his track suit bottoms.* SIMON *and* DORCAS *draw apart from their near violent encounter.*]

[*Brightly*] Good afternoon.

[MURPHY *nods but keeps his eyes gimlet-like on* SIMON, *as if appraising a felon. There is a stare-out for a moment as* SIMON *glares back and then* MURPHY *jogs off again, having seen his opposition.*]

Was that Murphy?

SIMON: That's Murphy.

DORCAS: Looks rather impressive, doesn't he?

SIMON: He's all right. He looks better when he's got his walking stick.

[*He begins to remove his track suit, moving towards the start.*]

DORCAS: Good luck.

SIMON [*smiling and winking at her, affectionately*]: You need a bit of taking in hand, I can see that.

DORCAS [*wincing but managing to smile*]: Good luck.

SIMON: Yes.

[SIMON *jogs out. As he goes, he passes* MELVYN *returning with* BRENDA *in tow, still carrying the glider.*]

MELVYN: Good luck.

SIMON [*off*]: Ta.

MELVYN [*to* DORCAS]: Do you know what you're doing then?

DORCAS: Yes, I think so.

MELVYN: More than we do. We're just going to trip up Murphy as he comes past.

[MELVYN *and* BRENDA *start up the slope.*]

DORCAS: Mel.

MELVYN: Yep?

DORCAS: Just a second, would you?

MELVYN: What?

[*He stops somewhat reluctantly. After a look between them,* BRENDA *moves on.*]

DORCAS: Why didn't you tell me, Mel? About Brenda?

MELVYN: Oh, that.

DORCAS: Yes.

MELVYN: Well ...

DORCAS: I mean, it's a bit hurtful, Mel.

MELVYN [*uneasy*]: Yes, well ... I thought you might have gone on a bit.

DORCAS: I see.

MELVYN: So.

[*He looks at her, shrugs, then runs up the slope.*]

DORCAS: Mel?

[MELVYN *turns.*]

Did you tell Abi?

MELVYN: No fear. She'd've gone on even more, wouldn't she?

DORCAS [*smiling*]: Yes.

[MELVYN *and* BRENDA *go out over the hill. From off, the sound of the starter, Group Captain Brodie, getting the race under way, finishing with the starter's pistol.* DORCAS, *alone, does her own start and runs round her flags.*]

Hup, hup.

[*An almost unrecognizable* STAFFORD *enters. He wears an impressive sporting cap and a smart expensive coat.*]

STAFFORD: Hallo.

DORCAS [*caught in her running but not recognizing him*]: Oh, hallo. Sorry, I was just – My God. Stafford?

STAFFORD: Yes.

DORCAS: Staff, what are you – ? Heavens. Staff, you look – you look so different.

STAFFORD: Yes.

DORCAS: How are you?

STAFFORD: I'm – I'm doing fine.

DORCAS: Why are you here? Didn't you go home to Leicester?

STAFFORD: No – I – well – I did what you said once. You said, write to the Arts Council, for money, you know. For my writing. So I wrote to them. But they said no. So then I got this job, you see.

DORCAS: What job?

STAFFORD: With the *Gazette*.

DORCAS: The *Pendon Gazette*?

STAFFORD: Yeah.

DORCAS: As a reporter?

STAFFORD: Yeah.

DORCAS: I didn't know ...

STAFFORD: Well, I wanted to get the job first and surprise you. You know.

DORCAS: Well. Wow. You look very smart.

STAFFORD: Well, I'm doing weddings and funerals, you see.

DORCAS: Why are you here?

STAFFORD: I'm writing about the race. I do Sports as well, sometimes. On Saturdays. I thought you might be here with –

DORCAS: Simon.

STAFFORD: Simon, yeah. I was actually looking for someone who might be able to help me with my report. Get some terms. Technical terms, you know.

DORCAS: What, about running?

STAFFORD: Yes.

DORCAS: Well, you could ask Uncle Len. Have you seen him yet?

STAFFORD: Yes.

DORCAS: What did he say when he saw you?

STAFFORD: I don't think he remembered me.

DORCAS: No.

STAFFORD: He kept calling me 'squire'. The berk. You don't happen to know any terms, do you?

DORCAS: Running terms? Er ... Well ... Flags.

STAFFORD [*nodding*]: Yes.

DORCAS: Runners. Er ... start ... finish ...

STAFFORD [*consulting his notebook*]: Yes, I think I've got most of those down here.

DORCAS: Well, I'm a steward of the course.

STAFFORD [*nodding reporter-like*]: Uh-huh ... [*He writes painfully in his notebook.*]

DORCAS: And this is Checkpoint 7.

STAFFORD: Uh-huh, uh-huh.

DORCAS: What else? Oh yes. You go left round the red flags and right round the blue ones.

STAFFORD: Steward of the course, and checkpoint ...?

DORCAS: Checkpoint 7. 7.

STAFFORD [*closing his notebook, seemingly satisfied*]: Yes, I think I can build a story round that O.K.

DORCAS [*suspiciously*]: Stafford, are they printing the bits you write for them?

STAFFORD: Well, possibly.

DORCAS: What do you mean, possibly?

STAFFORD: I only started on Friday.

DORCAS: What, Friday yesterday?

STAFFORD: Yes. I meant to start on Monday only I was in bed. [*Explaining*] Ill.

DORCAS: So this is your first job?

STAFFORD: Yes, first assignment.

DORCAS [*very doubtfully*]: I hope this works out for you, Stafford.

STAFFORD: Yes.

[*Offstage, the loudspeaker is heard again.*]

LEN [*over loudspeaker*]: Just to keep you posted, ladies and gentlemen, boys and girls. The athletes should just about now be turning off the B481 and in another minute or so our spotters should be able to glimpse the front runners moving along Durkin's Ridge, preparatory to moving down into Hackett's Field. Thank you.

DORCAS: Shouldn't you be watching?

STAFFORD: No, no. I want to get the atmosphere first.

DORCAS: That's where the finish is, you see. They'll be coming down this hill soon. They have to do three laps, you see.

STAFFORD [*not interested by this*]: Ah.

DORCAS: How's the poetry? Have you been writing lately?

STAFFORD: No.

DORCAS: Have you been on the novel?

STAFFORD: No, no. I've stopped all that.

DORCAS: Stopped writing?

STAFFORD: Yes.

DORCAS: You can't.

STAFFORD: I have.

DORCAS: Stafford, that is criminal. You can't give up your writing. I absolutely forbid it. You have a great talent. A fine talent, so let's not hear any more of that nonsense. Do you hear me?

STAFFORD: How are you?

DORCAS: I'm fine. Do you hear me?

STAFFORD: Yes. Anyway, so here I am.

DORCAS: Yes.

STAFFORD: Back again.

DORCAS: Yes.

STAFFORD: So. Hi.

DORCAS [*suspiciously*]: What are you talking about?

STAFFORD: You and me.

DORCAS: I thought that's what you meant. I'm permanently with Simon now.

STAFFORD: Ah yes, but that was before.

DORCAS: Before what?

STAFFORD: Before I got this job and a suit and money and everything. See? So now you have to say yes.

DORCAS: Oh, don't be so totally daft.

STAFFORD: O.K. What else do you want? Do you want me to run in this race, is that it? O.K. I'll run in this race. [*He starts to take his coat off.*]

DORCAS: Stafford!

STAFFORD: Look, why else do you think I've sold out like this? I've only sold out for your sake.

DORCAS: Why does everyone keep doing things for my sake?

STAFFORD: What else do you want?

[MELVYN *appears on the ridge with his binoculars.*]

MELVYN [*excitedly*]: I can see the first two. It looks like Murphy with Simon close behind him.

DORCAS: Oh. Good.

MELVYN: They'll be here soon. Oh, hi there, Staff. Didn't recognize you.

STAFFORD: Hi, Mel.

MELVYN: Win the Pools?

STAFFORD: No.

MELVYN: Must get back.

[MELVYN *goes.*]

DORCAS [*suddenly amused*]: Oh Staff, you really are ridiculous.

STAFFORD: Ha!

DORCAS: What are you doing, working for the *Pendon Gazette*? I mean, honestly. And more important what made them take you on?

STAFFORD: I think I had good references.

DORCAS: Who from?

STAFFORD: Well, your father.

DORCAS: Pa wrote you a reference?

STAFFORD: Yes.

DORCAS: Well, he's mad anyway.

STAFFORD: Yes, he must be. He made out I was Lord Northcliffe. Then I told this assistant editor I'd had this very sporting youth, you see.

DORCAS [*giggling*]: What?

STAFFORD: I said I'd been given a trial for Manchester United, only I had to ... [*He breaks off, laughing; a strange honking sound.*]

DORCAS: Why are you laughing?

STAFFORD [*still laughing*]: I said I had to quit the game because of my pigeon toes ...

DORCAS [*helpless*]: You didn't?

STAFFORD: And he believed me.

DORCAS: Oh, dear God.

[*They lie on the bank laughing.* MURPHY *appears at the top of the slope,*] *glistening, breathing heavily and working hard. He descends the slope with much panting and grunting.*]

DORCAS [*springing up*]: Oh no.

    [*She runs to her post.*]

  [*As she does so*] Don't let Simon see you.

    [STAFFORD *obligingly stands well clear of the runners, his cap pulled well down.*]

  [*Waving* MURPHY *along*] To your left round the red flags, right round the blue flags. Thank you.

    [MURPHY *looks at her dangerously.* SIMON *appears only a few yards behind at the top of the hill.*]

  [*Seeing him*] Oh, hooray, hooray.

    [SIMON *does not acknowledge this, looking grim and determined.*]

  [*Also getting business-like*] To your left round the red flags, right round the blue flags. Thank you.

    [MURPHY *has gone off.*

    SIMON *now follows him.*]

Did he see you?

STAFFORD: I don't think so.

DORCAS: Good, because I don't think he'd be too pleased at present.

STAFFORD: Yes. Anyway, then I told this editor . . .

DORCAS: Stafford, shouldn't you be writing any of this down? You know, Constable Murphy after one lap was being hotly pursued by Simon Grimshaw . . .

    [STAFFORD *doesn't seem to think so.*

    MELVYN *appears at the top of the slope.*]

MELVYN: Did you see that? Did you see that?

DORCAS: Mel, get back.

MELVYN: There's no one coming yet, it's all right.

    [MELVYN *goes.*

    The loudspeaker is heard offstage.]

LEN [*on loudspeaker*]: The two runners coming through at the moment leading the field, perhaps predictably, Number 17, John Murphy, who has just registered an official first lap time of 8 minutes 34.4 seconds which constitutes a new first lap record for this particular course. Close behind him is Number 8, Simon Grimshaw, in a time of 8 minutes 42.1 seconds. So as you can see, there is very little in it at present. Thank you.

DORCAS: Isn't that good? Sorry, you were saying?

STAFFORD: Then I told this editor that I went from there into teaching, you see. P.E. and so on.

DORCAS: Why P.E.?

STAFFORD: It sounded good, and then I got offered this job, you see, with this firm in Africa that sold machine tools.

DORCAS: Stafford. Did you mention Simon's firm?

STAFFORD: Yes. B.L.M. Ltd. I remembered it.

DORCAS: But they might check.

STAFFORD: That's all right. I gave them his name as well.

DORCAS: Just a second. You've told the *Gazette* that your name is Simon Grimshaw?

STAFFORD: Yes.

DORCAS: For heaven's sake, Stafford, they're bound to find out you're not. What happens when they find out you're Stafford Wilkins?

STAFFORD: That's all right, I told them that Simon Grimshaw was just my nom de plume.

DORCAS: And they believed that?

STAFFORD: Well, it sounded reasonable. Nobody in his sane mind would write under the name of Stafford Wilkins.

DORCAS: All the same it's going to be very confusing when you report this race, isn't it? Simon Grimshaw reports on Simon Grimshaw.

STAFFORD: That's O.K. I shan't mention him, don't worry.

[DORCAS *gives up.*

LEN *enters from the starting area, looking worried.*]

LEN: Excuse me – [*Seeing* STAFFORD] Oh, talking to the Press, are you?

DORCAS: No, just passing the time of day.

LEN: Enjoying the race, Squire?

STAFFORD: Rather.

DORCAS: Uncle Len, this is Mr ...

STAFFORD: Mr S. Grimshaw. Hallo.

LEN [*briefly shaking his hand*]: How do you do. Len Coker. [*Heading for the slope*] Excuse me, I just have to ... [*Stopping*] It's odd that. We've got a namesake of yours running in this race. Another Grimshaw. Coincidence.

STAFFORD: Ah well. It's a common enough name.

LEN [*dubious*]: Yes, yes. You've covered this race before, haven't you?

STAFFORD: Ha ha.

LEN: Thought so. Never forget a face. Excuse me. [*Shouting*] Mel! Mel!

MELVYN [*off, distant*]: Hallo.

LEN: Mel!

[MELVYN *arrives to join* LEN *at the top of the slope.*]

MELVYN: Yes?

LEN: We can't see anyone on Durkin's Ridge at all. Can you see anyone?

MELVYN: No.

LEN: Bloody odd. I mean, the field's often spread out but not as thin as this. I mean, it's been, what, three or four minutes since those two came through. They'll lap 'em all in a minute at this rate. [*To* STAFFORD] Excuse me. [*To* MELVYN] Keep your eyes peeled.

    [MELVYN *goes off.*

    LEN *comes down the bank.*]

I think there may be some records broken today, Mr Grimshaw.

STAFFORD [*nodding hawk-eyed*]: Uh-huh, uh-huh.

LEN: If you'd care to join us afterwards, we'll be having an informal cup of tea in the Range Rover.

STAFFORD: Possibly will, possibly will.

    [MELVYN *appears at the top of the slope again.*]

MELVYN [*calling*]: Uncle Len.

LEN: Yes. What is it, son? [*Moving away, to* STAFFORD] Excuse me.

MELVYN: I can see one more.

LEN: Only one?

MELVYN: Yes, he's running very slowly.

LEN: This is very peculiar. I mean, there's supposed to be eighteen runners out there somewhere. They can't have disappeared. Let's have a look.

DORCAS: Anything I can do?

LEN [*running up the slope and grabbing* MELVYN's *binoculars*]: No. No. [*Looking through the glasses*] That's George Lidgett. That's Major Lidgett, that is. He shouldn't be running in third place.

MELVYN: There's something wrong, isn't there?

LEN: Sssh. Keep your voice down. The Press are just there. They'd have a field day over this.

MELVYN: It's all right. He won't say anything, he's –

LEN: Sssh. Keep your voice down and get back to your post.

    [MELVYN *goes.*

    LEN *runs down the hill.*]

[*To* STAFFORD] Excuse me.

DORCAS: Shall I stay here?

LEN: Yes, don't move whatever you do. You're always welcome to stroll this way, Mr Grimshaw, if you'd like a better view. [*He goes back to the starting area.*]

DORCAS [*laughing*]: Mr Grimshaw! [*Becoming serious*] Nevertheless, Stafford, let us be quite clear ...

STAFFORD: Uh?

DORCAS: I have one Mr Grimshaw. He is quite sufficient. I do not want two.

STAFFORD: Then get rid of him.

DORCAS: No.

STAFFORD: I was here first.

> [MAJOR LIDGETT *appears at the top of the hill. He is wiry but seems quite frail, and runs very slowly and carefully. Nevertheless he is running. He wears a running cap, shorts and running vest with Number 23.*]

DORCAS [*seeing him*]: Good lord. [*Gently, to* LIDGETT] Left round the red flags, right round the blue flags. Thank you.

> [LEN *re-enters from the starting area. He sees* LIDGETT.]

LEN: Ah, Major Lidgett. [*He falls into step beside him in order to talk to him.*] Major Lidgett, where are the others?

> [LIDGETT, *with a wave of his hand, disclaims any knowledge.*]

Yes, but where are the rest of the field? They can't have vanished ...

> [LIDGETT *runs off, with* LEN *in pursuit still talking.*
> MELVYN *appears at the top of the hill again.*]

MELVYN: Did you see that?

DORCAS: Yes.

MELVYN: He nearly fell down this hole here. It's very dangerous.

DORCAS: Well, move the flag.

MELVYN: Do you think I should?

DORCAS: If it's dangerous, someone will get hurt, won't they?

MELVYN: Yes, but ...

DORCAS: Move the flag.

MELVYN: O.K.

> [MELVYN *goes off over the slope.*
> LEN, *simultaneously, returns with furrowed brow.*]

LEN: Dorcas, could you spare me one moment, please.

DORCAS [*moving to him*]: Yes?

LEN [*to* STAFFORD]: Excuse me.

STAFFORD: Yes.

LEN [*to* DORCAS, *in an undertone*]: It would appear that we have lost the rest of the field.

DORCAS [*exclaiming*]: Lost it?

LEN: Please ... Don't raise your voice. Our friend from the Press there will have it in headlines two foot high. And he'd love it, the bastard, he'd love it. It appears that vandals have removed one of our flags.

DORCAS: Oh no.

LEN: Causing the majority of the competitors to go straight on up the B481, failing to turn off at the footbridge over Pendon Trickle. Thus they have joined the A4155 with the result they are, to the best of my knowledge, halfway to Reading.

DORCAS: Oh dear.

LEN: I've sent the loudspeaker van to hail them back but quite evidently the race is null and void.

DORCAS: Oh dear. Major Lidgett got through.

LEN: I should bloody well hope so. He's been running it for 27 years.

DORCAS: Why didn't the rest of them follow him?

LEN: How could they follow him? He was half a mile behind them.

DORCAS: Are we stopping then?

LEN: Well, normally that would be the procedure but young Murphy, at present, is running an extremely promising time. In the circumstances, we feel he should be allowed to run on if he so wishes. I shall be acquainting the remaining runners of the position as they complete the second lap. I'd be grateful, meanwhile, if you could keep this Press man occupied and as far from the fact as possible.

DORCAS: How?

LEN: Distract him, girl, distract him.

DORCAS: O.K.

[MELVYN *appears again.*]

MELVYN: Here they come.

LEN: Right, right.

[*He runs up the hill.*]

MELVYN: Simon's in the lead. [*He goes.*]

LEN [*going off over the hill*]: Simon is?

DORCAS [*rather automatically*]: Hooray, hooray.

STAFFORD: Anything wrong?

DORCAS: No. Just stewards' talk.

STAFFORD: Ah. There don't seem to be a lot of runners in this race. Is that normal?

DORCAS: Oh yes, quite normal.

STAFFORD: Ah.

[SIMON *and* LEN *appear side by side at the top of the slope.*]

DORCAS [*to* STAFFORD]: Look out.

[STAFFORD *moves away.* SIMON *runs down the hill, looking decidedly more tired, but he remains grim and determined.* LEN *runs beside him talking softly.*]

LEN: ... so the position is that the rest of the field are now on the A4155 so the question is, do you wish to continue the race or stop at the end of this lap? The decision is entirely in your hands ...

[LEN *and* SIMON *run off, still talking.*]

DORCAS [*over this last*]: Left round the red flag, right round the blue flag. Thank you.

STAFFORD: Listen, Dorc, I don't think you've quite got my argument. I'm back, that's the point I'm making. I'm back.

DORCAS: Stafford, please, I'm ...

[LEN *runs in past her and up the hill.*]

LEN [*as he passes*]: He wants to carry on. [*Waving the watch*] 17 minutes, 22 seconds. It's a good one.

DORCAS: Good.

[LEN *runs off over the hill.*]

STAFFORD: What I'm saying is, let's pick it up again now. I mean, as far as I'm concerned nothing's happened. It can all be the same as it was.

DORCAS: But, Staff, a hell of a lot has happened ...

[*She breaks off for* MURPHY *has now appeared on the slope, again shadowed by* LEN *in similar fashion as before.*]

LEN: ... so the position is that the rest of the field are now on the A4155, so the question is do you wish to continue the race or stop at the end of this lap? The decision is entirely in your hands ...

[LEN *and* MURPHY *exit together, still talking.*]

DORCAS [*under this last*]: Left round the red flags, right round the blue flags. Thank you.

STAFFORD: What are you saying's happened?

DORCAS: Well, perhaps nothing has to you. I don't know. Apart from criminally impersonating someone to obtain employment by false pretences. But for me, quite a lot has happened.

STAFFORD: What, what?

[LEN *re-enters. He holds the stopwatch.*]

LEN [*to himself*]: 17 minutes, 48 seconds. [*To* STAFFORD] Excuse me.

DORCAS [*moving to* LEN]: Yes.

LEN [*sotto*]: Murphy would prefer to stop.

DORCAS: Oh. You're not going to let him, are you?

LEN: No. The record is still vulnerable. I told him to pull his finger out and get moving. [*Patting her on the arm and nodding at* STAFFORD] Good girl, keep him busy.

[LEN *moves off to the starting area again.*]

STAFFORD: The question is, Dorc, what else do you want me to do? What do you want from me? There is a major demonstration of workers' solidarity going on in Slough at this very minute. I should be there. Don't you see, I have given up my politics, I have given up my poetry, I hope you've noticed I've even given up smoking. Look, I've shaved, for God's sake. I promise I will never write on your bedroom ceiling again. I won't wake you up in the night to say I love you. I won't ring in on your phone-in programmes to read you love poems.

DORCAS: Shut up, Stafford.

STAFFORD: I won't be there, I promise, when you come home at night with your cocoa.

DORCAS: I said, shut up. I know what you're doing so shut up.

STAFFORD: Look, Dorc, look. Look at me. I'm really boring and ordinary now, you know. I mean, you stand me next to the real Grimshaw, you'll never know the difference, I promise. I'll do exercises and grow unnecessary muscles, if that's what you'd like.

DORCAS: Stafford.

STAFFORD: Yes.

DORCAS: I'm going to hit you with a pole in a minute.

STAFFORD: Go on, go on. Yes, yes, yes.

DORCAS: Why the hell do I always get landed with the lame ducks?

STAFFORD: You know what they say?

DORCAS: What?

STAFFORD: If you don't like lame ducks, you really must stop stamping on their toes.

[MELVYN *appears at the top of the hill.*]

MELVYN: Here comes Major Lidgett again.

LEN [*running on from the starting area*]: Is that Major Lidgett?

MELVYN: Yes, he's on his way. [*He runs off.*]

DORCAS: Hooray, hooray. He's jolly good for his age, isn't he?

LEN: Yes, he should do this lap in ...

[*A distant feeble cry.*]

What's that?

MELVYN [*appearing again*]: Major Lidgett's fallen down a hole.

LEN [*running up the hill*]: Oh, my God.

[LEN *goes off.*]

DORCAS [*to* MELVYN]: Oh dear, didn't you move the flag?

MELVYN: Yes, he fell down the hole on the other side.

STAFFORD [*at his notebook*]: How do you spell Lidgett?

[LEN *returns wearily.*]

DORCAS: How is he?

LEN: He's all right, he's all right. No thanks to someone.

DORCAS: Why?

LEN: Some vandal moved that flag as well, you know. Two yards to the right. He saw the blue flag. Went round the right hand side, quite correctly and finished up in a seven-foot hole. Now, that's not accidental. It's an inside job by someone with prior knowledge. It's political, I'm convinced of that. They'll do anything for publicity. [*To* STAFFORD] Don't you dare print this.

DORCAS: Is he all right? Major Lidgett?

LEN: Fortunately, yes. He's not substantially damaged. But it's taken the edge off his enthusiasm, you know. He's given up the race. Brenda's walking him home. [*As he goes*] Tragic, isn't it? First time in twenty-seven years. Tragic.

[LEN *goes out*.]

DORCAS: What are you writing?

STAFFORD: How do you spell last Will and Testament?

DORCAS: You're being very unfair to me, Stafford. I thought I'd got my life sorted at last. I'd found Simon. For the first time in my life, I'd actually got something Abigail wanted and couldn't have. I mean, that's incidental, I think, but it wasn't a bad feeling after so many years. Suddenly I was O.K. I had a man who was looking after me instead of me looking after him.

STAFFORD: But if that's ... ?

DORCAS: That's what it was, Stafford. Always. Me looking after you. Me making decisions. Me telling you what to do next, where to go.

STAFFORD: Because that's what you wanted to do.

DORCAS: My God, did you think that?

STAFFORD: Well, tell me this. How do you like it the other way round, eh? How do you like being told by him?

DORCAS: He doesn't.

STAFFORD: He will.

DORCAS: He won't.

STAFFORD: He'll keep at you till he does. He won't stop till he's running everything. I've seen that type before. They're office managers, all of them. He'll get his way. Even if he has to do it by force.

DORCAS: Well, perhaps that's what I do want then.

STAFFORD: You don't want that. If you'd've wanted that, you'd've married your brother-in-law, wouldn't you? Patrick?

DORCAS: All right, what do I want then? You say.

STAFFORD: Me.

DORCAS: No, Staff, I'm sorry. There's got to be more to life than nurse-maiding you.

STAFFORD: Ah-ha, but will you ever find it?

DORCAS: What can you offer me?

STAFFORD: Think.

DORCAS: That nobody else can.

STAFFORD: Think.

DORCAS: That Simon can't.

STAFFORD: Think hard.

DORCAS: What is there about you that is so marvellous?

STAFFORD: Think, think.

DORCAS: No good.

STAFFORD: Think, remember.

DORCAS: I can't.

STAFFORD: Rack your brains. Rack your loins. It is I, Stafford T. Wilkins alias S. Grimshaw, ace reporter ...

[STAFFORD *is very close to* DORCAS *now.*
LEN *comes on hurriedly and goes straight up the hill, hardly noticing them.*]

LEN [*stopwatch in hand*]: Your lad's doing well. He's heading for the record.

MELVYN [*coming on over the hill*]: He's coming.

LEN: Come on, Grimshaw.

MELVYN: Grimshaw.

STAFFORD [*to* DORCAS]: Hear that, they're shouting for me.

LEN: Come on, Grimshaw.

MELVYN: Come on, Grimshaw.

[*Other voices are heard at the finishing line shouting for Grimshaw.*]

STAFFORD: Come on, Grimshaw.

DORCAS [*lying back against the bank*]: Come on, Grimshaw.

STAFFORD: That's it. Let's hear it again.

DORCAS: Come on, come on, come on.

MELVYN: Come on, Grimshaw.

LEN: Here he comes.

STAFFORD: Here comes Grimshaw.

DORCAS: Here comes Grimshaw.

[STAFFORD *lies with* DORCAS.]

MELVYN: Bravo!

[SIMON *runs on, a look of triumph in his eye. A man with a record in sight. He reaches the bottom of the bank. As he does so,* STAFFORD *and* DORCAS, *locked together, roll into his path.*]

LEN: Keep going, keep going. You've got it.

[SIMON *stops, breathing heavily. He stares at* DORCAS *and* STAFFORD.]

DORCAS [*sitting up*]: Oh. God. Look, Grimshaw ... I mean, Simon ...

[SIMON *stares, shaking his head trying to get his breath.*]

LEN: Go on, man, go on. You can't stop. You've got 10 seconds. 9 seconds to beat that record.

STAFFORD [*to* SIMON]: You want to hit me? Hit me.

LEN: 8.

STAFFORD: I've chosen for her, you see.

LEN: 7.

STAFFORD: You don't need her.

LEN: 6.

STAFFORD: She needs me.

LEN: 5.

STAFFORD: It's no use asking her to choose.

LEN: 4.

STAFFORD: She only chooses wrong.

LEN: 3.

STAFFORD: Always.

LEN: 2.

STAFFORD: Go on.

LEN: 1.

STAFFORD: Win your race. Leave her alone.

LEN [*banging his stopwatch in irritation*]: Oh God. Well, that's it, isn't it? All over, there goes the record. What's the matter with the lad?

> [MURPHY *appears at the top of the hill. He is completely clapped out. He stands clasping his side in great pain from a stitch. He surveys the scene.*]

MELVYN [*seeing* MURPHY]: Look out, Simon.

> [MURPHY *sees* SIMON.]

LEN: Come on, Murphy. You can still win, boy.

DORCAS [*gently*]: Go on, Simon. Left round the red flag, right round the blue one.

> [SIMON *looks at* DORCAS *and* STAFFORD, *then at* MURPHY. MURPHY *starts to come down the slope.*]

LEN: Run, Murphy. Run, lad.

DORCAS: Run, Simon.

MELVYN: Go on, Simon, run.

> [SIMON *exits round the flags followed by* MURPHY. MELVYN *follows.*]

LEN [*following, and looking at his stopwatch in disgust: to* STAFFORD]: And I rather expect the Press to conduct themselves better than that, you know. That's an accredited steward.

> [LEN *goes off to the finishing line. As he goes, the sound of cheers.*]

MELVYN [*returning from the finishing line, briefly*]: He's won. Simon's won. He's won.

> [MELVYN *goes off.*]

DORCAS: Well? You want to come home to tea?

STAFFORD: O.K.

DORCAS: What about your story? Do you have to file it or whatever you call it?

STAFFORD: No, no. It'll keep, it'll keep. We'll probably put it on the spike, you know. Run it as a colour feature later.

DORCAS [*in realization*]: You aren't working for any newspaper at all, are you?

STAFFORD: No.

DORCAS: You haven't given up writing poetry?

STAFFORD: No.

DORCAS: Or your politics?

STAFFORD: No.

DORCAS: Or smoking?

STAFFORD: I'm trying.

DORCAS: You've still got no money.

STAFFORD: No.

DORCAS: You little – maggot. Where did you get those clothes, then, if you've got no money?

STAFFORD: I found them on the bench over there [*Indicating the starting area.*] I think they belong to that old git, Major Lidgett.

DORCAS [*closing her eyes in exasperation*]: All right, that's it. That is finally it. You have just thrown away your very last . . . Aaark!

[STAFFORD *has lifted her off her feet. He swings her over his shoulder cave-man fashion. He now lopes up the hill with her.*]

Stafford! Stafford, put me down, Stafford. Where are we going . . .

STAFFORD [*with a leer*]: We're going for a run . . .

DORCAS [*resignedly*]: Oh, Stafford.

[*They disappear over the hill.*]

End of Act Two Scene One D
Act Two Scene Two follows.

ACT TWO
SCENE TWO

Footnote

The scene change has again been swift. It is a Saturday afternoon in November at about three o'clock. A cold but dry day, slightly frosty. As the scene starts, immediately, RALPH comes hurrying on. He is dressed very smartly in his best suit and a colourful tie. He has his hat on but no coat. The effect is ruined somewhat by his footwear. A pair of cheerful, worn bedroom slippers. In his buttonhole, a carnation. He is followed by LEN, also in his best suit, probably the same as at the start though his tie, too, is brighter, reflecting a more cheerful occasion. He, also, wears a carnation. On his arm is RITA, dressed in her wedding outfit with floral spray, doing her best to add cheer to the proceedings, through her usual tide of troubles.

RALPH: ... Now I know none of you are going to love me for this but I think you're going to thank me for it when you've seen this view. Now, this here ... Len, Rita ... this spot here ... the day I got married to Amy, we came to this very spot and we rushed up that hill, Amy still in her long wedding dress ... yes. [*He muses.*]

RITA: It must have got very muddy.

RALPH: I remember we stood there for so long watching the sun going down, back there the whole reception sitting there waiting for us. They couldn't start, you see.

RITA: Must have caused a bit of a stir.

LEN: It did.

RALPH: Oh well ... We were all mad in those days.

LEN: Yes.

RITA: Yes, yes. Don't spoil your bedroom slippers, will you, Ralph?

RALPH: No, no.

LEN: Find them more comfortable to wear these days, do you?

RALPH: Not really.

LEN: Ah.

RITA: Yes, yes.

RALPH: Where are the rest of them? [*Shouting back*] Come on, you lot. I'm waiting to show you this view.

[MELVYN *enters with* BRENDA.
BRENDA *in full conventional wedding dress.*
MELVYN *in his suit and carnation.*]

MELVYN: Sorry.

LEN: Ah, the happy couple.

RITA [*without a lot of fire*]: Hooray, Hooray.

[MELVYN *is kissing* BRENDA.]

RALPH: Don't keep doing that, boy. You'll give her some dreadful disease. Now, we're all going up the slope.

MELVYN: Here we go again.

RALPH [*greatly amused by this*]: Here we go again, he says. Here we go again. [*Seizing* RITA's *arm*] Come on, Rita, we'll get you up there.

RITA: Oh, I don't know if I can ...

RALPH: Come on, come on.

LEN: Careful with her now, Ralph, the ground's a bit hard.

RALPH [*to* RITA]: We'll get you over the difficult bits, don't you worry.

MELVYN: Why don't you put your shoes on, Dad? Have you lost them again?

RALPH: Lost them, he says. 'Course I haven't lost them, you daft dimple. Now I've told you before, I've told you this – listen to your feet. Listen to your feet. And you know why? Because where are your feet?

MELVYN [*repeating as if by heart*]: On the other end of my body to my head.

RALPH: Correct. On their own. Right down there.

LEN [*anxiously watching* RITA *as* RALPH *gesticulates with her*]: You'll be careful with her, won't you, Ralph?

RALPH: Yes, yes. You see, your feet are your distant branch offices. They're your outposts. If you're going to get trouble, it generally starts miles from your H.Q. [*He taps his head.*] If you neglect your feet, they get a chip on their shoulder. Talk to your feet and you'll live to be ninety-nine. Chat to your tootsies. I've told all my patients that. Bit by bit, none of them needed to come back. Never saw them again. All cured.

LEN: That's a very interesting theory.

RALPH [*heaving her up the remaining slope*]: All right, Rita. [*Over his shoulder*] And don't make them wear shoes if they don't want to. They never asked to, did they?

LEN [*to* MELVYN *nervously, as he watches*]: As long as he doesn't push her down that hole again. The last time it didn't do her a scrap of good, you know.

[RALPH *and* RITA *stop for a breather.*]

[*To* MELVYN *and* BRENDA] I hear you two are going to open a shop.

MELVYN: That's right.

LEN: Where did you find the money for that then?

MELVYN: We borrowed it.

LEN: Dear, dear, dear. Into debt before you've begun. What sort of start is that, eh?

MELVYN: It'll be O.K.

LEN: It'll be O.K. till you have to pay it back. [*Wagging a finger at* BRENDA] Money has to be paid back, you know.

BRENDA: Well, in our case, I think the risks are fairly minimal. I've negotiated the interest at a fixed 8% and it's compounded at monthly stops with the repayment of the initial capital and the corresponding payment of interest only becoming due at the start of each new financial year.

LEN [*digesting this*]: Oh well then, you'll probably be just about all right then.

RALPH: Come on, you lot. Rita and I have scaled the mountain.

MELVYN: Hang on.

[MELVYN *sweeps* BRENDA *up in his arms.*]

LEN: What sort of shop are you opening then?

MELVYN: A toyshop.

[*He runs up the slope carrying* BRENDA.]

LEN [*muttering*]: I don't know why I bothered to ask. [*He starts to follow.*]

RALPH [*meanwhile watching* MELVYN'S *antics*]: Bravo, bravo.

[DORCAS *appears dressed attractively for the wedding. Following her a little way behind is* STAFFORD *who has been given a new outfit for the occasion but manages to make it look already quite old.*]

DORCAS [*calling*]: Pa, we're paying for these cars by the hour, you know.

RALPH: Come up here, Abi. It's glorious, glorious.

DORCAS: Dorcas, father.

RALPH: That's right, bring Dorcas as well. We want all of you up here. And the best man. Where's the best man? Where's that young Simon?

[RALPH *goes out over the hill, following* MELVYN *and* BRENDA *who have already disappeared.*]

RITA [*who has been abandoned suddenly*]: He's not right, you know, is he?

DORCAS: He certainly isn't.

LEN: He's got this thing about feet. He keeps grabbing folk by the feet all the time.

RITA: I mean, when he does it suddenly he upends you, you know.

LEN: He upended Rita.

DORCAS: Oh dear.

RITA: He did. I went right over, didn't I?

LEN: Right. Over she went. Chest over cheeks.

[LEN *and* RITA *disappear over the hill.* DORCAS *stands impatiently, unsure how to recall the party.* STAFFORD *stands ruminatively.*]

DORCAS [*absently*]: Stafford, tuck your shirt in, love. Well, I hope they hurry up. [*To* STAFFORD *again*] Now that wasn't too bad, was it? I mean, you stood in the church and you weren't struck by lightning. O.K.?

STAFFORD: Yeah.

DORCAS: You'll get something to eat in a minute. That'll cheer you up.

STAFFORD: Great. Yeah ...

[ABIGAIL *comes on hurriedly, also dressed well and expensively.*]

ABIGAIL: What the hell is Pa playing at? Brenda's mother is droning on in that car there, she's driving Patrick mad. I can see he's beginning to foam.

DORCAS: She's driving us all nuts. What are you talking about?

ABIGAIL [*calling up the slope*]: Pa! [*Slight pause*] Father dear.

DORCAS: It's no use.

ABIGAIL: Well, we're going to have to drive off and leave him in a minute. The whole wedding's a fiasco anyway. That large pregnant thing lumping up the aisle.

DORCAS: It doesn't show.

ABIGAIL: Well, I'll give them a year. I mean, opening a toyshop. Honestly. Who needs a toyshop in this place?

DORCAS: People who have children. You will soon.

ABIGAIL [*laughing drily*]: We'll see. I think Patrick plans to wean our child straight on to calculators.

[STAFFORD *is wandering away, head down, punching with one arm.*]

DORCAS: Don't wander too far off, will you, Staff?

STAFFORD: No.

[STAFFORD *goes off.*]

DORCAS [*semi-apologetically*]: He's writing a poem. At least I think he is.

ABIGAIL: He's looking a bit better, isn't he? Has he been washing more?

DORCAS: No, no, no. That's next year's job.

ABIGAIL: Look, if father really does drive you potty and you can't stand looking after him another minute, then he'll have to come and live with us. But now with the baby coming, I really don't think ...

DORCAS: No, no, that's O.K. He's fine. Except he thinks I'm you half the time.

ABIGAIL: How extraordinary. We're hardly alike. And you really won't miss your job?

DORCAS: No. And it means Stafford's got to work, which is good. It'll give him an incentive.

[PATRICK *arrives, similarly dressed to the others.*]

PATRICK [*to* ABIGAIL]: Darling, could you possibly whistle your father and put him back on his lead, please. I am stuck in the back of a car with a woman who has the political views of Attila the Hun and I'm about to let her have it between her hat.

ABIGAIL: Please be polite to the bride's mother.

PATRICK: The bride is shortly to be orphaned. Hurry up.

[PATRICK *turns to go, nearly colliding with* SIMON *who is hurrying on.*]

SIMON: Sorry. Beg your pardon. After you.

PATRICK: No, after you. You're the best man after all.

SIMON: Yes, true ...

PATRICK: Well, for today anyway.

[PATRICK *goes.*

SIMON *laughs.*]

SIMON [*to the women*]: Is the old boy coming then?

ABIGAIL: I've no idea.

SIMON: Only the drivers are getting a bit stroppy. I slipped them both a quid. All the same ... I'll give him a yell, shall I? [*No reply*] Yes. Sorry. I'm afraid mother's going on a bit. Proud mama, you know. Yes. Right.

[SIMON *runs up the slope. He stops briefly, aware that both women are staring at him. He turns, smiles at them both and winks rather self-consciously. He goes off over the hill.*]

ABIGAIL [*when he has gone*]: I have to say it, he's a very silly man, isn't he? I mean, when I first met him, I don't think I realized quite how silly he was. I suppose I was taken in by all that sunburn and teeth and things. Well, weren't we all?

DORCAS: Yes, I know what you mean.

ABIGAIL: I don't know about you but I'm absolutely certain I made the right decision there. I expect you feel the same.

DORCAS: Yes. [*With less conviction*] Oh yes ... I think so.

ABIGAIL: Aren't you sure?

DORCAS: No. What I mean is, I think I made a decision.

ABIGAIL: Well, you decided, didn't you? You decided, whatever the temptations, to stay with thingy – Stafford. And I decided, God help me, to stick with Patrick.

DORCAS [*not really convinced*]: Yes, I expect we did. Anyhow, the important thing is for us to *feel* we've made decisions, isn't it? Otherwise, everything would be just so pointless ...

ABIGAIL: Yes, quite right. Now, next decision. Which of us is to travel home the rest of the way in the car which contains the bride's mother and her hat?

DORCAS: Tell you what. I'll toss you for it. [*They move off, linking arms.*]

ABIGAIL: God, she's a dreary woman. I was talking to her in the car just now. Everything I said ... [*Hearty impersonation*] Nnnyaaa-ha-ha-

DORCAS [*copying*]: Nnnyaaa-ha-ha-

ABIGAIL: Oh, she'll have to go. Mel's not getting stuck with that ...

[*They have gone, leaving the Common deserted.*]

BLACKOUT

FOR THE BEST IN PAPERBACKS, LOOK FOR THE 🐧

Hugh Leonard in Penguin Plays

DA/A LIFE/ TIME WAS

Da

'A beguiling play about a son's need to come to terms with his father and himself ... in a class with the best of Sean O'Casey' – *The New York Times*

A Life

'Even better than its famous predecessor (*Da*): as human and funny, but richer in texture and even more cannily aware of the sad complexity of life' – *Daily Telegraph*

Time Was

'Proves once again that he's Ireland's funniest playwright ... snappy, witty, polished ... Leonard's observations on Dublin suburbia are acidly accurate' – *Sunday Press* (Dublin)

Also by Hugh Leonard in Penguins

HOME BEFORE NIGHT

A delightful evocation of his Dublin childhood in the thirties and forties, Hugh Leonard's autobiography is like an Irish *Cider With Rosie* – crammed with people and conversations, rich in poetry, full of love, laughter and rare pleasures.

'Entrancing ... the playwright author's gift of language and apparently total recall make his account of growing up in the thirties and forties absolutely irresistible' – *Sunday Telegraph*

'Impossible to put down ... a brilliant, multi-faceted gem' – *Hibernia*

'An unqualified delight ... (he has) a marvellous eye for character, the ability to weave show-stopping funny stories into larger narrative and to recreate the past with the sensuous immediacy of childhood' – Irving Wardle in *Books and Bookmen*

'Superb ... moving and very funny' – William Trevor

John Mortimer in Penguin Plays

A VOYAGE ROUND MY FATHER/THE DOCK BRIEF/WHAT SHALL WE TELL CAROLINE?

A Voyage Round My Father
'John Mortimer's funny, subtle, touching portrait. It is his father's enigmatic endurance that concerns him and enriches us' – J. W. Lambert in the *Sunday Times*

The Dock Brief and *What Shall We Tell Caroline?*
'There is hardly a line in these plays which does not create a vivid picture in the hearer's mind, and stir his memory, and disturb his imagination, and fill it with vague, impalpable feelings of remembered disappointments and delights' – Harold Hobson in the *Sunday Times*

Also by John Mortimer in Penguins

RUMPOLE OF THE BAILEY

Horace Rumpole ... sixty-eight next birthday, with an un-surpassed knowledge of Blood and Typewriters, a penchant for quoting from the *Oxford Book of English Verse*, and a habit of referring to his judge as 'the old darling' ... Rumpole now takes up his pen in pious hope of making a bob or two that the egregious taxman, or She Who Must Be Obeyed (Mrs Rumpole), or his clerk, Henry, won't benefit from. In doing so he opens up some less-well-charted corners of British justice.

'Rumpole has been an inspired stroke of good fortune for us all' – Lynda Lee Potter in the *Daily Mail*

David Storey in Penguin Plays

HOME/THE CHANGING ROOM/MOTHER'S DAY

Home

'As a view of crippled lives and wintry tenderness between them, the play is beautifully spare and sustained in tone' – Ronald Bryden in the *Observer*

The Changing Room

Behind the ribbing, and the swearing, and the showing off, the piece is permeated by a Wordsworthian spirit. You can, if you listen, hear through it "the still, sad music of humanity"' – Harold Hobson in the *Sunday Times*

Mother's Day

'Mr Storey's farcical invention is tireless, and has the advantage of unlimited permissiveness' – *Financial Times*

EARLY DAYS/SISTERS/LIFE CLASS

Early Days

'It has the insidious simplicity of a piano piece by Satie or a Wordsworth lyrical ballad ... it touches deep chords' – Michael Billington in the *Guardian*

Sisters

'Deals in betrayal, love and finally, madness ... A remarkable, stimulating, and unsettling gem of a play' – Gerard Dempsey in the *Daily Express*

Life Class

'Art itself may have moved into happenings some years ago; but, to my knowledge, this is the stage's first tribute of that event, and we are not likely to see it bettered' – Irving Wardle in *The Times*